THE
IRISHMAN

"A page-turning account of one man's descent into the mob."
—*Delaware News Journal*

"Charles Brandt has solved the Hoffa mystery."
—Professor ARTHUR SLOANE, author of *Hoffa*

"Sometimes you can believe everything you read."
— WILLIAM "BIG BILLY" D'ELIA, successor to Russell
Bufalino as godfather of the Bufalino crime family

"One of Frank Sheeran's virtues was his gift as a storyteller; one of his flaws
was his tendency to murder, in mobster jargon, 'to paint houses.' . . . Although
he professed his loyalty to Hoffa — he said on one occasion, 'I'll be a Hoffa
man 'til they pat my face with a shovel and steal my cufflinks' — Sheeran
acknowledged that he was the one who killed the Teamsters boss. . . . On July
30, 1975, Hoffa disappeared. Sheeran explains how he did it, in prose remi-
niscent of the best gangster films."

— *Associated Press*

"My source in the Bufalino family . . . read *The Irishman*. All the Bufalino
guys read it. This old-time Bufalino guy told me he was shocked. He couldn't
believe Sheeran confessed all that stuff to [Brandt]. It's all true."
— JOSEPH COFFEY, New York Police Department
organized crime homicide detective

"If the made men Brandt rubbed up against during his five years with Sheeran
suspected what Sheeran was confessing to him on tape, they'd both have been
promptly whacked."
— JOE PISTONE, retired FBI deep undercover agent
and the author of *Donnie Brasco*

"*The Irishman* is the best Mafia book I ever read, and believe me, I read them
all. It's so authentic."
— STEVEN VAN ZANDT, featured actor, "Silvio Dante," in *The Sopranos*
and musician in Bruce Springsteen's E Street Band

"Is Sheeran believable? Very . . . and *The Irishman* is a very enjoyable book."
—*Trial Magazine*

"Sheeran's confession that he killed Hoffa in the manner described in the
book is supported by the forensic evidence, is entirely credible, and solves
the Hoffa mystery."

— MICHAEL BADEN M.D., former Chief
Medical Examiner of the City of New York

THE
IRISHMAN

Frank Sheeran
AND
Closing the Case
ON
Jimmy Hoffa

Originally published as
I Heard You Paint Houses

Charles Brandt

STEERFORTH PRESS
Lebanon, New Hampshire

For information about permission to reproduce
selections from this book, write to:
Steerforth Press L.L.C., 31 Hanover Street, Unit 1,
Lebanon, New Hampshire 03766

The Library of Congress has cataloged the hardcover edition as follows:

Brandt, Charles.
I heard you paint houses: Frank "the Irishman" Sheeran and
closing the case on Jimmy Hoffa / Charles Brandt.
p. cm.
Includes bibliographical references.
ISBN 1-58642-247-9 (alk. paper)
1. Gangsters—United States. 2. Mafia—United States. 3. Teamsters—United States.
4. Hoffa, James R. (James Riddle), 1913- 5. Sheeran, Frank. I. Title.
HV6446.B73 2004
364.1'06'0973—dc22

2004006625

ISBN 978-1-58642-246-2 (paperback)

EXPANDED PAPERBACK EDITION
Printed in the United States of America
Book Design by Peter Holm, Sterling Hill Productions

1 3 5 7 9 10 8 6 4 2

To my wife,
NANCY POOLE BRANDT,
our children and their spouses,
TRIPP and ALLISON, MIMI and JOHN, JENNY ROSE and ALEX,
and our granchildren,
MAGGIE, JACKSON, LIBBY, and ALEXANDER

To the memory of our parents,
CAROLINA DIMARCO BRANDT,
CHARLES P. BRANDT
and
MAGGIE and CAPT. EARLE T. POOLE

*To the memory of my maternal grandparents from
Le Marche, to whom I owe everything,*
ROSA and LUIGI DIMARCO

···

Contents

...

Acknowledgments

I owe a debt of gratitude to my incredibly beautiful, talented, and wonderful wife, Nancy, who gave each chapter and each revision a hard, honest, and sensible edit before I sent it to the publisher. While I was in New York and Philadelphia working on the book Nancy took care of everything else and gave me daily inspiration, encouragement, and support. On the times Nancy would accompany me to visit Frank Sheeran, he would light up like a young man. And I owe a deep sense of gratitude for the encouragement of our supportive children Tripp Wier, Mimi Wier, and Jenny Rose Brandt.

I owe a debt of gratitude to my remarkable mother, who at 89, cooked Italian food for me, put up with me, and encouraged me during the long weeks I stayed in her Manhattan apartment and sat at my laptop.

I owe a debt of gratitude to my dear friend, the publishing icon William G. Thompson — first to publish both Stephen King and John Grisham — who generously lent his expertise as editorial advisor in developing and executing the project.

I struck pay dirt when Frank Weimann of the Literary Group agreed to be my agent. Frank took the project to heart as a piece of history that would otherwise be lost, gave the book its title, and gave Frank Sheeran a nudge in the right direction for his final taped interview.

When the late Neil Reshen suggested that my agent contact Steerforth Press we suddenly had my book accepted by a publisher who is always thinking, always hands on, and now always my dear friend. Thank you Neil, for steering us to the exceptional Chip Fleischer and his aide, Helga Schmidt.

Thanks to those writers, such as Dan Moldea, Steven Brill, Victor Riesel, and Jonathon Kwitny, whose skillful investigative reporting, at risk of physical harm, uncovered and preserved so much of the history of Jimmy Hoffa, his times, and his disappearance.

Thank you Special Agent Robert A. Garrity, retired, for the excellent, thorough and professional job you did as the Hoffa Case Agent for the FBI. The job that you and your colleagues did made my job doable.

Thank you to those agents, investigators, and prosecuting attorneys and their staff whose efforts created many of the headlines and news stories I consulted.

Thanks to my creative cousin, Carmine Zozzora, for his daily encouragement that kept me focused when the going was rough and for his wise counsel every bit of the way, especially when I would bellyache and he would repeat: "Just write the book; the rest will take care of itself."

How blessed have I been to have had by my side through life my sister and brother-in-law Barbara and Gary Goldsmith and their family Denis, Laura Rose, Danny, Pascal, Lucas and Rose.

A big heap of gratitude to all my superb friends and family who rooted for this book and for its new Conclusion, and to those pals to whom I repeatedly turned for advice, encouragement, and support, especially Marty Shafran, Peter Bosch, Steve Simmons, Jeff Weiner, Tracy Bay, Theo Gund, Joe Pistone, Lin DeVecchio, Al Martino, Leslie Little, Roland DeLong, Colin Jensen, Ed Gardner, Cheryl Thomas, Kathleen and Jerry Chamales. I owe a deep debt in countless ways to Rob Sutcliff.

Thanks Lynn Shafran for all your advice, and especially for bringing the late Ted Feury to Nancy and me. Thank you, Ted, so much.

Thanks to the award-winning illustrator, author, and artist, my friend Uri Shulevitz, who more than twenty years ago encouraged me to start writing professionally.

A toast of lemon and water to my late uncle from Sassano, Prof. Frank Zozzora, who mentored me through the University of Delaware and beyond.

And a belated thanks to my inspiring eleventh-grade English teacher at Stuyvesant High School in 1957, Edwin Herbst.

THE
IRISHMAN

"Russ & Frank"

In a summer cottage by a lake in a room full of tearful and anxious members of Jimmy Hoffa's family, the FBI found a yellow pad. Hoffa kept the pad next to his phone. On the pad Hoffa had written in pencil "Russ & Frank."

"Russ & Frank" were close friends and staunch allies of Jimmy Hoffa. The giant, iron-muscled Frank was so close and loyal to Jimmy throughout Jimmy's ordeals with the law and with Bobby Kennedy that Frank was thought of as family.

On that day by the lake the family in the room feared deep in their souls that only a very close friend, someone trusted, could have gotten near enough to harm a cautious, vigilant Jimmy Hoffa — a man who was keenly aware of his deadly enemies. And on that day "Russ & Frank," mob enforcer Frank "The Irishman" Sheeran and his godfather, Russell "McGee" Bufalino, became leading suspects in the most notorious disappearance in American history.

Every book and serious study on the Hoffa disappearance has alleged that Frank "The Irishman" Sheeran, a staunch Hoffa supporter within the Teamsters, had turned on his friend and mentor. These studies allege that Sheeran was a conspirator and perpetrator, present when Hoffa was killed, and that the killing was sanctioned and planned by Russell "McGee" Bufalino. Among these studies are meticulously researched books, including *The Hoffa Wars,* by investigative reporter Dan Moldea; *The Teamsters,* by Court TV's founder Steven Brill; and *Hoffa,* by Professor Arthur Sloane.

On September 7, 2001, more than twenty-six years after the mystery began, a family member who had been at the cottage by the lake sharing that terrifying time with his mother and his sister held a press conference. Hoffa's son, Teamsters President James P. Hoffa, had just had his hopes raised by a new development in his father's disappearance. The FBI revealed that a DNA test done on a strand of hair proved that Jimmy Hoffa had been inside a car long suspected of being used in the crime. Fox News's senior correspondent Eric Shawn asked James if his father could have been lured into that car by several of the other well-known suspects. James shook his head in response to each man on the list and at the end said, "No, my father didn't know these people." When Shawn asked if Frank Sheeran could have lured his father into the car, James nodded his head and said, "Yes, my father would have gotten into a car with him."

In closing his press conference, James expressed to the media his wish that the case would be solved by a "deathbed confession." At the time he made this request, Frank Sheeran was the only man among the original suspects who was still living and sufficiently aged to give a "deathbed confession." The press conference took place four days before the tragic events of September 11, 2001. James P.'s scheduled appearance on *Larry King Live* for the next week was canceled.

A month later, and with the Hoffa story crowded off the front page, Jimmy's only daughter, Judge Barbara Crancer, telephoned Frank Sheeran from her chambers in St. Louis. Judge Crancer, in the manner of her legendary father, got to the point pretty quickly and made a personal appeal to Sheeran to provide her family closure by telling what he knew about her father's disappearance. "Do the right thing," she said to him. Following his attorney's advice, Sheeran revealed nothing and respectfully referred Barbara to his counsel.

This wasn't the first time Judge Barbara Crancer had written or called the Irishman with the aim of unlocking the secrets in his soul. On March 6, 1995, Barbara had written Frank: "It is my personal belief that there are many people who called themselves loyal friends who know what happened to James R. Hoffa, who did it and why. The fact that not one of them has ever told his family — even under a vow of secrecy — is painful to me. I believe you are one of those people."

On October 25, 2001, a week after Barbara's telephone call, Frank "The Irishman" Sheeran, then in his eighties and using a walker to get around, heard a knock on the patio door of his ground-floor apartment. It was two young FBI agents. They were friendly, relaxed, and very respectful to this man nearing the end of his life. They were hoping he had softened with age, perhaps even repented. They were looking for that "deathbed confession." They said they were too young to remember the case, but they had read thousands of pages of the file. They were up front about the recent phone call Sheeran had received from Barbara, telling him straight out they had discussed the call with her. As he had done repeatedly since July 30, 1975, the day Jimmy disappeared, Sheeran sadly directed the FBI agents to his lawyer, the former district attorney of Philadelphia, F. Emmett Fitzpatrick, Esq.

Failing to persuade Sheeran to cooperate and give a "deathbed confession," the FBI announced on April 2, 2002, that it had turned over its complete, 16,000-page file to the Michigan district attorney and had released 1,330 pages of that file to the media and to Jimmy Hoffa's two children. There would be no federal charges. Finally, after nearly twenty-seven years, the FBI had given up.

On September 3, 2002, almost a year to the day after James P's press conference, the State of Michigan gave up too and closed its file, expressing "continued condolences" to the Hoffa children.

In announcing his decision at a press conference Michigan District Attorney David Gorcyca was quoted as saying: "Unfortunately, this has the markings of a great 'whodunit' novel without the final chapter."

• • •

The Irishman is a "whodunit," but it is not a novel. It is a history based on one-on-one interviews of Frank Sheeran, most of which were tape-recorded. I conducted the first interview in 1991 at Sheeran's apartment, shortly after my partner and I were able to secure Sheeran's premature release from jail on medical grounds. Immediately after that 1991 session Sheeran had second thoughts about the interrogative nature of the interview process and terminated it. He had admitted far more than he was happy with. I told him to get back in touch with me if he changed his mind and was willing to submit to my questioning.

In 1999 Sheeran's daughters arranged a private audience for their aging and physically disabled father with Monsignor Heldusor of St. Dorothy's Church in Philadelphia. Sheeran met with the monsignor, who granted Sheeran absolution for his sins so that he could be buried in a Catholic cemetery. Frank Sheeran said to me: "I believe there is something after we die. If I got a shot at it, I don't want to lose that shot. I don't want to close the door."

Following his audience with the monsignor, Sheeran contacted me, and at Sheeran's request I attended a meeting at his lawyer's office. At the meeting Sheeran agreed to submit to my questioning, and the interviews began again and continued for five years. I brought to the interview process my experiences as a former homicide and death penalty prosecutor, a lecturer on cross-examination, a student of interrogation, and the author of several articles on the U.S. Supreme Court's exclusionary rule regarding confessions. "You're worse than any cop I ever had to deal with," Sheeran said to me once.

I spent countless hours just hanging around with the Irishman, meeting alleged mob figures, driving to Detroit to locate the scene of the Hoffa disappearance, driving to Baltimore to find the scene of two underworld deliveries made by Sheeran, meeting with Sheeran's lawyer, and meeting his family and friends, intimately getting to know the man behind the story. I spent countless hours on the phone and in person, prodding and picking away at the storehouse of material that formed the basis of this book.

More often than not, the first rule in a successful interrogation is to have faith that the subject truly wants to confess, even when he is denying and lying. This was the case with Frank Sheeran. The second rule is to keep the subject talking, and that was never a problem with the Irishman either. Let the words flow and the truth finds its own way out.

Some part of Frank Sheeran had been wanting to get this story off his chest for a long time. In 1978 there had been a controversy about whether Sheeran had confessed over the phone, perhaps while he was under the influence of alcohol, to Steven Brill, author of *The Teamsters*. The FBI believed Sheeran had confessed to Brill and pressured Brill for the tape. Dan Moldea, author of *The Hoffa Wars*, wrote in an article that over breakfast at a hotel, Brill told Moldea he possessed a tape-recorded confession from Sheeran. But Brill, perhaps wisely to keep from becoming a witness in need of protection, denied it publicly in the *New York Times*.

Accordingly, throughout most of the arduous interview process, an effort was made to protect and preserve Sheeran's rights, so that his words would not constitute a legally admissible confession in a court of law.

As the book was written, Frank Sheeran read and approved each chapter. He then re-read and approved the entire manuscript.

On December 14, 2003, Frank Sheeran died. Six weeks earlier, during his final illness, he gave me a final recorded interview from his hospital bed. He told me that he had made his confession and received communion from a visiting priest. Deliberately omitting the use of any protective legal language, Frank Sheeran faced a video camera for his "moment of truth." He held up a copy of *The Irishman* and stood behind all the material in the book you are about to read, including his role in what happened to Jimmy Hoffa on July 30, 1975.

The following day, a week or so before he lost his strength and stamina, Frank Sheeran asked me to pray with him, to say the Lord's Prayer and the Hail Mary with him, which we did together.

Ultimately, Frank Sheeran's words are admissible in the court of public opinion and so to be judged by you, the reader, as part of the history of the past century.

The thread of this story is Frank Sheeran's unique and fascinating life. The witty Irishman was raised a devout Catholic and was a tough child of the Great Depression; a combat-hardened hero of World War II; a high-ranking official in the International Brotherhood of Teamsters; a man alleged by Rudy Giuliani in a Civil RICO suit to be "acting in concert with" La Cosa Nostra's ruling commission — one of only two non-Italians on Guiliani's list of twenty-six top mob figures, which included the sitting bosses of the Bonnano, Genovese, Colombo, Luchese, Chicago, and Milwaukee families as well as various underbosses; a convicted felon, mob enforcer, and legendary stand-up guy; and a father of four daughters and a beloved grandfather.

Because of all that was positive in Frank Sheeran's complex life, including his military service and his love for his children and grandchildren, as a pallbearer I helped to carry the Irishman's green coffin draped with an American flag to his final resting place.

Here is the final chapter of the Hoffa tragedy, a crime that has hurt and haunted everyone connected with it, including those who carried it out, but a crime that has especially hurt and haunted the family of Jimmy Hoffa in their effort to lay to rest their father's fate.

Author's Note: The portions of this book in Frank Sheeran's voice, derived from hundreds of hours of interviews, are indicated by quote marks. Some sections and some chapters written by me add critical detail and background information.

chapter one

"They Wouldn't Dare"

I asked my boss, Russell "McGee" Bufalino, to let me call Jimmy at his cottage by the lake. I was on a peace mission. All I was trying to do at that particular time was keep this thing from happening to Jimmy.

I reached out for Jimmy on Sunday afternoon, July 27, 1975. Jimmy was gone by Wednesday, July 30. Sadly, as we say, gone to Australia — down under. I will miss my friend until the day I join him.

I was at my own apartment in Philly using my own phone when I made the long-distance call to Jimmy's cottage at Lake Orion near Detroit. If I had been in on the thing on Sunday I would have used a pay phone, not my own phone. You don't survive as long as I did by making calls about important matters from your own phone. I wasn't made with a finger. My father used the real thing to get my mother pregnant.

While I was in my kitchen standing by my rotary wall phone getting ready to dial the number I knew by heart, I gave some consideration to just how I was going to approach Jimmy. I learned during my years of union negotiations that it always was best to review things in your mind first before you opened your mouth. And besides that, this call was not going to be an easy one.

When he got out of jail on a presidential pardon by Nixon in 1971, and he began fighting to reclaim the presidency of the Teamsters, Jimmy became very hard to talk to. Sometimes you see that with guys when they first get out. Jimmy became reckless with his tongue — on the radio, in the papers, on television. Every time he opened his mouth he said something about how he was going to expose the mob and get the mob out of the union. He even said he was going to keep the mob from using the pension fund. I can't imagine certain people liked hearing that their golden goose would be killed if he got back in. All this coming from Jimmy was hypocritical to say the least, considering Jimmy was the one who brought the so-called mob into the union and the pension fund in the first place. Jimmy brought me into the union through Russell. With very good reason I was concerned for my friend more than a little bit.

I started getting concerned about nine months before this telephone call that Russell was letting me make. Jimmy had flown out to Philly to be the featured speaker at Frank Sheeran Appreciation Night at the Latin Casino. There were 3,000 of my good friends and family, including the mayor, the district attorney, guys I fought in the war with, the singer Jerry Vale and the Golddigger Dancers with legs that didn't quit, and certain other guests the FBI would call La Cosa Nostra. Jimmy presented me with a gold watch encircled with diamonds. Jimmy looked at the guests on the dais and said, "I never realized you were that strong." That was a special comment because Jimmy Hoffa was one of the two greatest men I ever met.

Before they brought the dinner of prime rib, and when we were getting our pictures taken, some little nobody that Jimmy was in jail with asked Jimmy for ten grand for a business venture. Jimmy reached in his pocket and gave him $2,500. That was Jimmy — a soft touch.

Naturally, Russell Bufalino was there. He was the other one of the two greatest men that I ever met. Jerry Vale sang Russ's favorite song, "Spanish Eyes," for him. Russell was boss of the Bufalino family of upstate Pennsylvania, and large parts of New York, New Jersey, and Florida. Being headquartered outside New York City, Russell wasn't in the inner circle of New York's five families, but all the families came to him for advice on everything. If there was any important matter that needed taking care of, they gave the job to Russell. He was respected throughout the country. When Albert Anastasia got shot in the barber's chair in New York, they made Russell the acting head of that family until they could straighten everything out. There's no way to get more respect than Russell got. He was very strong. The public never heard of him, but the families and the feds knew how strong he was.

Russell presented me with a gold ring that he had made up special for just three people — himself, his underboss, and me. It had a big three-dollar gold piece on top surrounded by diamonds. Russ was big in the jewelry-fencing and cat-burglar world. He was a silent partner in a number of jewelry stores on Jeweler's Row in New York City.

The gold watch Jimmy gave me is still on my wrist, and the gold ring Russell gave me is still on my finger here at the assisted-living home. On my other hand I've got a ring with each of my daughters' birthstones.

Jimmy and Russell were very much alike. They were solid muscle from head to toe. They were both short, even for those days. Russ was about 5'8". Jimmy was down around 5'5". In those days I used to be 6'4", and I had to bend down to them for private talks. They were very smart from head to toe. They had mental toughness and physical toughness. But in one important way they were different. Russ was very low-key and quiet, soft-spoken even when he got mad. Jimmy exploded every day just to keep his temper in shape, and he loved publicity.

The night before my testimonial dinner, Russ and I had a sit-down with Jimmy. We sat at a table at Broadway Eddie's, and Russell Bufalino told Jimmy Hoffa flat-out he should stop running for union president. He told him certain people were very happy with Frank Fitzsimmons, who replaced Jimmy when he went to jail. Nobody at the table said so, but we all knew these certain people were very happy with the big and easy loans they could get out of the Teamsters Pension Fund under the weak-minded Fitz. They got loans under Jimmy when he was in, and Jimmy got his points under the table, but the loans were always on Jimmy's terms. Fitz bent over for these certain people. All Fitz cared about was drinking and golfing. I don't have to tell you how much juice comes out of a billion-dollar pension fund.

Russell said, "What are you running for? You don't need the money."

Jimmy said, "It's not about the money. I'm not letting Fitz have the union."

After the sit-down, when I was getting ready to take Jimmy back to the Warwick Hotel, Russ took me aside and said: "Talk to your friend. Tell him what it is." In our way of speaking, even though it doesn't sound like much, that was as good as a death threat.

At the Warwick Hotel I told Jimmy if he didn't change his mind about taking back the union he had better keep some bodies around him for protection.

"I'm not going that route or they'll go after my family."

"Still in all, you don't want to be out on the street by yourself."

"Nobody scares Hoffa. I'm going after Fitz, and I'm going to win this election."

"You know what this means," I said. "Russ himself told me to tell you what it is."

"They wouldn't dare," Jimmy Hoffa growled, his eyes glaring at mine.

All Jimmy did the rest of the night and at breakfast the next morning was talk a lot of distorted talk. Looking back it could have been nervous talk, but I never knew Jimmy to show fear. Although one of the items on the agenda that Russell had spoken to Jimmy about at the table at Broadway Eddie's the night before my testimonial dinner was more than enough to make the bravest man show fear.

And there I was in my kitchen in Philadelphia nine months after Frank Sheeran Appreciation Night with the phone in my hand and Jimmy on the other end of the line at his cottage in Lake Orion, and me hoping this time Jimmy would reconsider taking back the union while he still had the time.

"My friend and I are driving out for the wedding," I said.

"I figured you and your friend would attend the wedding," Jimmy said.

Jimmy knew "my friend" was Russell and that you didn't use his name over the phone. The wedding was Bill Bufalino's daughter's wedding in Detroit. Bill was no relation to Russell, but Russell gave him permission to say they were cousins. It helped Bill's career. He was the Teamsters lawyer in Detroit.

Bill Bufalino had a mansion in Grosse Pointe that had a waterfall in the basement. There was a little bridge you walked over that separated one side of the basement from the other. The men had their own side so they could talk. The women stayed on their side of the waterfall. Evidently, these were not women who paid attention to the words when they heard Helen Reddy sing her popular song of the day, "I Am Woman, Hear Me Roar."

"I guess you're not going to the wedding," I said.

"Jo doesn't want people staring," he said. Jimmy didn't have to explain. There was talk about an FBI wiretap that was coming out. Certain parties were on the tape talking about extramarital relations his wife, Josephine, allegedly had years ago with Tony Cimini, a soldier in the Detroit outfit.

"Ah, nobody believed that bull, Jimmy. I figured you wouldn't go because of this other thing."

"Fuck them. They think they can scare Hoffa."

"There's widespread concern that things are getting out of hand."

"I got ways to protect myself. I got records put away."

"Please, Jimmy, even my friend is concerned."

"How's your friend doing?" Jimmy laughed. "I'm glad he got that problem handled last week."

Jimmy was referring to an extortion trial Russ had just beat in Buffalo. "Our friend's doing real good," I said. "He's the one gave me the go-ahead to call you."

These respected men were both my friends, and they were both good friends to each other. Russell introduced me to Jimmy in the first place back in the fifties. At the time I had three daughters to support.

I had lost my job driving a meat truck for Food Fair, when they caught me trying to be a partner in their business. I was stealing sides of beef and chickens and selling them to restaurants. So I started taking day jobs out of the Teamsters union hall, driving trucks for companies when their regular driver was out sick or something. I also taught ballroom dancing, and on Friday and Saturday nights I was a bouncer at the Nixon Ballroom, a black nightclub.

On the side I handled certain matters for Russ, never for money, but as a show of respect. I wasn't a hitman for hire. Some cowboy. You ran a little errand. You did a favor. You got a little favor back if you ever needed it.

I had seen *On The Waterfront* in the movies, and I thought I was at least as bad as that Marlon Brando. I said to Russ that I wanted to get into union work. We were at a bar in South Philly. He had arranged for a call from Jimmy Hoffa in Detroit and put me on the line with him. The first words Jimmy ever spoke to me were, "I heard you paint houses." The paint is the blood that supposedly gets on the wall or the floor when you shoot somebody. I told Jimmy, "I do my own carpentry work, too." That refers to making coffins and means you get rid of the bodies yourself.

After that conversation Jimmy put me to work for the International, making more money than I had made on all those other jobs put together, including the stealing. I got extra money for expenses. On the side I handled certain matters for Jimmy the way I did for Russell.

"So, he gave you the go-ahead to call. You should call more often." Jimmy was going to act nonchalant about it. He was going to make me get to the reason Russell granted me permission to call him. "You used to call all the time."

"That's the whole thing I'm trying to say. If I called you, then what am I supposed to do? I got to tell the old man — what? That you're still not listening to him. He's not used to people not listening to him."

"The old man will live forever."

"No doubt, he'll dance on our graves," I said. "The old man

is very careful what he eats. He does the cooking. He won't let me fry eggs and sausage because one time I tried to use butter instead of olive oil."

"Butter? I wouldn't let you fry eggs and sausage either."

"And you know, Jimmy, the old man is very careful how much he eats. He always says you got to share the pie. You eat the whole pie you get the bellyache."

"I got nothing but respect for your friend," Jimmy said. "I would never hurt him. There are certain elements Hoffa will get for fucking me out of the union, but Hoffa will never hurt your friend."

"I know that, Jimmy, and he respects you. Coming up from nothing, the way you did. All the good things you've done for the rank and file. He's for the underdog, too. You know that."

"You tell him for me. I want to make sure he never forgets. I've got nothing but respect for McGee." Only a handful of people referred to Russell as McGee. His real name was Rosario, but everybody called him Russell. Those who knew him better called him Russ. Those who knew him best called him McGee.

"Like I say, Jimmy, the respect is mutual."

"They say it's going to be a big wedding," Jimmy said. "Italians are coming from all over the country."

"Yeah. That's good for us. Jimmy, I had a talk with our friend about trying to work this thing out. The timing is good. Everybody being there for the wedding. He was being very encouraging about the matter."

"Did the old man suggest working this out or did you?" Jimmy asked quickly.

"I put the subject on the agenda, but our friend was very receptive."

"What'd he say about this?"

"Our friend was very receptive. He said let's sit down with Jimmy at the lake after the wedding. Work this thing out."

"He's good people. That's what McGee is. Come out to the lake, huh?" Jimmy's tone of voice sounded as if he were on the verge of showing his famous temper but maybe in a good way. "Hoffa always wanted to work this fucking thing out, from day one." More and more these days Jimmy was calling himself Hoffa.

"This is a perfect time to work it out with all the concerned parties in town for the wedding and all," I said. "Settle the thing."

"From day one Hoffa wanted to work this fucking thing out," he hollered just in case everybody in Lake Orion didn't hear him the first time.

"Jimmy, I know you know this matter's got to be settled," I said. "It can't go on like this. I know you're doing a lot of puffing about exposing this and exposing that. I know you're not serious. Jimmy Hoffa's no rat and he never will be a rat, but there is concern. People don't know how you puff."

"The hell Hoffa's not serious. Wait till Hoffa gets back in and gets his hands on the union records, we'll see if I'm puffing."

From growing up around my old man and from union work, I think I know how to read the tone of people's voices. Jimmy sounded like he was on the verge of showing his famous temper back the other way again. Like I was losing him by bringing up the puffing. Jimmy was a born union negotiator, and here he was coming from strength, talking about exposing records again.

"Look at that matter last month, Jimmy. That gentleman in Chicago. I'm quite certain everybody thought he was untouchable, including himself. Irresponsible talk that could have hurt certain important friends of ours was his problem."

Jimmy knew "the gentleman" I was talking about was his good friend Sam "Momo" Giancana, the Chicago boss who just got killed. Many times I brought "notes" — verbal messages, nothing ever in writing — back and forth between Momo and Jimmy.

Before he got taken care of, Giancana had been very big in certain circles and very big in the media. Momo had spread out from Chicago and moved into Dallas. Jack Ruby was a part of Momo's outfit. Momo had casinos in Havana. Momo opened a casino with Frank Sinatra in Lake Tahoe. He dated one of the singing McGuire sisters, the ones who sang on

Arthur Godfrey. He shared a mistress with John F. Kennedy, Judith Campbell. This was while JFK was president and he and his brother Bobby were using the White House for their own motel room. Momo helped get JFK elected. Only Kennedy then stabbed Momo in the back. He paid him back by letting Bobby go after everybody.

The way it went with Giancana is that the week before he got hit, *Time* magazine brought out that Russell Bufalino and Sam "Momo" Giancana had worked on behalf of the CIA in 1961 in the Bay of Pigs invasion of Cuba and in 1962 in a plot to kill Castro. If there was one thing that drove Russell Bufalino nuts it was to see his name in print.

The U.S. Senate had subpoenaed Giancana to testify about the CIA hiring the mob to assassinate Castro. Four days before his appearance Giancana was taken care of in his kitchen in the back of the head and then under the chin six times, Sicilian style, to signify he was careless with his mouth. It looked like it was done by some old friend that was close enough to him to be frying sausages in olive oil with him. Russell often said to me: "When in doubt have no doubt."

"Our Chicago friend could have hurt a lot of people, even you and me," Jimmy yelled. I put the phone away from my ear and still could hear him. "He should have kept records. Castro. Dallas. The gentleman from Chicago never put anything in writing. They know Hoffa keeps records. Anything unnatural happens to me, the records come out."

"I'm no 'yes man,' Jimmy. So please don't tell me 'They wouldn't dare.' After what happened to our friend in Chicago, you gotta know by now what it is."

"You just be concerned for yourself, my Irish friend. You're too close to me in some people's eyes. You remember what I told you. Watch your own ass. Get some people around yourself."

"Jimmy, you know it's time to sit down. The old man is making the offer to help."

"I agree with that part of it." Jimmy was being the union negotiator, conceding just a little bit.

"Good," I jumped on that little bit. "We'll drive out to the lake on Saturday around 12:30. Tell Jo not to fuss, we'll leave the women at a diner."

"I'll be ready at 12:30," Jimmy said. I knew he'd be ready at 12:30. Russ and Jimmy both went by time. You didn't show time, you didn't show respect. Jimmy would give you fifteen minutes. After that you lost your appointment. No matter how big you were or thought you were.

"I'll have an Irish banquet waiting for you — a bottle of Guinness and a bologna sandwich. One more thing," Jimmy said. "Just the two of you." Jimmy wasn't asking. He was telling. "Not the little guy."

"I can relate to that part. You don't want the little guy."

Want the little guy? Last I knew Jimmy wanted the little guy dead. The little guy was Tony "Pro" Provenzano, a made man and a captain in the Genovese family in Brooklyn. Pro used to be a Hoffa man, but he became the leader of the Teamsters faction that was against Jimmy taking back the union.

The bad blood that Pro had with Jimmy began with a beef they had in prison where they almost came to blows in the dining hall. Jimmy refused to help Pro go around the federal law and get his $1.2 million pension when he went to jail, while Jimmy got his $1.7 million pension even though he went to jail, too.

A couple of years after they both got out they had a sit-down at a Teamsters Convention in Miami to try to square the beef. Only Tony Pro threatened to rip Jimmy's guts out with his bare hands and kill his grandchildren. At the time, Jimmy told me he was going to ask Russell for permission for me to take care of the little guy. Since Pro was a made man, a captain even, you didn't take care of Pro without getting approval from Russell. But then I never heard a peep. So I figured it was a fleeting thought during one of Jimmy's tempers. If anybody was serious, I'd hear about it the day they wanted me to do it. That's the way it's done. You get about a day's notice when they want you to take care of a matter.

Tony Pro ran a Teamsters Local in north Jersey where the Sopranos are on TV. I liked his brothers. Nunz and Sammy were good people. I never cared for Pro himself. He'd kill you for nothing. One time he had a guy killed for getting more votes than him. They were on the same side of the ticket. Pro was at the head of the ticket, running for president of his local, and this poor guy was below him, running for some lesser office, I forget what. When Tony Pro saw how popular the guy was compared to him, Pro had Sally Bugs and an ex-boxer with the Jewish mob, K.O. Konigsberg, strangle him with a nylon rope. That was a bad hit. When they made deals with the devil trying to nail the handful of us Hoffa suspects on any charge they could get, they got a rat to testify against Pro. They wound up giving Pro life for that bad hit. Pro died in jail.

"I won't meet with the little guy," Jimmy said, "Fuck the little guy."

"You're making me work hard here, Jimmy. I'm not trying to go for the Nobel Peace Prize here."

"Help Hoffa square this beef and I'll give you a peace prize. Remember, just the three of us. Take care."

I had to be content that at least the three of us were going to sit down by the lake on Saturday. Jimmy sitting down with "Russ & Frank" with our names on that yellow pad he kept near his phone for anybody to find.

The next morning was Monday the 28th. My second wife, Irene, the mother of the youngest of my four daughters, Connie, was on her own line with her girlfriend. They were trying to decide what Irene should pack for the wedding when my line rang.

"It's Jimmy," Irene said.

The FBI has a record of all these long-distance calls back and forth. But I don't think Jimmy had these kinds of records on his mind when he made his threats about exposing this and that. People couldn't tolerate threats like that very long. Even if you don't mean them yourself you send the wrong message to the people at the bottom of the chain of command. How strong are the leaders if they tolerate people talking about ratting? God forbid he'd expose the Vegas skim.

"When are you and your friend getting in?" Jimmy said.

"Tuesday."

"That's tomorrow."

"Yeah, tomorrow night around dinnertime."

"Good. Call me when you get in."

"Why wouldn't I?" Whenever I got into Detroit I would call the man out of respect.

"I've got a meeting set up on Wednesday afternoon," Jimmy said. He paused. "With the little guy."

"Which little guy?"

"That little guy."

"You don't mind me asking what changed your mind about meeting with that individual?" My head was spinning.

"What have I got to lose?" Jimmy said. "McGee would expect Hoffa to try to square his own beef first. I don't mind making one last try before you come out to the lake on Saturday."

"I gotta urge you to take along your little brother." He knew what I meant, a gun, a piece, not the peace prize, a peace-maker. "Precautionary."

"Don't you worry about Hoffa. Hoffa doesn't need a little brother. Tony Jack set the meet up. We'll be at a restaurant out in the public. The Red Fox on Telegraph, you know the place. Take care."

Anthony "Tony Jack" Giacalone was with the Detroit outfit. Tony Jack was very close to Jimmy and his wife and kids. But Jimmy wasn't the only one in the picture that Tony Jack was close to. Tony Jack's wife was a first cousin to the little guy, Tony Pro. That's serious with the Italians.

I could understand why Jimmy would trust Tony Jack. Tony Jack was very good people. He died in jail in February 2001. The headline read: "Reputed U.S. Mobster Takes Hoffa Secret to Grave." He could've told some things.

Word was out for a long time that Tony Jack had been trying to arrange another sit-down between Jimmy and Tony Pro after the fiasco in Miami, but Jimmy went thumbs down on that idea like Siskel and Ebert. Now all of a sudden Jimmy was agreeing to meet with Pro, the same Pro that threatened to rip his guts out with his bare hands.

Looking back, you know hindsight and all, maybe Jimmy was the one setting Pro up to go to Australia. Maybe Jimmy was counting on Pro to act like Pro. Tony Jack would sit there at the restaurant and watch Jimmy being reasonable and Pro being an asshole. Maybe Jimmy wanted Russell to know on Saturday by the lake that he had tried everything humanly possible with the man, but now Pro had to go.

"Out in a public restaurant, that's good. Maybe this wedding really is bringing everybody together," I said. "Smoking the peace pipe and burying old hatchets. Only I'd have more comfort if I was there for backup."

"All right, Irishman," he said, as if he was trying to make me feel better, even though he's the one that asked me when I was getting in to Detroit in the first place. As soon as he asked me when I was getting in, I knew what he wanted. "How about you take a little ride and meet me there on Wednesday at 2:00? They're coming at 2:30."

"Precautionary. But however, you can rest assured, I'll bring my little brother. He's a real good negotiator."

I called Russ right away and told him the encouraging news about Jimmy's meeting with Jack and Pro, and that I was going to be with Jimmy for backup.

I've thought a lot about it since, but I can't recall Russell saying anything.

chapter two

What It Is

When my wife, Irene, and I got to Kingston in upstate Pennsylvania near Wilkes-Barre that Monday night, our plan was to have dinner with Russ and his wife, Carrie, and her older widowed sister, Mary. Irene and I would spend the night at the Howard Johnson that Russ owned a piece of. Then early Tuesday the five of us would start off for Detroit in my new black Lincoln Continental. (It was a car they said I got under the table. When they were trying to get the eight of us Hoffa suspects on anything they could, they used the car to send me to jail in 1981 on labor racketeering.)

The drive would take us about twelve hours because Russell didn't allow smoking in the car. Russ quit smoking on a bet with Jimmy Blue Eyes, who was with Meyer Lansky, on a boat they took out of Cuba in 1960 when Castro kicked them all out and took away their casinos. They lost a million dollars a day on account of Castro. They were all mad as hell at Castro, especially Russell and his two very close friends, Carlos Marcello, the New Orleans boss, and Santo Trafficante, the Florida boss. Castro had the nerve to actually put Trafficante in jail. I heard that Sam "Momo" Giancana had to send Jack Ruby to Cuba to spread some green stamps around to get Trafficante out of jail and out of Cuba.

Being so fuming mad, Russell smoked cigarette after cigarette and softly cursed Castro on that boat. So Jimmy Blue Eyes saw an opportunity to bet Russ twenty-five Gs Russ couldn't go a year without smoking. Russ threw his cigarette overboard and never picked up a cigarette again, even a year later after the bet was over and Jimmy Blue Eyes had paid up.

But the ladies in the car made no such bet with anybody. We'd be stopping along the way for their smoke breaks, and that would slow us down. (Smoking is one vice I never had to confess to the priest when I was a kid. I never got started on tobacco, not even in the war, not even pinned down at Anzio with nothing else to do in a dugout for four months but play cards, pray to God, and smoke. You need your wind in this life.)

Another reason it would take so long is that Russell always had business stops to make along the way whenever or wherever we went together — instructions to give about certain matters, cash to pick up, stuff like that.

On Monday night Irene and I had dinner with Russell, Carrie, and her sister Mary at Brutico's in Old Forge, Pennsylvania. Russ had special restaurants that met his standards. Otherwise, if he didn't cook it himself, most of the time he didn't eat it.

If it weren't for Russ's gray hair there's no way you would know he was in his seventies. He was very spry. He was born in Sicily, but he spoke perfect English. He and Carrie never had any children. Many a time Russ reached up and pinched my cheek and said, "You should've been Italian." He's the one named me "The Irishman." Before that they used to call me "Cheech," which is short for Frank in Italian — Francesco.

After we had our meal, which was something like veal and peppers with spaghetti marinara, a side dish of broccoli rabe, and a nice salad with dressing Russell made in the back, we sat and relaxed with our coffee laced with Sambuca.

Then the owner came over and whispered to Russ. This was before portable phones. Russ had to leave the table to take the call. He came back business-like. He had that smile on his round, craggy face you get when you squint at the sun. He had muscle deterioration in his face that gave him a lazy eye. If you didn't know him you would think he was blinking or drinking. With his good eye he looked through his wide glasses into my blue eyes.

Russell didn't say anything at first, like he was trying to think how to say it by studying my eyes. Russell had a voice that crackled like a rattle, but the madder he got the softer Russell talked. He was very soft-spoken that night before my testimonial dinner at Frank Sheeran Appreciation Night when he warned Jimmy to back off from trying to take back the union.

At the table at Brutico's, Russell was talking so soft I had to lean my extra-large head real close. In a raspy whisper he said, "We got a little change in plans. We're not leaving tomorrow. We stay put 'til Wednesday morning."

The news hit me like a mortar shell. They didn't want me in Detroit Wednesday afternoon at that restaurant. They wanted Jimmy alone.

I stayed bent over close to Russell. Maybe he'd tell me more. You listen. You don't ask questions. It seemed like it took him a good while. Maybe it just seemed like a long delay to me before he spoke. "Your friend was too late. There's no need for you and me to meet him on Saturday by the lake."

Russell Bufalino's penetrating good eye stayed on mine. I moved back up in my seat. I couldn't show anything in my face. I couldn't say a word. That's not the way it works. The wrong look in my eyes and my house gets painted.

Jimmy warned me to watch myself back in October at the Warwick Hotel in Philly when I tried to tell him what it is. He said, ". . . watch your ass . . . you could end up being fair game." Just yesterday he got done warning me again on the phone that I was too close to him "in some people's eyes." I put the coffee and Sambuca up to my nose. The licorice didn't smell strong enough against the smell of the coffee so I added some Sambuca.

I didn't have to be told that I better not even think about calling Jimmy when Irene and I got back to the Howard Johnson motel for the night. From this point on, whether it was true or not, I would have to assume that I was being watched. Russell had a piece of that Howard Johnson's. If I used the phone that night it is quite likely that Irene and I never would have made it out of the parking lot the next morning. I would have gotten what some people thought was coming to me anyway, and poor Irene just would have been in the wrong place at the wrong time with the wrong Irishman.

And there was no way in the world Jimmy could call me. In case the feds were listening, you never said on the phone where you'd be staying when you got to where you were going. There were no cell phones then. Jimmy just wouldn't get a call from me Tuesday night in Detroit, and that would be that. He would never know why. He'd go alone to his meeting on Wednesday. My little brother and I wouldn't be there for backup.

I sat there in silence with the ladies talking among themselves about who knows what. They might as well have been on the other side of the bridge over the waterfall in Bill Bufalino's basement.

I was reviewing things fast. Right after I called Russell that morning about Jimmy calling me, Russell would have called certain important people. He would have told these people about me going to the restaurant with Jimmy and taking my little brother. Right or wrong, the best I could figure at that moment was that these people called Russell and told him they wanted us to stay put for a day so they could get Jimmy alone.

Only before they called Russell they must've been reviewing things themselves. All day certain people in New York, Chicago, and Detroit must have been deciding whether or not to let me be there with Jimmy on Wednesday. That way one of the closest Hoffa supporters in America would go to Australia with Jimmy. Whatever secrets Jimmy may have told me after Broadway Eddie's that night at the Warwick and over the years would die with me. In the end they made the decision to spare me out of respect for Russell. It wouldn't be the first time Russell saved me from something serious.

I don't care how tough you are or how tough you think you are, if they want you you're theirs. It's usually your best friend that walks up to you talking about a football bet and you're gone. Like Giancana got it frying eggs and sausages in olive oil with an old friend he trusted.

This was the wrong time for me to sound like I was worrying about Jimmy. Still, I couldn't help myself. Without making it sound like I was trying to save Jimmy, I got right next to Russell's ear. "The nuclear fallout from the feds." I tried not to stammer, but I probably was stammering. He was used to it; it was the way I talked since childhood. I wasn't worried that he might view it as some kind of sign that I was having a problem with this particular matter because I was very loyal to Jimmy and very close to Jimmy and his family. I bowed my head and shook it from side to side. "The nuclear fallout's going to hit the fan. You know, Jimmy's got records stashed away in case something unnatural happens to him."

"Your friend made one threat too many in his life," Russell shrugged.

"I'm only saying the nuclear fallout's going to hit the fan when they find his body."

"There won't be a body." Russell went thumb down on the table with his right hand. Russell had lost the thumb and index finger on his left hand when he was young. He moved the thumb he still had around like he was grinding something into the white tablecloth and said, "Dust to dust."

I leaned back and sipped my Sambuca and coffee. "That's what it is," I said. I took another sip, "So, we get in on Wednesday night."

The old man reached up and pinched my cheek like he knew what was in my heart. "My Irishman, we did all we could for the man. Nobody could tell that man what it is. We get into Detroit together Wednesday night."

I put my coffee cup down into its saucer, and Russell moved his warm, thick hand to the back of my neck and left it there and whispered, "We'll drive so far, and we'll stop for the women someplace. We'll go do some business."

Sure, I thought, and nodded. Russell had business all along the route from Kingston to Detroit. We'd drop the women at some roadside diner and go do our business while they smoked and had coffee.

Russell leaned toward me, and I bent down and leaned close to him. He whispered, "There'll be a pilot waiting. You take a quick fly over the lake and do a little errand in Detroit. Then you fly back. Pick the women up. They won't even notice we're gone. Then we take our time. Nice, leisurely drive the rest of the way to Detroit. The scenic route. We're in no hurry. That's what it is."

chapter three

Get Yourself Another Punching Bag

What were the twists and turns that brought me to that exact moment in a small Italian restaurant in a coal-mining town in Pennsylvania, where I listened carefully to whispered orders? Orders I had to follow for the part I had to play in the plot against my friend Jimmy Hoffa.

I wasn't born into that Mafia way of life like the young Italians were, who came out of places like Brooklyn, Detroit, and Chicago. I was Irish Catholic from Philadelphia, and before I came home from the war I never did anything really wrong, not even a pinch for disorderly conduct.

I was born into some rough times, not just for the Irish, but for everybody. They say the Depression started when I was nine years old in 1929, but as far as I'm concerned our family *never* had any money. Nobody else's family did either.

My first taste of enemy fire came from farmers in New Jersey when I was a young lad. Philadelphia sits across the wide Delaware River from Camden, New Jersey. Both cities got their start as ocean-going port towns and are connected by the Walt Whitman Bridge. It's hard to believe now, when you drive out past Camden and you see that there's hardly any free land for so much as a tiny Victory garden, that in the Roaring Twenties when I was a kid it was all flat, fenced-in farmland. New Jersey was the sticks compared to Philadelphia. It was real peaceful out there.

My father, Tom Sheeran, would borrow a big old clumsy car with a running board. He'd drive me out to the farm fields outside of Camden from the time I was very little. He'd drop me off where the Camden Airport is now so I could do a little harvesting.

We'd go in the early evening when it was still light enough to see, but getting dark. That's the time of day when the farmers were expecting to have their own dinner. I would climb over the farmer's fence and toss back to my father samples of the crop I was harvesting. It could be ears of corn or tomatoes or whatever was in season. That's what you had to do to get by and put food on the table.

But the farmers weren't any too happy with our ideas about sharing in nature's bounty. Some nights they'd be waiting for us with shotguns. Some farmer would chase me, and I'd jump over the fence and get hit in the butt with birdshot.

One of my earliest childhood memories is getting birdshot picked out of my backside by my mother, Mary. My mother would say, "Tom, how come I'm always picking this stuff out of Francis's behind?" My father, who always called her Mame, would say, "Because the boy doesn't run fast enough, Mame."

I get my size from my mother's Swedish side of the family. Her father was a miner and a railroad worker in Sweden. Her brother was a doctor in Philadelphia, Dr. Hansen. My mother was about 5'10" and never weighed less than 200 pounds. She ate a quart of ice cream every day. I used to go down to the ice-cream parlor for her every night. You would bring your own bowl and they would give you so many dips of ice cream. They knew to expect me. My mother loved to cook and make all her own bread. I can still smell the aroma of her roast pork, sauerkraut, and potatoes simmering on the coal stove. My mother was a very quiet woman. I think she showed her love for us through her cooking.

My folks got married very late in life for those days. My mother was forty-two when they had me, their first kid, and my father was forty-three. They had us a year apart. My brother was thirteen months younger than me, and my sister was thirteen months younger than him. We were what they used to call Irish twins because the Catholic Irish popped those babies out so close together.

Even though my mother was Swedish my father raised us Irish. His people were from outside of Dublin, and I never met any of my grandparents on either side. People in those days didn't display affection like they do today. I'm still learning how to be affectionate to my grandchildren. I don't ever remember getting a kiss from my mother. I never even saw her kiss my kid brother, or my kid sister, Margaret. Not that anyone meant to play favorites, but Tom was my father's favorite and Peggy was my mother's. I guess I was so big, and being the oldest, they expected me to be more grown up than the two younger ones. I even got that in school from teachers who talked to me like I was an older kid and expected me to understand what they were talking about.

My folks did the best they could with what they had. Every Easter, Tom and Peggy would get some new clothing to wear, but my parents would never have any money to get me anything. Getting a new outfit for Easter was big in the Catholic neighborhoods I grew up in. I can remember one Easter when I complained to my father about never getting anything for Easter and he told me, "Take Tom's new hat and put it on your head and stand in front of the window and the neighbors will think you got a new hat, too."

I can't remember any of us Sheeran kids ever having a toy of our own. One Christmas we got a pair of roller skates to share. They were metal skates, and you could adjust the size. We learned to go without. And if we wanted something we had to fend for ourselves. I had my first job when I was seven, helping a guy clean out the ashes from cellars. And if I managed to get some work cutting somebody's grass for spending money and my father found out about it, he'd wait up the block until I got paid, and then he'd come down and take the big coins and leave me maybe a dime.

We lived in a lot of different Catholic neighborhoods, but mostly in the same parish. We'd spend a few months some-where, and then my father would get behind in the rent, and we'd sneak out in a hurry and move to another apartment. Then we'd do it again when that rent came due. When he got work my father worked as a steel worker, high up on tall buildings, walking on beams like those Mohawk Indians. It was dangerous work. People were always falling to their death. He worked on the building of the Ben Franklin Bridge in Philadelphia and on the few high-rise buildings they could afford to build in the Depression. He was about two inches shorter than my mother, maybe 5'8", and weighed about 145 pounds. For a long time the only work my father could get was as the sexton and the school janitor at the Blessed Virgin Mary Church and School in Darby, Pennsylvania.

The Catholic religion was an important part of our lives. It was mandatory. If I had to say what my mother's hobby was, I'd say she was very religious. I spent a lot of time inside Catholic churches. My father had studied for five years at a seminary to be a priest before he dropped out. His two sisters were nuns. I learned all about confession as a way to get absolution for your sins. If you died on your way to confession before you could tell the priest what you had done wrong you would burn in hell for all eternity. If you died on your way home from confession after confessing your sins you would go straight to heaven.

I was an altar boy at Mother of Sorrows Church until I got kicked off for trying the sacramental wine. I don't blame the other altar boy who snitched on me. He wasn't really a rat. Father O'Malley — believe it or not that was his name, just like the priest Bing Crosby always played — saw the wine was missing and told the boy that whoever took the wine wouldn't go to heaven. I guess the other kid figured he had a shot to go to heaven so he squealed on me. And the worst part about it is I didn't even like the wine they used.

My father did like his beer. My father used to bet on me a lot in the speakeasies. We'd be in a new section of Philadelphia where they didn't know us too well yet and he'd go in a speakeasy and bet somebody that he had a ten-year-old kid who could lick any fourteen- or fifteen-year-old boy. He'd bet some kid's father a quarter for beer, and us kids would have to fight it out in front of all the grown men. If I won, which was almost always the case, he'd toss me a dime. If I lost he'd cuff me hard on the back of the head.

We lived for a while in a mostly Italian neighborhood, and I had to fight to get home from school every day. I learned a lot of Italian words as a kid that helped me later on in the Sicilian and Italian campaigns during the war. While I was over there I learned to speak Italian pretty good. While I was learning it, mostly to get along with the Italian women, I didn't realize that the people I would get involved with after the war would be very impressed with how well I spoke Italian. They took it as a sign of respect toward them. It made it a lot easier for them to confide in me and trust me and respect me.

My father, Thomas Sheeran, was an amateur boxer for Shanahan's Catholic Club. He was a tough welterweight. Many years later after the war I would go on to play football for Shanahan's. When I was a kid a lot of our activities were supplied by the church. This was way before television. Very few people had radios and the movies cost precious money. So people came and watched the church events or participated in them. My father competed a lot in the ring.

He also competed a lot at home. Whenever he thought I'd done something wrong, he'd toss me the boxing gloves. But I wasn't allowed to hit back. My father was untouchable. He would jab my face and throw hooks and overhand rights. Being a steel worker, he could hit. I would bob and weave and try to block the blows with my own gloves. If I was foolish enough to try to punch him I'd really get hammered. I was the only one in the family he ever tossed the gloves to. No matter what Thomas Jr. (who was named after him) did wrong, he never got cuffed around.

But then Tom never played the pranks I did either. Nothing bad, but I was always a rebel. One time in the seventh grade, when I was attending the Blessed Virgin Mary elementary school, I took Limburger cheese out of the old ice-box tray at home and brought it to school. Schools were pretty cold when you first got there until the heat came up, and we all sat with our sweaters and jackets on in the winter. They had steam heat in the school. The heat came from radiators and we'd have to wait for them to warm up. I stuck the Limburger in the radiator. It heated up and got softer and softer and slowly stunk the whole room up. They called my father, who was the school janitor. He followed the smell and found the Limburger, and then some other kid ratted me out. My old man said he'd see me when he got home.

When I got home and waited for him I knew that as soon as he got home he was going to get the boxing gloves out and toss them to me. Sure enough, when he came through the door he calmly said, "What do you want to do, eat first or eat after I kick your ass?" I said, "I'll eat first." I knew I wouldn't feel like eating dinner afterward. I got it pretty good that night, but at least I got some food in me.

I stammered a lot as a young fellow coming up, and I still do when I talk too fast, even today at eighty-three. Stammering as a kid will get you in a lot of fights. Boys who didn't know how good I could fight would make fun of me, but they'd pay for it.

We kids fought a lot for fun, too. Every Friday night we would have boxing matches on the corner. Nobody got hurt too bad. It was all for the sport of it, and that's how you learned how to fight, by getting your ass kicked once in a while. I thought about becoming a boxer, but I knew I could never be as good as Joe Louis, and if you couldn't be the champ, boxing was no life. Kids today play soccer and Little League. I love to go to my grandchildren's soccer games. But back then we had to amuse ourselves, and fighting seemed to be all we had. Looking back, it was good for us. You got a lot out of your system. And you learned a lot. And then when our country needed soldiers we were in shape. We already had a mental toughness.

I graduated from the eighth grade at Blessed Virgin Mary, where my father worked and where I had to watch my step. For high school I got switched to public school, which had a less restricted atmosphere. They enrolled me in the ninth grade at Darby High School. I didn't get very far in the ninth grade, though. One morning in assembly the principal was on the stage singing and leading us in the old song "On the Road to Mandalay." He would emphasize by winking after each line of the song like some vaudeville singer. Being so tall I stood out and he could look right at me. So every time he would wink I would imitate him and wink back at him.

When we got done with the assembly he told me to wait in his office for him. I went and sat there in the chair in front of his desk. He was a pretty big man, my height, only he outweighed me. He walked into the office, came up behind me, and cuffed me hard on the back of the head just the way my father used to whenever I lost one of his beer bets for him. "You fat fuck," I said and jumped up and decked him. I broke his jaw, and they expelled me permanently on the spot.

Naturally, I knew what to expect when my father got home. I had a lot of time to think about it, but all I could think about was breaking the principal's jaw with just one punch, a grown man.

My father walked in the door steaming mad and threw the boxing gloves at me hard. I caught them, but this time I threw them back at him. I said, "You better take another look." I was sixteen, almost seventeen, by then. "I won't hit you," I said. "You're my father. But you better get yourself another punching bag."

chapter four

Little Egypt University

And then I joined the carnival. The highlight of every spring in Philadelphia was the arrival of the Regent traveling carnival. They would set up their tents on Seventy-second Street near Island Avenue. There was absolutely nothing out there then but long stretches of grassland. It was just the way the Indians left it. Today it's wall-to-wall car dealerships.

As big a city as it was and as close as it was to New York City, Philadelphia had a small-town feel to it. The Commonwealth of Pennsylvania had blue laws that didn't allow bars to be open on Sunday. No stores were open. It was the day of worship. Even later on when night baseball came in, the Philadelphia Phillies and the Philadelphia Athletics could play baseball at Shibe Park on Sunday only while there was daylight. They weren't allowed to turn on the stadium lights on Sunday. Many a Sunday game was called on account of darkness. You never picked up a paper and read about Prohibition gangland killings or any of that stuff that went on in New York, just a couple of hours away on the Pennsylvania Railroad. So the carnival coming to Philadelphia was very big entertainment.

After I got expelled from Darby High, I had been working at odd jobs, bagging groceries at Penn Fruit, and, depending on the weather, hitchhiking up to Paxon Hollow Golf Course to caddy. I was living at home, which still meant moving around a lot to beat the rent. Maybe all that moving around every time the rent came due gave me my restless streak, and that restless streak burst out like so many buds on a tree that spring when the carnival arrived.

My best buddy at the time was Francis "Yank" Quinn. He was a year older than me and had finished high school. A few years later he went on to college and into the service as a second lieutenant. He saw plenty of combat in Europe. But I never ran into him over there. Later on after the war we played football together at Shanahan's Catholic Club. Yank was the quarterback.

One warm night Yank and I, with a dollar between us to spend but not a steady job between us, went to the carnival to look around, and the next thing you know we both had taken laborer jobs to travel with the show on their New England tour. All my young life I wanted to get out of Philadelphia and see the world, and now I was doing it and getting paid for it.

I worked for the barker in the girlie show. Regent had two girlie dancers, something like the old go-go dancers they came out with in the seventies. Only the carny dancers had more clothes on. They left a lot up to the imagination of the customers. The two girlie dancers were Little Egypt, the brunette who dressed as if she had oozed out of an Aladdin's lamp, and Neptune of the Nile, the blond who wore a series of blue veils as if she had bubbled up out of the deep blue sea. They worked one at a time and did their exotic dances on a stage inside their own tent. The barker would promote the show, and I would collect fifty cents from the customers and give them their tickets.

The Regent shows were pure variety entertainment, like the old Ed Sullivan show on TV. They had jugglers, acrobats, games where people could win Kewpie dolls, a knife thrower, a sword swallower, and a band playing circus songs. There was no gambling going on. The customers didn't really have any money to gamble. It was the height of the Depression. No matter what they say, the Depression didn't end until the war came. And we laborers certainly didn't have any money to gamble. The laborers were mostly runaways and people without roots. Everybody was very decent, though — no troublemakers.

Yank and I would help set up the tents and the seats for the customers and take it all down when we traveled on. If there was any trouble — maybe fighting going on among the customers — the local law would just tell us to pack up and leave town. If business was good and we were getting a good reception from the crowds we'd stay about ten days. Otherwise, if we weren't making any money, we would pack up and move on in search of a better reception. We played a lot of small towns in places like Connecticut, Vermont, New Hampshire, and outside of Boston.

We moved around in run-down trucks and old beat-up cars, and we slept outdoors on blankets under the stars. This was no Ringling Brothers; it was a honky-tonk carnival. I guess you could say that my childhood of moving around with my family like nomads in the desert prepared me for the inconveniences of this life.

They didn't pay us much, but they fed us and the food was good and solid. Lots of hearty beef stew that smelled wonderful in the outdoors. It couldn't touch my mother's cooking, but not much could. If it rained we'd sleep under the trucks. I got my first taste of moonshine on the road with that carnival under a truck in the rain. I really didn't care for it. I actually didn't develop the drinking habit until during the war. I did my first real drinking in Catania, Sicily. The first time I tasted red wine it became my drink of choice and stayed that way all my life.

One morning at a stop on the road in Brattleboro, Vermont, the rain came pouring down and didn't let up all day. There was mud everywhere. And no customers, no fifty cents to collect, and no tickets to give out. Little Egypt saw me standing around breathing hot air into my hands trying to keep warm and took me aside and whispered in my ear. She asked me if I wanted to spend the night in her tent with her and Neptune. I knew they liked me and I said "yeah, sure." Yank would have to sleep under a truck, but I was going to be nice and dry for the night.

After the show I took my blankets and went to their dressing room, which smelled like perfume the second you walked in. Their dressing room was in a tent that they also slept in. Little Egypt was resting on her bed with pillows fluffed up behind her and she said, "Why don't you take your clothes off and get comfy? They must be wet."

By this time I was seventeen. I hesitated a little bit, not sure if she was kidding, and she asked me: "Have you ever been with a woman?"

And I told her the truth, which was "no."

"Well you're going to be with one tonight," Little Egypt said and laughed. She got up from the bed and lifted my shirt up over my head. I was standing there topless.

"Make that two women," Neptune of the Nile chimed in from behind me, also laughing. Then she whistled at me. I must have turned red.

And that was the night I lost my cherry. I had been stored up for years before then. I didn't believe in masturbation. The church was against it, but I was, too. There was something about it that I didn't think was right.

After I had my first lovemaking session with Little Egypt in control, Neptune asked me to come over to her bed and Little Egypt gave me a little shove. When I got there, Neptune of the Nile asked me first to lick her. I stammered and said, "I waited long enough for this much, I can wait a little longer for that." In those days, believe it or not, oral sex on a woman was considered a sin and a scandal. At least in Philadelphia.

When I got inside of Neptune of the Nile, she looked as if she was watching my face for a reaction. When she saw my eyes suddenly pop open real wide Neptune said, "Get all of this while you can, young fellow, it'll make you a complete man. I've got a snapper. You won't see a snapper too often." And oh Mother of Mercy did she ever! I thought *I* had muscles.

All that night I made up for a lot of lost time, going from bed to bed with those two highly experienced grown women. Those two were wild women. I was young and strong then. The next morning I thought, how long has this been going on? What the hell have I been missing? Little Egypt and Neptune of the Nile gave me a college education in how to please a woman. There were no books in those days and around the neighborhood you got your sex education from your bragging friends who knew less than you did.

I spent a lot of nights in that tent, mostly with Little Egypt, falling asleep in her bed with her long brown hair all over us, smelling of perfume, and cuddling together. Poor Yank, sleeping out in the cold on the damp ground. I don't think he ever forgave me. (Yank was a good man who lived a good life. He never did anything wrong. He died before his time, while I was still in jail. They wouldn't let me come home on a pass for his funeral. Not even for my brother's or sister's funerals. Yank managed O'Malley's Restaurant on the West Chester Pike, and he wrote me in jail that he was going to throw a great big welcome home party for me when I got out, but poor Yank got a heart attack and it killed him.)

When we reached Maine with the carnival the summer was mostly over. It was around September, and the Regent show always went south to Florida to spend the winter down there. We were in Camden, Maine, when the show closed. About forty miles away there was a logging camp that we heard was doing some hiring, so off Yank and I went on a dirt road into the woods on foot. I knew I was going to miss Little Egypt, but there was no more work for me with the carnival once we tore down camp for the last time and got the trucks loaded.

The logging company hired us both. They put Yank in the kitchen helping the cook. On account of my size they put me on a two-man saw. I was too young to fell the big trees, but I sawed the branches off the trees and turned them into logs once they were on the ground. Then bulldozers would push the logs into the river and they'd float downstream to a point where trucks would load them. Sawing those trees all day was hard work. I was only about 6'1" then and weighed about 175 pounds, and after nine months of that work there wasn't an ounce of fat on me.

We slept in little shacks they had set up with potbellied woodburning stoves and we ate — you guessed it — stew and more stew. After a day of sawing logs by hand you never tasted food so good.

We saved what little money we made because there was no place to spend it. Neither Yank nor I played cards with the men or they'd have cleaned us out.

They had a wild form of rugby they played on Sundays. I played a lot of that. I never did catch on to the rules, if there were any. It was just a lot of knocking each other down.

It seemed like every night that it didn't snow we had boxing matches in a roped-off section that was like a ring. They didn't have any gloves up there, and so the fighters would wrap their fists in bandages. Everybody wanted to see the big kid fight the men who were in their late twenties and thirties, so by popular demand I participated a lot in those matches. It reminded me of my father pairing me up with older boys to win beer bets. Including my own father, it seemed like I was always matched against people older than me. Only these loggers could hit even harder than my father. I lost many a fight, but I could always hit, too, and I learned an awful lot of tricks.

I think you're born with the ability to hit. Rocky Marciano didn't start boxing until after the war when he was already twenty-six, but he was a natural hitter. You need leverage, but a lot of your power comes from your forearm down into your wrist. There's a snap to your punch that comes from your wrist to your fist, and that's what knocks the other guy out. You can actually hear that snap; it sounds like a pistol shot when it's working to perfection. Joe Louis had that famous six-inch punch. He'd knock a guy out with a punch that only traveled six inches. His power came from the snap. It's like snapping a towel at somebody's butt. There's no power in your arms.

Then if you learn a trick or two besides, you're set for life. They say Jack Dempsey learned all the tricks of fighting as a thirteen-year-old working in the mining camps of Colorado. I can believe that about Dempsey after my nine months in the deep woods of Maine.

We hitchhiked back to Philly that next summer, and all of a sudden we found we had a new interest besides boxing — chasing girls. I worked two or three jobs, whenever I could find work, until I got an apprenticeship at the Pearlstein Glass Company at Fifth and Lombard. It was a commercial area then just off South Street; now it's where the young kids go to shop. I was studying to be a glazier. I learned how to set windows in all the big buildings in town. Sometimes I worked in the shop grinding bevels on the glass. I learned a lot, and it was nowhere near as hard work as logging. At the end of a workday I still had plenty of energy left to compete against Yank for the neighborhood girls.

My secret weapon against Yank was my dancing. Most big men are clumsy and heavy-footed, but not me. I had a good sense of rhythm and I could move every part of my body. I had very fast hands, too, and good coordination. Swing music was sweeping the country and social dancing was all the rage. I went dancing six nights a week (never on a Sunday) to a different hall every night. That's how you learned the dances. You learned by going dancing. They all had certain steps, unlike today where you just make it up as you go along. After the war, one of the jobs I had was a ballroom dance instructor.

In 1939, when I was nineteen, my dance partner, Roseanne De Angelis, and I took second place in the fox-trot competition against 5,000 other couples in Madison Square Garden in the Harvest Moon Ball dance contest. Roseanne was some graceful dancer. I met her up at the Garden before the contest when her partner got hurt on the dance floor during practice. My partner got tired and worn out, so Roseanne and I teamed up. The Harvest Moon was the biggest event in dancing in the whole country. It was sponsored every year by the *New York Daily News.* Many years later I taught my daughters how to dance, every kind of dance, even the tango and the rumba.

I made good money at Pearlstein's, almost $45 a week. That was more than my father made at the Blessed Virgin Mary. Out of that money I paid room and board at home so we didn't have to keep moving. My sister, Peggy, was still in school and worked after school at the A&P as a stocker. My brother, Tom, was out of the house. He had dropped out of school and joined the CCC, a youth conservation corps that

Roosevelt had set up to provide jobs for the youth on account of the Depression. The young men would go to camps set up in rural areas around the country, and they'd work on conservation projects.

Most of the money I had leftover from paying my parents out of my Pearlstein's pay was spent in the dance halls. There wasn't a lot left over to spend on dates with the girls, but Yank and I found ways to have fun without money. One afternoon I took a pretty young Irish girl with freckles buck-bathing in the creek off Darby Road, where Mercy Fitzgerald Hospital is now. The creek was about a hundred yards from the road. Yank snuck up on us and swiped our clothes. Then he stood up at the top of the hill near the road and yelled down for the girl I was with to come out of the water, get dressed, and go with him or he'd leave with her clothes, too. So she came out and went off with him and he gave a kid a quarter to hold onto my clothes until Yank and the girl got out of sight and then drop them back down by the creek and run like hell.

I'm sure I played a trick back on him; I just don't remember exactly which trick it was. Did I spread the rumor that a pregnant girl he didn't even know was his responsibility? Probably. Did I give him a hot foot? No doubt. But that's about all we did. Played jokes. Walked around and messed around. We were no longer boxers and fighters and road warriors; we were lovers and dancers. I had been to the Little Egypt University and the Neptune of the Nile Graduate School, and it was my duty to the young maidens of the City of Brotherly Love not to let all that good education go to waste.

I had the ideal carefree young man's life — the Life of Riley — popular with the girls, good pals, no responsibilities; a life where your only real job is to build memories for the rest of your days. Except I couldn't stay put. I was impatient. I had to move on. Pretty rapidly I found myself halfway around the world. But by then I no longer could have the luxury to be impatient. I had to do things the Army's way: hurry up and wait.

chapter five

411 Days

I first heard the song "Tuxedo Junction" in 1941. I was an MP in Colorado, pulling guard duty at Lowry Field for the Army Air Corps. Most people think it was Glenn Miller who first made that song famous, but it was a black bandleader named Erskine Hawkins. He wrote the song and had the first hit with it. That song stayed with me like a theme song through the whole war. After the war I had my first date with Mary, my future wife, to see Erskine Hawkins at the old Earl Theater in Philly.

One cold night in December 1941 I won a dance contest jitterbugging to "Tuxedo Junction" at the Denver Dance Hall. The next thing I knew I was on a troop train at four in the morning heading for the West Coast to defend California. The Japanese had bombed Pearl Harbor. I just turned twenty-one and I was 6'2". Four years later when the war ended I got my discharge one day before I turned twenty-five; I was 6' 4". I had grown two inches. People forget how young we were. Some of us were not full-grown yet.

I spent the war as a rifleman in Europe in the Thunderbird Division — the 45th Infantry Division. They say the average number of days of actual combat for a veteran is around eighty. By the time the war was over the Army told me I had 411 combat days, which entitled me to $20 extra pay a month. I was one of the lucky ones. The real heroes, some of them with only one combat day, are still over there. As big a target as I was and as many fire fights as I was in, I never got hit by a German bullet or shrapnel. I said a lot of foxhole prayers, especially pinned down in a dugout in Anzio. And whatever anybody wants to say about my childhood, one thing my childhood did teach me was how to take care of myself, how to survive.❞

Eliciting information from Frank Sheeran about his combat experiences was the most difficult part of the interview process. It was two years before he could accept the fact that his combat experience was even worth discussing. And then it became painstaking and stressful for both a respectful questioner and his reluctant subject, with many stops and starts.

To help me understand his combat days, Sheeran tracked down the 45th Infantry Division's hardbound, 202-page official Combat Report, issued within months of World War II's end. The more I learned from both this report and Frank himself, the clearer it seemed to me that it was during his prolonged and unremitting combat duty that Frank Sheeran learned to kill in cold blood.

The Combat Report states: "The 45th paid heavily for maintaining our American heritage: 21,899 battle casualties." Considering that a fully staffed division has 15,000 members, Sheeran saw replacements march in and be carried out on a daily basis. The report asserts a record of "511 days of combat" for the division itself; that is, 511 days of shooting and being shot at on the front lines. The Thunderbird Division fought valiantly from the very first day of the war in Europe to the very last.

With time out for rest and rehabilitation along the way, Private Frank Sheeran, with 411 combat days, experienced more than 80 percent of the division's total "days of combat." Sheeran was conditioned for the rest of his life by the experience of killing and maiming day after day, and wondering when he would be next. Not all people are affected the same way by the same events. We are each our own fingerprints and the sum of our own life's experiences. Other combat veterans I have interviewed drop their jaws and gasp at the thought of 411 days of combat.

"I ought to kick your ass," Charlie "Diggsy" Meiers said. I was two years older than Diggsy and a foot taller. We had been pals since grade school.

"What did I do wrong? What do you want to kick my ass for, Digs?" I asked and smiled down at him.

"You had a noncombat gravy job in the MPs. You could have sat out the whole friggin' war in the States. You must be crazy transferring over here. I always knew you had a screw loose, but this takes the cake. You think we're having fun over here?"

"I wanted to see some action," I said, already feeling like a jackass.

"Well, you'll see it."

A blast like thunder and a loud, whistling buzz shot across the sky. "What's that?"

"That's your action." He handed me a shovel and said, "Here."

"What the hell is this for?" I asked.

"Your foxhole. Start digging. Welcome to Sicily."

After I got done digging, Charlie explained to me that an exploding shell is going to spread its shrapnel on an angle upward. You get down and stay down and let it sail over you. Otherwise it cuts you in half right across your chest. When we were kids I looked out for Diggsy, but now it was going to be the other way around.

How did I end up with a shovel in my hand in Sicily in 1943?

In August 1941 I had enlisted in the army. The rest of the world was already in the war, but we were neutral and weren't in it yet.

Biloxi, Mississippi, was where I did my basic training. One day a Southern sergeant addressed the recruits and said he could lick any one of us and if anybody thought otherwise they should step forward now. I took a giant step forward, and he had me digging latrines for five days. It was just a trick to get us to respect his rank and rank in general. They were getting us ready for a war.

After basic training, the army took one look at me and sized me up as a perfect specimen for the military police. They didn't ask you what you thought of your new assignment, and before the war started there was no way out of the MPs.

But after Pearl Harbor, with a war going on, they let you transfer out of the military police if you were willing to go into combat. I liked the idea of dropping out of the sky and into combat, and I signed right up for the Army Airborne and transferred to Fort Benning, Georgia, for paratroop training. I was in real good shape, so the rigid training of a paratrooper came easy for me. I liked the whole idea of finally seeing some action. When your parachute landed, you'd be on your own a lot, kind of self-reliant. I thought I was something special until I jumped from a tower during training and dislocated my right shoulder. I had landed wrong, and they gave you only one mistake. They cut me from the team. I was now going to go into the infantry as a combat foot soldier.

Meanwhile, no amount of authority or military discipline could stop me from getting into my little scrapes. I was in one scrape after another in my army career. I went into the army as a private, and I came out four years and two months later as a private. They gave me combat promotions from time to time, but then I'd have my fun and get busted back down. All in all I had fifty days lost under AWOL — absent without official leave — mostly spent drinking red wine and chasing Italian, French, and German women. However, I was never AWOL when my outfit was going back to the front lines. If you were AWOL when your company was going back into combat you might as well keep going because your own officers would blow you away, and they didn't even have to say it was the Germans. That's desertion in the face of the enemy.

While I was waiting to be shipped overseas they had me at Camp Patrick Henry in Virginia, and I gave some lip back to one of those Southern sergeants, so they put me on

KP (kitchen patrol) peeling potatoes. First chance I got I bought some laxative at the PX and put it in the giant coffee urn. Everybody wound up with bad diarrhea, including the officers. Unfortunately, I was the only one who didn't report in sick at the infirmary. They had that caper solved before they put in a requisition for extra toilet paper. Can you guess which brilliant criminal ended up on his knees scrubbing bathroom floors?

I set sail on July 14, 1943, for Casablanca in North Africa, assigned to the 45th Infantry Division as an infantry rifleman. While you couldn't choose your division, you could choose a particular company in the division if they had an opening. A company is about 120 men. Our church in Philly put out a newsletter keeping tabs on where all the neighborhood boys were stationed, so I knew Diggsy was with the Thunderbird. I asked to be in his company and got it. That didn't mean I'd end up in his platoon of about thirty-two men or end up in his eight-man squad in his platoon, but I did, and we stayed together in the same squad.

In the fall of 1942, while they were still being trained for combat in the States and had yet to go overseas, General George S. Patton addressed Diggsy and the men of the 45th from the stage of a theater in Fort Devens, Massachusetts. General Patton told the impressionable boys of the 45th — boys away from home for the first time, about to be sent overseas to fight and die — that he had a special role in the war for their division.

As reported by Colonel George E. Martin, chief of staff to the commanding officer of the 45th Infantry Division:

> [General Patton] had much to say, all interlarded with shockingly coarse and profane language. . . . He was telling of occurrences when British infantry moving forward to attack would bypass enemy pockets, only to find themselves engaged

by this enemy to the rear. Then when the British turned to mop-up, the German soldiers would fling down their weapons and raise their hands in surrender. If this should happen to us, said General Patton, we should not accept their surrender; instead we should kill every last one of the bastardly S.O.B.s.

We were then told that our Division probably would see more combat than any other American division, and he wanted us to be known to the Germans as the "Killer Division."

In a follow-up speech on June 27 in Algiers, North Africa, as reported by an officer of the division who was present, Patton told the men of his "Killer Division":

. . . to kill and to continue to kill and that the more we killed the less we'd have to kill later and the better off the Division would be in the long run. . . . He did say that the more prisoners we took the more men we would have to feed and not to fool around with prisoners. He said that there was only one good German and that was a dead one.

Another officer listening to the speech reported Patton's position on the killing of civilians: "He said something about if the people living in the cities persisted in staying in the vicinity of the battle and were enemy, we were to ruthlessly kill them and get them out of the way."

66 After I got my foxhole dug, Diggsy told me there were two big scandals going on. Everybody hated snipers. Both sides hated snipers, and if you captured one it was okay to kill him on the spot. They had some sniping going on outside Biscari airfield and a bunch of Americans had been hit. When about forty Italians soldiers surrendered, they couldn't tell which ones had done the sniping so they lined them all up and shot them. Then a sergeant took about thirty prisoners back behind the line. When they got some distance he grabbed a machine gun and let them have it. That got my attention like the whistling shell that had sailed over us. It made you think twice about surrendering yourself if it ever came to that.

In his last speech to the 45th Infantry Division in August 1943, following their combat success in Sicily, at an outdoor address, Patton told the men and officers of the 45th: "Your division is one of the best if not the best division in the history of American arms." By his praise Patton was reinforcing his faith in his "Killer Division." They were doing things the way he wanted their division to do things and the way he had instructed them to do things in prior speeches.

At the time he uttered these words to the men of the 45th, two of their comrades were facing courts-martial for murder. Captain John T. Compton had ordered a firing squad to shoot approximately forty unarmed prisoners of war, two of whom were civilians, following a battle to take Biscari airfield in Sicily on July 14, 1943. In a separate incident Sergeant Horace T. West had personally machine-gunned thirty-six unarmed prisoners of war that same day following that same battle.

Patton's personal diary for July 15, 1943, a day after these killings, reads:

> [General Omar] Bradley — a most loyal man — arrived in great excitement about 0900 to report that a Captain in the 180th Regimental Combat Team, 45th Division [Sheeran's actual regiment within the division], had taken my injunction to kill men who kept on shooting until we got within 200 yards seriously, and had shot some fifty prisoners in cold blood and in ranks, which was an even greater error. I told him that it was

probably an exaggeration, but in any case to tell the officer to certify that the dead men were snipers or had attempted to escape or something, as it would make a stink in the press and also would make the civilians mad.

General Omar Bradley, Patton's equal in rank, did no such thing. Bradley engaged in no cover-up, and his investigation led to murder charges against the captain and the sergeant.

Captain John T. Compton was tried by a military court, but he was acquitted on the grounds that he was merely following Patton's explicit instructions to the 45th to shoot prisoners in cold blood.

Sergeant Horace T. West was also tried by a military court for murder, and he used the same defense as Captain Compton. A lieutenant testified for the sergeant that the night before the invasion of Sicily, Lieutenant Colonel William H. Schaefer went on the ship's loudspeaker and reminded the men of Patton's words: they "would not take any prisoners."

Sergeant Horace T. West, however, was convicted and given life in prison. The unremitting outcry that ensued following the acquittal of an officer and the conviction of an enlisted man for essentially the same course of conduct, on the same day, following the same battle, in the same campaign, from the same 45th Infantry Division, led to the sergeant's prompt release and return to combat, where he served out the balance of the war as a private. Four months after his acquittal, Captain Compton was shot and killed as he approached German soldiers who were displaying the white flag of surrender as a deadly trick.

There were hushed reports of other atrocities in Sicily as well. In his book *General Patton: A Soldier's Life,* Stanley P. Hirschson cites one well-known British newspaperman of the day who witnessed two busloads of about sixty prisoners each being shot, but who chose not to report the story after Patton gave his word he would put a stop to all atrocities. The newspaperman, however, told a friend, and that friend prepared a memorandum that recounted the events. The memo states: "Patton's bloodthirsty way of talking, and wording of his instructions, before the landing in Sicily was taken too literally by the American troops of the 45th Division particularly."

" Later that day, Diggsy asked me about a rumor he had heard from a neighborhood pal he had run into overseas that I had enlisted because Yank knocked a girl up and blamed me. Can you imagine, halfway around the world and rumors are going around about me. I knew Yank was out there in college somewhere still having his little jokes. "

chapter six

Doing What I Had to Do

For me the easiest part of the war was Sicily. The Italians were terrible soldiers. The Germans were keeping the backbone in the Italians. We'd advance, and sometimes the Italian soldiers actually would be standing there at attention with their suitcases packed. While I was in Sicily, Mussolini surrendered and the Germans took over the war from the Italians. The Sicilian people were very friendly. Once we drove the Germans out I got to see Catania, where every house had homemade spaghetti drying on the clothesline. After the war Russell Bufalino liked the fact that I went right through his town.

My first new pal was a tough guy in our squad out of the Jewish section of Brooklyn named Alex Siegel. We had our picture taken together in Sicily with my arm resting on his shoulder, but he got killed a month later in a strafing on the beachhead at Salerno.

Salerno is a town just below Naples on the western coast of Italy. In September 1943, we jumped off landing craft into the Mediterranean with German shells exploding all around us. Salerno was the worst of the three invasion landings I made. Those of us who made it ashore had the goal of getting about 1,000 yards up to secure the beachhead. Each soldier had a shovel on his pack, and we began digging in. No matter how tired you are, when you hear enemy artillery, you dig with a passion.

Our position was pounded by artillery and strafed by German planes. If you saw German soldiers coming at you, you shot your rifle. I know I was there shooting. I know I asked myself why the hell did I volunteer for this, but I have no recollection of the first time I fired at an enemy soldier in Salerno.

We almost got pushed off the beach by the Germans. But I know I stayed there the same as everybody else did. Everybody's scared. Some don't want to admit it. But it doesn't make a difference whether you admit it or not, you're still scared.

The Combat Report quotes an on-the-scene general of another division who said: "The 45th prevented the Germans from driving the Allied invaders into the sea."

When our Navy artillery brought in heavy firepower, the Germans retreated back out of the range of the Navy's guns. That gave us a chance to move up, and we advanced off the beach and hooked up with other divisions for a push north.

Riflemen would do whatever we were assigned to do. If you didn't follow an order in combat they can shoot you automatically, right then. Jimmy Hoffa was never in the service. He got a hardship of some kind to keep out. In combat you learned fast, if you didn't know it already, certain rules are strict rules and nobody's above those rules. Before combat I was never much on following orders myself, but I learned over there to follow orders or else.

Sheeran was there following orders for what the Combat Report calls the "sickness and exhaustion that had developed among the troops" in the "fatiguing and heart-breaking fighting over rough terrain" in the drive from Salerno north to Venafro. In unrelenting succession came the "suffering attendant to a winter campaign in the cold vastness" of the

Apennine Mountains under the guns of the German-held monastery at Monte Cassino.

> We pushed north in Italy from Naples toward Rome, and by November 1943, we got as far as the foothills where we began being shelled by Germans above us on the mountains around Monte Cassino. We were pinned down there for over two months. There was a monastery on top of Monte Cassino that the Germans used as an observation post so they could see our every move. It was an ancient monastery, and certain factions didn't want it bombed. When they finally did bomb it, they made the whole situation worse because now the Germans could get protection from the rubble. In January 1944 we tried to assault the German line but got thrown back down the mountain. Some nights we'd go out on patrol to capture a German soldier for interrogation. Most nights we just tried to stay dry from all the rain and keep from getting hit.
>
> By then I was learning not to get close to too many people. You get to liking people and you see them get killed. A nineteen-year-old kid would come in as a replacement, and before his boots got a chance to dry he was dead. It's got to affect you mentally. I was close to Diggsy and that was it. It was tough enough seeing Diggsy get shot twice.
>
> Then came the worst of it. They decided to send some of us back to a rest area near Naples in Casserta. It had been the Italian king's palace. We had it easy for about ten days and then we took off in landing craft for Anzio. This was a coastal town that was north of the German line at Monte Cassino but south of Rome. The idea was to attack the German flank and give our main force a chance to break through at Monte Cassino.

The 45th Division was pulled back from the repeatedly unsuccessful and costly Allied attacks against the monastery at Monte Cassino to open up another front on the German flank by the amphibious invasion of Anzio. In moving the 45th away from the front line at Monte Cassino, General Mark Clark wrote, "For the past seventy-two days the 45th Infantry Division has been engaged in continuous combat against strong enemy forces and under extreme combat conditions." General Clark reflected upon the "bitter cold, wet and almost constant enemy artillery and mortar fire" to which the 45th Division — and Private Frank Sheeran — had been subjected at Monte Cassino. What the general didn't know was that he was taking the 45th out of the frying pan of Monte Cassino and putting them right into the fire that was the hell of Anzio.

66 Before a battle or a landing, you get a little nervous tension. Once the shooting starts it goes away. You don't have time to think. You just do what you have to do. After the battle it sinks in.

We took the Germans by surprise at the Anzio beach, taking a couple of hundred prisoners. Everything was quiet that first twenty-four hours as we moved up off the beach, but instead of advancing, the general in charge thought it was a trap. He decided to play it safe and wait for our tanks and artillery to land. This delay in advancing gave the Germans time to get their tanks and artillery into position above us and to dig in so they could pin us down and keep our tanks and artillery from landing. 99

As Sir Winston Churchill put it, and despite his expressed wishes to the contrary, "But now came disaster. . . . The defenses of the beachhead were growing, but the opportunity for which great exertions had been made was gone." Hitler poured in reinforcements, pinned the Allies down, and ordered that his army eliminate what he called the "abscess" of the Allied beachhead at Anzio.

Then along came their heavy artillery and their airplanes strafing us. We had to dig deep because foxholes wouldn't do us any good. We ended up in dugouts that went down about eight feet that we dug with our shovels. We used foot ladders to climb out, and we put boards and tree branches on top to protect us from the rain and to absorb the shrapnel from the constant shelling.

We stayed like that under a never-ending attack for four solid months. You couldn't leave your dugout during daylight or they'd pick you off. Where are you going to go anyway? You'd take your chances and come out at night to relieve yourself or empty your helmet of your body waste if you couldn't hold it in during the day and you had to go in your helmet. You ate K-rations out of a can. They couldn't get any cooked food to you. The Germans bombed our supply ships. You played cards and you talked about what you were going to do after the war. And most of all, you prayed. I don't care who you were or who you thought you were, you prayed. I said more Hail Marys and more Our Fathers than I could count. You promised to sin no more if only you got out of this alive. You swore to give up women and wine and cursing and anything you ever did that you could use to offer up in your prayers.

The worst shelling was done at night by what we nicknamed the Anzio Express. It was a giant piece of artillery that the Germans kept camouflaged during the day so our airplanes couldn't find it. It was kept on a railroad track outside of Rome. They'd bring it out and put it into position after dark, when our planes were on the ground, and fire round after round at us. Its incoming shell sounded like a boxcar on a freight train overhead in the night sky. It was so loud and scary it was demoralizing every time you heard it, and you never let yourself think too long that some poor GIs not far from you were on the receiving end of it and getting blown all to hell so there'd be no bodies left even to send home to their families. And you could be next.

You took your turn on point a hundred yards out on the perimeter as an outpost so the other guys could get some sleep, but there wasn't much sleeping during those four months. I've found better places to be than to be out on point all night. Nighttime is always scarier than daytime. Even without the Anzio Express at night you're getting conventional shelling all day long. It rattles your nerves, and you harden up inside to keep from rattling all over. It's got to affect you unless you're a complete nut. Twice the Germans advanced on our position trying to drive us off the beach, but we held on.

The Combat Report states that the 45th "ripped to shreds" the German attempt to "erase the beachhead." This period of repelling the German assault was followed by "the long months of holding and waiting" at Anzio and constant bombardment and loss of more than 6,000 Allied lives. In May the main force that had been at a standoff broke through the German line at Monte Cassino. By the end of that month, 150,000 weary but happy soldiers moved out of their dugouts in Anzio and linked up with the main force advancing from the south toward Rome. Meanwhile, on June 6th, the Allies landed in Normandy and opened up another front.

We marched into Rome without a fight. Rome was what they called an open city, which meant neither side would bomb it, but there was a little bombing. Rome is the first time I ever saw a sidewalk café. We'd sit there and relax, eat our lunch, and drink a little wine. I saw my first blond Italian women in Rome parading by the cafés. I had a few adventures. It wasn't hard to do. We were issued chocolate bars and tins of cheese and chopped eggs in a can. That's all it took. The people had nothing so you can't judge them on morals. Fraternizing with the local women was against regulations, but what were they going to do, send us to a combat unit?

We fought the Germans in Italy for a while, and then we got put on landing craft for the invasion of southern France called Operation Dragoon on August 14, 1944. We had some resistance as we landed. It was more harassment than real fire power. But fire is fire. Two shots of fire is still bad.

Running up out of the surf on to the beach at St. Tropez I thought I was shot. I looked down and saw red all over my uniform. I hollered for the medic and Lieutenant Kavota from Hazleton, Pennsylvania, came running over to me and shouted, "You son of a bitch, that's wine. You ain't shot. Get up and get going. They shot your canteen." He was a good Joe.

We finally drove the Germans back and we entered the Alsace-Lorraine region, which is part French and part German. I had a pal from Kentucky that we called Pope. He was a damn good soldier. You can't say such and such a guy is a coward. You can only absorb so much. In Alsace-Lorraine I saw Pope stick his leg out from behind a tree to get a million-dollar wound so he'd be sent home; only a heavy round came in and took his leg off. He survived and went home with one leg missing.

Another way I saw guys snap a little bit is when it came to taking prisoners. Here these Germans were shooting at you, trying to kill you and blowing your pals all to hell, and now you've got a chance to get them back, and they want to surrender. Some people take that personally. So maybe you didn't understand what they were saying. Or if you did take them alive and you took them back behind your own line, maybe they tried to escape. I don't mean a massacre. If you had a load of prisoners you took them back, but with a handful of Germans or less you did what you had to do and what everybody else expected you to do. The lieutenant gave me a lot of prisoners to handle and I did what I had to do.

In a fire fight in the Alsace, Diggsy got hit in the back halfway up a hill. The medics got him and started bringing him down the hill. I didn't have much emotion left by this time in the war, but I have to say seeing little Diggsy hit on that hill and I was emotional. I saw his rifle on the ground where he fell. They didn't want you to lose your rifle over there. I must have snapped or something. So I called for cover from the other guys, and I crawled up and got Diggsy's rifle for him. When we all crawled back down the hill, Digs said to me,

"You got to be nuts. You could have been killed for this friggin' m-1." I said, "Ah, the Germans didn't know they had us outnumbered." It was the second time I had seen him get shot.

In Alsace-Lorraine we heard that the Germans had launched a desperate counteroffensive up north through a forest in Belgium to halt our advance after Normandy in what they called the Battle of the Bulge. The Germans were advancing in a bulge and so Allied troops were needed to be sent from our southern front to reinforce their northern front. Our company was left to cover the division's whole southern front, which meant 120 men were covering a front that might have been covered by a full division of 10,000 or 15,000 men.

All we did was retreat. We walked the whole night New Year's Eve of 1945. We watched the French people of the Alsace pulling in the American flags on their houses and start putting the German flags back up. But soon reinforcements came in, and we built up our strength and pushed back into the German part of the Alsace.

From there we fought our way to the Harz Mountain concentration camps. One night we intercepted a mule train with hot food for the German guards on top. We ate what we wanted and soiled the rest with our waste. We left the German women alone. They were like our WACs. They had prepared the food. We just left them there. But the mule teams were driven by a handful of German soldiers. We had no intention of taking them back down the mountain, and we couldn't take them with us as we advanced up, so we gave them shovels, and they dug their own shallow graves. You wonder why would anyone bother to dig their own graves, but then I guess you cling to some hope that maybe the people with the guns would change their mind, or maybe your own people would come along while you were digging, or maybe if you cooperated and dug your own grave you'd get a good clean hit without any brutality or suffering. By this time, I thought nothing of doing what I had to do.

From the Harz Mountains we made a right turn and kept on heading in a direct line south in Germany, taking

Bamberg and then Nuremberg. That town had been practically bombed to the ground. Nuremberg had been the place where Hitler held all his big rallies. Every single symbol of the Nazis that survived the bombing was systematically destroyed.

Our goal was Munich in Bavaria in southern Germany, the town where Hitler had gotten his start in a beer hall. But on the way, we made a stop to liberate the concentration camp at Dachau.

The Combat Report states that inside the camp there were "some 1,000 bodies. . . . Gas chamber and crematoriums were conveniently side-by-side. Clothing, shoes, and bodies were stacked alike in neat and orderly piles."

We had heard rumors about atrocities at the camps, but we were not prepared for what we were seeing and for the stench. If you see something like that it gets printed on your mind forever. That scene and that smell when you first saw it never goes away. The young, blond-haired German commander in charge of the camp and all his officers were loaded in jeeps and driven off. We heard gunfire in the distance. In short order all of the rest of them — about 500 German soldiers guarding Dachau — were taken care of by us. Some of the camp victims who had the strength borrowed our guns and did what they had to do. And nobody batted an eye when it was done.

Right after that we marched down and took Munich, and about two weeks later the war in Europe ended with Germany's unconditional surrender.

All these years later and from stirring it up I started having dreams again about the combat, only the dreams were all mixed in with things I started doing for certain people after the war.

I was discharged on October 24, 1945, a day before my twenty-fifth birthday, but only according to the calendar.

chapter seven

Waking Up in America

By coincidence I ran into my kid brother, Tom, on the dock in Le Havre, France, in October 1945. The war was over and we were both shipping back to Philly, but on separate ships. Tom had seen a little bit of combat. I said, "Hi, Tom." He said, "Hi, Frank. You've changed! You're not the same brother I remember from before the war." I knew just what he meant. That's what 411 days of combat does to you. He could see it on my face, maybe in my stare.

Thinking about what my brother said to me on the dock in Le Havre makes me wonder if he was looking into my soul. I knew something was different about me. I didn't care anymore about things. I had been through practically the whole war; what could anybody do to me? Somewhere overseas I had tightened up inside, and I never loosened up again. You get used to death. You get used to killing. Sure, you go out and have fun, but even that has an edge. Not to bellyache or anything, because I was one of the lucky ones to come out in one piece. But if I hadn't volunteered for action I never would have seen any of what I saw or did any of what I had to do. I would have stayed in the States as an MP jitterbugging to "Tuxedo Junction."

You step on shore from overseas and everywhere you look you see Americans, and they're not wearing a uniform, and they're speaking English, and you get a big boost in morale.

The Army gives you $100 a month for three months. The

men who didn't go seem to have all the good jobs and you just go back to where you came from and try to pick up where you left off. I went back to live with my parents in West Philly and back to Pearlstein's to pick up where I left off as an apprentice. But I couldn't handle being cooped up in a job after living outdoors all that time overseas. The Pearlstein family was good to me, but I couldn't take supervision and I quit after a couple of months.

Many a morning I found myself waking up in America and being surprised to find myself in a bed. I had been having nightmares all night long, and I didn't know where I was. It would take me awhile to adjust, because I couldn't believe I was in a bed. What was I doing in a bed? After the war I never slept more than three or four hours a night.

In those days you didn't talk about stuff like that. There was no such thing as war syndrome, but you knew something was different. You tried not to remember anything from over there, but things came back to you. You had done every damn thing overseas, from killing in cold blood to destroying property to stealing whatever you wanted and to drinking as much wine and having as many women as you wanted. You lived every minute of every day in danger of your own life and limb. You couldn't take chances. Many times you had a split second to decide to be judge, jury, and executioner. You had just two rules you had to obey. You had to be back in your outfit when you went back on the line. You had to obey a direct order in combat. Break one of those rules and you could be executed yourself, right on the spot even. Otherwise, you flaunted authority. You lost the moral skill you had built up in civilian life, and you replaced it with your own rules. You developed a hard covering, like being encased in lead. You were scared more than you'd ever been in your life. You did certain things, maybe against your will sometimes, but you did them, and if you stayed over there long enough you didn't even think about them anymore. You did them like you might scratch your head if it itched.

You had seen the damnedest things. Emaciated bodies stacked up like logs in a concentration camp; young kids barely shaving and lying about their ages to get into combat and then getting blown away; even your own buddies lying down dead in the mud. Imagine how you feel when you see only one body laid out in a funeral parlor; there you're seeing body after body.

I used to think a lot about dying when I got home. Everybody does. Then I thought, what are you worrying about? You have no control over it. I figured everybody is put here with two dates already determined for them; a date for when they're born and a date for when they go. You don't have any control over either one of those dates, so "what will be will be" became my motto. I got through the war, so what can happen to me? I didn't care so much anymore about things. What will be will be.

I did a lot of wine drinking overseas. I used the wine over there the way the jeeps used gasoline. And I kept it up when I got back home. Both of my wives complained about my drinking. I often said that when they put me in jail in 1981 it was not the FBI's intent, but they saved my life. They only have seven days in a week, and by the time I went to jail I was drinking eight.

That first year home I tried different jobs. I worked for Bennett Coal and Ice whenever they needed me. I hauled ice in the summer — two cakes in the icebox — lots of people didn't have electric refrigerators after the war. In the winter I delivered coal for heating. It was funny that my first job at seven was cleaning out the ashes that the coal leaves behind and now I had made it all the way up to delivering the coal. I worked for a moving company for a month. I stacked cement bags at a cement plant all day long. I worked on construction as a laborer. Whatever I could get. I didn't rob a bank. I was a bouncer and taught ballroom dancing at Wagner's Dance Hall part time on Tuesday, Friday, and Saturday nights. I kept that job for about ten years.

I had too many jobs to remember. One job I do remember was taking hot blueberry pie mix coming out of a cooker onto an ice-cold aluminum conveyor. The more I raked, the cooler the blueberries got before they went into the Tastykake pies.

The job pusher kept on me to rake harder. He said, "You're a little lax on that rake." I tried to ignore him, and he said, "You hear what I said, boy?" I asked him who the hell did he think he was talking to. He said: "I'm talking to you, boy." He said that if I didn't put more effort into the job he'd stick the rake up my butt. I told him I'd do him one better and stick the rake down his throat. He was a big black guy, and he came at me. I tapped him and put him on the conveyor belt unconscious. I stuffed blueberries in his mouth. That took care of him. The cops had to take me out of there.

After that my mother went over to see a state senator named Jimmy Judge. My mother had some political connections. One of her brothers was a doctor in Philly. Another one was big in the glass union and was a freeholder, which is like a councilman, in Camden. He's the one who got me the union apprenticeship at Pearlstein's. Anyway, one morning when I woke up she told me she had arranged with the senator to get me on the Pennsylvania State Police. All I had to do was pass the physical. I wanted to be grateful, but that was the last thing I wanted to do, so I never went down to pay my respects to the senator. Years later when I told my lawyer, F. Emmett Fitzpatrick, that one he said, "What a cop you'd have made!" I said, "Yeah, a rich one." Rape, child abuse, things like that I'd have arrested you for. Anything else and you'd have been on your way with an out-of-court settlement.

I tried to be easygoing again like I was before I went in the war, but I couldn't get the hang of it. It didn't take much to provoke me. I'd just flare up. Drinking helped ease that a little. I hung around with my old crew. Football helped a little, too. I played tackle and guard for Shanahan's. My old pal Yank Quinn was the quarterback. They had leather football helmets in those days, but with my oversized head I couldn't get comfortable in one. So I played with a woolen cap on my head, not for bravado or anything, but it's the only thing I could get to fit my big head. There's no doubt if I was born later on in better times I would have loved to try out to be a professional football player. I wasn't just big. I was very strong, very fast, very agile, and a smart player. All my team-mates but one are gone now. Like I said, we're all terminal; we just don't know the date. Like all young people we thought we had forever to live back then.

One afternoon a bunch of us went downtown to sell our blood for $10 a pint to get some more money to keep drink-ing shots and beer. On the way back we saw a sign for a carni-val. It said that if you could last three rounds with a kangaroo you'd win $100. That was a better deal than the blood money we had just made. So off we went to the carnival.

They had a trained kangaroo in the ring with boxing gloves on. My pals put me up to fight the kangaroo. Now a kangaroo has short arms, so I'm figuring I'll knock his ass out. They put gloves on me and I start jabbing away at him, but what I didn't know is that a kangaroo has a loose jaw so when you hit them it doesn't go to their brain and knock them out. I'm only jabbing at him, because who wants to hurt a kangaroo? But when I couldn't' get anywhere with him with my jab I let loose with an overhand right, a real haymaker. Down the kangaroo goes and I feel this hard whack on the back of my head where my old man used to whack me. I shake it off and go back to jabbing the kangaroo who's hopping all over the place, and I'm trying to figure out who the S.O.B. was who clipped me from behind.

You see, another thing I didn't know is that the kangaroo defends itself with its tail. It has an eight-foot tail that comes whipping up behind you when you knock the kangaroo down. And the harder I hit him, the harder and faster his tail came up behind me. I never saw that tail come whipping up behind me, and I never paid attention to the boxing glove on the tail. He had an eight-foot reach I didn't know about.

Actually, my attention was on a pretty Irish girl sitting in the stands with the sweetest smile on her face. I was trying to show off for her. Her name was Mary Leddy, and I had seen her in the neighborhood, but I had never spoken to her. Pretty soon she was going to change her name to Mrs. Francis J. Sheeran, but she didn't know that then sitting there in the third row, laughing along with the rest of the crowd.

Between the first two rounds my buddies are laughing like hell, but I don't know what's going on. I came out for the second round, and it was more of the same only this time I knocked the kangaroo down twice — which isn't easy to begin with — and I got hit on the back of the head twice. I was starting to get groggy from drinking all day, selling my blood, and getting whacked on the back of the head. I wasn't looking too good to the girl in the third row, either.

Between the second and third rounds I asked my buddies what the hell was going on. "Who's hitting me on the head?" They told me it's the referee, that he doesn't like Irishmen. I walked over and told the referee if he hits me on the back of the head one more time I'm going to knock him out. He said, "Get back in there and fight, rookie."

I came out now with one eye on the kangaroo and one eye on the referee. I'm really steaming mad now, and I creamed that kangaroo. His tail hit me so hard my head ached for three days. I jumped off at the referee and decked him. The referee's people jumped in the ring after me, and my pals jumped in after them. The cops had a hell of a time in that ring sorting things out.

I got taken down to Moko, which was our name for the city jail at Tenth and Moyamensing. In those days they'd keep you informally for a while and let you go without any legal proceedings. They didn't work you over or anything, unless you asked for it. They picked their shots. When they thought I had enough punishment they released me.

I headed straight for Mary Leddy's house, knocked on her door, and asked her out. We made a date to go see Erskine Hawkins's big band at the Earl Theater. We had a ball. She was a real strict Catholic, and I was very respectful. She had beautiful dark-brown hair and the prettiest Irish face I had ever seen. And boy could she dance. I had in my mind that night that this was the girl I was going to marry. I wanted to settle down. I had done enough roaming. I meant well.

They say good girls like bad boys. Opposites attract. Mary loved me, but her family hated me. They thought I was what they used to call shanty Irish, and I guess they thought they were what they used to call lace-curtain Irish. Or maybe they saw something in me; that as hard as I was trying I was still too unpredictable for their Mary.

Mary went to church every Sunday, and I went with her. I did try hard. In 1947 we got married at Mother of Sorrows Church, where I had gotten bounced as an altar boy for drinking the wine. I was still without a steady job, picking up work where I could, and working at Wagner's.

I went around to four finance companies and borrowed a hundred bucks from each one so we could get married. Then when the collectors came around I persuaded them that they couldn't find me. One of them that I convinced had my case taken over by his supervisor, who decided not to cooperate with my disappearance and showed up one night at Wagner's looking for Frank Sheeran. He didn't know it was me at the door. I said to follow me and I'd take him in to see Mr. Sheeran. He followed me into the bathroom and I gave him a shot to the body and a shot to the jaw and down he went. I didn't give him the boot or anything. I just wanted to make sure he understood that Mr. Sheeran was too busy to see him that night or any other night. He got the message.

Mary had a good job with the Philadelphia College of Pharmacy as a secretary. We couldn't afford our own place in the beginning, and so like most of our friends we lived with her parents to start off our married life. I wouldn't advise that to anyone who could help it. The night of the wedding we had a reception at her parents' house, and I had a few drinks in me and I announced that I was going to return all the wedding gifts to her side of the family. If they didn't want me I didn't want their gifts. I wouldn't advise that either. I still had that hair-trigger from the war.

According to my rap sheet, my first real legal proceeding was on February 4, 1947. Two big stiffs on a trolley must have said something I didn't like, or maybe they looked at me the wrong way. It didn't take much in those days. The three of us got off the trolley to fight. I was beating the both of them when the cops pulled up and told us to get going. The two stiffs were happy to get off the corner. I told the cop I wasn't going anywhere until I was finished with them. Next thing you know I'm fighting three cops. This time they booked me for disorderly conduct and resisting arrest. I had a pocket-knife in my pocket. So to keep the bail high they threw in a charge for a concealed weapon. If I was ever going to use a weapon it wouldn't be a pocketknife. I paid a fine, and they put me on probation.

We saved our money and didn't stay too long with the Leddys, and I kept looking for work I could stay with. I worked at Budd Manufacturing where they made auto body parts. It was a slave pit, a real butcher shop. They had no decent safety standards. Every so often somebody would lose a hand or a finger. People today forget how much good the unions did in getting decent working conditions. I didn't feel like donating an arm to Budd so that's another place I quit, but that job made an impression on me when I got into union work later.

In desperation for a job, I went walking down Girard Avenue among the real butcher companies. I saw a black guy lugging hindquarters and loading them onto a truck for Swift's meat company. I asked him about work, and he sent me to a guy and the guy asked me if I thought I could handle loading hindquarters. Three days a week I was going to the gym and hitting the heavy bag, the speed bag, lifting weights, and playing handball. Plus I was teaching dancing, so I picked up a hindquarter like it was a pork chop, and I got the job.

The black guy was Buddy Hawkins and we became friends. Every morning for breakfast Buddy had a triple shot of Old Grand-Dad and a double piece of French apple pie. Buddy introduced me to Dusty Wilkinson, a black heavyweight who once fought the champ Jersey Joe Wolcott. He gave Wolcott a hell of a fight. Dusty was good people and we became friends. He was a good fighter, but he didn't like to train. He worked as a bouncer at a black dance club called the Nixon Ballroom and at a bar, the Red Rooster, at Tenth and Wallace. I'd stop in and hang out with Dusty at the bar and drink for free.

With a steady paycheck coming in and a baby on the way, Mary was able to give notice at her job, and we were able to afford our own place to live in. We rented a house in Upper Darby. We paid half the rent in exchange for Mary taking care of the landlady's daughter during the day.

And then we had our first baby girl, Mary Ann, born on Mary's birthday. There's no greater feeling than that. I made a vow to make as much money as I could for my family. Being Catholic we were going to have as many children as God provided to us. We had a nice christening for Mary Ann at the house. Dusty came to the house, which was a little unusual in 1948 in Philadelphia. The Phillies were the last major league team to get a black player.

After loading trucks for a while, I finally got a good steady union job as a truck driver with Food Fair. I kept that job for ten years. I delivered hindquarters and chickens mostly. Dusty showed me how to make a little extra on the side. I'd set aside some chickens and replace them with ice so the weight of the crates remained the same. I'd drive by the Red Rooster bar, and Dusty would have the people lined up to buy their chickens. He'd sell whole, fresh-killed chickens for a buck apiece, and we'd split the money down the middle. If I had sixty extra chickens, that was $30 apiece.

My daughter Peggy was born a little over a year later, and with the steady work at Food Fair, the extra job at Wagner's, and the money from the chickens, things were looking prosperous around the Sheeran household. Mary's mother helped out with the two babies.

Then I switched over a couple of nights from Wagner's Dance Hall to the Nixon Ballroom as a bouncer with Dusty. The black girls would hit on me to make their boyfriends jealous, and I'd have to settle everybody down. One day Dusty came up with an idea. He told me that the men were beginning to think I was afraid to fight them because I would only settle them down. So we worked out a deal where I would back down and keep backing down while Dusty made bets that I would kick a guy's ass. When the bets were in Dusty would nod his head and I'd knock the guy out. I don't know if you've ever knocked anybody out, but the best place to hit them is where the jaw meets the ear. If you catch them right they fall forward. They were always grabbing at my shirt on the way down and ripping it, so I had a deal with Nixon that I got a new white shirt every night as part of my pay. Anyway, Dusty and I would split the profit on the bets. Unfortunately, that didn't last too long. Pretty soon there were no volunteers.

We had our third daughter in 1955, Dolores. Mary and I went to church every Sunday, and the children had their own mass. Mary went to novenas when they had them and made all the sacraments. Mary was a terrific mother. She was a very quiet girl like my mother, but she showed our girls affection. That was hard for me to do, because I never got it as a kid. I learned how more with my grandchildren than with my own children. Mary did the raising of the girls. All my daughters never gave me a headache on their behavior. Not due to my care. Due to their mother's attention and the way she raised them.

I used to take my second daughter, Peggy, to Johnny Monk's club with me. Mary Ann liked to stay at home with her mother and the new baby, Dolores. Johnny Monk was the ward leader. His joint had very good food. We'd go there for New Year's Eve, even though Mary was no drinker. Mary liked to arrange picnics with the kids, and we'd take them to the Willow Grove Amusement Park. I wasn't always running. When they were smaller I used to take them out. I was very close to Peggy, but she doesn't talk to me any more, not since Jimmy disappeared.

The whole thing changed when I started hanging around downtown. Some of the drivers at Food Fair were Italian, and I started going downtown with them to the bars and restaurants that certain people also hung out in. I got into another culture.

I feel very bad about it now. I wasn't an abusive father, but I started getting a little neglectful, and Mary was too good a woman, too easy on me. Then at some point, I just joined that other culture and I stopped coming home. But I brought cash over every single week. If I did good, Mary did good. I was a selfish bastard. I thought I was doing good by giving money, but I didn't give the kids enough family time. I didn't give my wife enough time. It was different in the sixties when I married my second wife, Irene, and I had my fourth daughter, Connie. By then I was with Hoffa and the Teamsters, and I had steady money coming in and I was older and home more. I wasn't out maneuvering. I was already in position.

Sometime in the fifties I remember seeing *On the Waterfront* in the movies with Mary and thinking that I'm at least as bad as that Marlon Brando character and that some day I'd like to get in union work. The Teamsters gave me good job security at Food Fair. They could only fire you if they caught you stealing. Let me put it another way, they could only fire you if they caught you stealing and they could prove it.

chapter eight

Russell Bufalino

In 1957 the mob came out of the closet. It came out unwillingly, but out it came. Before 1957 reasonable men could differ over whether an organized network of gangsters existed in America. For years FBI director J. Edgar Hoover had assured America that no such organization existed, and he deployed the FBI's greatest resources to investigate suspected Communists. But as a result of the publicity foisted on the mob in 1957, even Hoover came on board. The organization was dubbed "La Cosa Nostra," meaning "this thing of ours," a term heard on government wiretaps.

Ironically, the publicity-shy Russell Bufalino had something to do with the mob's unwanted publicity in 1957. Russell Bufalino helped organize the famous meeting of godfathers from around the nation at the town of Apalachin (*apa-lake-in*), New York, in November 1957. The meeting had been called to settle down the potential problems that could have erupted in the wake of the October 1957 shooting of godfather Albert Anastasia in a barber's chair with a hot towel over his face in New York's Park-Sheraton Hotel.

The Apalachin meeting did the mob much more harm than good. The police in Apalachin were suspicious of all the mob activity in the area and raided the house in which the meeting was being held. This was before the U.S. Supreme Court changed all the laws on search and seizure. Fifty-eight of the most powerful mobsters in America were seized and hauled in by the police. Another fifty or so got away running through the woods.

Also in 1957 the public was getting a close look at organized crime on TV every day during the televised sessions of the McClellan Committee Hearings on Organized Crime of the United States Senate. Live for all America to see in black and white as no newspaper could convey it were tough mobsters wearing diamond pinkie rings conferring quietly with their mob lawyers, then shifting in their chairs to face the senators and their counsel, Bobby Kennedy, and in gruff voices taking the Fifth Amendment as to every single question. Most of these questions were loaded with accusations of murder, torture, and other major criminal activity. The litany became a part of the culture of the fifties: "Senator, on advice of counsel, I respectfully decline to answer that question on the grounds that it might tend to incriminate me." And, of course, the public took that answer as an admission of guilt.

No major decision of the Commission of La Cosa Nostra was made without Russell Bufalino's approval. Yet the public knew nothing of him before Apalachin and the McClellan Committee hearings. Unlike the Al Capones or the Dapper Don–types who flaunt their status, the quiet Bufalino could have been mistaken for a typical Italian immigrant.

Born Rosario Bufalino in 1903 in Sicily, in the years following Apalachin and the McClellan hearings the Justice Department almost succeeded in having Bufalino deported, along with his close friend and ally Carlos Marcello, crime boss of New Orleans. With his plane tickets already purchased and arrangements made to take some of his money with him, Bufalino succeeded in beating his deportation charges in court.

Not wanting to take their chances in court with Carlos Marcello, the FBI literally picked Russell's good friend Carlos up off the streets of New Orleans and put him on a plane to Guatemala. Carlos had a Guatemalan birth certificate, and according to the FBI he had no rights of an American citizen. Fuming and enraged, Marcello flew back and also beat his deportation charges in court.

Despite the government pressure Bufalino continued to conduct his business and flourish. The Pennsylvania Organized Crime Commission's 1980 report "A Decade of Organized Crime" revealed that by that time: "There are no more Magaddino . . . or Genovese crime families — the members in these families are now under the control of Russell Bufalino."

Bufalino was identified by the Pennsylvania Organized Crime Commission as a silent partner of the largest supplier of ammunition to the United States government, Medico Industries. Russell Bufalino had secret interests in Las Vegas casinos and not-so secret connections to the Cuban dictator Fulgencio Batista, whom Fidel Castro toppled in 1959. With Batista's blessings Bufalino had owned a racetrack and a major casino near Havana. Bufalino lost a great deal of money and property, including the racetrack and the casino, when Castro booted the mob off the island.

Time magazine reported in June 1975, a week before the assassination of Sam "Momo" Giancana in Chicago and a month before the disappearance of Jimmy Hoffa in Detroit, and during the time of the Church Committee Senate hearings on the CIA's ties to organized crime, that Russell Bufalino's help had been successfully recruited by the CIA in a mysterious CIA-gangland plot to kill Castro. Senator Frank Church's committee concluded that Bufalino was part of a bizarre conspiracy to assassinate Castro with poison pills just before the April 1961 Bay of Pigs invasion was to take place.

Bufalino had three acquittals for organized crime activity in the seventies. The last, a federal extortion case, came down a mere five days prior to Jimmy Hoffa's disappearance. The *Buffalo Evening News* reported on July 25, 1975: "'It turned out the way I anticipated,' said Bufalino, who has been linked to the CIA's plotting of the Bay of Pigs invasion." That same day the Rochester, New York, *Democrat* and *Chronicle* reported: "When asked if he will retire, Bufalino said, 'I'd like to retire, but they won't let me retire. I've got to pay my lawyers.'"

Russell Bufalino's organized crime territory included Pennsylvania outside of Philadelphia, upstate New York including Buffalo, and interests in Florida and Canada, parts of New York City, and parts of northern New Jersey. But his true power was in the respect he got from every mob family in the country. In addition, his wife, Carolina Sciandra, known as Carrie, was related to the Sciandra line of La Cosa Nostra. Although no Sciandra ever rose to godfather status, members of the family went back to the earliest days of the American Mafia.

Perhaps Bufalino's closest friend was Philadelphia crime boss Angelo Bruno. Law enforcement referred to Bufalino as "the quiet Don Rosario"; Bruno was known as the "Docile Don" for his similar low-key approach to heading a major crime family. Like Bufalino's family, the Bruno crime family was not permitted to deal in drugs. Because of his perceived old-fashioned ways Bruno was killed by greedy underlings in 1980. Bruno's demise would lead to everlasting anarchy in his family. His successor, Philip "Chicken Man" Testa, was literally blown up a year after taking over. Testa's successor, Nicodemus "Little Nicky" Scarfo, is now serving multiple life sentences for murder, having been betrayed by his own underboss and nephew. Little Nicky's successor, John Stanfa, is serving five consecutive life sentences for murder. Frank Sheeran got a Christmas card every year from John Stanfa in his Leavenworth cell. John Stanfa's successor, Ralph Natale, is the first boss to turn government informant and testify against his own men. Frank Sheeran calls Philadelphia "the city of rats." On the other hand, Russell Bufalino lived a long life. He died of old age in a nursing home in 1994 at the age of ninety. He controlled his "family" until the day he died, and unlike Angelo Bruno's Philadelphia family, not a sign of discord has been reported in the Bufalino family since his death.

Frank Sheeran said that of all the alleged crime bosses he ever met, the mannerisms and style of the Marlon Brando portrayal in *The Godfather* most nearly resembled Russell Bufalino.

In a report of its findings the McClellan Committee on Organized Crime of the United States Senate called Russell

Bufalino "one of the most ruthless and powerful leaders of
the Mafia in the United States."

Yet in the summer of 1999 I picked up a man, his wife, and
his son along an interstate in upstate Pennsylvania. Their
car had broken down, and they needed to get to a rest area.
The man turned out to be the retired chief of police of the
town where Russell Bufalino had lived and where his widow
Carrie still lived. I identified myself as a former prosecutor
and asked if the man could tell me anything about Russell
Bufalino. The retired police chief smiled and told me that
"whatever he did in other places he kept it out of our juris-
diction. He was old-school, very polite, a perfect gentleman.
You wouldn't know he had two dimes to rub together from
looking at his house or the car he drove."

chapter nine

Prosciutto Bread and Homemade Wine

The day I met Russell Bufalino changed my life. And later on, just being seen in his company by certain people turned out to save my life in a particular matter where my life was most definitely on the line. For better or for worse, meeting Russell Bufalino and being seen in his company put me deeper into the downtown culture than I ever would have gotten on my own. After the war, meeting Russell was the biggest thing that happened to me after my marriage and having my daughters.

I was hauling meat for Food Fair in a refrigerator truck in the mid-fifties, maybe 1955. Syracuse was my destination when my engine started acting up in Endicott, New York. I pulled into a truck stop and I had the hood up when this short old Italian guy walked up to my truck and said, "Can I give you a hand, kiddo?" I said sure and he monkeyed around for a while, I think with the carburetor. He had his own tools. I spoke a little Italian to him while he was working. Whatever it was, he got my horse started for me. When the engine started purring, I climbed down and I shook his hand and thanked him. He had a lot of strength in his handshake. The way we shook hands — warmly — you could tell that we both hit it off with each other.

Later on when we got to know each other he told me that the first time he saw me he liked the way I carried myself. I told him that there was something special about him, too, like maybe he owned the truck stop or something, or maybe he owned the whole road, but it was more than that. Russell had the confidence of a champ or a winner while still being humble and respectful. When you went to church for confession on Saturday you knew which priest's line to get on. You wanted to go to the fairest one that didn't give you a hard time; he was like that priest. At the time we shook hands that first time I ever laid eyes on him I had no idea who he was or that I would ever see him again. But change my life he did.

Around that same time I had already started going downtown to the Bocce Club at Fifth and Washington with a bunch of Italian guys I worked with at Food Fair who lived in South Philly. It was a new crowd for me. From there we'd go over to the Friendly Lounge at Eighth and Washington, owned by a guy named John who went by the nickname of Skinny Razor. At first I didn't know anything about John, but some of the guys from Food Fair pushed a little money on their routes for John. A waitress, say, at a diner would borrow $100 and pay back $12 a week for ten weeks. If she couldn't afford the $12 one week she'd just pay $2, but she'd still owe the $12 for that week and it would get added on at the end. If it wasn't paid on time the interest would keep piling up. The $2 part of the debt was called the "vig," which is short for vigorish. It was the juice.

My Italian Food Fair buddies made a few bucks that way, and one time when we were at the Friendly Lounge they introduced me to Skinny Razor, and I got started doing it on my route. It was easy money, no muscle, strictly providing a service for people who had no credit. This was before credit cards when the people had nowhere to go for a couple of bucks between paychecks. But technically, pushing money was all illegal since it was the alleged crime of loan sharking.

Pushing money was a natural for me, because I was already pushing football lottery tickets in the White Tower hamburger joints on my route for an Irish muscle guy and ex-boxer named Joey McGreal, who was a Teamster organizer out of my Local 107. My Italian pals at Food Fair bought lottery tickets from me. I wasn't backing the lottery. I couldn't afford to do that in case somebody hit big. McGreal was backing the thing, and I took my cut on commission. I played the lottery tickets myself. Soon I began selling them downtown to people in the bars. The real bookmakers like Skinny Razor didn't care if I sold them right in the bar, because they didn't mess with football lotteries. It was small stuff. Even so, they were illegal in those days; I guess they still are.

You could tell Skinny Razor was successful with his side businesses of bookmaking and loan sharking from the way he conducted his business and the kind of respect he got from people who came in to talk to him. He looked like he was an officer or something and everybody else was an enlisted man. But none of my Italian friends identified him as any kind of a gangster big shot or anything like that. What kind of a big shot has the nickname of Skinny Razor?

John got the name Skinny Razor because he used to own a live chicken store and the Italian ladies would come and pick out a chicken they wanted from looking at the chickens in the cages all lined up. Then John would take out a straight razor and cut the chicken's throat, and that was the chicken the Italian ladies would take home and pluck and cook for dinner.

Skinny Razor was very well liked and he had a great sense of humor. He called everybody "mother" in an affectionate way, not like they use that term today. He was very lean and went about 6'1", which was very tall for downtown. He looked a little like a skinny straight razor. Skinny was very good for the underdog. If you made a mistake you could always cop a plea with him, unless what you did was "severe." If it was a misdemeanor he'd give you a break, but he wasn't going to adopt you.

As hard as it is to believe today, people didn't really know that there was a mob organization in those days. We heard about individual gangsters, sure, like Al Capone with their own gang, but a national Mafia with a hand in just about everything — not too many people knew about that. I was in the know about a lot of things, but I didn't know about that even a little bit. Like everybody else, I didn't know that the neighborhood bookie was tied in with the cat-burglar jewel thief or the hijacker of trucks or the labor boss or the politician. I didn't know there was this big thing I was getting exposed to little by little in the beginning, when I was getting exposed to their culture. In a way it was like a dock worker being exposed to asbestos every day and not knowing how dangerous it is. They didn't want people to know.

The Italian guys I worked with at Food Fair who pushed money for him didn't even know how big the guy was that they called Skinny Razor.

Shooting the breeze over a bottle of homemade red wine, I bragged to my Food Fair buddies about the deal I had going with Dusty on the chickens and they put me wise to more money that could be made. After your truck was loaded with hindquarters the yard manager where you loaded your truck would put an aluminum seal on the lock and off you'd go. When you got to the Food Fair store with your delivery of hindquarters the store manager would break the aluminum seal and you'd load the meat into the store's refrigerator. Once the seal was broken it could never be put back together again, so you couldn't break the seal on your way to the store with the meat delivery. Only the store manager could break the seal. But on cold bitter days the yard manager who was supposed to put the seal on after the meat was loaded onto your truck would get a little lazy and hand you the seal to put on for him. If you palmed the seal, you could deliver, say, five hindquarters to a guy waiting for it at a diner. He'd deliver it to restaurants and split the money with you. After you gave this guy at the diner his five hindquarters, you'd put the seal on your lock. When you got to the store your seal would be intact and would then be broken by the store manager and everything would be copacetic. Then you'd be a nice guy and tell the butcher you were going to pack the meat for him in his icebox. You'd go in and there'd be hindquarters on hooks on the right rail. You'd take five off and put them on the left rail. Then instead of delivering twenty-five hindquarters you'd add the twenty you had left to the five you already had put on the left rail. The store manager would count your twenty-five and sign off on it. At inventory they'd see that they had a shortage, but they wouldn't know who was responsible or how it happened. The yard manager would never admit he handed you the seal to put on yourself and that he was too lazy to go out in the cold and do his job the right way.

That's how it worked in theory, but in reality nearly everybody was in on the deal and got a little piece of the pie for looking the other way.

Before the war I earned everything I ever had. During the war, you learned to take whatever you want, whatever you could get away with taking, not that there was much over there worth taking. Still, you took wine and women and if you needed a car you took it, too — stuff like that. After the war, it just seemed natural to take what you could take wherever you could take it. There was only so much blood you could sell for $10 a pint.

I got a little carried away one day and sold my entire load of meat on my way to a delivery in Atlantic City. I put the seal on my lock after the whole load of meat was transferred to the guy. When I got to Atlantic City the seal was broken by the manager and there was no meat inside and I was mystified. Maybe the guys who loaded the truck forgot to load it. The store manager asked me didn't I realize I was driving a light truck? I said I thought I had a good horse. After that incident Food Fair put signs up in the stores for all managers to keep a sharp eye on me. But then, like I said, a lot of them were in on the thing anyway.

The signs didn't stop me. They knew things were missing wherever I went, but they had no proof against me. They knew I was doing it, but they didn't know how I was doing it. And under the contract, management couldn't fire a Teamster unless they had certain grounds. They had none. Stealing was grounds only if they could prove it. Besides, I worked hard for them when I wasn't stealing from them.

But on November 5, 1956, they decided to take a shot with what they had, and they got me indicted for stealing in interstate commerce. My lawyer wanted me to take a plea and turn on the people who were in it with me. But I knew that all the people in it with me were the witnesses the government planned on using in their case against me. If they put me in jail they'd have to bring a wagon to court to cart away their own witnesses. If they had me, they had everybody. All they wanted me to do was name names and they'd let me go. I put the word out to the witnesses against me to be stand-up, that I wasn't going to rat anybody out. They should keep their mouths shut and act like they don't know anything. Meanwhile, I took the opportunity to break into the office and swipe the records about all the things Food Fair could not account for besides the meat I delivered.

The government witnesses, one after another, couldn't pin anything on me. I got my lawyer to put in the Food Fair records about all the things they had missing all the time, all the shortages. The government objected because they said I swiped the records. I said some anonymous guy swiped it and left it in my mailbox. The judge threw the case out and said that if he owned stock in Food Fair he would sell it. Food Fair then made an offer to me through my lawyer that if I would resign they would give me $25,000. I told them I couldn't afford the cut in pay.

We celebrated downtown, and I could see that Skinny Razor and some of the other people he sat with were most impressed that I didn't rat anybody out. Not ratting was more important to them than winning the case.

Somewhere in that time period when I started hanging out downtown we went into the Villa d'Roma on Ninth Street for dinner. One night I spotted this guy and I recognized him as the old guy who got my horse started at the truck stop. I went over and paid my respects, and he invited me to sit down with him and his friend. It turned out that his friend was Angelo Bruno, and I would later learn that Angelo Bruno was Skinny Razor's boss and the boss of all of Philadelphia and that Angelo Bruno was a silent partner in just about everything downtown, including the Villa d'Roma.

I had a glass of wine with them and Russell told me that he comes down to Philly a lot to pick up prosciutto bread. That's bread made with prosciutto and mozzarella baked in it. You slice it down and eat it like a sandwich. It's almost like a sandwich, but it's not. I thought he was serious that that was the only reason he came to Philly, and the next time I had a delivery up his way I brought him a dozen loaves of prosciutto bread. It shows you how much I knew. He was very gracious.

Then I began seeing Russell in different places downtown, and he was always with his friend Angelo Bruno. Whenever I was up his way, I started bringing him Roselli's sausages, because he said he came to Philly for them, too. Meanwhile, the more prosciutto bread and sausages I'm dropping off to him the more I keep seeing him in Philly. He always invited me to sit down and drink red wine and dunk bread in it. He loved the fact that during the war I had been to Catania, the town where he was born in Sicily. I told him about the maca-roni hanging out on the line like laundry to dry on Sunday in Catania. Sometimes he'd invite me to eat with him and we'd talk a little Italian. He'd actually buy a two-dollar football lottery ticket off me and play the card. It was just social.

Then my plans to become a permanent partner in the Food Fair chain came to an abrupt halt. They put Globe Detective Agency to watch a certain restaurant they suspected, and they caught the guy who brought the meat to the drops. He didn't work for Food Fair. He was just a guy who hung around downtown at Skinny Razor's place. He used a pickup truck and it was loaded with Food Fair meat I had given him. Once again they had nothing on me, because they couldn't identify the meat as being meat that any particular driver ever had on his truck. All they had me for was wishful thinking. But they knew it was me and they came to me and said that if I resigned they would let that guy go. I asked for the $25,000 if I resigned and they laughed at me. They figured I wasn't going to let that guy go down, and they were right. I resigned.

Next thing you know when I'm in the Villa d'Roma I run into Russell and he knows all about it and says I did the right thing. He says that the guy has a wife and kids and I did the right thing saving him from jail. Meanwhile, I've got a wife and kids, too, and I'm out of a job.

I started picking up jobs out of the union hall. You'd work your turn for companies where their driver was out sick.

You shaped up like the longshoremen in *On the Waterfront*. Some days you worked, some days you didn't, and all the time you're hoping to pick up a steady job. I still had the ballroom jobs. But I lost my Food Fair routes, and without my routes it was hard to push money for Skinny Razor and sell lottery tickets for Joey McGreal.

Being out of work meant I had more time on my hands to hang around downtown and try to earn a buck here or there. My Italian Food Fair buddies would brag about how I could bench press 400 pounds and how I would do reps of straight presses of 275 without jerking when we worked out at the gym. One day a numbers writer named Eddie Rece came up to me and wanted to know if I wanted to earn some money. He wanted me to take care of a little matter for him. He gave me a few bucks to go see a guy in Jersey who was messing around with the girlfriend of one of his relatives. He gave me a gun to show the guy, but he told me not to use it, just to show it. That's the way it was in those days. You showed a gun. Now they don't show you the gun, they just shoot you with it. In those days they wanted their money today. Now they want their money yesterday. Half of them today are doing drugs themselves, and it makes them impulsive. It distorts their thinking. More than half of them. Some of the bosses, too.

I went over to Jersey and talked to the guy. I told him not to be cutting somebody else's grass, to cut his own grass in his own yard. I told him this one's spoken for. I told him to go get his own trim — which is what we called it in those days, getting trim. I told him to look for your trim elsewhere. Right off I could tell Romeo wanted no trouble from me, so I never even bothered to show him the gun. He knew what it was.

That little errand for Eddie Rece turned out all right and that led to more errands for people. Maybe some guy owed one of the men downtown some money and I'd go collect it. One time Skinny Razor told me to go to Atlantic City and bring back a guy who was late paying his vig on a loan. I went and got the guy. This one I had to show the gun to in order to get him into my car. He was peeing in his pants by the time we got to the Friendly Lounge. Skinny Razor took a look at him and told him to come back with his money. The guy asked Skinny how he was going to get back to Atlantic City to get his money, and Skinny told him to take a bus.

No doubt I was getting a reputation for being efficient, but also for being somebody you could trust. Quitting the job at Food Fair to save that guy from jail kept being brought up by people as proof that I was a stand-up guy. They started calling me "Cheech," which is short for Frank in Italian — Francesco. They started inviting me into the Messina Club at Tenth and Tasker, which is a members-only joint where you get the best sausage and peppers you ever ate. You'd play cards there; just hang out without the public citizens being at the next table. It's still there, and it still has the best sausage and peppers in all of South Philly.

A couple of times when I ran into Russell on a Wednesday he'd tell me to go home and get my wife. Then he and his wife, Carrie, would meet us at the Villa d'Roma for dinner. Wednesday night was the night that you went out with your wives, that way nobody was seen out with his *cumare*, his mistress, whatever you want to call it. Everybody knew not to be out with their *cumare* on Wednesday night. It was like an unwritten rule. Mary and I would have a pleasant evening on many a Wednesday with Russ and Carrie.

Automatically I started going downtown if there was no work out of the union hall. It was comfortable down there. I always had a glass of red wine in my hand. I started staying out later and later and sometimes not going home at all. On Sunday nights I'd go to the Latin Casino, a fancy night club in Cherry Hill, New Jersey, where I'd see everybody that hung out downtown during the week. Frank Sinatra would play there, all the big stars would. I'd bring Mary once in a while, but it wasn't her kind of crowd, and a baby sitter was a luxury we couldn't afford too often with me out of work. Mary was lighting candles that I'd get a steady job. I began sleeping late on Sundays after Saturday night at the Nixon Ballroom with Dusty, and Mary would go by herself to mass and the kids would go to their mass.

Once in a while Russell would call me from upstate and ask me to drive up and take him someplace. He had business all over, from Endicott to Buffalo in New York; from Scranton to Pittsburgh in Pennsylvania; and in north Jersey and New York City. He seemed to know where I was during the day when he would call me to come up and get him. I enjoyed his company, and I never asked him for a dime. He knew he was doing me good by my being seen with him. I didn't know how good until one day in November 1957. He asked me to drive him to a small town across the border in upstate New York called Apalachin. He told me that when he got done in Apalachin he was going to Erie, Pennsylvania, and then to Buffalo and that he had a ride lined up to Erie and Buffalo and back again to his home in Kingston. So I took him to this house in Apalachin and dropped him off. I didn't see anything unusual.

The next day this meeting at Apalachin is the biggest thing to ever happen to Italian gangsters in America. All of a sudden they had arrested about fifty gangsters from every part of the country, and one of them was my new friend Russell Bufalino. It was front page every day for days. It was the hottest thing on television. There really was a Mafia, and it covered the whole country. All these individual gangsters had their own territory. Now I understood why Russell would ask me to drive him to different places and wait for him in the car while he did a little business in somebody's house or in a bar or a restaurant. They did all their business in person and in cash, not over the phone or with banks. Russell Bufalino was as big as Al Capone had been, maybe bigger. I couldn't get over it.

I read every article. Some of these guys wore silk suits, some others dressed plain like Russell. But they were all powerful men with big criminal records you could brag about, not just fighting with cops after a brawl that started on a trolley, not lifting a little meat from Food Fair. These partners of Russell Bufalino and Angelo Bruno were involved in every type of crime from murder and prostitution to drugs and hijacking. Loan sharking and gambling were described as big business for these men. So was labor racketeering. Russell had not been coming to Philly just for prosciutto bread and sweet and hot sausage from Roselli's, not even extra-hot sausage. He had business interests with Angelo Bruno, their own kind of business.

And Russell Bufalino was one of the biggest bosses in their business, and I was his friend. I was seen with him. I drank wine with him. I knew his wife. He knew my wife. He always asked about my kids. I talked Italian with him. I brought him prosciutto bread and sausages. He gave me gallons of home-made red wine. We would dunk the prosciutto bread in the wine. I drove him places. I even drove him to that meeting in Apalachin.

But after all this hit the paper I didn't see him downtown anymore for a while and he didn't call me to drive him anywhere. I figured he was avoiding publicity. Then I read where they were trying to deport him because he was forty days old when he arrived in America from Sicily. The deportation proceedings and appeals would last for fifteen years, but they were always hanging over Russell's head. In the end when he lost his last appeal and had packed his bags and had his tickets, I recommended a lawyer to him who went through the Italian government, spread a little lira, and got it so the Italian government refused to take Russell, and that was that. America had to keep him. Russell was very grateful for my recommendation on that deportation thing, but when I first read about it in the paper, who could have imagined I would have worked my way that far up the ladder to be help-ing save Russell Bufalino from deportation.

Another thing is that downtown people were saying that it looked like Russell was the boss who had called the Apalachin meeting to prevent a gang war over the whacking of the New York waterfront boss Albert Anastasia in a barber's chair the month before. Russell Bufalino, the mechanic who started my horse for me at a truck stop in Endicott, New York, was getting bigger and bigger every day in my eyes. And I've got to say, if you've ever met a movie star or somebody famous, there was an element of that. Although he hated it, Russell was a tremendous celebrity, and anybody who was seen with him downtown or wherever had some of that status rub off on them.

Then one day this guy, Whispers DiTullio, came over to my table at the Bocce Club and bought me a glass of wine. I had seen him around, but I didn't know him too well. He had the same last name as Skinny Razor, but they were not related. I knew he pushed money for Skinny Razor, but way bigger money than me and my friends pushed. He pushed money to restaurants and legitimate businesses, not just to waitresses at White Tower joints. Whispers told me to meet him at the Melrose Diner. So I went around there. You wouldn't expect to see any people from downtown at the Melrose Diner. It's more for the crowd grabbing a bite to eat before they go to a Phillies game. You get a nice piece of apple pie there with hot vanilla syrup on it. Whispers sat down and asked me if I could use ten grand. I told him to keep talking.

chapter ten

All the Way Downtown

Whispers was one of these short Italian guys in his early thirties that you'd see all around South Philly, just trying to get by with one hustle or another. This is not the same Whispers they blew up when they bombed his car around the same time. This is the other Whispers. I didn't know the one they blew up; I just heard about it.

I didn't know anything about "made men" back then. That's a special status in the alleged mob where you go through a ceremony and after that you are then untouchable. Nobody can whack you without approval. You get extra respect wherever you go. You are part of the "in" crowd, the inner circle. It only applies to Italians. Later on I got so close to Russell that I was higher up than a made man. Russell even said that to me. He said, "Nobody can ever touch you because you are with me." I can still feel him gripping my cheek with that strong grip of his and telling me, "You should have been an Italian."

If I had known about made men then I would have known that Whispers was nowhere near a made man. He hung around downtown and did whatever he had to do. He knew everybody, and he had more experience downtown than I did. Sunday nights he would sit with Skinny Razor and his wife at the Latin Casino. By now, after Apalachin, I already knew that Skinny Razor was Angelo's underboss. That meant Skinny Razor from the Friendly Lounge was the number two man in Philly.

Having the same last name, I'm quite sure Whispers wanted people to think that he was up there with John "Skinny Razor" DiTullio. He wanted to increase his status and look like a made man.

The only thing is that Whispers had the worst breath known to man or beast. He suffered from halitosis so bad you'd think he was growing garlic in his belly. No amount of chewing gum or mints did him any good. So he was only allowed to whisper when he talked to people. Nobody wanted a full dose of Whispers's breath when he opened his mouth. Of course, out of respect and knowing his proper place in things, he wouldn't have done much talking anyway when he sat with Skinny Razor and his wife at the Latin.

After we had a little something to eat, which wasn't an easy thing to do sitting across from him, Whispers and I left the Melrose and took a walk around the block. Whispers explained to me that he had pushed a lot of money to a linen supply house, more money than he had ever loaned out before. It was his big stake, and it was turning into a big mistake.

Linen supply was ordinarily good money. They supplied fresh linen to restaurants and hotels. It was like a big laundry. They would pick up the linen, wash and iron it, and deliver it fresh. It was a license to print money.

But this linen supply house Whispers had pushed money to was having a hard time of it. It was getting competition from the Cadillac Linen Service down in Delaware, which was beating them out of contracts. If it kept going that way, it would take forever for Whispers to get all of his big stake back. The only money the linen company was able to afford was the vig, and sometimes they were late with that. Whispers was more than a little bit concerned that he could even lose the whole capital he had loaned.

I didn't know what he was getting at for me, but I listened. Did he want me to drive down to Delaware and show a gun and collect his money? You don't pay ten grand for that service. Delaware's only thirty or so miles south of Philly. Ten grand then is like fifty grand today or better.

Then he peeled off two grand and handed it to me.

"What's that for?" I asked.

"I want you to bomb or torch or burn to the fucking ground or do whatever you choose to do to disable the Cadillac Linen Service. Put those fuckers out of business. That way my people will get back their contracts and I can get back my money out of this fucking thing. I want this Cadillac business permanently disabled. No flat tires. No scratching the paint. Gone for good. Closed down. A thing of the past. Permanent press. No starch on the shirts. Go fucking let them collect their insurance if they got any — which being Jews you know they do — and let them learn to leave my customers the fuck alone."

"You said ten grand."

"Don't worry. You get the other eight when you achieve success in closing them the fuck down for good. I don't want them starting up again in a couple or three weeks and then I'm out ten grand besides."

"When do I get the other eight?"

"That depends on you, Cheech. The more damage you do the quicker I'll know they are permanently out of business. I want you to burn those Jew fucking washerwomen to the ground. You were in the war; you know what the fuck to do."

"Sounds good. The money part is all right. I'll look the place over. I'll see what I can do."

"You were in the war, Cheech. Listen, I took you out here by the Melrose away from the neighborhood to talk because this has got to be just between you and me. You understand what I'm trying to tell you?"

"Sure."

"I don't want you using nobody else to help you neither. I hear you can keep your mouth shut. I hear that you work alone. I hear good things about your work. That's what I'm paying the strong money for. Ten grand is strong money for this. I could get it done for a grand or two. So don't say nothing to Skinny Razor or nothing to nobody. Ever. You hear? You start opening your mouth about what you're doing and it reflects bad on you. You hear?"

"You sound a little nervous, Whispers. If you don't think you can trust me, get somebody else."

"No, no, Cheech. I never used you before, that's all. Just between you and me. If we gotta talk again, we come out here to talk. Downtown we just say hello, that's all, like regular."

That night I went straight home. I took the two grand and handed $1,500 straight to Mary for child support. I told her I hit the number on a $4 bet. The bookies paid 600-to-one, but you always gave the bookie a $100 tip for each dollar bet. Most bookies took it out automatic. She was very appreciative, and she knew I was keeping $500 for myself. Mary was getting used to getting cash in different amounts at different times whenever I got it.

The next morning I drove down to the Cadillac Linen Service and started to look the plant over. I drove around the block a few times. Then I parked across the street and went over and took a quick peek inside the plant a little. It looked easy to get in the place. A place like that in those days had no burglar alarm or any kind of real security. There was nothing to steal and there were no homeless or crack addicts to worry about breaking in. It looked like a big job, but it was big money I was getting. Not the couple of hundred to drive to Jersey to straighten somebody out.

Then I came back at night to see what it looked like after dark. When I went home I thought about it and started working on a plan, and the next day I went back for another look, cruising past the place a few times. I figured I'd burn it down to the ground. That way I'd get my other eight grand right away. It had to go up in flames fast before the firemen could put out the fire, so I'd soak the whole place real good with kerosene.

The next day I walked into the Friendly Lounge, and Skinny Razor said there was somebody in the back who wanted to talk to me. I walked down to the back room with Skinny Razor right behind me. I went into the room and there was nobody in there. I turned to leave and Skinny was standing in my path. He shut the door and folded his arms.

"What the fuck you doing at Cadillac?" he asked me.

"Trying to make a little money, that's all."

"Doing what?"

"For a guy."

"What guy?"

"What's going on?"

"I like you, Cheech. Angelo likes you, but you got some explaining to do. They seen a blue Ford like yours with Pennsylvania tags on it, and they seen a giant motherfucker get out of it. That's you; that's how easy that was. That's all I'm going to say to you. You did the right thing not trying to deny it. Angelo wants to see you right now."

Now I'm walking over there and I'm thinking, what the hell is going on? What kind of shit has Whispers got me into?

I walked into the Villa d'Roma, and Angelo was sitting at his table in the corner and who's sitting there with him but Russell. Now I'm doing some serious thinking. What have I got myself into, and is it something I can get out of? These are the same powerful men they wrote all that stuff about after Apalachin, but now these men are not sitting here in the capacity of my friends anymore. Like I said, growing up around my old man, I knew when something was wrong. Something big was wrong, and I was in the jackpot. It looked like a court-martial. But a court-martial for desertion in the face of the enemy, not just some bullshit AWOL drinking spree.

Now maybe I didn't know much when I first started hanging around downtown with my Italian friends from Food Fair, but by then, after Apalachin and after the Senate hearings they had been having on television, I knew these were not people you disappointed.

Then it dawned on me that the restaurant was empty except for the bartender in the front room, and I could hear the bartender making moves to come out from behind the bar. Every sound was magnified for me like when you're on a landing craft heading for an invasion on a beachhead. All your senses are sharpened by the occasion. Crystal clear I heard his footsteps walking around from the bar, and I heard him lock the door and put a closed sign up. The locking of the door was a loud snap that almost echoed.

Angelo told me to sit down.

I sat in the chair he pointed to. Then he said, "All right, let's have it."

"I was going to put Cadillac out of commission."

"For who?"

"Whispers. The other Whispers."

"Whispers? He fucking knows better than that."

"I was just trying to make some money." I looked over at Russell and he had no expression on his face.

"You know who owns Cadillac?"

"Yeah. Some Jews in the laundry business."

"You know who's got a piece of Cadillac?"

"No."

"I do."

"You know who?"

"No. I do. I do got a piece. Not I do know who got a piece."

I almost wet myself. "I didn't know that, Mr. Bruno. That's something I did not know."

"You don't check these things out before you go around doing things in this part of the country?"

"I figured Whispers already checked it out."

"He didn't tell you it was the Jew mob?"

"He didn't tell me a thing about that. He told me it was some Jews. I figured it was just some Jews in the laundry business."

"What else did he tell you?"

"He told me to keep this matter to myself; that I should work alone. That's about it."

"I'll bet my next meal he told you to keep it to yourself. That way you'd be the only one looking bad here when you got seen maneuvering around down there in Delaware."

"Should I give him back his money?"

"Don't worry, he won't need it."

"I'm real sorry for not checking. It won't happen again."

"You get one mistake. Don't make another one. And thank your friend here. If it wasn't for Russ, I wouldn't be wasting my time. I'd have let the Jews have you. What do you think they were made with, a finger? They're not fucking stupid. They're not going to let somebody drive around their block and not check them out."

"I certainly apologize. Thank you, too, Russell; it won't happen again." I didn't know if I should have called him Mr. Bufalino, but I was so used to calling him Russell by that point in the thing that "Mr. Bufalino" would have been too phony. It was bad enough calling Angelo "Mr. Bruno."

Russell nodded and said softly, "Don't worry about it. This Whispers had aspirations. I know these people who get too ambitious. They want the whole pie. They get jealous of other people moving up. He saw you sit down with me and drink with me and eat with me and sit down with our wives, and I don't think he liked that. Not a bit did he like that. Now you gotta square this up right here and now and do the right thing. Listen to Angelo here, he knows what it is."

Russell got up and left the table, then I could hear the bartender open the door for him and he was gone.

Angelo said to me, "Who else is involved with this besides you and Whispers?"

"Nobody that I know of. I didn't tell a soul."

"Good. That's good. This fucking Whispers put you on the fucking spot, my young fellow. Now it becomes your responsibility to make this come out right."

I nodded my head and said, "Whatever I gotta do."

Angelo whispered, "It's your responsibility to take care of this matter by tomorrow morning. That's the chance you get. Capish?"

I nodded my head and said, "Capish."

"You gotta do what you gotta do."

You didn't have to go down the street and enroll in some courses at the University of Pennsylvania to know what he meant. It was like when an officer would tell you to take a couple of German prisoners back behind the line and for you to "hurry back." You did what you had to do.

I got a hold of Whispers and told him where to meet me later that night to talk about the thing.

The next morning it was front page. He was found lying on the sidewalk. He had been shot at close range with something like a .32, the kind of gun the cops used to call a woman's gun because it was easier to handle and had less of a kick than even a .38. Being a smaller caliber it didn't do the damage a .38 does, but all you need is a little hole if you put it in the right place. The good feature is that it makes a little less noise than a .38 and a whole lot less noise than a .45. Sometimes you want a lot of noise, like in the middle of the day to scatter bystanders; sometimes you don't want a lot of noise, like in the middle of the night. What do you want to go around disturbing people's sleep for?

The paper said it was an unknown assailant and that there had been no witnesses. So laying there on the sidewalk he really did not need his money back. I never could find my .32 after that, the one that Eddie Rece had given me to show to that Romeo in Jersey. It must have ended up someplace.

That morning I just sat there staring at the paper. I must have sat there for over an hour. I kept thinking, "That could have been me."

And it would have been me if it weren't for Russell. Whispers knew what he was doing. I didn't even know it was the alleged Jew mob that owned Cadillac. I just thought it was some Jews. Whispers was going to leave me out there. I was the one the Jew mob would have seen nosing around, and I was the one they would have whacked after the thing happened. Whispers would have gotten the place burned down and after the Jews got done with me he never would have had to pay me the other eight grand.

No questions asked one way or the other, either before or after I did the job, I would have been gone to Australia. If it weren't for Russell, no questions asked I'd have been history right then and there, and I wouldn't be here now talking about all this stuff. I owed that man my life. And that was only the first time.

Whispers knew the rules. He broke the wrong rule, that's all.

When I finally got off my ass and went around to the Friendly, I could tell that everybody that sat down with

Skinny Razor had a bigger respect for me. Skinny Razor bought me a bunch of drinks. I went to the Villa d'Roma and checked in with Angelo and gave him a report. He was satisfied. He bought me dinner on the house, and he told me to just be careful who I got involved with next time. He said that Whispers knew what he was doing and that he was greedy.

Then two men came in and sat down with us. Angelo introduced me to Cappy Hoffman and Woody Weisman. They were the two Jewish mobsters who owned Cadillac with Angelo. They were real friendly to me, very courteous men with good personalities. When Angelo left with them, I stayed at the bar in the front room. The same bartender who locked the door behind me yesterday wouldn't take my money for my glasses of wine. Even the waitresses could tell I was getting all this respect and they started flirting. I tipped everybody real good.

Looking back on that twenty-four-hour period between the time I met with Angelo and Russell and the time I met with Angelo again, after that particular matter with Whispers on the sidewalk, it got easier and easier not to go home anymore. Or it got harder and harder to go home. Either way, I stopped going home.

Once that line was crossed into the new culture there was no more confession on Saturday, no more church with Mary on Sunday. Everything was different. I had been drifting downtown and now I was all the way down there. It was a bad time to leave the girls. It was the worst mistake I made in my life. But no time is a good time to leave your wife and kids.

I got myself a room around the corner from Skinny Razor's and I took my clothes over there. I still went down to the Teamsters hall for trucks, and I still had the ballroom jobs, but I kept getting more and more jobs from downtown. I was now running. I was a part of the culture.

chapter eleven

Jimmy

It is no doubt difficult for some people today to appreciate the degree of fame or infamy that Jimmy Hoffa enjoyed in his heyday and before his death, a span of roughly two decades from the mid-fifties to the mid-seventies.

While in his heyday he was the most powerful labor leader in the nation, how can that mean anything in these times when labor leaders are virtually unknown to the general public? Labor union strife? Bloody labor wars? The closest thing to a labor war today is a threatened baseball player's strike and whether the major league baseball season will be shortened and whether there will be a World Series. However, in the first two years following World War II, years in which Frank Sheeran looked for steady work and got married, there were a combined total of 8,000 strikes in 48 states. That's more than 160 separate strikes per year per state, and many individual strikes were nationwide.

Today Jimmy Hoffa is famous mostly because he was the victim of the most infamous disappearance in American history. Yet during a twenty-year period there wasn't an American alive who wouldn't have recognized Jimmy Hoffa immediately, the way Tony Soprano is recognized today. The vast majority of Americans would have known him by the sound of his voice alone. From 1955 until 1965 Jimmy Hoffa was as famous as Elvis. From 1965 until 1975 Jimmy Hoffa was as famous as the Beatles.

Jimmy Hoffa's first notoriety in union work was as the leader of a successful strike by the "Strawberry Boys." He became identified with it. In 1932 the nineteen-year-old Jimmy Hoffa was working as a truck loader and unloader of fresh fruits and vegetables on the platform dock of the Kroger Food Company in Detroit for 32¢ an hour. Twenty cents of that pay was in credit redeemable for groceries at Kroger food stores. But the men only got that 32¢ when there was work to do. They had to report at 4:30 p.m. for a twelve-hour shift and weren't permitted to leave the platform. When there were no trucks to load or unload, the workers sat around without pay. On one immortal hot spring afternoon, a load of fresh strawberries arrived from Florida, and the career of the most famous labor leader in American history was launched.

Hoffa gave a signal, and the men who would come to be known as the Strawberry Boys refused to move the Florida strawberries into refrigerator cars until their union was recognized and their demands for better working conditions were met. Their demands included a four-hour-per-day guarantee of hourly pay per twelve-hour shift for the platform workers. Fearing the loss of the crates of strawberries in the heat of the day, Kroger folded and acceded to young Jimmy Hoffa's demands and gave the new one-company union a one-year charter.

Born on St. Valentine's Day in 1913, Jimmy Hoffa was seven years older than Frank Sheeran. Yet both grew to manhood in the same Great Depression, a time when management normally held the upper hand and people struggled just to put food on the table. Jimmy Hoffa's father, a coal miner, died when he was seven. His mother worked in an auto plant to support her children. Jimmy Hoffa quit school at age fourteen to go to work to help his mother.

Hoffa and his Strawberry Boys' victory in 1932 was a rare labor victory in those days. In that same year a group of World War I veterans and their plight came to symbolize the powerlessness of the working man in the Depression. In 1932 thousands of veterans, tired of broken promises, marched on Washington and refused to leave the Mall until their promised bonuses, not due until 1945, were granted by Congress now when they needed them most. President Herbert Hoover ordered General Douglas MacArthur to evict the Bonus Marchers by force, and MacArthur, astride a white horse, led an assault of troops, tanks, and tear gas against the veterans without giving them a chance to leave quietly. The U.S. Army opened fire on its own unarmed former soldiers, killing two and wounding several others, all veterans of a bloody world war that had ended fourteen years earlier, a so-called War to Save Democracy.

The next year, Kroger refused to negotiate a new contract, and Hoffa's victory was short-lived. But on the strength of his stand with the Strawberry Boys, Jimmy Hoffa was recruited by Detroit's Teamsters Local 299 as an organizer. Hoffa's job was to encourage men to join the union and through solidarity and organization to better their lives and the lives of their families. Detroit was home to America's auto industry. As the auto industry's chief spokesman, Henry Ford's position on the labor movement in general was that "labor unions are the worst thing that ever struck the earth."

In fighting such a monstrous evil as labor unions, companies believed any means were justified. Both big and small business had no compunction about hiring thugs and goons as strikebreakers to break the heads and the will of strikers and union organizers.

Once it is organized, a union's only negotiating weapon is a strike, and a strike cannot succeed if a sufficient number of people show up for work and do their jobs. Because jobs were scarce during Hoffa's rise, management had little difficulty hiring nonunion "scab" workers to replace striking union workers. When union strikers on the picket lines refused to allow nonunion scabs to cross the lines and go to work, management goons and thugs would wade into the picket line, clearing a path. Sicilian mobster Santo Perrone of Detroit provided hired muscle for Detroit's management. Perrone sent Sicilian goons to break strikes in Detroit with billy clubs, while cops either looked the other way or helped the strikebreakers.

As Hoffa put it, "Nobody can describe the sit-down strikes, the riots, the fights that took place in the state of Michigan, particularly here in Detroit, unless they were a part of it." And on another occasion he said, "My scalp was laid open sufficiently wide to require stitches no less than six times during the first year I was business agent of Local 299. I was beaten up by cops or strikebreakers at least two dozen times that year."

And on the other side of the ledger, unions like the Teamsters often employed their own muscle, their own reigns of terror, including bombings, arsons, beatings, and murders. The warfare and violence were not just between labor and management. It was often between rival unions vying for the same membership. Sadly, it was often violence directed at rank-and-file union members who urged democratic reform of their unions.

The alliances Hoffa made with mobsters around the country as he and his union rose together are now a matter of historical record. But in the 1950s it was a subject that was just beginning to be exposed to public light.

In May 1956, Victor Riesel, an investigative reporter for the daily *New York Journal American,* featured anti-Hoffa Teamsters on his daily radio show. Riesel had been crusading against the criminal element in labor unions. The night of the radio broadcast, Riesel stepped out of the famous Lindy's restaurant on Broadway near Times Square and was approached on the sidewalk by a goon who threw a cup of acid in his face. Riesel was blinded by the acid's effect on his eyes. It soon became obvious that the attack had been ordered by Hoffa ally and labor racketeer John Dioguardi, aka Johnny Dio. Dio was charged with ordering the vicious crime, but when the acid thrower was found dead, and other witnesses got the message and refused to cooperate, the charges were dropped.

The image of a blind Victor Riesel wearing dark glasses and appearing on television still courageously urging labor reform so outraged the nation that the U.S. Senate responded by conducting live televised hearings on the influence of racketeers on the labor movement. These hearings came to be known as the McClellan Committee hearings, named after the

Arkansas senator, John L. McClellan, who presided over them. Future presidential candidates Senator Barry Goldwater of Arizona and Senator John F. Kennedy of Massachusetts were members of the committee. The committee's chief counsel and principal interrogator was the future president's younger brother and the nation's future attorney general, Bobby Kennedy. As a result of his aggressive work on the committee, Bobby Kennedy was to become Jimmy Hoffa's mortal enemy.

Johnny Dio took the Fifth Amendment on every question posed to him, including whether he had ever met Jimmy Hoffa. Because of his union position, Jimmy Hoffa could not take the Fifth Amendment without forfeiting his job. He answered question after question with doubletalk and a memory incapable of being refreshed. When confronted with wiretap tape recordings of conversations he had had with Johnny Dio, Hoffa could not remember ever asking Johnny Dio to do any favors for him. At one point Hoffa told Bobby Kennedy regarding the tapes, "To the best of my recollection, I must recall on my memory, I cannot remember."

There would have been considerably more outrage had the public known what Hoffa had told his staff when he had heard about Riesel's blinding: "That son of a bitch Victor Riesel. He just had some acid thrown on him. It's too bad he didn't have it thrown on the goddamn hands he types with."

When asked by Bobby Kennedy where he'd gotten $20,000 in cash to invest in a business venture, Hoffa replied, "From individuals." When asked to name them Hoffa said, "Offhand, that particular amount of money I borrowed I don't know at this particular moment, but the record of my loans, which I requested, I have, and out of all the moneys I loaned over this period of time I went into these ventures."

Well, that explained that.

Bobby Kennedy called Jimmy Hoffa "the most powerful man in the country next to the president."

Part of Hoffa's mystique when he became famous in the fifties came from his in-your-face rebel tough-guy image on television. He was antiestablishment before people used that word. The closest thing today to what Hoffa's public image was then might be some heavy metal band. There are simply no public figures today who so challenge the elite business and government establishment and so champion the working class as Jimmy Hoffa did almost daily and with arrogance.

Television was in its infancy when Jimmy Hoffa became president of the International Brotherhood of Teamsters on October 14, 1957, a month before Apalachin. Hoffa was a frequent guest celebrity on the news talk shows of the day, such as *Meet the Press.* Microphones were stuck in his face wherever he went, and if Jimmy Hoffa called a press conference the world press showed up.

Jimmy Hoffa had two philosophies that guided his actions. One way or another he expressed them daily and often through word or deed. The first of these philosophies was "the ends," the second was "the means." The "ends" was his labor philosophy. Hoffa often said that his labor philosophy was simple: "The working man in America is being shortchanged every day in America." The "means" was his second philosophy and can be summed up by a remark he made to Bobby Kennedy at a private party in which they found themselves together: "I do to others what they do to me, only worse." Simply put, Jimmy Hoffa believed that the "ends" of improving the lot of working Americans, with his union leading the way, justified whatever "means" were used to accomplish it.

His popularity with his own membership reflected their willingness to reap the tangible rewards he obtained for them in wages, vacations, pensions, and health and welfare benefits. As Hoffa told Johnny Dio in one of those wiretapped conversations that he couldn't remember: ". . . treat them right and you don't have to worry."

Although others may have shared his zeal to improve the lives of American working men and women and their families, Jimmy Hoffa had the power to do something about it. His ardent supporter Frank Sheeran said that "Jimmy Hoffa was ahead of his time when it came to labor. There were only two things that mattered in his life: the union and his family. Believe it or not, as strong as he was for the union, his wife and his daughter and his son came first to him. Unions to him were a thing that helped not just the men, but it helped the men's families, too. They talk all about family values these days. Jimmy was ahead of his time on that, too. Those two things were his whole life."

Jimmy Hoffa once said to Frank Sheeran enthusiastically, "If you got it, Irish, a truck driver brought it to you. Don't ever forget that. That's the whole secret to what we do." That "you got it" part covered food, clothing, medicine, building materials, fuel for home and industry, just about everything. Because a nationwide trucking strike could literally starve and shut down the nation, Bobby Kennedy called Jimmy Hoffa's Teamsters "the most powerful institution in the country aside from the United States government. . . . and as Mr. Hoffa operates it, this is a conspiracy of evil." Senator John L. McClellan took the image a step further. McClellan called "the Teamsters under Mr. Hoffa's leadership" a "superpower in this country — a power greater than the people and greater than the government."

From the time in 1957 that his predecessor and mentor Dave Beck abdicated the presidency and went to jail for embezzling $370,000 from the Western Conference of Teamsters, to finance, among other things, the building of a house for his son, the new president Jimmy Hoffa wielded his power absolutely. Perhaps it is true that all power corrupts, and that absolute power corrupts absolutely. If it is so, Jimmy Hoffa was not apologetic about the criminal records of the men with whom he allied himself to accomplish his goals.

Hoffa once announced to a television audience: "Now, when you talk about the question of hoodlums and gangsters, the first people that hire hoodlums and gangsters are employers. If there are any illegal forces in the community, he'll use them, strong-arm and otherwise. And so if you're going to stay in the business of organizing the unorganized, maintaining the union you have, then you better have a resistance."

Hoffa's "resistance" consisted of close alliances with the most powerful godfathers of the newly uncovered, secret tangled web of Apalachin gangsters who had carved America into twenty-four territories of organized crime and who ran their organizations (called families) with a military structure. They were "bosses," the godfathers who were the equivalent of generals; "underbosses" and "consiglieres," who were the equivalent of top brass; "capos," who were the equivalent of captains; and "soldiers," who, as soldiers, followed the orders from upstairs. In addition, there were associates like Frank Sheeran who had whatever status they earned, but who were not permitted an official rank in the Italian families' military structure.

From the historical record there can be little doubt that Hoffa knew full well that the vast majority of mobsters who constituted his "resistance" had little regard for his ideals. Johnny Dio himself owned and operated a nonunion garment industry dress shop. Many of these dark figures looked upon unions as just another means to aid them in the commission of more crime, and to aid them in the accumulation of more wealth and greater power.

Meanwhile, in speech after speech to his rank and file, Hoffa told his brother Teamsters, "All this hocus-pocus about racketeers and crooks is a smokescreen to carry you back to the days when they could drop you in the scrap heap like they do a worn-out truck."

On the other hand, in his book, *The Enemy Within,* Bobby Kennedy wrote about his experiences and observations as chief counsel for the McClellan Committee hearings on organized crime and labor unions, saying: "We saw and questioned some of the nation's most notorious gangsters and racketeers. But there was no group that better fits the prototype of the old Al Capone syndicate than Jimmy Hoffa and some of his chief lieutenants in and out of the union."

Twentieth Century Fox commissioned a screenplay of Bobby Kennedy's book. Budd Schulberg, the celebrated writer of *On the Waterfront,* wrote the screenplay, but the project was abandoned by the studio. Columbia Pictures then expressed interest in picking up the project but abandoned it as well. In an introduction he wrote to a 1972 book written about Hoffa by Bobby Kennedy's chief aide, Walter Sheridan, Budd Schulberg explained why the two studios abandoned the project: "A labor tough walked right into the office of the new head of [Twentieth Century Fox] to warn him that if the picture was ever made [Teamster] drivers would refuse to deliver the prints to the theaters. And if they got there by any other means, stink bombs would drive out the audiences."

This threat to Twentieth Century Fox was backed by a warning letter to Columbia Pictures from Teamsters lawyer Bill Bufalino, who at the time was also Hoffa's lawyer. Budd Schulberg wrote about Bufalino's letter: "It stated flatly that Twentieth Century Fox had wisely abandoned the project as soon as all the possible eventualities had been pointed out to them, and he felt confident that Columbia would be smart enough to do likewise."

chapter twelve

"I Heard You Paint Houses"

My restless streak never went away. And it seems like my whole life when I could still get around pretty good on my legs I had a lot of gypsy in me.

Working out of the union hall on a day-by-day basis with no commitment gave me the freedom to be wherever I needed to be on any given day. On the days I had a downtown odd job, I just didn't bother going down to the union hall to get a truck. Little by little as my reputation increased I did more and more odd jobs downtown. I supported myself, and I dropped by and paid support to Mary and the girls depending on how much I had that week. Everything I did downtown was a cash business; even the dance halls paid me in cash.

If I had a truck for the day, however, there was no cash attached to it. You couldn't do any larceny on the side with a truck you only had for a day. You needed more than a day here and there to establish a system, like the hindquarter thing with Food Fair. So going downtown and hanging around the bar was like shaping up for extra cash.

I learned the ropes from Skinny Razor and a lot of his people. It was like they were the combat veterans in this line of work and I was the new recruit just coming in to the outfit. In people's eyes I appeared to be closer to Angelo and his people than I was to Russell. But my allegiance was to Russell. I just saw more of Angelo and his people, because he was downtown and Russell was mostly upstate. Angelo said he loaned me to Russell, but it was really the other way around. Russell loaned me to Angelo. Russell thought it would be good for me to learn and earn downtown with Angelo's people. One day Russell called me his Irishman, and then everybody else downtown started calling me Irish or the Irishman instead of Cheech.

After the Whispers matter I started having a piece available to me for whatever purpose at all times. If I was driving I had one in the car's glove compartment. One night, coming home around two in the morning from the Nixon Ballroom, I stopped at a red light on a dark corner on Spring Garden Street where the streetlight was busted. I was alone and my window was down. This young black guy came up waving a gun under my nose. I figured he's the one who must have put the streetlight out on that corner by breaking the lightbulb. It was his corner. He had a partner standing behind him for backup without an obvious piece on him. The one with the gun told me he wanted my wallet. I told him, "Sure, but it's in my glove compartment." I told him to "settle down" and "don't do anything rash, young fellow." I reached across into the glove compartment and took hold of my snub-nosed .38, which the bandit couldn't see at all because my broad shoulders were blocking his view. And then when I turned back to him he couldn't see it because of my big hand and because I swept around as fast as the tail on a kangaroo. He had his empty hand out for what he thought was going to be my wallet. I shot him in the kneecap, and when he started to double down I shot him in his other kneecap. In my rearview mirror while I pulled away I could see him rolling around in the street, and I could see his buddy running straight down Spring Garden Street. Something told me his buddy wasn't running for help or for more backup. Something told me the one rolling on the ground would never do anymore running of his own. From now on every time he took a step when he walked he'd feel it in what was left of his kneecaps and he'd think of me.

Just to be on the safe side I got rid of that .38. If you kept a piece around the car or the house it was best to have a brand-new piece, one that was never fired. That way it could never be linked to anything. You never would know with an old piece whether somebody else used it in something that you didn't even do. So I recommend a brand-new piece out of the box.

I was getting a little stronger into pushing money, starting to get into bigger sums. People knew where to find me and they would come to me for it. I didn't need a truck route anymore. Those days of pushing $10 loans to waitresses at the White Tower hamburger joints were over.

I had this one guy who I made a loan to who I thought was avoiding me. I couldn't find him anywhere. No vig, no nothing. One night one of the guys came into the Friendly and told me they had seen this guy I was looking for over at Harry "The Hunchback" Riccobene's bar called the Yesteryear Lounge. When I caught up with him playing cards in Harry's bar, the guy told me his mother died and the funeral set him back the money he was saving to give me. I felt bad for the guy, and I went to the Friendly and told Skinny Razor I found the guy at Harry's. Skinny said, "Did you get any of your money?" I said, "Not yet," and Skinny said, "Don't tell me. Let me guess. His mother died." So I said, "Yeah, poor guy. I guess you heard." Skinny Razor said, "His fucking mother's been dying over and over again for ten years."

I felt more than a little bit taken advantage of because I was new. Imagine a guy using his mother's name like that. So I went back down to Harry's and told the deadbeat to get up from the card table. He was my height but he outweighed me a little bit. He got up ready and threw a punch at me, and I beat him to the punch. I decked him, and down went the card table, chairs flying. He came up with a chair in his hand, and I snatched it away from him and threw it at him and proceeded to beat him to a bloody pulp and left him unconscious on the floor.

All of a sudden Harry came in, looked around, and went nuts. He had a hunchback, but he was still tough and he was still a made man and very high up with Angelo. He started yelling at me for trashing his bar, getting the guy's blood on the barroom floor. I told him I'd pay for the damage. He said it didn't matter, what kind of respect was I showing trashing his bar? I could have taken the guy outside into the street to fight him. Not right in the bar. I didn't know Harry too good, but I told him the guy swung at me. I told him the guy owed me money and he wouldn't even come up with the juice. Harry said, "This bum had the balls to go out on the street and borrow more money? He owes everybody already." I said, "I didn't know that when I loaned him the money." Then Harry "The Hunchback" walked over to the guy on the floor and pulled him up by his hair and began beating his face for him, too.

Meanwhile, when I'd go into his place, Skinny Razor started making comments to me that I shouldn't just be driving a truck. Skinny said, "How come you're doing nothing, mother? You should be doing something." He said that they should be doing something for me. I shouldn't just be out maneuvering. I should start going up the ladder. I should be in with the big shots. He kept it up a few different times. One of these times I told him I liked the movie *On the Waterfront*. I said I wouldn't mind getting started in some kind of union work. I liked the way the organizers like Joey McGreal and the business agents handled themselves for the betterment of the men in my union, the Teamsters. Skinny Razor must have talked to Angelo, and Angelo must have talked to Russell. A little later I started getting hints from Russell when we would sit down and dunk the bread in the wine. Russell started saying things like, "You ain't going to be driving a truck forever, my Irishman."

Then one time this other guy got a load of hijacked jewelry and never came up with the money. When you do something like that, you know there's going to be aggravation. But a lot of these people just don't know how to tell the truth or how to be square with people and live on the level. Getting over on everybody is like a habit for them, like chewing gum. Some of them have drinking problems or gambling problems that affect their judgment. I don't know if he did or not; I don't know what his problem was. The only thing I do know is that he had a problem.

I got sent around to give the deadbeat a message. I know some other people tried to tell him what it is. But he was giving everybody a different story. Downtown they told me to stay close to him. I started hanging out with him a little bit. One night I was with him at the Haverford Diner at Sixty-third and Harrison. I left him there at 8:30 because he was staying behind and waiting for another guy he knew.

Later that night the deadbeat got shot in his own basement with a .357 Magnum. I was living then on City Line Avenue and the cops came busting in and took me in for questioning. They could do that back then, before the Supreme Court changed the rules. Now they got all these people out there running around that killed their wives or their girlfriends and nobody can take them in and ask them their name even. They grabbed us whenever they felt like it. They sat us down and fired questions at us from all corners of the interrogation room. It was the real third degree.

They found a .357 Magnum in my apartment, but it had never been fired, which is my point. They had a witness at the Haverford who said I kept asking the waitress out loud what time it was during the time I was in the deceased's company. They said I asked her again for the time just when I got up to leave at 8:30.

According to them this was me trying to establish an alibi in the mind of the waitress so that nobody could say I was with the man later on in the night when he got whacked. Then they told me they found a fingerprint of mine on his banister going into the basement. I told them that the day before I had picked up a baby's crib I was borrowing from him and they could find my prints all over his basement because the crib had been in his basement. It's a good thing I had become close to the man or that fingerprint would have gone against me. They asked me if I had anything I wanted to get off my chest and I told them, "I got nothing to get off my chest because I didn't do anything." They asked me to take a lie detector test, and I reminded them that I wasn't made with a finger, and I told them very respectfully that I thought they should take a lie detector test themselves on whether they ever had occasion to help themselves to some loot they recovered, which went on a lot in those days.

As I learned the ropes I learned that for many good and sound reasons the bosses and the captains sent a guy to whack you who was your friend. The obvious factor was that the shooter could get close to you in a lonely spot. A less obvious factor is that if any evidence is found against the shooter, if he is your friend, there are many innocent explanations on how it got there in your house or in your car or on your body.

Take the Jimmy Hoffa hair they found in the car, for instance. Jimmy was close to Tony Giacalone and his family. Jimmy's hair easily could have been on the clothing of one of the Giacalones. The hair could then have been transferred in passing from the clothing of one of the Giacalones to the Giacalone kid's car. Or Jimmy himself could have been in that car on a prior occasion. Or it could have come from Chuckie O'Brien's clothing to the car. There were a million possibilities besides that car being used on that day to pick Jimmy Hoffa up and take him somewhere.

Anyway, I had been at the guy's house the day before, picking up a crib. The cops thought I was there to get a lay of the land, so to speak, to become familiar with the basement where his body had been found, maybe to leave a window or a door unlocked or something in the basement. But they never did charge anybody with that case, even though they tried like hell to pin it on me.

If a guy will welsh out on a load of hijacked jewelry, there's no telling what he's capable of doing. And there's no telling what he's capable of saying if pressure's put on him. He's a rat in the making. If you want to have an orderly society, this kind of thing is like treason. Even the government executes you for treason. That kind of mistake is "severe," especially if they give you many a chance to make it right, like they did with the guy. There are certain rules that you follow and that's what it is.

By this time I was a major part of the culture, and as a friend of both Russell and Angelo I had a great deal of respect. I know some of it went to my head. Because we were Catholic, Mary and I hadn't gotten a divorce, but we were separated and I lived whatever life I wanted to live.

The Golden Lantern was a restaurant that was across the street from the Nixon Ballroom. One summer from Memorial Day to Labor Day the place had forty-four waitresses, and I had sex with thirty-nine of them. Little Egypt and Neptune of the Nile had been good teachers, and I was very popular with the women. Word must have spread among them and they each wanted a turn. Women found me attractive and I liked the feeling. I was single. But what was it all about? Ego, that's all. There was no love there. Just a lot of drinking and a lot of ego. Both of them will kill you.

They gave me a job at a nightclub called Dante's Inferno. It was owned by a guy named Jack Lopinson, but Lopinson owed a lot of money on the place to a loan shark named Joseph Malito who hung out there. My job was to watch the money for Lopinson and for Malito, the money man on the thing, to make sure the money was ending up in the cash register and not in the bartenders' pockets, and to keep the customers in line if any of them would get out of line.

A loudmouthed Teamsters organizer for Local 107 named Jay Phalen, one of Joey McGreal's men, used to come in and get drunk, and I'd have to tell the bartenders when he had his limit and to stop serving him. One night Phalen pulled a gun on some other customer and I came up and dropped him. I lifted him up off the floor and threw him out into the street and told him never to come back in there again. He was banned for life, and he stayed out as long as I was there at Dante's Inferno.

Whenever I thought about what Skinny Razor said to me about them doing something for me, I got more and more tired of people like Phalen and jobs like Dante's Inferno. In one way it was good that I wasn't cooped up all the time in one humdrum routine, but a lot of it was like the army, where you hurry up and wait, a lot of boredom in between the combat. Every so often I would think about what it would be like to get in union work, get a steady paycheck, and advance in that organization. That way I'd no doubt have more money to give to Mary every week, or at least it would be a set amount each week instead of feast or famine, and I'd be someplace else instead of in bars all the time and maybe that way I'd cut down on the drinking.

Whenever Russell said something about me not driving a truck forever, I started telling him outright that I would like to get with the union. He said, "Then why don't you, Irish?"

I said, "I already looked into it, with Joey McGreal, the one I do the football lotteries for. He's a Teamsters organizer out of 107. McGreal told me they didn't have any vacancies. I told him there's an organizer I eighty-sixed out of Dante's they should get rid of. McGreal told me it wouldn't matter. They had other guys in line. He told me you've got to know somebody high up in the thing. You need a rabbi to support you and vouch for you. Besides McGreal, the only other one I know is my own shop steward and he doesn't have any juice to spare my way. Whatever juice he has he needs to try to advance himself. He wants to be an organizer, too."

Russell said something in Sicilian about stormy weather conditions that roughly translates into "You never can tell how things are going to work out. The weather's in God's hands."

I walked into the Friendly one afternoon before going to Dante's for work. Skinny Razor said to me, "Russell's coming in tonight and he wants you here before 8:00. He's getting a call from a guy. He wants you to talk to somebody." I didn't know what Russell wanted or who he wanted me to talk to, but I knew enough to be prompt.

I got back to the bar about 7:30 and Russell was outside talking to some people. He told me to go on inside and to come out and get him when he got a call. At 8:00 exactly the bar phone rang and Skinny Razor answered it. I got up from my table to get Russ, but Russ came walking in; he must have heard the phone ring from outside. I had taken the table near the phone. Skinny said to the party on the other end, "How you doing? Good. And the family? Yeah, we're all good. Knock wood. Oh yeah, Angelo's fine. He got a good physical with the doctor last week. He's in the pink. Knock wood again. Let me give McGee the phone. You take care of yourself, you hear." Skinny handed the phone to Russ.

Russ took the phone, but he didn't talk into it. He brought the phone over to my table and sat down. He put an envelope on the table.

"I got that friend I told you about. He's sitting here with me. He's a good union man. I want him to meet his president. See what you think of him." Russell turned his head and said to me, "Say hello to Jimmy Hoffa." Then Russ handed me the phone.

I reached for the phone and I thought, can you imagine this? Jimmy Hoffa calling to talk to me? "Hello," I said. "Glad to meet you."

Jimmy Hoffa didn't even say hello. He got right to the point. The next thing I heard were the first words Jimmy Hoffa ever spoke to me.

"I heard you paint houses," Jimmy said.

"Y-Y-Yeah, and I d-do my own carpentry work, too." I was embarrassed because I was stammering.

"That's what I wanted to hear. I understand you're a brother of mine."

"That's right." I was keeping my sentences short and my words few. "Local 107. Since 1947."

"Our friend speaks very highly of you."

"Thank you."

"He's not an easy man to please."

"I do my best," I said.

"The best thing, and the most important thing the labor movement cannot do without, and must have and fight to keep, is solidarity. Big business has been on the attack and on the offensive; they are financing splinter groups whose very goal is to tear the union apart. Big business is right now as we speak behind some aggressive tactics of certain AFL-CIO unions trying to steal our locals out from under us right here in my home base in Detroit and elsewhere. Big business is working with the government right now to block us at every turn and embarrass us to the public and our own membership, that way sowing the seeds of dissent at a time when we need unity. We need solidarity more than ever before in our history, not just our history but the history of the working man's struggle in America. You want to be a part of this fight?"

"Yes, I do."

"You want to be a part of this history?"

"Yes, I do."

"Can you start tomorrow in Detroit?"

"Sure."

"Come to Local 299 and report to Bill Isabel and Sam Portwine. They're in charge of public relations for the International."

We hung up and I thought, boy, he's a speaker. For a minute there, I thought it was Patton.

"Russ," I said. "This was quite the surprise. I didn't think it was Christmas so soon, and I know it's not my birthday."

"Don't worry; he needs you as much as you want to be in with him. I hate to lose you. I hope he doesn't keep you out there in Detroit too long."

"That's right, yeah. I told him I'd be in Detroit tomorrow. I better start driving right now."

"Don't be in such a hurry," Russ said, and handed me the envelope that he had placed on the table when he sat down. "Go ahead, open it."

In it was a plane ticket to Detroit and a pile of $100s.

All of a sudden I started laughing. I just sat there and laughed. "What can I say," I said. "Nobody ever did anything like this for me in my life. I won't ever forget this."

"You got it coming, Irish. Nobody's giving you nothing. You earned it. Let's go eat and meet Angelo."

"What about Dante's?" I asked. "I'm supposed to work there tonight."

"Skinny Razor already took care of that. They got somebody covering for you until you get back from Detroit. And don't bother getting a cab to the airport. Angelo is sending somebody to get you in the morning. You don't want to be late for Jimmy Hoffa. He's worse than me about time."

I started laughing again. I was afraid Russ maybe thought I was going nuts. But this was very funny to me. I don't know why. I guess maybe I was embarrassed at how much the old man was taking care of me.

chapter thirteen

They Didn't Make a Parachute Big Enough

At the time of the Frank Sheeran job interview by long-distance phone call, Jimmy Hoffa was coming off a period full of accomplishment and notoriety. In the mid- to late fifties Jimmy Hoffa had bulldogged and bluffed his way through the McClellan Committee hearings. He had become president of the International Brotherhood of Teamsters. And he had survived several criminal indictments.

More significantly for his future and that of his rank and file, in 1955 Jimmy Hoffa had created a pension fund whereby management made regular contributions toward the retirement of their Teamsters employees. Before the creation of the Central States Pension Fund, many truckers merely had their Social Security to fall back on when they retired.

Jimmy knew how to use his temper. I wasn't with him when he got that pension fund off the ground, but Bill Isabel told me how he exploded at the trucking companies at their meetings. He threatened them with everything. He wanted the fund, he wanted the fund set up in a certain way, and he wanted to have control of the fund. He wanted it set up so certain people he approved of could borrow money from the fund. Now don't get me wrong, the fund managers charged interest on the loans, like the loans were an investment of the fund's money. The loans would be secured and all. But Jimmy got it the way he wanted it. So he could lend out the money to certain people. Right away the fund kept getting bigger and bigger, because the men it covered weren't retiring yet, and the companies kept putting in so much for every hour worked by every man into the fund. By the time I came on there was about $200 million in the fund. By the time I retired there was a billion. I don't have to tell you how much juice comes out of that kind of money.

The Teamsters pension fund organized by Hoffa almost immediately became a source of loans to the national crime syndicate known to the public as La Cosa Nostra. With its own private bank, this crime monopoly grew and flourished.

Teamsters-funded ventures, especially the construction of casinos in Havana and Las Vegas, were dreams come true for the godfather entrepreneurs. The sky was the limit and more was anticipated. At the time of Jimmy Hoffa's disappearance in 1975 Atlantic City was about to open up to legalized gambling.

Jimmy's cut was to get a finder's fee off the books. He took points under the table for approving the loans. Jimmy helped out certain friends like Russell Bufalino, or New Orleans boss Carlos Marcello, or Florida boss Santo Trafficante, or Sam "Momo" Giancana from Chicago, or Tony Provenzano from New Jersey, or Jimmy's old friend Johnny Dio from New York. They would bring customers. The bosses would charge the customers 10 percent of the loan and split that percentage with Jimmy. Jimmy did a lot of business with our friends, but he always did it on Jimmy Hoffa's terms. That pension fund was the goose that laid the golden eggs. Jimmy was close with Red Dorfman out of the Chicago outfit. Red got the Waste Handlers Union in Chicago in 1939, when the president of that union got whacked. They say Red had Jack Ruby with him as the other officer in the union. That's the same Jack

Ruby who whacked Lee Harvey Oswald. Red was tied in with
Ruby's boss Sam "Momo" Giancana and Joey Glimco and all
the rest of the Chicago Italians. Plus Red was big on the East
Coast with people like Johnny Dio.

Red had a stepson named Allen Dorfman. Jimmy put Red
and Allen in charge of union insurance policies, and then he
put Allen as the man to see for a pension fund loan. Allen was
a war hero in the Pacific. He was one tough Jew, a Marine.
He was stand-up, too. Allen and Red took the Fifth a grand
total of 135 times during one of those Congressional hearings
they used to have. Allen Dorfman had a lot of prestige in his
own right. Allen would collect the points and then split it
with Jimmy — nothing big, just a taste. Jimmy always lived,
not poor, but modest. Compared to Beck and the ones that
came after Jimmy, you might as well say Jimmy took home
company stamps.

However, Jimmy Hoffa had at least two little business
secrets that became a source of concern to him. In both of
these secret ventures Hoffa's business partner was his close
Teamsters ally Owen Bert Brennan. Brennan was president
of his own Detroit Teamsters local and had an arrest record
for violence that included four incidents of bombing company trucks and buildings. Brennan referred to Jimmy as his
"brains."

Hoffa and Brennan formed a trucking company called Test
Fleet. The "brains" and his partner put that company in their
wives' maiden names. Test Fleet had only one contract. It was
with a Cadillac car carrier that had been having union problems with its Teamsters union independent owner-operator
car haulers. This group of Teamsters held an unsanctioned
wildcat strike. Angered by this break of union solidarity,
Jimmy Hoffa ordered them back to work. With Hoffa's blessings the Cadillac car carrier then terminated its leases with
the independent Teamsters haulers, put many of them out
of business, and gave hauling business to Test Fleet. This
arrangement helped Josephine Poszywak, aka Mrs. Hoffa,

and Alice Johnson, aka Mrs. Brennan, make $155,000 in dividends over ten years, without doing a single minute's work for the Test Fleet company.

Hoffa and Brennan had also invested in a Florida land development deal called Sun Valley and had committed $400,000 in interest-free union money as collateral to further their investment. When he entered into these deals, Jimmy Hoffa had little reason to believe he would soon be a worldwide figure who would be held up to public scrutiny and have to answer for sins of the past, however small they may have seemed to him.

Justly concerned that the McClellan Committee would soon be discovering many of his little secrets, including the pension fund goose that laid the golden eggs, Jimmy Hoffa became obsessed with deflecting the committee's attention from himself.

When the committee was formed in early 1957, its target was the then-Teamsters president Dave Beck. According to Bobby Kennedy's right-hand man, Walter Sheridan, Hoffa secretly provided Kennedy with details of Beck's wrongdoings. Sheridan wrote in his 1972 book, *The Fall and Rise of Jimmy Hoffa:* "He went about this by arranging for one of Beck's own attorneys to feed information to Kennedy about Beck."

That simple sentence is a courageous one by Mr. Sheridan. Although Hoffa was still alive when the book came out and had literally just walked out of jail, Bobby Kennedy had been dead for four years. Had Kennedy been alive, and had anyone picked up on the implications of that sentence, an ethics probe would have been fully warranted. Depending on the facts, Kennedy could have been disbarred for his complicity in allowing Beck's attorney to violate his ethical duty to his client and secretly "rat" on Beck on Hoffa's behalf.

Sheridan went on to say that Hoffa "had that same attorney arrange a meeting between him and Kennedy where he would offer to cooperate with the committee."

Can there be any question that Hoffa's own godfather pals took notice of these two sentences when Sheridan's book came out in 1972? To ruthless and powerful men such as Bufalino, Trafficante, Marcello, Provenzano, and Giacalone being a rat is a severe character defect and ratting on your ally is a severe mistake; such a person can never be trusted again, and the offense is unpardonable, to say the least. Hoffa landed on the streets of Detroit from prison around the same time Sheridan's book landed in the bookstores. The book labeled Hoffa a "rat," and Hoffa leant credence to the label when, in pursuit of the IBT presidency, he publicly threatened to expose the mob's influence in the Teamsters Pension Fund under Fitzsimmons. But all that came many years later. In the late fifties Hoffa's Machavellian strategy of feeding his union brother Dave Beck to the wolves was a win-win strategy. By focusing its resources on Beck the committee put Hoffa's Test Fleet and Sun Valley deals on a back burner and Hoffa had Beck out of his way.

> ❝Jimmy liked to control his environment. He didn't drink, so no one took a drink in his presence. He didn't smoke, so nobody lit up around him. Sometimes he'd get all riled up. He'd get impatient and he'd do things that would remind you of a kid scratching chicken pox. You couldn't tell him he was going to end up with pockmarks. You couldn't say a word. You just listened.❞

Jimmy Hoffa became impatient and obsessed with finding out as much as he could about the inner workings of the McClellan Committee.

In February 1957, Hoffa contacted a New York lawyer named John Cye Cheasty. Cheasty had been in the Navy and the Secret Service. His law practice had a subspecialty in conducting investigations. Hoffa told Cheasty that the committee was hiring investigators. If Cheasty would take a job with the committee and report on its activities to Hoffa there was $24,000 in cash in the deal for Cheasty at the rate of $2,000 a month for a year. Hoffa gave Cheasty a down payment of $1,000 for his expenses in getting the job. However, in his impatience, Hoffa had not sufficiently checked Cheasty out. This was an honest New York investigator and a patriot. Cheasty reported the bribery scheme straightaway.

Bobby Kennedy gave Cheasty a job with the committee at a salary of $5,000 a year. The FBI planted microphones and set up cameras. Cheasty notified Hoffa that he had an envelope with sensitive committee documents and wanted another cash installment in exchange for the envelope. The two men met near DuPont Circle in Washington, D.C. Cheasty handed the envelope to Jimmy Hoffa. Hoffa handed Cheasty $2,000 in cash. The exchange was photographed. The FBI moved in, catching Jimmy Hoffa red-handed with the documents. They arrested Jimmy Hoffa on the spot.

When a reporter asked Bobby Kennedy what he would do if Hoffa were acquitted, Bobby Kennedy, who said he had "never considered that possibility" with such an "air-tight case," remarked, "I'll jump off the Capitol."

In June of 1957 Hoffa went on trial in Washington, D.C., on a charge of passing a bribe to a McClellan Committee investigator for inside information on the committee's activities.

The jury was composed of eight blacks and four whites. Hoffa and his attorney, the legendary Edward Bennett Williams, struck only white jurors in the selection process. Hoffa had a black female lawyer flown in from California to sit at counsel table. He arranged for a newspaper, *The Afro-American,* to run an ad praising Hoffa as a champion of the "Negro race." The ad featured a photo of Hoffa's black-and-white legal team. Hoffa then had the newspaper delivered to the home of each black juror. Finally, Hoffa's Chicago underworld buddy Red Dorfman had the legendary boxing champion Joe Louis flown in from his Detroit home. Jimmy Hoffa and Joe Louis hugged in front of the jury as if they were old friends. Joe Louis stayed and watched a couple of days of testimony.

When Cye Cheasty testified, Edward Bennett Williams asked him if he had ever officially investigated the NAACP. Cheasty denied he had, but the seed was planted.

Hoffa was acquitted.

Edward Bennett Williams sent a wrapped box with a ribbon around it to Bobby Kennedy. Inside was a toy parachute for Kennedy's jump from the Capitol Building.

> Jimmy never met Joe Louis before that trial, only the jury didn't know that. But Jimmy was strong for civil rights. That part is true. The only thing is, every time he won a trial, he thought he could never lose. And have no doubt: he hated Bobby with a passion. I heard him call Bobby a spoiled brat to his face in an elevator and start after him. I held Jimmy back. Many a time Jimmy said to me they got the wrong brother. But he hated brother Jack, too. Jimmy said they were young millionaires who had never done a day's work.

In *The Enemy Within,* Bobby Kennedy asserted that after the trial, Joe Louis, who was out of work and deeply in debt at the time, was immediately given a well-paying job with a record company that got a $2 million Teamsters pension fund loan. Joe Louis then married the female black lawyer from California whom he had met at the trial. When Bobby Kennedy's right-hand and chief investigator, the future author Walter Sheridan, tried to interview Joe Louis for the McClellan Committee about the record company job, the ex-champ refused to cooperate and said about Bobby Kennedy: "Tell him to go take a jump off the Empire State Building."

Still, Bobby Kennedy expected to have the last laugh by the end of 1957.

Hoffa's need to control his environment had led to a federal indictment for hiring a friend of Johnny Dio to illegally wiretap and bug Teamsters offices to make sure that none of his own officers were feeding the McClellan Committee information against him, as he had done against Beck. Hoffa's coconspirator in the bugging offense was Owen Bert Brennan, his partner on his Test Fleet and Sun Valley ventures, a man well motivated by his own potential legal problems involving these two ventures.

In addition to the pending bugging indictment, Bobby Kennedy brought a separate perjury indictment in Washington because Hoffa had lied about the bugging incidents in his testimony before the McClellan Committee.

At the time Hoffa had these two indictments hanging over his head, the Teamsters union was, and for decades had been, affiliated with the AFL-CIO, the world's largest labor organization. In September 1957 the Ethics Committee of the AFL-CIO charged that Dave Beck and Jimmy Hoffa had used "their official union positions for personal profit." The AFL-CIO further charged that Hoffa "had associated with, sponsored, and promoted the interests of notorious labor racketeers."

The response of the International Brotherhood of Teamsters was to elect Jimmy Hoffa, while under indictment in two federal jurisdictions, to his first term as president.

In those tight-reined days, the president was elected not by the rank and file, but by handpicked delegates to the International Convention held every five years. And just to be on the safe side, there were no secret ballots. In his acceptance speech Jimmy Hoffa said, "Let us bury our differences."

How many dissidents had Jimmy Hoffa and his racketeers already buried? How many houses would be painted in the future?

We do know that as a result of his ascendance to president, Jimmy Hoffa was able to advance his mob allies. Although it was to change by the seventies, Anthony "Tony Pro" Provenzano was in 1957 a staunch Hoffa man and president of Local 560 in Union City, New Jersey, one of the largest locals in the nation. Hoffa immediately gave Provenzano a second paycheck by naming him president of New Jersey's Joint Council 73, with its one hundred thousand members. By 1959 the government had installed a Board of Monitors to oversee the Teamsters. The Board of Monitors ordered Hoffa to purge Provenzano from the union. Instead, in 1961 Hoffa added a third paycheck and enormous power to his

ally by making him an International vice president. In that
same year, Provenzano "buried his differences" with popular
reform-minded Local 560 member Anthony "Three Fingers"
Castellito by having him strangled to death and buried on
a farm in upstate New York by K.O. Konigsberg, Salvatore
Sinno, and Salvatore "Sally Bugs" Briguglio.

Ten days after Hoffa took the oath of office in 1957, the
AFL-CIO kicked out the Teamsters, saying that they could
get back in only if they got rid of "this corrupt control" of the
union by Jimmy Hoffa and his racketeer union officials.

On November 15, 1957, the public was greeted with the
news of the Apalachin conference. Notwithstanding J. Edgar
Hoover's protestations to the contrary, there appeared to be a
national crime syndicate that operated like a separate country
and whose capital appeared to be New York City.

Ten days later a federal jury in New York City was impaneled to try Hoffa and Brennan on the bugging charges.
The jury hung at eleven to one. Promptly a new jury was
impaneled. During the second trial a member of the jury
came forward to report a bribe attempt. He was excused and
replaced by an alternate. This jury found Jimmy Hoffa not
guilty.

A crushed Bobby Kennedy still had the perjury charge
against Hoffa to fall back on. But not for long. The perjury
indictment relied on wiretapped conversations between
Johnny Dio and Jimmy Hoffa. The wiretap had been
authorized pursuant to New York State law and was a valid
search and seizure of the telephone conversation under
existing New York law. Unfortunately for Bobby, this was
the beginning of the age of the Warren Court's expansion of
its control over state and local police procedures. The U.S.
Supreme Court ruled that such state-sanctioned wiretaps
were unconstitutional and that any evidence obtained by the
wiretaps or derived from them was "fruit of the poisonous
tree." As a consequence there was no admissible evidence
with which to bury Jimmy Hoffa, and the perjury indictment
was dismissed.

I went to work for the union around the time all this was going on, right after Jimmy got the president's job. After the wiretap trial everybody was saying they didn't make a parachute big enough to save Bobby Kennedy's ass when he jumped off the Capitol.

chapter fourteen

The Gunman Had No Mask

I flew to Detroit and reported to Local 299 on Trumbull Avenue. That was Jimmy's home local. It was down the street from Tiger Stadium. Local 299 was having an organizing drive to unionize the cab drivers of Detroit. Right across the street from the union hall there was a big taxicab garage, and when my cab pulled in to Local 299 I could see the Teamsters picketers across the street. That was going to be me. I knew I was right where I belonged. I was very happy to be an organizer attached to Local 299, and if I worked out on this job they'd make me an organizer back in Philly at Local 107, even if they had to create an extra position for me. I had a chance to get the head rabbi as my rabbi.

I already had my sights set on becoming an International organizer some day. That's a position at the very top. You worked out of the national office. You traveled all over the country in that position, wherever they needed you. You could do a lot of favors that were legitimate and still help yourself. If that thing hadn't happened to Jimmy at the end, I would have been an International organizer.

In Detroit I was assigned to Bill Isabel and Sam Portwine. They worked as a team, doing public relations, but actually Sam looked to Bill as boss of the team. Bill was about 5'8" and was known for his ability with candy, not the kind you eat, the kind you use to blow things up with — dynamite. Bill was proficient in bombing, and he always packed. Bill was born in Ireland, but he sounded American. He came up through the ranks as a trucker. He was stationed in St. Louis and was listed as an organizer for a St. Louis local and as an organizer for the Joint Council in St. Louis that a real good union man named Harold Gibbons headed. Harold Gibbons was the one Jimmy should have appointed to take his place instead of Frank Fitzsimmons when Jimmy went to school in 1967.

Sam was out of Washington, D.C., and was a little taller and heavier and quite a bit younger than Bill, more my age. I was about thirty-seven. I think Sam came out of college and went straight to work for the union. They were both very tight with Jimmy Hoffa.

There were about eight organizers assigned to the taxi driver organizing drive. We would assemble every morning and then go to a place to picket and hand out flyers that Bill and Sam put together as the public relations men on the thing. Sometimes we would picket the taxicab garage across the street from the union hall. Other times we would put up informational picket lines at cab stands around the city, like at the big convention center Cobo Hall or at the Warner Hotel.

You'd take cabbies aside and you'd explain the benefits of being organized, and you'd ask them to sign a union card. If you got 30 percent of the workers to sign, then the labor law entitled you to an election to see if the workers wanted the union or not. But Bill taught me that you would never ask for the election until you had better than 50 percent, because with less than that you were sure to lose. Bill also explained to me that if you did get the right to hold an election, another union could come in and try to take it from you. If they got 10 percent of the cards they could intervene in the election and maybe beat your union out after you did all the work. Once we were kicked out of the AFL-CIO we were always concerned about one of their unions coming in on one of our elections to intervene and steal the election or siphon off enough of our votes so that nobody won. It was dog-eat-dog there for a while. You didn't know who to trust, but you kept taking cabbies aside and persuading them to sign a card. For some reason there were a lot of lesbians who were working as cabbies at that time in Detroit. They liked to be treated like men, and you had to respect that or you wouldn't get a signature.

If they did sign the card that didn't mean they had to vote for the union later on in the election, because those elections were supervised and they were by secret ballot, so the cabbies could sign just to get rid of you and then vote whichever way they wanted to, and you couldn't do anything about it.

I was staying at the Holiday Inn, and the union was picking up my hotel bill and giving me meal money and daily-expense money, and I got a paycheck besides. You could have more than one full-time union job in those days and pick up as many full-time paychecks as Jimmy or whoever was your rabbi got for you. I had the one, but I know Bill and Sam got paid out of several different accounts.

It seemed like easy money, and Detroit was a lot like Philly. There was plenty to do and never a dull moment. We'd go to the fights or a football game or whatever was in town. Bill and Sam were both heavy drinkers and so we did a lot of that together.

They taught me that the word *union* means something. Everybody's got to be united in the same direction or there is no progress for the worker. A union is only as strong as its weakest member. Once there is dissension the employer senses it and takes advantage of it. Once you allow dissension and rebel factions to exist you are on the way to losing your union. You can have only one boss. You can have helpers, but you can't have nine guys trying to run a local. If you did, the employer would make side deals and split the union. The employer would illegally fire the strongest union men and get away with it while the union was split in half.

"Rebel factions are like Nazi collaborators during the war, like they had in Norway and France," Bill Isabel told me. "Jimmy Hoffa will never tolerate rebel factions. He's worked too hard to build what we have. He's the first one up in the morning and the last one in bed at night. Look at how much better off we all are today. The rebels didn't give us shit. Jimmy won it all. The pension, the hospitalization covering your whole family every time you're sick. He's fighting for a Master Freight Agreement where every trucker gets the same wage all over the country. And whatever Jimmy gets for us, the do-gooders in the AFL-CIO tag along and get the same for its members. Then they complain that Jimmy's tactics are too rough. You were in the war; you know what you got to do to get from point A to point B. I say if a few pints of Guinness get spilled along the way, that's tough shit, my fine colonial boy."

One night the three of us were out on the town. Bill was driving us to an Italian restaurant. I had been on my new job just a few weeks. I was in the backseat and Bill was watching me in the rearview mirror. Bill said to me, "We heard from Jimmy that you paint houses."

I didn't say anything. I just nodded my head "yes." Okay, here it is, I thought. So much for getting away from the downtown culture and getting into a new line of work.

"We got something in Chicago that needs to be straightened out. We got a friend there named Joey Glimco. He runs the cab local there, 777. He's got the trucks on the waterfront, too. Ever heard of him?"

I still didn't say anything. I just shook my head "no." A couple of weeks later Russell told me that Joey Glimco was Giuseppe Primavera. He had been with Al Capone and was very big with the Chicago outfit. He had a big record, a couple of murder arrests. He took the Fifth on every question during the McClellan Committee hearings, including whether he knew Jimmy Hoffa.

"There's a guy there needs straightening out," Bill said. "We want you to fly to Chicago tomorrow morning. Somebody will meet you at the airport."

And that was it. Don't ask me who or what because I don't know. It's not something I want to talk about anyway. It was a problem that needed squaring away and I squared it away for them. By now it seemed like it was something I was doing all my life. If you count my father sending me out to beat up other boys so he could win beer bets, maybe it was.

Evidently they needed somebody unknown to the guy, because everybody the guy knew on the street was a person he had screwed and he'd be leery of. The guy wouldn't be concerned about some Irish-looking fellow walking by him on the street. And they wanted the guy left right there on the sidewalk as a message to those who needed to know the guy did not get away with whatever it was he had done.

Anytime you read in the paper about a masked gunman, rest assured the gunman had no mask on. If there are any eyewitnesses on the street, they always say the gunman had a mask on, so everybody on the shooter's side of the thing knows the eyewitnesses didn't see a thing and the eyewitnesses don't have to worry about a thing.

I was used to getting put on landing craft and now I was moving up in the world, invading Chicago on a plane. I was in Chicago maybe an hour. They supplied me the piece and they had one guy right there to take it from me after the thing and get in one car with it and drive away. His only job was to break the piece down and destroy it. They had other guys sitting in crash cars to pull out in front of cops who might go after the car I got in. The car I got in was supposed to take me back to the airport.

I relaxed when I saw the airport coming up. I knew that they used "cowboys" sometimes and then took care of the "cowboys" when the matter was completed. The "cowboys" were expendable. Russell had told me how Carlos Marcello liked to send to Sicily for war orphans with no families. They would get smuggled in from Canada, like through Windsor, right across the water from Detroit. The Sicilian war orphans would think they had to take care of a matter and then they could stay in America and maybe they'd be given a pizza parlor or something. They would go paint a house and then they would get in the getaway car and be taken somewhere and their house would get painted and nobody back in Sicily would miss them. Because they were orphans and had no family there would be no vendettas, which are very popular things in Sicily.

Carlos Marcello and the war orphans did cross my mind during the drive, and I sat the whole way facing the driver. He was a little guy, and if he took his hand off the steering wheel I was going to take his head off for him. I flew back to Detroit, and Bill and Sam were waiting at the airport for me. We went to dinner. Bill handed me an envelope. I handed it back to him. I told him, "I'll do a friend a favor." Russell had taught me well. Don't cheapen yourself. "If you do a friend a favor," Russell had said, "then sometimes he does you a favor."

Bill and Sam had a chance to evaluate my work and they recommended to Jimmy Hoffa to keep me with them. That way I had a better chance to learn.

We flew to Chicago, and we stayed at the Edgewater Beach Hotel. The union kept a suite on the eighteenth floor with two bedrooms and two beds in each room. Sam and Bill had one and I slept in the other. The second night in Chicago, I got introduced to Joey Glimco. Bill told me that Joey handled important problems for all the locals in Chicago, not just his own, and that I would probably be sent to him in the future.

The next night Jimmy Hoffa came to Chicago and I met him at Joe Stein's across the street from the Edgewater. Jimmy Hoffa was very personable. He was a charming man who was a good listener for all the talking he did. He asked me all about my daughters. He told me the reason the union was kicked out of the AFL-CIO was that the AFL-CIO leaders were scared if they crossed that "spoiled brat" Bobby Kennedy they'd end up getting investigated themselves and they'd end up with all the legal hassle Jimmy had. For all the pressure on the man he seemed very at ease, a man you'd like to have with you in a foxhole.

When the waiter came I ordered a glass of Chianti, and Bill kicked me under the table and shook his head "no." I stuck to my guns and drank my wine, but I do know there was a little tension in Bill's face after that at the table every time I lifted my glass. Bill and Sam stuck to ginger ale. Bill later told me that before the dinner he had been recommending me to Jimmy and he wanted me to make a good impression.

During the dinner Bill said something to Jimmy I'll never forget. He said, "I've never seen a man walk straight through a crowd of people like the Irishman does and never touch a single person. Everybody automatically parts out of the way. It's like Moses parting the Red Sea."

Jimmy looked at me and said, "I think you should stay in Chicago for a while."

And what a town that turned out to be. If you can't make money in Chicago you can't make money anywhere. They leave the bodies right on the sidewalk. If your dog was with you, your dog goes, too.

They sent me to Cicero to see Joey Glimco about a problem he was having and I got lost and went into a bar. Cicero was the town Al Capone used to own. As soon as I walked into the bar to ask directions I was surrounded by about twenty rough-looking men and every one of them had a piece. Something told me I was in the right neighborhood. I told them I was looking for a friend and they told me to sit down until they made some calls. Joey Glimco himself came into the bar to get me and take me to the right bar I was supposed to meet him at.

Glimco was having a problem with a freight hauler that was resisting the union and wouldn't rehire a shop steward they had fired. It made Joey Glimco look bad to his men, and he wanted me to take care of the matter. I told him nobody needed to paint anybody's house. I told him to give me a case of Coca-Cola that used to come in those old-fashioned bottles. I said give me one of your men and we'll handle it. I got on a bridge just down the street from the freight company. When a truck would pull out and drive down to go under the bridge, the man and I dropped bottles of Coke down on the truck. It sounded like bombs going off, and trucks were crashing into the bridge abutment without knowing what was happening. Finally, the drivers refused to take trucks out of the yard, and the freight company came around and rehired the shop steward, but he didn't get his back pay. Maybe I should have used two cases of Coke.

I spent nights at the Edgewater, mostly rooming with Jimmy Hoffa when he came in from his home in Detroit. Sam and Bill and I would cut a hole in a watermelon and fill it with rum so Jimmy didn't know we were drinking. "Boy, you men sure like your watermelon," Jimmy would say. One night Jimmy wasn't supposed to be coming home and I had a gallon of wine in the window cooling off. Jimmy came in while I was asleep and the noise of him coming in woke me up. When he got in bed he said, "What's that in the window?" I said, "I think it's the moon, Jimmy." Sam and Bill said I got away with more shit with Jimmy than anybody else did.

Jimmy was the first one up every morning. Breakfast was at seven sharp and you'd better be up and ready or you got no breakfast. His kid, young Jimmy, would come around to the Edgewater. He was a good kid and he respected his father. Jimmy was very proud that his son was going to go to law school, which he did. He's now president of the Teamsters.

I got to meet a lot of important people. Sam "Momo" Giancana would come by the Edgewater. In the beginning I wouldn't stay for their business. But I would be there to greet him on his arrival at Jimmy's suite. Giancana was in the newspapers a lot in those days, dating celebrities. He was the exact opposite of Russell as far as publicity went.

Later on, when Jimmy got to know my work himself, I stayed in the room whenever something was going on. Once in a while Giancana would have a guy with him named Jack Ruby from Dallas. I met Jack Ruby a few times. I know Jimmy's kid met him, too, at the Edgewater. Ruby was with Giancana and he was with Red Dorfman. One time we all went out to eat and Ruby had a blond with him that he brought up from Dallas for Giancana. There is no doubt whatsoever that Jimmy Hoffa didn't just meet Jack Ruby, he knew Jack Ruby, and not just from Giancana, but from Red Dorfman, too.

In September 1978 Dan E. Moldea, author of *The Hoffa Wars*, tape-recorded a conversation with James P. Hoffa, Jimmy's son. Moldea wrote in a postscript to his meticulously researched and reasoned book on Jimmy Hoffa and his many wars: "When I reminded [young Jimmy] Hoffa that he had told me of his father's relationship with Jack Ruby,

Hoffa confirmed [it]. Unknown to Hoffa and for my own protection I secretly tape-recorded this telephone conversation with Hoffa."

One of the very hot topics between Jimmy and Sam Giancana was Senator John F. Kennedy's upcoming campaign for president. This was very controversial between them. Giancana had been promised by Kennedy's old man that he could control Bobby and nobody had to worry about Bobby if Jack got in. The Kennedy old man had made his money alongside the Italians as a bootlegger during Prohibition. He brought in whiskey through Canada and distributed it to the Italians. The old man kept his contacts with the Italians over the years as he branched out into more legitimate things, like financing movie stars like Gloria Swanson who he was having affairs with.

Sam Giancana was going to help John F. Kennedy against Nixon and so were Giancana's buddy Frank Sinatra and practically all of Hollywood. Giancana said he was going to fix the election in Illinois so Kennedy would win that state. Jimmy couldn't believe his ears. Jimmy tried to talk him out of it. Jimmy told him nobody could control Bobby because he was mental. Jimmy said people went to the old man during the McClellan Committee hearings and he couldn't do anything about either one of his millionaire kids.

Giancana told Jimmy that Kennedy was going to help them get Castro out of Cuba so they could get their casinos back. Jimmy said that they were crazy to trust those Kennedy boys after what they did in the McClellan hearings. Jimmy said Nixon was still going to beat Kennedy and Nixon would help them in Cuba. Giancana said the whole thing happened in Cuba under Eisenhower and Nixon, so what good were the Republicans? It was something to listen to this. It was only a couple of years after Apalachin let everybody know there was such a thing as this La Cosa Nostra. And here they were talking about whether the Chicago outfit should or should not fix a presidential election. Growing up wherever you grew up you knew the local elections were fixed. You knew the local Philly elections or whatever were fixed, but this was something, and this high-level talk was all going on right in front of me.

The Teamsters turned out to be the only union to back Nixon in the 1960 election. Now the History Channel makes no bones about it; one of the reasons Kennedy won that election was because Sam Giancana fixed Illinois for him with phony ballots from people who were dead, names taken off gravestones.

I knew how important Cuba was to my friends in the East and all their friends in the country. Russell had taken me with him to Cuba just when Castro was starting to kick everybody out and confiscate their casinos and racetracks and houses and bank accounts and everything else they owned in Cuba. I never saw Russell madder than on that trip to Cuba, and I wasn't even on the last trip he made where he was even madder because his friend Santo Trafficante from Florida had been arrested by the Communists and was being held in jail. I heard a rumor that Sam Giancana had to send Jack Ruby to Cuba to spread some money around to get Santo out.

Around that time I was getting more advanced in the union work, and I was going back and forth between Local 107 in Philadelphia and Local 777 in Chicago to be with Bill and Sam and Joey Glimco. I wouldn't just be walking on the picket line or getting workers to sign a card. I would be put in charge of making sure the pickets showed up. I was what they called "muscle" for the picket line. I'd make sure the picket line was orderly. If a striker didn't show up and pull his tour of duty, he didn't get paid for walking the picket line. I made sure he didn't get a strike check for that day.

Local 107 in Philly was the fourth-largest local in the country and it was always having a lot of problems. It was just too big to manage. They were investigated for corruption by the U.S. Senate, and the president, Raymond Cohen, was always on the hot seat. There were always factions at 107. Joey McGreal had his own muscle crew and he was always looking to sow

dissension so he could take over. I couldn't stand Raymond
Cohen. He tried to rule with an iron hand. He had no respect
for people. Every month I would make a motion to take away
his car or his expense account or something to harass him.
Cohen was a big supporter of Jimmy Hoffa in public and so
Cohen complained about me to Jimmy.

But what Cohen didn't know was that Bill and Sam were
encouraging me on orders from Hoffa. Cohen was big in
the International. He was one of the three trustees. But
Cohen was the kind of guy that backed Jimmy on the outside
publicly but bucked Jimmy on the inside when Jimmy wanted
to get something done. For example, he was against Jimmy's
biggest dream of a nationwide trucker's contract, the Master
Freight Agreement. Cohen was an embarrassment, and he
ended up getting indicted for embezzlement, and they eventually got rid of him.

Jimmy had a loyal supporter in Puerto Rico named Frank
Chavez. But however, Frank Chavez was a definite trouble-
maker. He was very hotheaded. He's the one who sent Bobby
Kennedy a letter from his local in Puerto Rico the day John F.
Kennedy got assassinated. He told Bobby that in honor of all
the bad things Bobby Kennedy had done to Jimmy Hoffa, his
Puerto Rican local was going to put flowers on the grave of
Lee Harvey Oswald and maintain them and keep them fresh.
That still has to make you cringe a little. Let the dead rest in
peace. You honor the dead, especially that man. He was a war
hero who saved his own men in that PT boat incident. Bobby
was a son of a bitch, but the man had just lost his brother and
he must have known it was all connected with him and that
it was his own fault, besides.

Frank Chavez was in a jurisdictional dispute with big Paul
Hall's Seafarers International Union in Puerto Rico. Paul Hall
was in the AFL-CIO, and they wanted to represent the drivers
down on the docks who carted away the ship's cargo because
they were on the waterfront. But because they were drivers,
Frank Chavez wanted them as Teamsters. Hoffa and Hall
hated each other. Paul Hall was one of those in the AFL-CIO
that threw the Teamsters out, and now Jimmy Hoffa believed

that Hall was trying to do whatever he could to bring Jimmy Hoffa and the Teamsters down. It was a bloody war. Both sides had their own hit squads.

One night I got a call in Philadelphia from Jimmy to grab a flight the next morning to Puerto Rico to straighten a couple of matters out, and then to fly to Chicago and straighten a matter out, and then to meet Jimmy at the Fairmont Hotel in San Francisco at 8:00 P.M.

Only in the movies or comic books do people say they want you to go and hit somebody. All they ever say is that they want you to go straighten a matter out. They say they want you to do whatever you've got to do to straighten a matter out. When you get there the people there have it all set up and you just do whatever you have to do, and then you'd go back to whoever sent you to give your report in case there was anything more they had to order to be done. It was like a report you might make in combat after you got back from a night patrol. Then you'd go home.

All in one day I flew to Puerto Rico and took care of two matters. Then I flew to Chicago and took care of one matter. Then I flew to San Francisco and stopped at a bar for a couple of glasses of wine, because I knew I wouldn't get anything to drink when I got to the Fairmont to meet up with Jimmy and give him the report. I walked into Jimmy's hotel room at exactly 8:00 P.M. and he yelled at me for keeping him waiting.

"I'm on time, Jimmy," I said. "It's 8:00."

"You couldn't have been early," Jimmy yelled.

Later that same year John F. Kennedy was elected president by a thin margin. The first thing he did was appoint his brother attorney general of the United States. This put Bobby in charge of the Justice Department, all of the United States attorneys, and of the FBI and the FBI director, J. Edgar Hoover. And the first thing Bobby Kennedy did was turn against the very men who helped elect his brother. For the first time in American history an attorney general committed his office to the eradication of organized crime.

Toward that end, Bobby Kennedy formed a squad of lawyers and investigators within the Justice Department, and he put in charge of that squad his old right-hand man during the McClellan Committee hearings, Walter Sheridan. Bobby Kennedy chose the members of the squad himself. He gave the squad a very limited job to do and gave the squad a very subtle name: "The Get Hoffa Squad."

66 Everything, and I mean everything, came as a result of that. 99

chapter fifteen

Respect with an Envelope

When I was home working out of Local 107 every once in a while I would go around my old Darby crowd and around my parents. That was the only time that I had a chance to smile a little for the Irish Catholics because Jack Kennedy was going to be sworn in. Back in the old Darby neighborhood, hanging with my old pals like Yank Quinn, this new Irish president John F. Kennedy was a little bit of a treat. He was the first Irish Catholic ever to get to be president. Not to mention he had done his time in the war just like us. When I was only a kid there was one other Irish Catholic politician around, named Al Smith, who tried to get to be president. He was out of New York. Al Smith was the one that made the saying, "I'd rather be right than president." Only at that time segments of the country were concerned that being a Catholic, Al Smith would take his orders from the pope. They say that's why the man lost the election.

It goes without saying that when I was around Jimmy Hoffa, I wouldn't bother to say a word about Jack Kennedy that was good. I would not bother to even mention the man's name after Jack Kennedy announced that he was going to make Bobby the attorney general. Jimmy knew even before that announcement that Kennedy's election was going to be bad for him, but Jimmy and Russell and everybody looked at this announcement as a really low blow from old man Joe Kennedy to his old friends. Jimmy knew that it was just a matter of time before the legal action against him would get worse and worse.

Jimmy would say things like, "That weasel Bobby knows full well the only reason he's attorney general is his brother. Without the brother he's nothing. Bobby was right there licking his chops when the votes were being counted their way. They're the worst kind of hypocrite. Our friends in Chicago were drinking idiot juice when they decided to be suckers for that Hollywood glamor and that Frank Sinatra crap. I tried to tell Giancana. Rat pack is the right name. A pack of no-good rats."

Russell himself had no great use for Frank Sinatra. I know Russell was no sucker for the Hollywood glamor. Russell wouldn't put up with Sinatra's loudmouth wise-guy routine. Frank Sinatra behaved himself around Russell Bufalino. One night at the 500 Club in Atlantic City I heard Russell tell Sinatra: "Sit down or I'll rip your tongue out and stick it up your ass." If he had a drink in him Sinatra was an asshole. He'd put on a gorilla suit when he got drunk. He'd go to fight some guy knowing somebody would stop it. He was a bad drinker. Me, if I drink, I want to sing and dance. I guess he figured he was already a singer and a dancer.

Bill Isabel told me that Jimmy was never the same after Bobby Kennedy crossed his path. It's like that old story about the guy who keeps chasing the white whale. Only with Bobby and Jimmy they both were the guy chasing the white whale. At the same time they both were the white whale being chased. Actually, one thing Jimmy did love to do, Jimmy used to love to go deep-sea fishing. The International kept a forty-foot fishing boat in Miami Beach for Jimmy. It had a full-time captain and bedrooms so that six people could sleep on it. Jimmy asked me to go deep-sea fishing with him once and I told him, "I don't go anywhere I can't walk back from."

One night in 1961 when I was in Philly I had dinner with Russell. I know it was way before Easter because every Easter and every Christmas you would meet with the particular boss at a party and you showed your respect with an envelope. Russell had done a lot for me that year, and I had given him the Christmas envelope at the party, and I hadn't given him the Easter envelope yet. In fact, it was probably no more than a few weeks after the Christmas party. The next year Russ stopped taking any envelopes from me. Instead, he started giving me gifts — like jewelry.

On this particular night Russell and I were having dinner alone at Cous' Little Italy restaurant, and Russell told me that President Kennedy was supposed to be doing something about Cuba. I already suspected from carrying notes — verbal messages — between Jimmy and Sam Giancana that something was going down in Cuba.

Russell told me during Prohibition old man Kennedy made a dollar on every bottle of scotch that came into the country. He told me the old man controlled the president, and he was supposed to get the president to help them in Cuba and help get the McClellan hearings stopped and get the government off everybody's back.

Looking back now, I've got to think the old man told President Kennedy to go ahead on this Cuba matter to pay off Sam Giancana for helping him in the election. Cuba would be a way to show respect for what was done for them; to give the envelope. Kennedy would look like he was helping the people get back their casinos and racetracks and other businesses they had down there. They had everything — shrimp boats and legitimate businesses.

Russell had a cataract problem and he didn't like to drive. If he had to drive a long distance and I was in the East, I still drove him places because I had a fair amount of free time. Local 107 in Philly didn't always have something for me to do. And if they did have something, Raymond Cohen didn't trust me to do it. At 107 at that time I was more like a fireman waiting for the fire to happen. In Chicago and Detroit when I was there it seemed like there was always a fire. Local 107 got hectic a couple of months later.

Russell would get in my Lincoln and he'd doze right off. Russ was good with sleep. He was disciplined about it. It was like medicine for him. He'd take a nap in the afternoon. He'd try to get me to do it, but I could never do that. After the war

I never got more than three or four hours' sleep a night. The war conditioned me to get by on less sleep. You had to learn how to do that over there, because you were always having to wake up and jump off. Whenever Russell spent the night at my apartment near the Philadelphia racetrack, we'd watch the fights, and at 11:00 he'd go to his room and he'd go straight to bed. I'd be up just listening to the radio, drinking wine, and reading until after two in the morning.

One night Russell asked me to drive him to Detroit. He got in the car and went right to sleep before I pulled out of the driveway. I had a CB radio and I kept an ear out for road-blocks or troopers. It was a quiet night, so I did 90 to 100 the whole way. When Russell woke up he opened his eyes and he was in Detroit. He looked at his watch and said, "Next time, I'll take a plane."

For as long as I knew him, Russell liked me to drive him out west to the Pittsburgh area and visit his very close friend Kelly Mannarino in New Kensington. They would both cook the tomato sauce, but they called it gravy, and it would cook all day and sometimes through the night. At dinner you had to eat what Russell cooked and you had to eat what Kelly cooked. You couldn't eat one meal without eating the other one's meal. Then at the end you would never be too full to dip your bread in the gravy on your plate. Russell made a good prosciutto gravy. Kelly was no slouch either. It was like a contest. But the winner was always the homemade wine and the relaxation. They both had a terrific sense of humor and they would joke about what the other one was cooking. Russell treated me like a son. He and Carrie never had any children. I don't know if I was a son to him or not. I know he liked having me around or I wouldn't be sitting here now. I'd be long gone.

The only time I saw Russ show any emotion was when Kelly got cancer in 1980, just before my first trial in Philadelphia. In six months Kelly went to 100 pounds, and Russell cried just looking at him.

Kelly had a candy company. The giant chocolate-covered Easter eggs were out of this world, filled with coconut nougat or peanut butter nougat. I always sent those eggs to my lawyers' wives when I was away in school.

Kelly and his brother were partners with Meyer Lansky in the San Souci casino in Havana. When people think of the alleged mob they think of the Mafia or the Italians, but the Italian thing is only one part of the bigger thing. There's a Jew mob and different other types. But they're all part of the same thing. Kelly and Russell were very tight with Meyer Lansky, and Lansky got a lot of respect.

Vincent "Jimmy Blue Eyes" Alo, the one that bet Russell he couldn't give up cigarettes on that boat on their way out of Cuba, was with Meyer Lansky. Jimmy Blue Eyes was Italian, and he was Meyer Lansky's best friend. They were like Kelly and Russell.

I was introduced to Meyer Lansky once at Joe Sonken's Gold Coast Lounge in Hollywood, Florida. I was walking in to meet Russell, and Meyer Lansky was leaving the table. I didn't even talk to him except to meet him, but when I was in school and my brother was dying of cancer and the VA doctor wouldn't give him morphine, Russell called Meyer Lansky from prison, and he got a doctor in there to help ease the pain for my brother. Meyer Lansky and Kelly and his brother had a lot taken away from them in Cuba just like Russell did.

Russell had a lot of business with Kelly. And both of them, just like Angelo, were dead set against drugs. There were no drugs where they were. Kelly had a good heart like Russell and Angelo. Russell took good care of the poor people in his area; they got food at Thanksgiving and Christmas, and really whenever they needed it, and they all got coal in the winter. Kelly was the same way.

I used to drive to Hollywood, Florida, with Russell for meetings at Joe Sonken's Gold Coast Lounge quite a bit. Once in a while we'd fly if there was some emergency, but most of the time I drove us down. Joe Sonken was with Russell's family. Everybody went to the Gold Coast for meetings. All the different people from all over the country met at the Gold Coast. They had the best stone crabs in Florida.

Russell would meet there with Santo Trafficante from Florida and Carlos Marcello from New Orleans many times over the course of a year. I met Trafficante's lawyer there, Frank Ragano. They loaned Frank Ragano to Jimmy to help him out with the trials he ended up having on account of Bobby and the Get Hoffa Squad.

I met Carlos Marcello's pilot there, too, a guy named Dave Ferrie. They later said he was gay, but if he was he didn't make a pass at me. He still had his hair when I met him. They say he went a little nutty later on and carried a makeup kit around with him. You could tell he hated Castro with a passion, and he was very close to the anti-Castro Cubans in Florida.

One morning a couple of weeks after the meeting at the Gold Coast where I met Dave Ferrie, I was back in Philly at the local and I got a call from Jimmy Hoffa, who told me to go check on that thing we talked about. That meant I should go to the pay phone I used to use and to wait for a phone call. I got over to the pay phone and when it rang I heard Jimmy's voice, say "Is that you?" I told him, "Yeah."

He said: "I talked to your friend and he told me to tell you. Get your hands on a safe rig tomorrow and go down to the Harry C. Campbell concrete plant on Eastern Avenue outside of Baltimore. You can't miss it. Bring somebody to help you drive. You're going over the road. And don't forget to call your friend."

I hung up and called Russell from the pay phone and I said to Russell that I had heard from that guy, and Russell said that was good and we hung up.

I drove up to Philly to see Phil Milestone at Milestone Hauling. He owed some big money that he couldn't pay, so he was doing favors instead, like he had me on the payroll but I didn't have to work. He was an old time bootlegger. Good people. He was safe to get a truck from; he was no rat. Phil ended up doing time for trying to bribe an IRS agent.

Phil gave me a truck and I got ahold of a young guy named Jack Flynn to drive with me. (Jack died young sitting in his car of a heart attack when I was back in school on a parole violation in 1995. I made a call and got his girlfriend a union death benefit.) We drove the Milestone Hauling truck to Baltimore and pulled into the Campbell plant. I've been down there lately to find it and it's got a new name, Bonsal. It's more built up, with a few more buildings, but the old stone buildings are still there. In 1961 when we drove in it had a little landing strip. The landing strip had a small plane on it, and Carlos Marcello's pilot who I had just met at the Gold Coast, Dave Ferrie, got out of the plane and came over to my rig and directed us to back up next to some army trucks. We backed up and all of a sudden this gang of soldiers came out of a building and began unloading military uniforms and weapons and ammunition from their army trucks and loading it all onto our truck.

Dave Ferrie told me that the war materiel being loaded was from the Maryland National Guard. He gave me paperwork on the load in case we got stopped. He told me to take it to the dog track in Orange Grove, Florida, outside of Jacksonville. He said I'd be met there by a guy with big ears named Hunt.

We drove straight down old Route 13. I used to drive coffee down to Florida for Food Fair and haul back oranges. I used to like to stop for those Lums chili dogs. You didn't get them in the North. It took us about twenty-one hours to get there, and we turned the load over to Hunt and some anti-Castro Cubans. Jack Flynn stayed down in Florida to drive the rig back and I flew back to Philly. Hunt later turned up on TV as the one in charge of the Watergate burglars, E. Howard Hunt, but at that time he was connected to the CIA somehow. Hunt also got some kind of operation on his ears, because the next time I saw him his ears were closer to his head.

I drove up to Kingston to give Russell a report on the matter, and he told me that something was going to be happening in Cuba and that's why Jimmy called me to drive the truck down to Florida. He told me that Jimmy Hoffa was keeping an open mind about the Kennedys. Jimmy was cooperating in this out of respect for Sam Giancana and out of respect for Russell, and because it would be good for everybody's sake to take back Cuba from the Communists. Even if it would turn out to be good for the Kennedys.

Then the next thing I heard on television that April was that President Kennedy had loused up the Bay of Pigs invasion against Castro. At the last minute Kennedy decided not to send American air cover for the infantry in the amphibious landing. I would have thought John F. Kennedy would have known better than that from having been in the war. You cannot have a landing invasion force without air support. The anti-Castro Cubans who invaded didn't even have ships offshore to shell the land above the beachhead. The invasion forces were sitting ducks on that beach. The ones that weren't killed outright were captured by the Communists, and who knows what happened to a lot of those guys.

These Kennedys could louse up a one-car funeral, I thought.

I flew down to the Gold Coast with Russell to meet with Santo Trafficante and some of the people. I never heard anything said by any of the people, including Russell, about any plot they had with the Kennedy government to assassinate Castro with poison or a bullet, but some of that came out about ten years later in the newspapers. They used to say the alleged mob only whacked their own. Maybe they figured Castro was a lot like them. In his way, he was a boss. Castro had a crew and he had a territory, and he violated his territory and he came into their territory and took over their valuable property and kicked them out. No boss is supposed to get away with that.

I can tell you that some of the different people at Joe Sonken's viewed old man Kennedy as one of their own. And in a way they no doubt viewed his sons Jack and Bobby as part of his crew.

In the summer of 1975 the U.S. Senate held closed-door hearings on the mob's involvement in both the Bay of Pigs invasion and a plot to assassinate Fidel Castro, primarily by poison. The Senate Select Committee was chaired by Senator Frank Church of Idaho and came to be known as the Church Committee. The committee heard testimony and gathered evidence regarding the suspected mob ties to the April 1961 Bay of Pigs invasion and to a suspected mob-CIA plot to assassinate Fidel Castro. At the onset of the 1975 hearings, in a shocking move, the CIA admitted to the Church Committee the mob's involvement and assistance in the Bay of Pigs invasion and the existence of the mob-CIA plot to kill Castro. This plot was called Operation Mongoose.

A few days before his scheduled testimony before the Church Committee, Sam "Momo" Giancana was assassinated. He would never testify. But Giancana's lieutenant did. The handsome and dapper Johnny Roselli testified under oath at length behind closed doors. A few months after his testimony, Johnny Roselli was assassinated and his body stuffed in an oil drum.

While the Church Committee was conducting its closed hearings, *Time* magazine reported in its June 9, 1975, issue that Russell Bufalino and Sam "Momo" Giancana were the crime bosses behind the mob's ties to the CIA and to the anti-Castro invasion and to the assassination plot to poison Castro.

As a result of its independent findings and the CIA's confession, the Church Committee drafted legislation restricting the CIA's involvement in the affairs of a sovereign nation. This legislation passed. The Church Committee's work, its findings, and its legislative reforms of the CIA became the subject of much debate following the 9/11 tragedy when certain pundits believed the Church Committee had gone too far in restricting the activities of the CIA.

Cuba or no Cuba, there was still a union to run. Somewhere around July 1961 Jimmy appointed me a sergeant-at-arms for the convention that was held at the Deauville Hotel in Miami Beach, Florida. The convention was held every five years for the election of officers and other matters. One of the other matters that I liked right away when I heard about it on the floor, and maybe the best thing to come out of this convention, was a big increase in the expense account. Being a guy brought up without a whole lot, I already thought the expense account was the best idea since sliced bread.

This 1961 convention was the first convention I ever attended. Raymond Cohen didn't want me to go, but it was Jimmy's wishes and Cohen had no say in the matter. As one of the sergeant-at-arms it was my job to check the credentials of anybody trying to get into the convention. The AFL-CIO tried to send in spies, and naturally, the FBI tried to get in. But they didn't give me a hard time. They gave it a try and when they were turned away they stayed away on the perimeter and tried to listen and peek in from a distance. Looking back, probably both the AFL-CIO and the FBI already had planted bugs in the convention room. By trying to get in the front door they wanted us to think we were keeping them out.

The big problem for me to deal with was the newspaper photographers. You'd push them back away from the opening, and they would try to sneak back in with their flash bulbs popping. One of them was especially annoying the hell out of me.

I turned to the cop who was assigned to the door and I said to him, "I think I'm going to need a surgeon. Can you radio in for a surgeon?"

"A surgeon?" the cop asked me. "What do you need a doctor for?"

"Not a doctor," I said. "I need a surgeon to perform an operation to get that photographer's camera out of his ass, which is where it's going the next time his flash bulb goes off."

Even the cop laughed.

I guess about a month before the 1961 convention Jimmy lost his good friend Owen Bert Brennan to a heart attack. Some of the men thought Brennan worried himself into the heart attack on account of his business dealings with Jimmy that Bobby was investigating.

Because his pal Brennan died, Jimmy had to replace Brennan as one of the International vice presidents, and he ended up choosing Frank Fitzsimmons over an old Strawberry Boy from the Kroger strike named Bobby Holmes.

Jimmy made his choice on the flip of a coin. Later on, this flip of the coin turned out to be what put Fitz in the position to succeed Jimmy when Jimmy went to school. Bobby Holmes was a very loyal Hoffa man. He was originally a coal miner from England. He was a part of Jimmy's first strike over the strawberries on the Kroger dock. There's no way Bobby Holmes ever would have betrayed Jimmy and done to Jimmy what Fitz did to him. I think if Jimmy had followed his gut instead of a flip of the coin everything would have worked out for everybody, and I would have retired someday as an International organizer.

At the convention Jimmy had a switch for the microphone and he turned it off if he didn't like what he was hearing. Jimmy would say things like, "You're out of order, brother, shut up." This is the convention where Jimmy said the line: "I may have faults, but being wrong ain't one of them."

Jimmy nominated Fitz, and Fitz got elected vice president at that 1961 convention. Fitz took the microphone and went on and on about Jimmy Hoffa. Fitz practically did the "Pledge of Allegiance" to Jimmy Hoffa, but we know how that went.

The other vice president vacancy was also filled by Jimmy Hoffa. He nominated, and the delegates elected Anthony "Tony Pro" Provenzano of north Jersey, "the little guy." And we know how that went.

chapter sixteen

Give Them a Little Message

Before the convention Jimmy sent me to Chicago, and again right away after the convention Jimmy sent me back to Chicago to work directly under Joey Glimco. A bunch of rebels wanted to take a taxicab local belonging to Joey Glimco and make it an independent. Everybody knew that Paul Hall's Seafarers Union with the AFL-CIO was behind the rebels and would take over the local once it became independent. It was Teamsters Local 777. The rebel leader was Dominic Abata. He had gotten enough cards signed by dissidents to bring the matter to an election.

I'm sure the rebels had their reasons for wanting to leave Joey Glimco. But Joey had fifteen cab locals in Chicago outright, besides all the other Teamsters locals he had in the other trades and all the other unions he controlled behind the scenes. So with all those other locals at stake, Joey Glimco was not a man who could afford to set a bad example by letting the rebels of Local 777 get away with leaving the Teamsters. He might lose them in the end, but he had to make their departure a painful experience. And the price they paid for their freedom had to send a message to the rest of his locals to stay in line.

Joey Glimco was shorter even than Jimmy. He was heavyset and very powerful. They claimed he was 5'4", and maybe he was in his younger days, but people lose height as they get older. I was 6'4". I'd hate to even measure my height today.

Glimco had a hawk nose and hawk eyes. He had beaten a couple of murder raps years ago. He talked like you would imagine that Al Capone talked.

Joey liked to eat and he was a hell of a gin player. Joey would beat the pants off Jimmy Hoffa in gin. Jimmy would tear up six decks of cards playing gin. Joey bought football lotteries from me, and then everybody started playing them. There were a lot of nice people in Chicago, and he was one of the best. He was very well respected. It was always hard to tell in Chicago who was boss because they all seemed to get along and go way back together. Some of the old-timers went back to the old days in Brooklyn, before they came out to Chicago.

They all liked to eat in Chicago, not just Joey. The Chicago outfit guys liked to eat even more than Russell and Kelly and Angelo. And that's saying something. How they all got together to eat in Chicago was in steam baths. The steam baths they owned were very popular eating places, and there were no outsiders to contend with. They would close the baths to the public and bring in the food and the wine and the booze and put it all on big tables in a big lounge area. It was a banquet with main dishes of veal, chicken, baccala, sausage, meatballs, different pasta dishes, vegetables, salad, a couple of different kinds of soup, fresh fruit and cheeses and all kinds of Italian pastry, not just cannolis. They'd sit in bathrobes like it was the beach. They'd eat and drink and smoke big cigars. In between card games they might get a massage. Then they'd eat again. All the while they're joking about sex and telling different funny stories and sometimes a couple of them would go off to the side and talk a little business. Next thing you know they'd drop off and go into the steam bath and sweat out all the food and alcohol they had put in their bodies. They'd come back out after a shower looking like a million dollars and start eating again. It was a hell of a thing to see. It put you in mind of the Roman baths in the movies.

Let's face it, cabbies are hard to organize to begin with, much less rebels that already signed more than enough cards to leave you. We had lost that first organizing drive I was on in Detroit, and there we had no other union against us. The lesbian cabbies beat us in Detroit. Cabbies usually have something else going on for themselves on the side. Pushing a couple of girls or making deliveries of one kind or another. Hustling customers for after-hours joints or for certain restaurants. Some of them even hustled jewelry in those days. They don't want to make waves with their bosses because their bosses look the other way on a lot of stuff they do. A lot of them are transient, anyway.

But Jimmy wanted to beat Paul Hall in Chicago and away we went.

One morning Glimco's scouts reported back that Dominic Abata was at a certain location with a couple of his men. This was before they gave him twenty-four-hour police protection. Joey Glimco told me, "Go out there and give them a little message." That means you don't bring a piece because you're only giving a message. It's a muscle job. I took two muscle guys from Philly that Jimmy had sent out to Chicago, and we went over to where Abata was supposed to be. We walked past a chain-link fence up to a cinder block building, and all of a sudden fifty guys poured out from the building right at us. The two I was with turned and ran. I stood my ground. The crowd came up to me. I said, "I know who you all are. If you go after me you better kill me. If you don't I'll be back and I'll kill you."

Abata made eye contact and said, "We know who you are."

I said, "Give me your two best men and I'll fight them right now. Maybe three, but I doubt it."

Abata said, "That's all right. You can go. You got a lot of balls. But I suggest you choose your company a little better next time."

When I got back to the Edgewater and saw Jimmy, I was so mad I said, "You better get those two yellow bastards on a plane and back to Philly before I find them myself." I never did see those two again.

When I told him what happened to me that night, Jimmy said, "You Irish son of a bitch. You could fall in a bucket of shit and come up with a brown suit."

The next morning I got on Glimco, too, about his information. It was the same during the war. If a patrol went out and came back and said there was a squad of Germans up ahead, you better not get up there and run into a full regiment. Your ass is going to shit. I said to Joey, "The next time you send me out to give a guy a message I better know how many you expect me to beat at one time."

The big thing that summer was hijacking cabs that had the rebel's sign on them or a Seafarers sign. If a rebel cabbie left his cab at a stand and went in for coffee he'd come out and find his cab gone. It had been hot-wired, or maybe he had left the keys in it. The cab would be driven down to Lake Michigan right past the cop car by the lake. You'd get out and let the car coast into the lake and sink into the water so the cabbie couldn't drive it. That way you'd cut the rebels' revenue and cost them money. Then your backup car would drive you out past the cop, and you'd hand the cop a paper bag with money in it. The bag was just so nobody could see the five $20 bills or whatever. You'd tell the cop the cab's brakes had failed or that it had run out of gas, and he'd laugh and you'd drive on out looking for another one to put in the lake.

The beef wasn't with management. It was two unions fighting each other. In the end Abata's rebels won that election in Chicago in the summer of 1961.

If that wasn't bad enough, just after Abata took over the rebel cab local, they held an AFL-CIO convention and Paul Hall took the microphone and called Jimmy Hoffa a "fink." And then big Paul Hall gave Abata's rebels a Seafarers charter and made them part of the AFL-CIO. Paul Hall had a lot of balls. You could tell by looking at him that he was a fighter. He was one of those guys you could probably beat, but you'd have to take a couple of days off before you thought about fighting him again.

Jimmy declared open warfare after that. Or I should say, the AFL-CIO declared this war, not Jimmy. Because you know Paul Hall didn't make his move in Chicago without the whole executive board of the AFL-CIO behind him, which Paul Hall was on anyway. And you know the AFL-CIO knew

Paul Hall's tactics were like Jimmy's. This taxicab thing in Chicago was going to turn into fighting fire with fire.

Jimmy sent me to do what I had to do on a couple of matters. One of them was in Flint, Michigan. The other one was in Kalamazoo, Michigan. But even though they were in Michigan, somehow I had the feeling both of those matters had to do with the Chicago taxicabs or Paul Hall. I know the Seafarers had their hit squad, too.

Right after Paul Hall gave the rebels the charter, Paul Hall and Dominic Abata were out celebrating in the cocktail lounge at the Hamilton Hotel in Chicago. Joey Glimco set up an informational picket line outside the hotel and a couple of dozen Teamsters began chanting "unfair." One of them went inside and began shouting at Hall and Abata, calling them every kind of curse word. The cops who were guarding Abata told him to leave, and the guy decked one of the cops. They arrested him and brought him outside, followed by Abata and Hall. And that was just what Joey Glimco had planned all along. He had decoyed them to come out of the hotel. The Glimco people jumped the cops and Hall and Abata, and for a few minutes before the squad cars started showing up all hell broke loose that night.

During the Chicago thing I flew back to Philly for the weekend and went over to Dante's Inferno. Who's sitting at the bar but Jay Phalen, the one I had flagged for pulling a gun on a customer. I asked the bartender what was going on. He shrugged and said Jack Lopinson, who owned the place, just started letting Phalen back in. An owner who lets a man back in who's barred for life for pulling a gun on a customer is an owner who is up to something. One look at Phalen and I knew something wasn't right. Call it instinct. Or call it that I knew Phalen was with McGreal, the one I sold the football lotteries for, and McGreal didn't keep Phalen around for his conversation skills.

I said goodnight and I went home to the rented room I was keeping for weekends. At two that morning I heard on the radio that there had been a double execution-style murder at

Dante's Inferno. Jack Lopinson's wife, Judith, and his "accountant," John Malito, had been shot to death, and Lopinson had been wounded in the arm by an unknown assailant. I got my ass dressed.

"Jesus, Mary, and Joseph," I thought. "Guess which one of Mame Sheeran's three children is about to get a knock on his door from Homicide."

I didn't feel a whole lot like spending the night under the hot lights in an interrogation room, so I took the prudent step of moving to a motel for the night, and on Monday morning I went back to Chicago. A contact I had in the district attorney's office returned my call out there to tell me the downstairs landlady had heard someone she assumed was me come in around ten and had heard someone come down the stairs and go out around two. She told Homicide that someone had eaten the pot of spaghetti and meatballs she had left outside my door for me around nine that night. The empty pot was outside her door when she woke up. Homicide was not too thrilled with this landlady because they thought for sure they finally had me dead to rights. I was tipped off that I'd be subpoenaed to come back for the coroner's inquest, and that Homicide was still working to build a case against me.

But before they had their inquest the detectives rounded up a bunch of witnesses, including Jay Phalen and Jack Lopinson, and put them all in a big room to sort through them and conduct interviews. They had brought in everybody they could find who had been in the bar that night and was still in the Philly area. Jay Phalen was sitting there and he didn't think he was getting enough attention. He kept hearing the detectives asking everybody questions about me. Finally, he jumped up and said, "How come you keep asking about Frank Sheeran? I'm the one who did it."

It turns out Jack Lopinson had hired Phalen to kill his wife, Judith, so he could end up with a blond and to kill his loan shark, John Malito, so he could end up with the money he owed Malito without having to pay the man back. When Phalen came up the stairs, Lopinson was going to shoot him and claim Phalen had tried to rob the joint and had killed his wife and friend. But as dumb and as nutty as Phalen was he outsmarted Jack Lopinson. Phalen had a hunch Lopinson was upstairs laying in wait for him. So, before he came up the stairs Phalen turned out all the lights in the joint and ended up winging Lopinson in the arm on his way out.

Judith Lopinson was a nice woman and a good-looking woman. All Lopinson had to do was divorce her. I didn't know John Malito very well, but he seemed like good people. I know he would have loaned Lopinson more money if Lopinson had asked him for it instead of having the man kissed by Phalen.

Both of these two bedbugs did life for that one. Homicide never even called me back from Chicago for the coroner's inquest.

Around that period I started dating the woman who would become my second wife, Irene, each time I was in Philly. She was younger than me and we fell in love. She wanted to have a family. I went to Mary and explained it to her and she agreed to a divorce. Irene and I got married right away, and the next year we had our daughter, Connie. Things were different with Irene. My running days were over. I gave up selling the football lottery. I had taken a few pinches on it, paid a few fines, and I got tired of doing business with the likes of Phalen's pal Joey McGreal. I didn't need that part of my life anymore, the downtown hustling. Even with the Teamsters culture that I had joined I slowed down my running. I stopped going across the bridge from Detroit to Windsor, Canada, with Bill Isabel and Sam Portwine. Windsor was a town where everything went in those days before America opened up in the sixties. Windsor was a very swinging place, a lot of action. But from now on with a new marriage I was a spectator. Maybe I was following the example Jimmy Hoffa set. During my marriage to Irene, I had good steady money coming in from more than one Teamsters job. This was before they outlawed that practice. There was money in my youngest daughter Connie's life, but not too much in my older daughters' lives.

Mary was a very good woman and a very good Catholic. I felt bad about the divorce, but she said herself it never would have worked out with us. Mary was the kind of woman you couldn't tell certain off-color jokes to. I feel very sad when one of my daughters comes back crying from visiting Mary today in the state nursing home where they have to keep her because of her Alzheimer's.

That same year we had all the problems in Chicago with Abata, things started to heat up in Philly at Local 107. A rebel faction was formed and called itself the Voice, which was short for the Voice of Teamsters Local 107. They were trying to do what Abata had done in Chicago, and Jimmy suspected that Paul Hall and the AFL-CIO was behind the Voice rebels, too.

Paul Hall brought a muscle crew into Philadelphia and had them bunking at the International Seafarers Union hall at Oregon Avenue and Fourth Street. Jimmy sent me back to Philly with a few of the Chicago crew. I went around to their hall to figure out how we could get inside. They kept the front door locked with a pretty good lock. I crouched behind the hedge they used to have on the sidewalk that bordered the street, and I looked in like a Peeping Tom. The wall on Fourth Street was plate glass and you could see rows of bunk beds set up inside in what was probably their lounge.

I left and borrowed a panel truck from the lot at 107 and filled it with eight or nine guys. I gave each one a white hat and told them, "Don't lose your hat, or I won't know which side you're on." I told one guy it was his job to drive the truck away and that the rest of us would get away on foot. At 6:30 in the morning I drove down Fourth Street and made a right turn into the bushes on the sidewalk that bordered the street. I drove the truck up the curb and up over the hedge and right between the two trees that are still standing today, and crashed it through the plate glass window. The glass went flying. The muscle that belonged to Hall were still sleeping, and we started swinging at them as they got out of their bunks. Just our fists. They were caught with their pants down, and they were groggy from sleep and they didn't have a chance. Cops came from all over the place. The truck made it out of there okay, and the rest of us scrambled and got away.

The Seafarers thing was just a message job. We weren't trying to seriously hurt anybody. We had the magistrate standing by to take our bail money if we got caught, but nobody got arrested on that one. There was a day we were battling the Voice that I got arrested twenty-six times in a twenty-four hour period. I'd get taken into Moko, post bail, and go back out to a picket line and get involved in another donnybrook with the Voice people.

At 107 we still had organizing drives, grievances, and other regular union work. One time I tried to organize the Horn and Hardart Restaurant chain in Philly. We had already organized the Linton Restaurants, and they were complaining that they were at a disadvantage because their competition, Horn and Hardart, didn't have to pay their help union wages and benefits. So, we kept trying to get the Horn and Hardart workers to sign cards, but we couldn't get anywhere with them. A lot of them were suburban housewives and they were just against unions. One day I walked into the Horn and Hardart with string tied around both of my pant cuffs. I held the ends of the string in my hands and walked across the floor of the restaurant. I got about halfway across and pulled the strings and released a herd of white mice out of each pant leg. My granddaughter Brittany wrote it up in junior high school like this: "They ran through this woman's spaghetti and she screamed and up the waitress's legs and she screamed and she dropped her tray. He was laughing so hard that he forgot to run away and he was caught." Yes, I told Brittany and her little brother Jake that I got caught and that I told the people at Horn and Hardart that I was very sorry for what I had done and that I would never do it again.

Jimmy Hoffa was more than a little bit concerned about Philly. He started keeping me there more and more. Two other rebel groups sprung up. The rebels couldn't even agree among themselves. Joey McGreal started a rebel group, but it wasn't legitimate. It didn't have a name, or if it did I never knew what it was. It was just some of his muscle guys trying to take over from Raymond Cohen so they could do the same stealing Cohen was doing. Shaking down businesses is an easy thing to do if you run a local. You get paid under the table by the employer so much a month for making sure there is labor peace. If you don't get paid there always seems to be one problem after another for the employer. The poor union worker is just a pawn in this. McGreal wanted this business for himself. When Jimmy Hoffa gave me my own local in 1966 in Wilmington, Delaware, the employers all had respect for me because I never shook a one of them down. The Betterment Committee was another rebel faction. It was a less radical group than the Voice and they were not muscle guys, more intelligent. Tempers in the City of Brotherly Love were flaring between us and Paul Hall and his shenanigans and the different rebel groups and Raymond Cohen at the top.

The Voice forced an election for 107. So to get support we held a rally at a big hall we rented and brought Jimmy Hoffa in to speak to the membership and give them some idea of all the good things he was doing for them. When Jimmy got there, the cops wanted to bring him in the back way so he could go right on stage and not walk down the aisles with all the Voice people at the rally holding up signs with wooden posts that they could have used as clubs.

Jimmy would have none of that back door nonsense. He told the cops: "Hoffa don't use the back door. And I don't want no cops escorting me down the aisle of my own membership. All I need is the Irishman." I walked down that aisle with Jimmy and there wasn't a single loud outburst along either side of the aisle. There were boos further back in the crowd of people, but nothing aggressive along the aisle where it would have been obvious. Jimmy was a hell of a speaker. Besides his speaking ability, Jimmy was telling them the truth; on the level he was doing a lot of good things for them and he needed solidarity to accomplish those goals and then everybody would be better off. Not everybody agreed with his positions, but a lot of them that came in to that rally against him left there respecting him. We won that election, not by much, maybe a few hundred votes, but we won. The Voice didn't go away, but it slowed them down. After that humbling experience of almost losing and needing Jimmy to save him, Raymond Cohen was a little easier to deal with, a little more gracious.

The most impressive thing about Jimmy's speech that day was that he was already under indictment in Nashville, Tennessee, for a Taft-Hartley criminal law violation on account of the Test Fleet car hauling company that Jimmy and Bert Brennan had set up in their wives' names. He was accused with the late Bert Brennan of grabbing "two plus two" — which is slang for $200,000. Yet when he spoke to our 107 membership in Philly he didn't look like he had a care in the world. Jimmy Hoffa had nerves of steel and balls of iron. But as hard as he tried he still couldn't do a whole lot more than a thousand important things at the same time.

Jimmy was something to behold at that period of time. He was involved in Teamsters beefs all over the country, mostly against rebels. At the same time he was trying to establish the first Master Freight Agreement that the Teamsters had been trying to get for twenty-five years, and he saw the trucking companies taking advantage of the rebel situations to fight the Master Freight Agreement. While at the same time Bobby Kennedy had grand juries meeting in thirteen states trying to build criminal cases against him. Still, every night for as long as I knew him, when his day was done, whether it was at eleven p.m. or at one a.m. that his day was done, he went to sleep. And the second Jimmy Hoffa's head hit the pillow he was sound asleep like somebody hit him with a sap. He was better than Russell at that. Without an alarm clock he was up at five. You didn't get a chance to stay home and lick your wounds too much around Jimmy Hoffa.

chapter seventeen

Nothing More Than a Mockery

One night in the summer of 1962 an enraged Jimmy Hoffa asked a burly Teamsters official if he knew anything about plastic explosives. The two men were alone in Hoffa's office at "the marble palace," Teamsters headquarters in Washington, D.C., looking out the window. Hoffa then told the official that he knew where to get a silencer for a gun. According to the man, Hoffa said, "I've got to do something about that son of a bitch Bobby Kennedy. He's got to go." Hoffa then described how easy it would be to kill Bobby Kennedy, because he takes no personal safety precautions, has no security detail, not even at his home, and he often travels alone in a convertible.

The official Hoffa was speaking to was Edward Grady Partin. He was president of Teamsters Local 5 in Baton Rouge, Louisiana. He was out on bail on a kidnapping charge stemming from a family custody squabble involving a trucker in his local. Partin was also under indictment for diverting $1,659 in union funds to his personal use. Partin was a big tough-looking man with an extensive criminal record as a youth. Hoffa misjudged the man and thought that because he was big and tough and had a criminal record and was out on bail and was from Louisiana, the home state of Carlos Marcello, the man must have been a guy who paints houses. But Hoffa never asked him that question before he made his comments that were part threat and part invitation for

Partin to do the job. Partin explained, "Hoffa always just assumed that since I was from Louisiana, I was in Marcello's hip pocket."

Partin reported the comments to the Get Hoffa Squad headed by Walter Sheridan. "It was an incredible story," Sheridan wrote in his book. After hearing it, Sheridan asked the FBI to administer a lie detector test to Partin, and Partin passed emphatically. Sheridan reported to Bobby Kennedy these threats on the attorney general's life.

Shortly thereafter at a private Washington dinner party, President John F. Kennedy leaked to journalist Ben Bradlee that Jimmy Hoffa was plotting to kill his brother Bobby. President Kennedy likely thought that leaking the story to the respected and influential Ben Bradlee, and having it published, might be a deterrent to Hoffa actually carrying out the threat. Ben Bradlee was to gain fame as the editor of the *Washington Post* who helped bring down President Richard M. Nixon during Watergate with the help of "Deep Throat." In his personal journal, Bradlee wrote that night that "the President was obviously serious." In his autobiography Bradlee said that when he approached Bobby Kennedy to confirm the assassination threat, Bobby begged him not to print the story, because it would scare off potential witnesses in the organized crime trials Bobby was then supervising. At that time, Bobby Kennedy was spearheading the biggest drive against organized crime the nation had ever known. Bradlee killed the story.

The trial against Jimmy Hoffa in the Test Fleet case for violating the Taft-Hartley labor racketeering law was scheduled for October 22, 1962. The Get Hoffa Squad later denied violating Hoffa's constitutional rights by encouraging Edward Grady Partin to go to that trial and become a member of Jimmy Hoffa's entourage. Whatever his motivation, Partin went to Nashville and served as a guard at the door to Hoffa's suite. However, Walter Sheridan did admit that they provided Partin with a recording device to tape any calls he had with Hoffa. Sheridan admitted that he instructed Partin that when he got to Nashville he was to be on the lookout for attempts to bribe any of the jurors.

Bobby Kennedy had already engineered three prior jury trials against Jimmy Hoffa and had yet to convict him of anything. Jury tampering was suspected in those trials. The Test Fleet charge against Hoffa was a misdemeanor. Jury tampering, if discovered, would raise the stakes to a felony.

The Test Fleet charges involved putting a car hauling company in the names of the wives of Jimmy Hoffa and the late Owen Bert Brennan. It involved activity that had ended five years earlier. It involved activity that had been thoroughly investigated by the McClellan Committee and the Justice Department. In his opening statement to the jury, prosecutor Charlie Shaffer said that Test Fleet was set up as part of "a long-range plan, whereby Hoffa would be continuously paid off by the employer." The government's theory hinged on the fact that the Test Fleet enterprise was created following a strike that Hoffa had settled favorably for the employer with whom Test Fleet was to then do business.

Hoffa's defense was that his lawyers had advised Brennan, Hoffa, and their wives that it was legal for their wives to own the company, and that once the McClellan Committee challenged its legality, his wife and Brennan's wife withdrew from Test Fleet. Jimmy Hoffa's lawyers were ready to testify on his behalf and confirm his version of their legal advice originally given in 1948.

The setting up of Test Fleet occurred ten days after the passage of the Taft-Hartley Act, and the lawyers were interpreting a law that had no case precedents on which to base a legal opinion. Furthermore, Hoffa was prepared to prove that the strike he had settled was an illegal strike by rebels and that he had settled it with the employer to avoid what Hoffa called a "very serious lawsuit" against the Teamsters by the employer.

To Hoffa, this case was the product of Bobby Kennedy's vendetta against him, and the staleness of the information proved how desperate Kennedy's Get Hoffa Squad was. The Get Hoffa Squad had already failed to get an indictment against him in any of the other thirteen grand juries that had been convened around the country for that purpose.

Jimmy Hoffa assembled the best legal talent he could find. His lead counsel would be Nashville's best, Tommy Osborn, a young lawyer who had successfully argued the landmark and very complex reapportionment case before the U.S. Supreme Court that resulted in the "one-man one-vote" rule. Among other lawyers assisting in Nashville were the Teamsters' attorney, Bill Bufalino, and Santo Trafficante and Carlos Marcello's attorney, Frank Ragano.

The trial judge, William E. Miller, was a man well respected for his fairness and not likely to favor either side.

Jimmy Hoffa set up base at the plush Andrew Jackson Hotel, down the street from the federal courthouse. He had lawyers in court and lawyers back at the hotel as part of a legal brain trust. The lawyers in the wings acted as advisers and as researchers. In addition he had a multitude of union allies and other friends in court and at the hotel to serve the cause, including a man known as Hoffa's "foster son," Chuckie O'Brien, and Hoffa's man on the pension fund, the ex-Marine Allen Dorfman. A number of the nonlegal entourage was from Nashville itself and would provide intelligence about, and insight into, the jurors during the selection process. These were the days before professional jury advisers.

Perhaps it would be more accurate to say that many of Hoffa's supporters were there at the Andrew Jackson in Nashville to serve the causes, rather than just the singular cause.

There would be two dramas unfolding in the courtroom at the same time over the next two months. The first would be the trial itself: the calling of witnesses, the cross-examination of witnesses, the lawyer's arguments, the objections, the motions, the trial rulings, the recesses, the side bars, and the oaths administered. But the trial, it turns out, was the B-picture. The other drama was the A-picture. It was the blatant jury tampering done all the while that a mole named Edward Grady Partin gave the Get Hoffa Squad all the details as they were unfolding. It was this jury tampering that ultimately would send Jimmy Hoffa to jail.

With a decent defense, with his defense well prepared, with his trial staff led by the respected and talented Tommy

Osborn and fortified by Bill Bufalino, Frank Ragano, and yet more legal talent in court and on call, and with a fair judge, why did Jimmy Hoffa resort to cheating? Why did he turn a misdemeanor into a felony?

" It was Jimmy's ego. Other than assaults and that kind of thing, Jimmy didn't have any convictions on his record for doing anything really wrong, and he didn't even want a misdemeanor. He wanted a clean record. He didn't want Bobby Kennedy causing him to have a record that involved a real crime.

You see, you've got to keep in mind that when Bobby Kennedy came in as attorney general, the FBI was still basically ignoring so-called organized crime. Don't forget, when I first got involved with the people downtown before the Apalachin meeting I didn't even know the extent of what I was getting involved in. For years and years since Prohibition ended, the only thing that the so-called mobsters had to contend with was the local cops, and a lot of them were on the pad. We never gave a thought to the FBI when I hung around Skinny Razor's.

Then came Apalachin and the McClellan hearings, and the federal government started getting on people's backs. Then Bobby Kennedy gets in and a bad dream turns into everybody's worst nightmare. All of a sudden everybody that's going along minding their own store starts getting indicted. People are actually going to jail. People are getting deported. It was tense.

Now in that Nashville trial on the Test Fleet case at the end of 1962, Jimmy's taking a stand against Bobby, in what was shaping up like a major war ever since Bobby got in as attorney general. "

On February 22, 1961, two days after being sworn in as attorney general, Bobby Kennedy had convinced all twenty-seven agencies of the federal government, including the IRS, to begin pooling all their information on the nation's gangsters and organized crime.

During the months preceding the Test Fleet trial the commissioner of the IRS wrote: "The Attorney General has requested the Service to give top priority to the investigation of the tax affairs of major racketeers." These racketeers were named and they would receive a "saturation-type investigation." The commissioner made it clear that the gloves were off: "Full use will be made of available electronic equipment and other technical aids."

Johnny Roselli was one of the IRS's first targets. He lived the glamorous life in Hollywood and Las Vegas, yet he had no job nor any visible means of support. Under prior attorneys general it had never occurred to him that he was vulnerable to the government. Roselli told the brother of the former mayor of Los Angeles: "They are looking into me all the time — and threatening people and looking for enemies and looking for friends." What made Roselli even angrier was that he suspected that Bobby Kennedy knew that Roselli was allied with the CIA in its operations against Castro. Roselli was later quoted as saying, "Here I am helping the government, helping the country, and that little son of a bitch is breaking my balls."

Around the same time, the IRS assessed Carlos Marcello $835,000 in back taxes and penalties. At that time Marcello was still fighting deportation and was under indictment for perjury and for falsifying his birth certificate. Russell Bufalino was also fighting deportation.

Prior to the Nashville trial Bobby Kennedy had been traveling around the country personally, like a general going to his troops, urging his department to focus on organized crime. He made a list of organized crime targets for the FBI and Justice Department to concentrate on. He expanded that list continually. He went to Congress and got laws passed to make it easier for the FBI to bug these targets and to use wiretaps in court. He got laws passed allowing him to more freely give immunity to cooperating witnesses.

Jury selection began in Test Fleet on the second day of the Cuban Missile Crisis. Bobby Kennedy was not in Nashville; he was needed at his brother's side as Jack Kennedy faced down Soviet Premier Nikita Khrushchev and ordered that all offensive nuclear weapons that were on their way in Soviet ships to Cuba be rerouted back to the Soviet Union or the U.S. Navy would open fire. The world was at the brink of nuclear war.

As Walter Sheridan wrote, "I went to sleep in the early morning hours thinking about the very real threat of nuclear war and the possibility that Jimmy Hoffa and I would end up very dead together in Nashville."

Instead, Walter Sheridan awoke the next day to his first instance of jury tampering. An insurance broker in the panel reported to Judge Miller that a neighbor of his had met with him over the weekend and offered him $10,000 in hundred-dollar bills to vote for acquittal should he be accepted on the jury. Hoffa's selection of the insurance broker made sense, because insurance men — being in a business that is ultra-suspicious about being ripped off and victimized by criminal fraud — are ordinarily considered death to criminal defense attorneys. They are normally struck before they get a chance to warm the seat. Surely, the government wouldn't strike the insurance man from the jury if he were selected from the panel.

The prospective juror was excused by Judge Miller after the judge forced the insurance broker to reveal his neighbor's name.

It was then revealed by a number of the prospective jurors that a man who identified himself as a reporter for the *Nashville Banner* named Allen had called them to find out their views on Jimmy Hoffa. There was no reporter on the *Nashville Banner* named Allen. Someone was illegally prying into some of the jurors' minds in search of jurors who might favor their side of the case. All of those tainted prospective jurors were dismissed.

After the jury had been selected and the trial had begun, Edward Grady Partin reported to Walter Sheridan that an attempt was going to be made by the president of a Nashville Teamsters local to bribe the wife of a Tennessee State Highway Patrol trooper. The wife was seated on the jury. Sheridan checked the data on the jurors and found among them the wife of a trooper. Agents followed the Teamsters official to a deserted road where the state trooper was waiting in his patrol car. The agents watched the two men sit in the trooper's patrol car and talk.

With this information in hand, but without revealing the source of the tip, the government prosecutors asked the judge to remove the trooper's wife from the jury, and Judge Miller held a hearing on the prosecution's request. The government called the agents who had followed the Nashville Teamsters president to his rendezvous with the trooper. The agents were questioned by the judge. The government then called the Teamsters official, and the man was brought in from a side room. According to Walter Sheridan, Jimmy Hoffa flashed the man the five-finger sign, and the official took the Fifth Amendment. Next, the State Highway Patrol trooper was brought into the courtroom. After first denying everything, the trooper admitted, under questioning by Judge Miller, that the Teamsters official had offered him a deal of promotion and advancement with the State Highway Patrol in exchange for an undisclosed favor. The trooper claimed that the Teamsters official never explained to him what that future favor might be.

Judge Miller excused the wife of the trooper and replaced her with an alternate. At her home that night the tearful woman told reporters she had no idea why she had been excused.

Speaking for Tommy Osborn and Frank Ragano and the rest of the team, Attorney Bill Bufalino said, "There was no fix. And if there was, it came directly out of Bobby Kennedy's office."

Young attorney Tommy Osborn was in a different sort of case than the one in which he argued about reapportionment before the U.S. Supreme Court. That case had already put him in line to be the next president of the Nashville Bar

Association and had helped him land the Hoffa case. The Hoffa case could best establish a national career if he got Jimmy off, and at the same time it was the case that could wreck his career if he became a part of the culture to which he was being exposed.

A Nashville police officer who moonlighted for Tommy Osborn as a private investigator doing legitimate jury pool research told the Get Hoffa Squad that Osborn had told him that he was working on putting one of the jurors into a land development deal. The Get Hoffa Squad found it hard to believe and already had their hands full. They stored the information away for a future day.

Strike three was a black juror whose son had been contacted by a black business agent from Jimmy Hoffa's home local in Detroit and offered a $10,000 bribe. According to a sworn affidavit the government prepared for Partin's signature, a $5,000 down payment on the bribe had been delivered and the deal struck before the trial began and the juror selected. Partin revealed in the affidavit that one day Jimmy Hoffa said to him, "I've got the colored male juror in my hip pocket. One of my business agents, Larry Campbell, came into Nashville prior to the trial and took care of it." The sealed affidavit was read by Judge Miller, who then denied the defense access to it, and excused the juror, who was replaced by yet another alternate. By this time, not knowing of Partin's defection, the defense was sure the government had been bugging and wire-tapping them since before the trial had even started.

I got a call from Bill Isabel that they needed me down there in Nashville, so I drove down. Over the phone he said they were expecting some protesters and they wanted me down there to help out if any protester got out of line with Jimmy. Now this was just something he was saying over the phone, because by then everybody was sure everything was bugged. It was like science fiction down there. What they really wanted me there for was to sit in the courtroom and make my presence felt by the jury in case any of the other ones they had reached out for on the jury got the idea to come out of the woodwork. Now nobody told me that directly, but I knew what it was when they told me to make eye contact with the jurors once in a while.

I stayed in the Andrew Jackson Hotel, but I wasn't a part of the thing. They had too many cooks already spoiling the broth. I remember the Southern-fried chicken at the hotel restaurant was out of this world. It was always good to see Sam and Bill again. I remember seeing Ed Partin in the restaurant but not thinking anything of it. He was just sitting there with Frank Ragano, and Ragano had no idea he was sitting there with a rat. Imagine the government today putting a planted rat inside your lawyers' offices. That hotel room they had was their lawyers' offices and Partin was right in there with them.

Of course, no protesters showed up. The place was loaded with FBI anyway. And then one day, almost to make Bill Isabel's reason for bringing me down come true, a nut came into the courtroom while I was standing in the back talking to Bill and Sam. It was on a recess and this young guy in a raincoat walks down to the front of the courtroom and gets behind Jimmy and pulls out a gun. I heard this gun going off and the first thing I saw was all the lawyers on both sides of the thing fighting for space while they were diving under the desks like they were foxholes. And there was Jimmy Hoffa charging at the nut with the gun. It turns out the nut had a pellet gun that looked real. It was the kind of gun used to kill squirrels and rabbits. He had fired it and hit Jimmy a couple of times in the back, but Jimmy had on a heavy suit. Jimmy swarmed the nut and decked him good. Chuckie O'Brien jumped on the nut and took him to the floor. Chuckie was a hefty guy and he was letting the nut have it real good. The marshals finally got over there, and one of the marshals sapped the guy with the butt of his revolver, but Chuckie kept whaling away at the guy. The marshals and Jimmy had to pull him off, or he'd have killed the guy.

I told Bill Isabel to be careful what he says next time about some protester getting out of hand. It turns out the guy claimed God told him to go kill Jimmy Hoffa. Everybody's got a boss, I guess.

The jury wasn't present in the courtroom for that pellet gun cowboy, but the defense filed for a mistrial. They claimed the nut in the raincoat was an example of how the population of Nashville was riled up against Jimmy Hoffa by all the anti-Hoffa government propaganda that was surrounding the case coming from Bobby Kennedy and his cohorts. It sounded good to me, but the judge denied it.

Bill Isabel told me that Jimmy said, "You always run away from a man with a knife and toward a man with a gun." I don't know about that. You have to know the circumstances. He's right if you can startle the man with the gun, because he doesn't expect you to come at him. Jimmy did the right thing in these circumstances. But if you go toward the man with a gun who cannot be startled, the closer you get the more you improve his aim. Most of the time you don't see the knife until you're cut with it. The best thing is to be a choirboy.

Jimmy said that "everybody'd been searched" by the marshals. That part was true all right. I got searched. The marshals had searched everybody who came into the courtroom. Jimmy said it wasn't a coincidence that this man had been able to walk right up behind him. The idea was that the government used a nut to whack him. Only this nut was too nutty to be able to get his hands on a real piece. Jimmy knew that nuts were used from time to time by certain people for certain matters. That same year of his Nashville trial Sam Giancana's friend Frank Sinatra had *The Manchurian Candidate* in all the theaters. It was a big movie out about the Communists using a nut to kill somebody running for president.

But in real life when a nut is used in America or in Sicily he's always disposed of right away, on the scene even. Like years later when Crazy Joey Gallo used that black nut to whack Joe Colombo, the boss of the Colombo family in Brooklyn. The nut got off three shots at Joe Colombo at a rally of the Italian-American Civil Rights League at Columbus Circle near Central Park. No doubt everything had been worked out in detail and rehearsed with the nut. He was shown exactly how he was going to be hustled into a car and driven away to safety. Naturally, the nut was laid out right on the sidewalk by certain people after the nut did his job and shot Colombo.

Russell never forgave Crazy Joey Gallo for that — for using a nut that way on Joe Colombo. I always thought Crazy Joey was a fresh kid anyway. Poor Joe Colombo laid in a coma like a vegetable for a long time before he died. That's the problem with using a nut. They're not accurate enough. Nuts can cause a lot of suffering. Like the nut who shot George Wallace and left the man paralyzed. Or the nut that shot Reagan and his press secretary, Brady.

The Nashville trial lasted forty-two days. The jury went out to deliberate just four days before Christmas. While the jury deliberated Walter Sheridan remained concerned that the government had not weeded out all those jurors who had been bribed. There may have been a bribed juror or two that had not been talked about in Edward Grady Partin's presence.

The jury was sequestered, and on the third day of deliberations they were dismissed by Judge Miller after repeatedly reporting that they were hopelessly deadlocked. However, before allowing them to step out of the jury box he turned from them as they sat in their seats and addressed the courtroom. Among other statements, the record reveals the following comments by Judge Miller.

> From the very outset, while the jury was being selected from a list of those summoned for jury service, there were indications that improper contacts had been made and were being made with prospective members of the jury. I have signed orders to convene another grand jury soon after the first of the year to investigate fully and completely all of the incidents connected with this trial indicating illegal attempts to influence

jurors and prospective jurors by any person or persons whomsoever and to return indictments where probable cause therefore exists. The system of trial by jury . . . becomes nothing more than a mockery if unscrupulous persons are allowed to subvert it by improper and unlawful means. I do not intend that such shameful acts to corrupt our jury system shall go unnoticed by this court.

Jimmy Hoffa, on the other hand, told a TV audience on Christmas Eve that it was "a disgrace . . . for anyone to make a statement that this jury was tampered with."

chapter eighteen

Just Another Lawyer Now

In 1963 Jimmy Hoffa told me he was determined to get a Master Freight Agreement by the end of the year. There were a lot of distractions for Jimmy in 1963, but by the end of the year he had it wrapped up. In the first contract we got a 45-cent-an-hour raise. Plus our pensions started going way up. A guy retiring out of a local today gets $3,400 a month. Add that to Social Security and you can live on it. All that came from Jimmy Hoffa that year, even with all the distractions. Once the Master Freight Agreement was signed Jimmy put me on the National Negotiating Committee for the union.

The dream of a Master Freight Agreement went all the way back to the Depression. With one agreement covering all the Teamsters in the country everybody would get paid the same hourly wage and get the same benefits and get the same pension. The best thing about it, though, was that there would be only one contract to negotiate. Instead of every trucking company negotiating individual contracts around the country, there would be a Management Negotiating Committee that would negotiate a single contract with the union National Negotiating Committee. If we had to strike because we couldn't come to terms there would be a nation-wide strike, but we never had to go that route. Jimmy never had a nationwide strike. Still, with the fear of it in manage-ment and the government's minds, you can imagine how hard that kind of thing was for Jimmy to accomplish. He had to get all the trucking companies to agree and all the locals in the union to agree. With a single contract the trucking companies couldn't divide and conquer anymore, and thieves like Raymond Cohen couldn't get paid under the table for sweetheart contracts. Cohen was that way.

That's why Jimmy had us fight so hard against the rebels and sometimes do what we had to do. Jimmy needed a solidified union. Philadelphia was the toughest nut for Jimmy to crack. First, Cohen was against giving up the power. Second, the Voice and the other rebel groups were still very active and agitating. The truckers in Philadelphia took advantage of the situation at 107. They wouldn't even cooperate on an area-wide agreement. They knew Cohen wouldn't strike. Jimmy brought them around by threatening to shut them down with strikes at their terminals outside of Philadelphia.

In February 1963 while the grand jury in Nashville was gathering evidence of jury tampering, Jimmy Hoffa spoke about the trucking companies in Philadelphia: "They've either got to live with us here or fight with us everywhere."

Hoffa addressed the problem of the rebel Voice, which he believed was then being supported and encouraged by the AFL-CIO and by Bobby Kennedy: "We have to convert them to our way of thinking."

And Hoffa addressed the legal proceedings in Nashville: "Something is happening in this country by the name of Bobby Kennedy. One man has assigned an elite squad of twenty-three deputy attorneys general to work his dictates on me."

Along with everyone else who had been part of Hoffa's Nashville entourage at the Andrew Jackson Hotel, Ed Partin was summoned to the grand jury in Nashville, and following the Hoffa party line he took the Fifth. Bill Bufalino wrote the precise language out for him on a card to take into the grand jury room. The government was determined to keep Partin's defection a secret. Meanwhile, people like the State Highway Patrol trooper began admitting the truth, and a jury-tampering indictment looked promising to the government.

Jimmy Hoffa spent fourteen weeks in Philadelphia at the Warwick Hotel campaigning against the Voice in the upcoming April election. In an election held a few months earlier the Voice had lost by only 600 votes in a local with 11,000 members. That election was set aside because of the anti-Voice violence that had dominated that election. Not resorting to violence this time, Hoffa campaigned vigorously and explained the benefits in pay and in pension that would come from the plans he had for the Teamsters Union. In the election of April 1963, Hoffa's Teamsters defeated the Voice again, bringing the fourth-largest Teamsters local back in line. Hoffa promised to "let bygones be bygones." Equally as important to Hoffa as defeating the Voice, Cohen now owed Jimmy Hoffa his complete loyalty in the matter of a Master Freight Agreement.

On May 9, 1963, Jimmy Hoffa was indicted in Nashville for jury tampering. At the entry of his not-guilty plea Hoffa held a press conference and said that Bobby Kennedy "has a personal vendetta against me and is trying to convict me with planted stories in the press. . . . Of course I'm not guilty. This indictment talks about ten people and I only know three of them."

On June 4, 1963, Cohen was convicted of embezzling union funds. There now would be no doubt about the dream of a Master Freight Agreement. Cohen would be removed as president of Local 107 and would go to jail. Cohen would be in no position to work secretly against Hoffa's negotiations with the Philadelphia trucking companies.

On the same afternoon of Cohen's conviction, a grand jury in Chicago indicted Jimmy Hoffa for fraudulent misuse of the Central States Pension Fund for personal profit. The principal charge against Hoffa dealt with the pledging of $400,000 of union funds at no interest to secure a personal loan for the Sun Valley land development deal in Florida. It was alleged that James R. Hoffa had a secret 22 percent ownership interest in the profits of that venture. Hoffa denied that he had any such secret interest.

" Right after Cohen went to school I went with Jimmy for a negotiating session against management, in a motel in Arlington, Virginia, outside of Washington. I grabbed some college kids and gave them $50 each to use all the public toilets and keep the elevators busy. Then I put laxatives in one of the coffee urns. Those of us on the union's team who drank coffee took our coffee from the other urn. Management was split about 50-50 on urn selection. Half of the people from management took coffee from the doctored urn. Pretty soon one guy ran into the one bathroom in the negotiating room and wouldn't come out. The other few guys went nuts running around the hotel looking for a toilet that wasn't being used. They all stayed out of the negotiations after that to rest up and change their clothes. I had thinned out the herd. It was easier to negotiate against a smaller group. Even with all the pressure on Jimmy, I never saw him laugh so hard as when we got back to our room.

During that summer and fall I didn't see that much of Jimmy. Jimmy met a lot with his lawyers about the new indictments. The first trial was going to be the one for so-called jury tampering. They had it scheduled in Nashville in October. I was planning on going down and getting to the Grand Ole Opry. The Chicago pension fund case involving the Sun Valley matter was scheduled for the spring of 1964. I most definitely looked for any excuse to go to Chicago.

The lawyer Frank Ragano claims in a book and on the History Channel that Jimmy Hoffa gave him a message to deliver to Santo Trafficante and Carlos Marcello — to kiss the president, John F. Kennedy. He said it happened in Jimmy's office in Washington while they were working on the trial preparation. I for one cannot see Jimmy delivering a message like that through that messenger with those words. "

In 1994 Frank Ragano wrote a memoir appropriately called *Mob Lawyer*. In the memoir, Ragano claims to have heard a discussion between Jimmy Hoffa, Joey Glimco, and Bill Bufalino in early 1963 while the grand juries were meeting in Nashville and Chicago, but before the indictments had been handed down. While playing gin with Glimco, Hoffa asked Bufalino, "What do you think would happen if something happened to Booby?" (Hoffa always referred to his archenemy as *Booby*.)

The consensus reached in the discussion was that if something happened to Bobby, Jack would unleash the dogs. But if something happened to Jack, Vice President Lyndon Johnson would become the president, and it was no secret that Lyndon hated Bobby. Lyndon, it was agreed, definitely would get rid of Bobby as attorney general. According to Frank Ragano's recollection, Jimmy Hoffa said, "Damn right he would. He hates him as much as I do."

A few months later, on Tuesday July 23, 1963, four months before President Kennedy was assassinated, Ragano claims to have been meeting with Hoffa about the new indictments that had recently been handed down in May and June. Hoffa was beside himself with rage. According to Ragano he was told by Jimmy Hoffa: "Something has to be done. The time has come for your friend and Carlos to get rid of them, kill that son-of-a-bitch John Kennedy. This has got to be done. Be sure to tell them what I said. No more fucking around. We're running out of time — something has to be done."

Okay, the way I look at Frank Ragano is that they didn't know about Partin. Jimmy was pretty sure they had a spy in their midst during that trial in Nashville. I know that everybody that was a part of that Andrew Jackson Hotel scene was a suspect in Jimmy's mind. Jimmy was just getting to know Frank Ragano back then. It's not like Bill Bufalino, where they had known each other for many years, did deals together, established a record of mutual respect together. Jimmy had a private jet at his disposal at all times. If he wanted to deliver a message that's as serious a message as a message can get, he would fly down to Florida. Jimmy kept a nice place down there in Miami Beach. Jimmy most definitely knew how to use a telephone to set up a meeting. That's how I met Jimmy — on a prearranged phone call at Skinny Razor's. Now don't get me wrong, they say Frank Ragano is good people, and Santo Trafficante and Carlos Marcello put a lot of trust in him as a lawyer. If Frank Ragano said that's the way he remembered it happened, I guess I have to go with his memory on that. But you're talking about something here that nobody in their right mind talks about the way he said Jimmy talked about it. If Jimmy said it to Ragano, and Ragano said it to those people, they had to wonder whether Jimmy was thinking clearly if he was talking out loud like that to Frank Ragano. Not to mention the position you put the person in who hears such a thing. Carlos used to have a sign in his office that said that three people can keep a secret if two of them are dead.

As if there weren't enough going on in 1963, word spread through the grapevine that the FBI got a certain soldier named Joseph Valachi to turn. Valachi was the first guy to roll over. He was just a soldier out of the Genovese family in New York. That was the family that Lucky Luciano started when Luciano and Meyer Lansky and the rest of them put the thing together years ago. Valachi wasn't too close to anybody big. I had never even heard of the man, much less met the man through Russell. If I'm not mistaken, Russell had never heard of the man either until the thing came out. But this Valachi knew all the old stories. He knew who whacked who and why. He told how Vito Genovese had a citizen thrown off a roof so he could marry the guy's wife, which he then went and did. He knew all the families and how everything was set up in the organization among the Italians.

Valachi was a born rat and a drug pusher, and his own boss Vito Genovese was going to have him kissed when they were in federal prison together on suspicion of being a jailhouse snitch and an informant. When in doubt have no doubt.

Joe Valachi ended up killing some innocent inmate that he

thought was going to kiss him, and after that he told everybody everything he knew about everything. He told about
how they get initiated into becoming made men. He told
Italian secrets I didn't even know about. He even told little
things like how Carlos Marcello didn't allow anybody from
any of the other families to so much as visit New Orleans,
not even for Mardi Gras, without first getting his approval.
Carlos Marcello was one boss that took no chances. The man
ran a tight ship.

A couple of weeks before Jimmy's jury-tampering trial
was scheduled Bobby Kennedy paraded this Joe Valachi on
television in some more of those McClellan hearings. It was
like propaganda in a war, like a publicity drive to sell war
bonds. Only Joe Valachi was Bob Hope. You could see after
the publicity over the Valachi hearing that the drive against
so-called organized crime was really going to open up even
bigger than it already was. There were a lot of interested
parties glued to their TV sets in bathhouses and private
Italian clubs all over the country.

In September 1963, about a month prior to Jimmy Hoffa's
scheduled trial for jury tampering, Joseph Valachi appeared
on television before the McClellan Committee and unveiled
to the public all the details of what Bobby Kennedy had called
"the greatest intelligence break-through in the history of
organized crime in America."

Joe Valachi's odyssey from low-level "button man" and
jailbird to media sensation and poster boy for Bobby
Kennedy began a year earlier in the summer of 1962 in
the Atlanta federal penitentiary. Valachi was serving time
on a drug-pushing charge at the same time his boss, Vito
Genovese, was serving time. To embarrass Valachi and make
it look as if he were cooperating, Federal Bureau of Narcotics
agents visited Valachi regularly. The idea was to make
Genovese paranoid around Valachi. That would put the fear
of death into Valachi and that pressure on Valachi would
cause Valachi to flip. This was a ruse that would later be used

at Sandstone Prison by the FBI unsuccessfully against Frank Sheeran to get him to talk about the Hoffa disappearance. In Valachi's and Genovese's cases it worked.

Vito Genovese walked up to his soldier, Joe Valachi, and, according to Valachi's testimony, Genovese slowly and thoughtfully said, "You know sometimes if I had a barrel of apples, and one of these apples is touched . . . not all rotten but just a little touched . . . it has to be removed or it will touch all the rest of the apples."

Genovese grabbed his soldier's head with both hands and gave Joe Valachi the "kiss of death" on the mouth.

When Valachi used a lead pipe on the first inmate to approach him and killed the man, the ruse had worked. To avoid the death penalty and in exchange for a life sentence, Joseph Valachi gave Jimmy Hoffa and his friends one more reason to hate Bobby Kennedy.

Bobby Kennedy was the first witness called by Senator McClellan before Joseph Valachi spoke at the September 1963 hearings. Bobby Kennedy told the committee and a nationwide television audience that "because of intelligence gathered from Joseph Valachi . . . we know that Cosa Nostra is run by a commission and that the leaders of Cosa Nostra in most major cities are responsible to the commission . . . and we know who the active members of the commission are today."

> Just after the Valachi hearings Jimmy's lawyers got the jury-tampering trial postponed until January 1964. And then for some reason or other the judge made a change of venue to Chattanooga because something was going on in Nashville. We were all going to be dancing to the "Chattanooga Choo Choo" for the New Year.

On November 8, 1963, the same Nashville police officer who had reported on Tommy Osborn during the Nashville Test Fleet case reported on Osborn again to the Get Hoffa

Squad regarding an attempt to tamper with a member of the
Nashville jury pool in the upcoming jury-tampering trial,
then scheduled for early 1964. This time the Get Hoffa Squad
got the goods on tape and reported it to Judge Miller, as chief
judge of the court.

Judge Miller called Tommy Osborn into his chambers and
confronted Osborn with an allegation from the Nashville
Police that Osborn had solicited a Nashville police officer
to seek out and bribe a prospective juror with an offer of
$10,000 for a vote of acquittal. The prospective juror would
get $5,000 should the juror be selected for trial and an
additional $5,000 when the jury subsequently reports itself
hopelessly deadlocked. Initially, Osborn denied the allegation. Judge Miller then told Osborn that the police officer
who had reported the clumsy solicitation to the Get Hoffa
Squad had secretly tape-recorded a confirming conversation
with Osborn. Tommy Osborn was given a Rule to Show
Cause why he should not be disbarred. Osborn reported the
matter to Bill Bufalino and Frank Ragano. Osborn returned
to the judge and admitted that it was his voice, but that it
was the police officer's idea and Osborn did not intend to
follow through on the idea. In other words, Osborn merely
had been puffing, talking tough. Ultimately, Osborn would
be convicted in a separate trial and serve a short prison
sentence. Upon his release from jail, filled with despair, he
would shoot himself in the head in 1970. But in late 1963,
Jimmy Hoffa's lead counsel for his upcoming jury-tampering
trial awaited word on whether he would be disbarred for yet
more jury tampering.

Considering the city of Nashville to be contaminated
beyond repair, the judge granted the defense request to move
the trial to Chattanooga for January 1964.

One morning, a few days to a week before November 22,
1963, I got a call from Jimmy to go to the pay phone. When I
got there the only thing Jimmy said to me was, "Go see your
friend."

I drove up to Russell's and when he answered the door all he told me to do was, "Go see our friends in Brooklyn. They've got something for you to take to Baltimore." That was not like Russell. He was setting the tone for whatever this was.

I turned around and drove to Monte's Restaurant in Brooklyn. It was a hangout for the Genovese people. It's the oldest Italian restaurant in New York City. It's in South Brooklyn, not far from the Gowanus Canal. Excellent food. To the left of the restaurant they have their own parking lot. I parked and went in and stood at the bar. Tony Pro got up from his table and went to the back and returned with a duffel bag. He handed it to me and told me, "Go down to Campbell's Cement in Baltimore where you went that time with the truck. Our friend's pilot will be there. He's waiting for this."

You didn't have to spend all that time in combat to know you had a duffel bag with three or four rifles in it. I knew it was rifles, but I had no idea what it was. And I knew not to look.

When I got there, Carlos's pilot, Dave Ferrie, was there with another guy I knew from Monte's who was with Genovese. He's gone now, but he has a nice family. There's no reason to bring his name into it. He said, "How's your friend?" I said, "He's doing good." He said, "You got something for us?" With the tone Russell had set, I didn't even get out of my car. I gave him the keys. He opened the trunk, took the bag, we said good-bye, and away I went home.

At the time of this exchange at Monte's, Provenzano was out on appeal from a June 13, 1963, labor-racketeering conviction. His bagman and fellow defendant, Michael Communale, a former Hudson County prosecutor, was also convicted. The June 1963 conviction would ultimately send Provenzano to Lewisburg prison for four and a half years, and because it was a labor-law violation he would be barred from union activity for five years after his release. During the trial *New York Post* writer Murray Kempton identified Provenzano as the "highest-paid labor boss in America."

At that time he was earning more salary from his three Teamsters posts than Jimmy Hoffa and more than the president of the United States.

Bobby Kennedy was the very visible driving force behind Provenzano's labor-racketeering conviction and hailed it roundly in the press. Provenzano in turn condemned the attorney general's tactic of sending investigators out to question his friends, neighbors, and, most unforgivably, his children. The *New York Times* reported that Provenzano had denounced Kennedy "in terms so obscene that the television film was unusable and reporters were unable to find a direct quote they could print."

In Nashville on November 20, 1963, Judge Miller disbarred Tommy Osborn.

Two days later, November 22, 1963, President John F. Kennedy was assassinated in Dallas.

Among the telephone calls a bereaved Bobby Kennedy made about those he suspected of involvement in his brother's murder was one to Walter Sheridan. Bobby Kennedy asked Walter Sheridan to check out the possible involvement of Jimmy Hoffa.

66 The union hall in Wilmington, Delaware, was down near the train station at that time. It was still a part of Local 107 in Philly. I had some union business down there and I had to stop at a couple of trucking terminals on my way down. When I walked into the union hall it was on the radio that Kennedy had been shot. When I first heard the news about Dallas it bothered me like it bothered everybody else in the world. He wasn't one of my favorite people, but I had nothing personal against the man, and he had a nice family. Even before Ruby whacked Oswald it crossed my mind whether it had anything to do with that matter at Monte's. I don't have to tell you there was nobody you could ask about something like that. 99

All the flags in Washington were put at half-staff as the news of the assassination spread and everyone who worked in or out of the government was sent home. When Jimmy Hoffa learned that International Vice President Harold Gibbons of St. Louis had put the Teamsters headquarters flag at half-staff and closed the building, Hoffa flew into a rage.

Jimmy never forgave Harold Gibbons for putting the flag at half-staff. I told Jimmy, "What was he going to do? All the buildings were at half-staff." Jimmy wouldn't listen to me. Later on when Jimmy was going off to school I told him to put Harold Gibbons in charge of the day-to-day instead of Fitz. There was no more dedicated or finer union man than Harold Gibbons. All Jimmy said to me was, "Fuck him."

On the day of President Kennedy's funeral procession, while the whole world mourned the young fallen commander in chief of the United States of America, Jimmy Hoffa went on television in Nashville to blast the government for framing Tommy Osborn and disbarring him. Hoffa said, "I feel that it's just a travesty of justice. That the government, the local officials, and the judges should have any part of trying to set up and entrap him and be able to take away from me a competent lawyer to represent me in my case."

Then, darkly relevant to the day's heartrending and solemn funeral, Jimmy Hoffa gloated to the Nashville television audience and said, "Bobby Kennedy is just another lawyer now."

chapter nineteen

Tampering with the Very Soul of the Nation

As early as December 9, 1963 — a mere seventeen days after his brother's assassination — Robert Kennedy spoke briefly about the possibility of mob involvement to Arthur M. Schlesinger Jr. A Pulitzer Prize–winning historian and former Harvard professor, Schlesinger had been a special assistant to President Kennedy. Schlesinger wrote in his two-volume biography, *Robert Kennedy and His Times,* that he and Robert Kennedy spent the evening of December 9 together and "I asked him, perhaps tactlessly, about Oswald. He said that there could be no serious doubt that Oswald was guilty, but there was still some argument if he had done it by himself or as part of a larger plot, whether organized by Castro or by gangsters."

Two years after the Warren Commission released its 1964 report, Bobby Kennedy told his brother Jack's former White House aide Richard Goodwin, "I never thought it was the Cubans. If anyone was involved it was organized crime. But there is nothing I can do about it. Not now."

At the time Bobby Kennedy made these statements to former White House officials who were his friends, he knew more about the inner game of organized crime than any "outsider" in the country. Bobby Kennedy certainly knew that, in the absence of a mob war, bosses did not ever eliminate another boss's underboss. It would bring major retaliation. To effect a desired change in policy, mob bosses have traditionally eliminated — and still eliminate — bosses, not underbosses. On an international scale it is called regime change. To the Italian bosses it is merely a matter of following the old Sicilian maxim that to kill a dog you don't cut off its tail, you cut off its head.

On the painful day his brother was shot to death in Dallas, Robert Kennedy was in Washington presiding over a two-day organized crime meeting of the federal attorneys on his staff. They had arrived from United States attorneys offices from all over the country to assemble at the Department of Justice for this pivotal meeting. The purpose of the meeting was to work out the details of the next phase of the attorney general's campaign against organized crime.

It was during a lunch break in the second day of meetings that Robert Kennedy heard the devastating news from Dallas.

The chief of the Organized Crime Section of the Criminal Division of the Department of Justice was an attorney named William Hundley. As Hundley expressed it, "The minute that bullet hit Jack Kennedy's head, it was all over. Right then. The organized crime program just stopped."

Exposing and ridding America of organized crime had been Bobby Kennedy's passionate obsession. It had been a very personal campaign for him, and he had made it a very personal campaign for his staff and for his enemies in organized crime. Bobby Kennedy brought to the campaign a fiercely competitive nature.

For the first three years of what would be a six-year campaign against organized crime, Bobby was chief counsel for the McClellan Committee. During those three years he grilled, taunted, and derided many of the most vicious and vengeful men in America. Kennedy asked loaded question after loaded question, and each answer came back the same: "I refuse to answer on the grounds that it might tend to incriminate me." During one such grilling, Bobby had stared into the eyes of Sam "Momo" Giancana and told him: "You are the chief gunman for the group that succeeded the Capone mob." Bobby Kennedy had grilled Frank Sinatra's pal and Cal-Neva Casino business partner about whether he disposed of his enemies by stuffing their bodies in trunks. When Giancana laughed and once again took the Fifth Amendment, Kennedy sneeringly remarked, "I thought only little girls giggled, Mr. Giancana."

When Bobby Kennedy made that remark he certainly knew that Sam "Momo" Giancana was notoriously sadistic in the methods of his murders. In December 1958 Giancana had ordered the brutal slaying of Mr. and Mrs. Gus Greenbaum in their Phoenix, Arizona, home. After they were both tortured, their throats were slit. Gus Greenbaum was an associate of Meyer Lansky. Greenbaum had succeeded Bugsy Siegel as head of the Flamingo Hotel and Casino in Las Vegas when Siegel was murdered. At the time of Greenbaum's murder he headed Sam Giancana's Riviera Hotel and Casino in Las Vegas. Giancana suspected Greenbaum of stealing. By having Greenbaum and his completely innocent wife tortured and killed, Giancana was sending a message to all those who worked for him to follow the rules.

In 1961 Giancana repeated the message to his crew. William "Action" Jackson was a 300-pound loan shark who worked for Giancana. Jackson was suspected of being a government informer. He was taken to a meatpacking plant and hung on a six-inch steel meat hook and tortured for two days. Jackson was systemically beaten, cut, burned, shot in the knee, and shocked with a cattle prod until he died. Photographs were taken of Jackson. All the men who worked for Giancana in his vast criminal empire, ranging from Chicago to Las Vegas to Dallas to Hollywood to Phoenix, were required to view the photographs.

At the conclusion of his three years with the McClellan Committee, Bobby Kennedy added a bestselling book to his fearless campaign. In his book Kennedy exposed organized crime in great detail, naming names and narrating deeds for a larger public. Bobby Kennedy labeled organized crime in the title of his book as *The Enemy Within*.

For the next three years of his campaign against organized crime, Kennedy was the attorney general, the nation's chief law-enforcement officer, the man to whom FBI Director J. Edgar Hoover reported. Bobby Kennedy drew up a list of gangsters to target, targeted them, and jailed them. Bobby Kennedy greatly expanded the use of informants and wiretapping. On an almost daily basis he taught America and the federal government, and especially FBI Director Hoover, about the existence of organized crime, about the need to rid the country of organized criminals, and how to use the enormous, heretofore dormant power of the federal government to do that.

And no more personal target or greater danger to the nation existed in Bobby Kennedy's heart and mind than Jimmy Hoffa. But so far Hoffa kept slipping through the net.

After Dallas, however, Bobby Kennedy's power source was unplugged. For any illegal acts Jimmy Hoffa and the friends of Jimmy Hoffa might venture into in the future, Bobby Kennedy would no longer be in the supremely powerful position of attorney general to his own brother and best friend.

However, for Hoffa's past sins, sins for which Hoffa was then under indictment, Bobby Kennedy continued to be very much the Attorney General of the United States.

Somehow Bobby Kennedy and Lyndon Johnson patched up their differences long enough to keep Kennedy on as attorney general until Hoffa's trials were over. The Get Hoffa Squad was kept intact, and their supervisor and chief strategist was to remain in command. Jimmy Hoffa's upcoming jury trials were both scheduled for early 1964. The jury-tampering trial would begin in Chattanooga on January 20, and the Sun Valley pension fund trial would begin in Chicago on April 27, 1964. The Get Hoffa Squad was counting on back-to-back justice that would land Jimmy Hoffa in jail.

Around the middle part of January, I was in Chicago with Jimmy for the final signing of the first Master Freight Agreement. I was working for the International and it was well represented in Chicago that day. There were four districts or conferences at that time, and each one had a vice president and they were all there. It was history in the making for the labor movement. It was a very ingenious thing. The locals still had to approve it, but it was basically a done deal in Chicago. Each local still had autonomy over local matters and their conference could negotiate a supplement to the national contract for their own or for their management's own special needs. Locals could negotiate better terms for themselves on something, but no one could negotiate less than what the Master Freight Agreement gave the workers. Unfortunately, there was still cheating after that. New York was notorious for giving their workers less. It was there for you to get in the national agreement, but it was up to your leadership to get it for you. Tony Pro was never going to get an Appreciation Night from his membership. A lot of his members took less or they didn't work, and Pro got paid under the table by management.

Four days after he signed the Master Freight Agreement, Jimmy was back down in a foxhole in Chattanooga for jury selection. After the trial started I went down to Chattanooga to sit in court with Bill Isabel and Sam Portwine. They had a new local lawyer now to replace the one that got disbarred. Bill Bufalino and Frank Ragano were there again. They had lawyers for all the other defendants. Allen Dorfman, who ran the pension fund, was one of those who were indicted for helping Jimmy on the jury tampering. Chuckie O'Brien was down there with Jimmy, no doubt keeping an eye out for any more nuts in the crowd with a gun.

And oh man, was it crowded in Chattanooga. The courtroom was packed. After I was there a couple of days I got the word that there was no need for my presence in the courtroom, and I left Chattanooga and went back to work. When I left Tennessee everybody thought the government had some cases against some of the people, but the government had no witnesses that could put Jimmy in the thing. They sounded like they were getting ready to send some more parachutes to Bobby Kennedy. They didn't know about Partin yet. The government saved Partin for last. He was their surprise witness.

There was no judicial requirement that government witnesses had to be identified in advance. Edward Grady Partin was kept out of sight in a cabin in Lookout Mountain, Tennessee.

The Chattanooga jury-tampering trial plodded along as government attorney James Neal called witnesses to build up case after case against Hoffa's accomplices, that is, against all those who had done the dirty work during the Nashville trial. Hoffa smiled cordially and exuded confidence.

Then on the final day, three months into the trial, when victory seemed assured for Hoffa, the government called its final witness. Edward Grady Partin walked in, and the courtroom erupted. Immediately, the defense attorneys cried foul. A motion was filed to exclude from the trial any testimony Partin might have to offer. The government was accused of planting a mole inside the defense camp in violation of Hoffa's constitutional right to counsel. If that were proven to be so, Partin's testimony would have to be excluded from the jury, and Jimmy Hoffa would walk out of court a winner once again.

The government's contention was that Edward Grady Partin was not planted by the prosecutors. Rather, he volunteered to attend the trial on his own. Partin did not report to the government prosecutors. Partin reported to the nonlawyer and former FBI agent Walter Sheridan. Partin merely had been instructed by Sheridan to be on the lookout for evidence of the ongoing crime of jury tampering. Partin reported such evidence of jury tampering to Walter Sheridan, and Sheridan reported it to the prosecutors, who reported it to the judge. Partin had never discussed with Walter Sheridan anything he may have heard in Nashville pertaining to the Test Fleet case itself or to any aspect of Hoffa's defense in the Test Fleet case.

The hearing on the defense motion lasted four hours. The judge accepted the government's version of the events, and Edward Grady Partin was permitted to testify before the jury, which was called back into the room. Jimmy Hoffa sat in his chair and glared at Partin. Partin was not intimidated. Partin proceeded to link Jimmy Hoffa to the specific instances of jury tampering by repeating to the jury the bragging Hoffa had done to Partin about certain attempts to bribe jurors either before they occurred or while they were occurring. With each sentence it became clearer and clearer that Jimmy Hoffa had been the puppeteer pulling the strings in Nashville.

At the next break Jimmy Hoffa picked up a heavy desk chair in the defense room at the courthouse and flung it across the room.

Partin testified for the government, and then the defense began questioning Partin. The cross-examination lasted almost five days, and instead of breaking down, Partin just got stronger with each passing day. On one occasion a defense lawyer accused Partin of memorizing and rehearsing his testimony, and Partin replied, "If I had it rehearsed you would have heard a lot more than you did. I forgot some things."

One night early in Partin's testimony a shotgun was fired into the Baton Rouge home of Partin's business agent and good friend.

At breaks during Partin's testimony, Jimmy Hoffa began to hurl loud obscenities at Walter Sheridan whenever their paths crossed. On one occasion Hoffa made the bizarre observation to Sheridan that he had heard that Sheridan had cancer (which wasn't true) and wondered, "How long does it take to work?" On another occasion Hoffa said to Sheridan, "You don't have an ounce of guts in your body." He began yelling at his own attorneys in public. Newsmen who overheard the defense attorneys being bawled out reported comments such as, "I don't care if you have to stay up all night." This treatment at the hands of Hoffa incited at least one defense attorney to erupt loudly and often at the trial judge, to the point of being held in contempt of court. At one break Jimmy Hoffa said to the prosecutor, James Neal, "I'll hound you for the rest of your life, Neal. You won't be in the government forever." After Partin finished testifying, Jimmy Hoffa took the stand. However, by this time he was spooked. He didn't know whether the government had tape recordings of anything he had said to Partin in Nashville. In fact, he was convinced the government had such tapes. As a consequence of his beliefs, he could not directly deny many of the things that were said against him. He hedged his answers and tried to explain away comments rather than flatly deny them.

Unfortunately for Hoffa, these were comments about actual jury-tampering events that had been proven to have transpired by the testimony of the bribed jurors. No amount of explaining could have helped him. The only explanation he could have given to satisfy a jury would have been an unequivocal denial that he had ever made such comments to the likes of Edward Grady Partin. But Hoffa's fear of electronic surveillance took that option away from him. Hoffa's performance on that Chattanooga witness stand was not vintage, in-your-face Jimmy Hoffa.

The rest of the defense was even weaker. Hoffa and his attorneys had clearly been unprepared for the bombshell surprise witness.

Frank Fitzsimmons testified for Hoffa that he had sent the black business agent Larry Campbell to Nashville to do some union organizing. This was weak testimony to imply that Campbell was not there for the purpose of jury tampering. Somehow it was intended to refute Partin's testimony that Hoffa said, "I've got the colored male juror in my hip pocket. One of my business agents, Larry Campbell, came into Nashville prior to the trial and took care of it."

Another defense witness was called to say that Edward Grady Partin was a dope addict. As weak as that evidence was on its face, it served the prosecution further by allowing the government to destroy it.The prosecution had Partin evaluated by two drug experts, physicians who treated addicts, who came to court to testify that there was no evidence that Partin was then on narcotics or that he had ever used them in his life.

In its desperation, and in a state of high paranoia, the defense filed a motion for a mistrial, accusing the government of employing electronic and nonelectronic surveillance against the defense team. The motions were supported by affidavits from experts in electronic surveillance and photographs of alleged FBI surveillance. Only one of the photographs had an FBI agent in it, and he happened to be a passing motorist. All the other photographs were of ordinary citizens of Chattanooga taking snapshots of the celebrity defendants. During an argument on the motion one of the defense attorneys, Jacques Schiffer, challenged prosecutor James Neal to a duel. Schiffer said, "You don't say that again unless you mean to back it up. I will meet you anywhere with anything. We will see who turns yellow first." Ultimately, the judge ruled that the motion for a mistrial based on alleged surveillance of the defense team by the FBI was "utterly without merit."

Next the defense filed a motion for a mistrial, alleging that the jury had overheard that same defense attorney, Jacques Schiffer, loudly arguing a legal point and that some of the jurors were overheard to be critical of Schiffer's boisterous and aggressive tactics. At the time of the alleged incident the jury was sequestered in the jury room and was not permitted to hear the legal arguments taking place in the courtroom. But for the loud volume of the defense attorney's argument, the jury would not have heard anything Schiffer had said. In support of its motion the defense alleged that defense attorney Frank Ragano, at the height of Schiffer's thunderous oration, had left the counsel table and gone back to the jury room door to listen to the jury to see if it could hear the arguments by Schiffer. An incredulous judge pointed out to Ragano that what he had done violated the sanctity of the jury room and that instead of manufacturing evidence for a mistrial he should have asked his cocounsel to quiet down, as the judge had been asking him to do throughout the trial.

In his closing summation, government prosecutor James Neal told the jury that what had occurred in Nashville was "one of the greatest assaults on the jury system known to mankind." As for the truthfulness of his star witness, Neal succinctly told the jury, "The reason the government says Partin is telling the truth is because it checked and found out that all he said was happening, and what he said was going to happen, did happen."

James Haggerty, the lead attorney for Jimmy Hoffa, called it all "a foul and filthy frame-up." Haggerty then played the Bobby card. By mentioning Bobby Kennedy and choosing words that would evoke slavery, Haggerty sought to appeal to a perceived Southern prejudice against Bobby Kennedy for his having put the Justice Department squarely behind integration and in support of the Rev. Martin Luther King Jr. Haggerty accused the man sitting in the back of the courtroom, a man who had not testified in the trial, Walter Sheridan, of being "the architect of the diabolical plot" against Jimmy Hoffa and of being "the servant of his master, Robert Kennedy."

The next defense summation also attacked Robert Kennedy and his "axe man Walter Sheridan."

The jury was not seduced away from the truth. Allen Dorfman, the marine combat veteran of the war in the Pacific, whose jury-tampering role had been minimal, was found not guilty. Jimmy Hoffa and three others who had done Hoffa's bidding were found guilty. In two separate trials, two other men who had acted on Hoffa's behalf were found guilty.

At sentencing on March 12, 1964, defense attorney Jacques Schiffer was sentenced to sixty days in jail for contempt of court. Attorney Frank Ragano received a public reprimand for standing outside the jury room door with his ear to the door to listen in on the jury.

Hoffa's three guilty codefendants in his trial got three years each. At sentencing in one of the separate trials, a Hoffa jury fixer got five years. At sentencing in the other separate trial, the Nashville lawyer, Tommy Osborn, who had crossed over the line into jury tampering for his client Jimmy Hoffa, got three and a half years.

Jimmy Hoffa, the architect of it all and the only person who could have profited from it all, got a sentence of eight years.

Judge Frank W. Wilson, in pronouncing sentence, said:

> Mr. Hoffa, it is the opinion of this court . . . that [in those jury-tampering incidents] of which you stand convicted . . . you [acted] knowingly and

you [acted] corruptly [even] after the trial judge
reported to you his information with regard to
an alleged attempt to bribe a juror. . . . [I]t is
difficult for the Court to imagine under those
circumstances a more willful violation of the law.
Most defendants that stand before this Court for
sentencing . . . have either violated the property
rights of other individuals or have violated the
personal rights of other individuals.

. . . You stand here convicted of having tampered, really, with the very soul of this nation.

chapter twenty

Hoffa's Comedy Troupe

66 Partin was no good to them dead. They needed him alive. He had to be able to sign an affidavit. They needed him to swear that all the things he said against Jimmy at the trial were lies that he got from a script fed to him by Bobby Kennedy's people in the Get Hoffa Squad. Partin had to say that he did all of this because he had kidnapping charges hanging over his head and not because Jimmy had made threats to whack Bobby. That was Jimmy's best chance on that jury-tampering matter. Partin knew nobody was going to kiss him as long as he strung them along. Partin gave Jimmy's lawyers useless affidavits and even a deposition. In the end, they never really got him to say that he railroaded Jimmy Hoffa. All they ever got out of him about railroading amounted to no more than, "Partin, me boy, is that the Chattanooga Choo Choo?" 99

Another reason Hoffa needed Partin alive for many years to come had to do with Hoffa's chances down the line before the parole board or for a presidential pardon. In his autobiography Jimmy Hoffa wrote that on March 27, 1971, Partin had given his lawyers a deposition that amounted to "a twenty-nine page confession." From Hoffa's written version alone it is clear to anyone who understands these things that it was not a "confession" of any railroading by Partin and the government. Furthermore, whatever it was, the deposition was given in exchange for the Hoffa camp putting Partin in a potentially lucrative business deal with Audie Murphy, the movie actor and "most decorated hero of World War II."

Still suffering nightmares from the war, Murphy had fallen on hard times. He had filed for bankruptcy in 1968 and had been acquitted on an assault-with-intent-to-murder charge in 1970. Still, to a southerner like Partin, the decorated soldier from Tennessee was a shining star. Hoffa brazenly wrote that for the deal to turn out profitable for Audie Murphy and Partin, an unspecified favor was needed from Jimmy Hoffa. Hoffa wrote that shortly after the deposition, "Senator George Murphy [California Republican and former movie actor] personally took [the deposition] to Attorney General John Mitchell, and Audie Murphy gave it to President Nixon."

I never met Audie Murphy, not with Jimmy and not overseas. We were in the same operations over there but in different divisions. He was a heavy drinker after the war like me. I heard he had business with Jimmy, but I didn't know what kind of business. He died in a crash of a small plane. Jimmy was in the coal business for a while, but I don't think Audie Murphy was in that.

Meanwhile, in the spring of 1964 in Philadelphia, the rebels in the Voice threatened to sue the International if any more money was spent on Jimmy's legal fees. Over a million already had been spent on the Chattanooga jury-tampering trial. And now the Chicago Sun Valley trial was coming up right around the corner. There would most definitely be more than a little bit of fees and expenses on that one with everything that was at stake. Jimmy had reserved a floor at the Sherman House Hotel in Chicago, and they had a fulltime chef lined up to cook for everybody. The Chicago trial was going to go on for months. They had half a platoon of lawyers. None of this was free. All this had to be paid for.

Jimmy told the International Executive Board not to worry about the Voice. He said that the lawyer for the International, Edward Bennett Williams, had told Jimmy that footing the legal bills was a perfectly legal union expense. Edward Bennett Williams was the lawyer Jimmy had used in the trial in Washington over trying to bribe the McClellan Committee investigator, where they brought Joe Louis into the courtroom and they sent Bobby Kennedy a parachute when they won. Jimmy gave Edward Bennett Williams the Teamsters business as a reward for the trial, and he figured Williams would go along with this. The International checked with Williams, and he told them that he had never said anything like that to Jimmy, and that paying the bills when Jimmy got convicted was not legal under the union's constitution.

I know I got reimbursed whenever I beat a rap, but I paid my own bills when I lost. Or I should say, somebody would hold a benefit and I'd get envelopes. I did collect a fair amount of private money to help out with my legal fees and expenses on those two cases I did lose. But in the end you're still short when you lose.

The trial in Chicago started about a month after Jimmy was sentenced to an eight-year bit in Chattanooga. I happened to be in Chicago for a part of that trial, and I stopped in and waited in the hallway for a break. I wished Jimmy luck and saw a big crowd of people coming out, mostly Teamsters, no alleged mob figures, not even Joey Glimco, who was also a Teamster. I chatted with Barney Baker. He was 6'6" and weighed about 350. He was a heavy eater. Believe it or not he boxed as a middleweight. He was supposed to have had something to do with getting Joe Louis to that trial in Washington. Jimmy liked him. He sold ties. He had a lot of neckties for sale all the time. Barney had a lot of balls. He'd be available to help. He was a good muscle man. He got investigated in the Warren Report thing because they traced some calls between him and Jack Ruby a few days before the Dallas matter.

Bill Bufalino was at the trial as a spectator, and Frank Ragano was there representing one of the other codefendants. Jimmy usually didn't listen to lawyers. Jimmy told them what he wanted done. And Jimmy had a good memory. He could tell the lawyers what the witnesses said two weeks ago better than the lawyers could tell from their notes. If the lawyer told Jimmy something he didn't want to hear, he'd say, "Well, you make it right." But in the hallway it looked to me like he might be doing a little more listening.

Jimmy told me to meet him back at the union office. At the Chicago office Jimmy told me point-blank to tell our friends back East that nothing should happen to Partin. Jimmy told me he had a good defense for the Chicago thing, and they were still working on Partin for an affidavit on the Chattanooga thing.

Besides that, they had a congressman in Chicago named Roland Libonti. I never met the man, but I heard about him. He was with Sam Giancana. Later on it came out in the papers that Giancana's son-in-law, Anthony Tisci, was on Libonti's congressional payroll. They had Libonti making resolutions for a congressional investigation of Bobby Kennedy. The idea was that Bobby Kennedy had violated Jimmy Hoffa's constitutional rights with illegal wiretapping and surveillance and by planting Partin in their rooms at the Andrew Jackson Hotel in Nashville. Jimmy was looking forward to turning the tables on "Booby" and getting him to have to take the Fifth at the congressional hearing. Jimmy claimed he had tapes of Bobby Kennedy and Marilyn Monroe having sex. Johnny Roselli and Giancana had Marilyn Monroe's house bugged. He never played me the tapes, but I got the impression that he planned on having them played, maybe during the congressional hearings if they ever had them.

I left Chicago and went back to the fun and games in Philly, and I passed the word among our friends about Partin. At 107 we still had the battles with the rebels and the battles with the other outfits from the AFL-CIO. We had a bar on Delaware Avenue where we used to keep shirts to change into. The cops would be looking for a guy in a green shirt, and I'd be sitting in the bar with a blue shirt on. I'd show the cop my bar tab. It would look like I was sitting there all day, only I could drink that much in an hour.

The Chicago trial of Jimmy Hoffa and seven codefendants began on April 27, 1964, five weeks after Hoffa had received a crushing eight-year sentence in Chattanooga. As had been done in Chattanooga, the identities of the prospective jurors in the jury pool were kept from both sides until the morning of jury selection.

The selection of jurors went without incident, and the government proceeded to put on a pension fund fraud case consisting of thirteen painstaking weeks of live testimony and the introduction into evidence of more than 15,000 documents for the jury to consider. It was a federal case in every sense of the phrase.

The pension fund fraud centered on the improvement of a tract of land in Florida that had been intended as a housing development for Teamsters willing to personally invest in it by purchasing lots, for either retirement or vacation homes. The tract was to be known as Sun Valley Village. While lots were sold to Teamsters, including Jimmy Hoffa, the land was never developed by the developer and the developer had since died. The Sun Valley Village development went into bankruptcy, and the undeveloped lots became worthless.

Unfortunately for Jimmy Hoffa, before Sun Valley went bankrupt in 1958, he had authorized the depositing of $400,000 in a non-interest-bearing account in a Florida bank as collateral to secure a loan to the benefit of the Sun Valley developer for the purpose of building roads and bringing utilities to the land. Jimmy Hoffa took that $400,000 that he pledged directly from the pension fund of his own Detroit local. When Sun Valley filed for bankruptcy, the bank held on to the $400,000 collateral. For Hoffa to get back the $400,000, he had to come up with a total of $500,000, which the developer had owed the bank altogether when he died.

To gather together the half-million it would take, according to the government, Hoffa went on a pension fund lending binge between 1958 and 1960. Hoffa and the seven codefendants began lending pension money left and right on speculative ventures, charging points and finder's fees, and funneling a portion of that money to Hoffa to pay off the

Florida bank loans. By 1960 the mission was accomplished and Hoffa not only paid off the Florida bank, he paid Local 299 $42,000 in lost interest when he repaid the $400,000 to the local's pension fund.

What turned all this into fraud, the government contended, was the fact that Jimmy Hoffa personally sought to profit while he encouraged Teamsters to invest in Sun Valley Village parcels; that he personally sought to profit while he pledged Local 299's pension fund money; and that he personally sought to profit while he scrambled his way through the Central States Pension Fund to siphon off enough money to pay back Local 299. The government contended that Hoffa's personal profit motive was contained in a document he had signed. The government contended that Jimmy Hoffa had signed a secret trust agreement with the developer whereby Hoffa was to receive 22 percent of all of the development's profits once the project was completely developed.

Jimmy Hoffa's defense was simple: He was going to deny that the signature was his. The developer was dead and couldn't testify that the signature on that trust agreement was Hoffa's. Jimmy Hoffa's partner, Owen Bert Brennan, was dead and couldn't testify that the signature was Hoffa's. Perhaps Bert Brennan had signed Hoffa's name and was going to keep the extra 22 percent profit himself. Perhaps the developer had signed Hoffa's name to gain credibility with other investors by claiming that Hoffa, with the might of his pension fund, was behind the project.

The government showed that the scrambling between 1958 and 1960 to get the money to pay the bank included things such as a $330,000 kickback on a $3.3 million loan for the building of the Everglades Hotel in Miami. On another scramble, $650,000 went to the Black Construction Company. There was no Black Construction Company; Cecil Black was a $125-a-week laborer, and he never saw a dime of the money.

What made this Chicago case particularly galling to Jimmy Hoffa was that all the scrambling he was alleged to have done between 1958 and 1960 was done in what he considered self-defense. All of this scrambling to repay the Detroit local its money was a direct result of the heat being put on by Bobby Kennedy during the McClellan Committee hearings and by the negative light being cast by Kennedy on that pledged, non-interest-bearing $400,000 deposit as collateral.

The chief witness in the Chicago trial against Jimmy Hoffa was an FBI handwriting expert who testified that the signature "J.R. Hoffa" on the trust agreement was a signature that was consistent with known handwriting exemplars of Jimmy Hoffa.

The government rested its case and Jimmy Hoffa took the stand. As expected, Hoffa denied it was his signature on the trust agreement. As was not expected, Hoffa went one step further and denied that he ever in his life signed a legal document "J.R. Hoffa." Jimmy Hoffa swore that he always signed all legal documents "James R. Hoffa."

While the government didn't have a surprise witness, it shuffled through its own mounds of documents to find a surprise document. On cross-examination Jimmy Hoffa was asked if he personally had leased a penthouse in Miami Beach at the Blair House. Confident that the penthouse lease could be justified as an appropriate union expense, Hoffa said that he had. When asked if he had personally signed the lease Hoffa said that he had. At that point the prosecutor asked Hoffa to authenticate the signature and handed the lease to Hoffa. To Jimmy Hoffa's everlasting dismay he had signed the lease "J.R. Hoffa."

What the Chicago case against Jimmy Hoffa was all about was eloquently stated by Walter Sheridan: "Hoffa was using funds reserved for the pensions of Teamsters members to extricate himself from a situation where he had misused funds belonging to Teamsters members for his own benefit." In dollars and cents, Jimmy Hoffa had swiped $400,000 from his union brothers, and to pay it back before it became a legal issue, he swiped another $500,000 from those same union brothers.

On July 26, 1964, the jury promptly found Jimmy Hoffa and his seven minions guilty of pension fund fraud. On August 17, 1964, Jimmy Hoffa was given an additional five years in jail to serve consecutively with the eight-year sentence he had received in Chattanooga.

This total of an unlucky thirteen years of sentences to be spent in a federal jail for Jimmy Hoffa was followed a week later, on August 25, 1964, by the news of Bobby Kennedy's resignation as attorney general and his announcement that he was running for the U.S. Senate from New York. Walter Sheridan resigned from the Department of Justice to help run Bobby Kennedy's campaign.

You got so used to Jimmy winning it was hard to picture him losing back to back to Bobby. You just knew he wouldn't take this lying down.

Still and all, the way he played the first trial in Tennessee he ended up turning a slap on the wrist into serious jail time. He kept going back with cash to bribe the jury even though he kept getting caught. It was like the kangaroo kept bopping the back of his head and he never caught on and he kept on walking into it.

Some of our friends questioned Jimmy's judgment, blabbing out loud like that to a man he hardly knew, Ed Partin. In our world you've got to keep things inside if you expect to be trusted. You don't want people losing respect for you.

I later heard from Harold Gibbons that after that thing in Chicago, Jimmy was careful to sign everything "James R. Hoffa."

At the time of his announcement for the U.S. Senate, Bobby Kennedy had spent three and a half years targeting Hoffa and the Teamsters. Bobby Kennedy's efforts had resulted in the indictment of 201 Teamsters officials and the conviction of 126 of them.

Thanks to Bobby Kennedy, mobsters everywhere were going to be under such public scrutiny that they wouldn't be able to gather together at a public restaurant without it being raided. On September 22, 1966, a table full of mobsters from around the country having lunch at La Stella restaurant in Forest Hills in Queens, New York, were arrested by the police. Included in the group that was taken in, harassed, and released without charges were Carlos Marcello, Santo Trafficante, Joe Colombo, and Carlo Gambino. A month later the same group defiantly held another meeting at La Stella, only this time they brought their lawyer, Frank Ragano, with them.

Bobby Kennedy's campaign against organized crime, and especially the methodology he devised — gathering intelligence, focusing on targets, making deals with informants, employing sophisticated electronic surveillance, and insisting on the pooling of information by disparate and often competitive government agencies — set the stage for every action the federal government has taken against organized crime since. Today no one questions the existence of organized crime or the commitment of the federal government and the FBI to its eradication. Today, thanks to Bobby Kennedy, organized crime is hardly thought of as a local police problem. The head may have been cut off, but the dog never died. The damage done by Bobby Kennedy to the power of organized crime and to mobster Teamsters was irreversible.

66 Jimmy Hoffa didn't care anything about money. He gave it away. But he did like the power. And jail or no jail, he wasn't about to give that power away. First, he was going to do whatever he could to keep from going to jail. If he went to jail he was still going to rule from jail while he did whatever it took to get out of jail. Once he got out of jail he was going to take back control of everything. And I was going to help him. 99

In 1965 a defense motion for a new trial was filed in Chattanooga on the grounds that jurors in that trial were having sex with prostitutes. The motion alleged that prostitutes had been arranged for and provided by U.S. marshals as inducement for the jurors to side with the government. The motion was accompanied by the affidavits of four Chattanooga prostitutes. One of them, a Marie Monday, claimed that the judge in Chattanooga had told her that he was out to "get Hoffa." One can only imagine the laughter that this bit of legal "improv" engendered in Chattanooga's hallowed halls of justice. The judge laughed the motion out of court. The government took one of the prostitutes to trial and convicted her of perjury. Whereupon Marie Monday promptly recanted her affidavit.

At the July 1966 Miami Beach Teamsters Convention, Jimmy Hoffa amended the IBT constitution to create a new office — the office of general vice president. That officer had all the power necessary to run the union in the event the president went to jail. Hoffa installed his perceived puppet, Frank Fitzsimmons, as the new general vice president. Hoffa gave himself a raise from $75,000 a year to $100,000 a year, the same salary as the president of the United States. Only Hoffa's salary would now contain a provision that the salary would continue to be paid in the event the president went to jail.

It was explained to the delegates that the reason Hoffa should continue to receive his pay while in prison was that prison is the equivalent of traveling for a rest period to conserve Hoffa's health, something like the expenses incurred in traveling to go deep-sea fishing. Hoffa had the delegates approve the payment of all past legal fees and expenses, regardless of whether he lost the case or not. Those expenses amounted to $1,277,680 as of the date of the convention. Hoffa had the delegates approve the payment of all of his future legal expenses, whatever they might turn out to be.

Meanwhile, Hoffa's Chattanooga appeal made it to the U.S. Supreme Court. The Supreme Court agreed to hear the appeal because it presented a novel issue involving Hoffa's constitutional right to counsel and whether that right was violated by Partin's presence at the Andrew Jackson Hotel. The appeal was being heard at the height of the "criminal law revolution," the decade from 1961 to 1971 when criminal rights were being created where none had previously existed. Hoffa's appeal was being handled competently by Joseph A. Fanelli, a seasoned appellate lawyer new to the Hoffa team. Walter Sheridan wrote that after oral argument in the Supreme Court the prosecution team was "not at all certain when it was over how the Justices would rule."

Just to be on the safe side, however, the Hoffa comedy troupe decided to strong-arm liberal Supreme Court Justice William Brennan. Walter Sheridan wrote about this bizarre act of appellate "improv": "A Teamsters official approached the brother of Supreme Court Justice William Brennan. The Justice's brother, who owned a brewery, was told that if his brother did not vote right on the Hoffa case, the brewery would be closed down and would never reopen."

Despite the strong-arm tactics, the Supreme Court ruled against Jimmy Hoffa on the merits of his appeal. Justice Brennan sided with the majority opinion, which was written by Justice Potter Stewart. Chief Justice Earl Warren wrote a minority opinion and voted to reverse Hoffa's conviction. Warren called the government's clandestine use of Partin "an affront to the quality and fairness of federal law enforcement."

Nine days after Justice Potter Stewart's opinion the justice received a letter from an old college chum on behalf of Jimmy Hoffa. The letter was from William Loeb, the owner and publisher of New Hampshire's influential *Manchester Union Leader*. Loeb informed his friend Justice Stewart that an unnamed high government official had assured him that Bobby Kennedy had used illegal wiretaps in his zeal to get Hoffa. An important fact Loeb had left out of the letter was that he had been promised a huge loan from the Teamsters pension fund, a loan he subsequently received. Had it been proved that Hoffa's attorneys put Loeb up to writing this letter they would have faced ethics proceedings, but the matter was not pursued.

Hoffa's lawyers filed a motion for a rehearing of Justice Stewart's decision. Such motions are routinely made but rarely granted, inappropriate letters from men of influence notwithstanding.

While the rehearing motion was pending the Hoffa troupe filed with the Supreme Court something novel to the law, something they called a "Motion for Relief Because of Government Wiretapping, Electronic Eavesdropping, and Other Intrusions." The motion was supported by an affidavit from a freelance wiretapper and electronic eavesdropping expert named Benjamin "Bud" Nichols. In his affidavit Nichols claimed that he had met with Walter Sheridan in Chattanooga just before the start of the jury-tampering trial. Nichols claimed that Sheridan had paid him to bug the phones in the jurors' rooms and he then planted bugs on the phones in the jurors' rooms at Sheridan's direction. There was a slight problem with the new Hoffa motion — there are no phones in jurors' rooms in Chattanooga or anywhere else in the country.

The laughter died down at 3:30 p.m. March 7, 1967, when, three years and three days after his conviction for jury tampering, Jimmy Hoffa entered the Lewisburg Federal Penitentiary in Pennsylvania. The March 17, 1967, issue of *Life* magazine featured a photo essay entitled, "Inmate 33298-NE: James Riddle Hoffa — A Swaggering Man on a Long Cold Walk." One of the photographs depicted a Valentine heart with Jimmy Hoffa's picture in the center and around the heart the words "Always Thinking of You." For years the Valentine had adorned Walter Sheridan's office door at the Department of Justice. Valentine's Day, February 14th, the day of the St. Valentine's Day massacre in Al Capone's Chicago, Jimmy Hoffa's birthday. The essay raised the question "Whether this spells the end of Hoffa's power in the huge union — or just a pause. Right now not many union men would bet against Hoffa's bounding back."

chapter twenty-one

All He Did for Me Was to Hang Up

Was Hoffa's incarceration on March 7, 1967, as *Life* magazine had put it, "the end of Hoffa's power in the huge union — or just a pause?" Was the transfer of leadership to Fitzsimmons a transfer of title only, or was there a substantive change blowing in the wind? From his perspective on the front lines of union combat and violence in Philadelphia in 1967, Frank Sheeran was likely the first Teamsters leader, the first "Hoffa man," to feel the chill of a new wind.

The night before Jimmy went to school I drove down from Wilmington to Washington to see him. Jimmy gave me $25,000 to give to the lawyers for Johnny Sullivan and the two others who got indicted for shooting John Gorey and his girlfriend Rita at the 107 union hall in 1964. Gorey was with the Voice, and the FBI tried to say he got whacked because he was a rebel. The girl was just in the wrong place at the wrong time with the wrong man, that's all — a civilian casualty.

Gorey was with the Voice all right, but if that was the case there were more important people than Gorey to whack. Charlie Meyers would have been the first to go, not Gorey. Meyers was the head of the Voice. Gorey was nobody big in the Voice. And what corruption was there to expose? There was nothing to expose. Everybody knew about the corruption.

Gorey was a gambler. More times if a guy owed money from gambling they would negotiate with him rather than do something drastic. But it all depends on the circumstances. Maybe the guy defied them, didn't show respect. Or maybe he owed too much money to negotiate about. Or maybe they'd been negotiating and negotiating with the guy and they ran out of patience. Or maybe they needed to send a message to other customers who started owing, say if the economy was bad or something. More likely they would just bust a guy up. Unless they started something and it got out of whack.

But that matter with Gorey, that was making unnecessary problems. Gorey didn't bother anybody. That could have been done by pushing him around a little bit. That was a waste, and the girl, too. I'll say one good thing about today. If you don't pay they just stop taking your bets. They put the word out and nobody takes your bets until you do pay.

I know they are trying to say Jimmy had it done. I can tell you without a doubt Jimmy Hoffa would not have somebody do something like that — whack a guy and his girlfriend right in the union hall. Why did Jimmy give me the money for the shooters' lawyers? All I know is he told me, "I made a promise." That was good enough for me. It's not my business why Jimmy gave me the $25,000 for the lawyers. That kind of money was nothing to Jimmy if he wanted to do a favor. He probably got asked to make a donation and that was his donation. Maybe after the fact, whoever asked Jimmy for a contribution told Jimmy that Gorey was a Voice trouble-maker anyway. I don't know about that, but he didn't get whacked on account of Jimmy. Gorey was a low-key Irish guy that didn't stand out in any way. I am sure Jimmy Hoffa did not even know who the man was.

Everybody downtown knew I was going to Teamsters headquarters in Washington to collect Jimmy's donation for the lawyers for Sullivan and them. When I got back to Philly, Big Bobby Marino asked me for the money. Bobby told me he'd give it to the lawyers for me. I asked him if he thought I was made with a finger. Thirteen years later I got indicted for having Big Bobby whacked, but the jury found me not guilty.

The next guy to come up to me to "help" me get the money to the lawyers was Harry "The Hunchback" Riccobene. I said, "No way. The only ones who are going to get this money are the lawyers." Guys like Harry the Hunchback and Big Bobby wouldn't give a crap about the guys going to trial. They wanted to get the money for themselves. There was always a lot of treachery among certain people downtown.

When I got arrested for the DeGeorge murder in 1967, shortly after Jimmy went to school, Big Bobby Marino went down to Washington to ask Frank Fitzsimmons for bail money for me. Fitzsimmons turned him down. Marino didn't go down to Washington to see Fitz for me. We had no business together. We were not social friends. Big Bobby was there for himself. They were trying to get it into their own pocket on your misery, that's the kind they were. I sat there in the Philadelphia Detention Center for four months until the judge let me sign my own bail. When I got out I chased Big Bobby down. He went about 6'6" and weighted 350 pounds easily. But he didn't want any trouble from me.

When I got out of jail I asked Fitz for my expenses and he turned me down. Jimmy would never hesitate to get you squared away. I called Russell, and Russell made a call and got my money for me from Fitz. I got thirty-five from Fitz down in Washington. They left it for me at the Market Inn. That was a dry spot.

A dry spot is a place where money is hidden. It's like a safe house that you lay low in for a while that nobody knows about. Only it's for hiding money. A safe house is like a civilian house on a normal street that's not connected to anybody. A dry spot could be temporary, until the money is picked up. The Market Inn was the place for that. It was a dry spot and it was a drop spot. You'd drop the package of money off there with the maitre d' until the party picked it up. The maitre d' didn't have to know what was in the package. It was safe until somebody came for it. I'm pretty sure the Market Inn is still there on E Street in Washington, but I don't know if they use it for that anymore.

The senators and congressmen and other people would go

in there to pick up small packages that were left for them. Nothing serious would be left like that. No half-million or anything like that, but sums under, say, fifty thousand. The Market Inn was quite a place in the old days. I had to go down there for the thirty-five and I had to go to New York for the fifteen to make fifty. I got the fifteen package from lawyer Jacques Schiffer's office.

The DeGeorge thing was at most a manslaughter, but Arlen Specter, before he became a U.S. senator, was the D.A. in Philly, and he was trying to make a name for himself. Specter had been the lawyer for the Warren Commission and he had a bit of limelight from inventing the single-bullet theory to explain all the bullet wounds in Dallas on President Kennedy and Governor Connelly.

The way the DeGeorge thing happened is, I was head of a local down in Delaware. About a year before he went to school Jimmy split 107 into three locals, figuring it would cut down on the violence that way. He gave me the charter for a new local in Wilmington, Delaware, Local 326. I became acting president of Local 326 until an election could be held and I could be voted in by the rank and file of that local. The first thing Jimmy wanted me to do was go up to Philly and fire these five disruptive organizers that the 107 president, Mike Hession, was afraid to fire. I drove up I-95 and fired Johnny Sullivan, who was with McGreal and was out on his appeal on the Gorey thing. I fired Stevie Bouras, who only got his job because he fired a gun into the ceiling and scared Hession. I fired another guy, but I don't remember his name. There was so much going on in those days it's hard to remember it all, but I do remember what Jimmy sent me up there to do. I fired Big Bobby Marino and Benny Bedachio. They had friends. I wasn't too popular up there, but nobody tried to shoot a gun into a ceiling around me.

After I fired them all I stayed in Philly awhile to make sure there was no backlash. Then I went back down to Delaware, which is about thirty miles south. I was learning my new position. I wanted to justify Jimmy's faith in me by giving me the charter. I spent two weeks driving a car hauler at the

Chrysler automobile plant in Newark, Delaware, for Anchor Motors. The car haulers have different issues than the freight haulers. I had only been a freight hauler and I didn't want anybody complaining that I didn't understand about car hauling. I learned how to drive the cars on the trailers so I would know what I was doing on grievances.

At 326 I covered all my barns (trucking companies) every morning. I got out. I didn't sit still. I like being with people. I checked in with the men to see how things were going. You make them feel respected. You don't buy respect. You earn it. I made sure the companies were putting into the pension fund and living up to their end. If the companies weren't putting into the fund and you weren't checking you could get sued.

That didn't mean you couldn't do some good for yourself. If you organized a new company you could give them a waiver of donating their share into the pension fund for up to a year. That way they could adjust to the thing. Maybe raise their rates to their customers or whatever, so they would have time to prepare for the extra overhead of the pension donations. Let's say the company has to donate $1 an hour for each employee. For a forty-hour week that's $40. If he's got a hundred employees, that's $4,000 a week. If you gave him a six-month waiver, that's a little over $100,000 he saves. Only it's more than $1 an hour to begin with. He puts his savings on the table and you both share it under the table — everybody's taken care of that way. Now the men don't get hurt at all. Because all Teamsters pensions are retroactive to the day you started with the company, even if the company wasn't contributing. They got their exact pension whether you gave the waiver or not.

After all the firings in Philadelphia the tensions kept heating up. Joey McGreal and his muscle crew decided they wanted to take over 107 once and for all and get all the union jobs for themselves so they could shake down the trucking companies and line their pockets. So one September night in 1967 they held a big rally in front of the 107 hall on Spring Garden Street. There must have been 3,000 people from all the different factions all stirred up. There were people walking up and down outside the building hollering and there were a few fistfights. Joey McGreal had muscle from downtown, not the Italians with Angelo, but muscle. Robert "Lonnie" DeGeorge and Charles Amoroso were part of McGreal's muscle. They wanted to take over the building. They were trying to scare all the organizers and business agents and local officers into stepping down. The mounted police had their hands full that night.

I wasn't there for any of that. I got a call late that night at home from Fitz to be there the next morning because after a rally like that you always figure it will get worse the next day. They'll come back looking for bear. Fitz said to me, "Get things under control." I know what that would have meant to Jimmy if Jimmy said that to me. I called Angelo Bruno and borrowed some Italian muscle. I had Joseph "Chickie" Ciancaglini and Rocco Turra and a few others. We had the good muscle. I had men inside the hall looking out the windows and men on the street. I had my back to the union hall. Two groups were walking toward each other from opposite ends of Spring Garden Street, the McGreal people coming from one direction and the people loyal to the local coming from the other direction.

All of a sudden shooting broke out. The first shot came from behind me and went whizzing past my head. They said I gave the signal for the shooting to begin. They said I pointed a finger at DeGeorge and somebody from our side shot him. There was so much shooting going on nobody could tell who was shooting at who or who started it. The cops on horseback had been there the night before, but they hadn't shown up yet that morning. That was some battle that morning. Chickie took two slugs in the belly. I grabbed Chickie and pulled him into a car and got him to my mother's brother who was a doctor. Dr. John Hansen told me to get Chickie to a hospital right away, because he was sure to die with the wounds he had. I went over to St. Agnes Hospital, which was right across the street from my uncle's office. I laid Chickie down and rattled the garbage cans until somebody came out to get him.

I drove down to Newport, Delaware, to hide out in an apartment over a bar until things died down. I called Fitz and I said to him, "One down. Two limping," and Fitz panicked and hung up the phone on me. That's the first time I knew things were going to be very different under Fitz. Still, at that point I had no idea the man was going to be capable of turning down my request for expenses when I got arrested for this on the thing that he had asked me to handle. I had no idea I was going to have to end up going to Russell to get taken care of on the matter. "One down. Two limping," and he hung up the phone on me.

The D.A.'s office put out an arrest warrant on me. They arrested Chickie, a black guy named Johnny West, and Black Pat, a white guy. I stayed in Delaware for a while, but I didn't want a flight charge on me, too. So I got Bill Elliot, who had been a big shot on the Wilmington Police Department, to drive me to Philly. I wore a granny dress and a bonnet and turned myself in to a *Philadelphia Bulletin* reporter named Phil Galioso, who took me to the police commissioner, Frank Rizzo. (It's funny when you think about it, but when Rizzo was mayor in 1974 he came to Frank Sheeran Appreciation Night.)

Chickie survived. He had an iron constitution. They tried to get the black guy Johnny West to turn on the three of us. They told him I had turned on him. He said, "Anybody but him, I'd believe you. But him, I'm keeping my mouth shut." They tried the three of them within six weeks and the jury found all of them not guilty. Meanwhile, I stayed in jail. My lawyer Charlie Peruto was on vacation in Italy while I rotted in a cell for four months and Fitz didn't lift a finger. He was probably too busy golfing or drinking. It cost me my union election at Local 326 in Wilmington. I couldn't campaign because I was sitting in jail. I still only lost by a few votes. Finally, the judge let me sign my own bail and I got out.

Around that time the 107 union hall burned to the ground. We figured it was the Voice or McGreal's faction, but we never found out. Right after that, Mike Hession stepped down as president. Hession was the kind of a guy who would fight you in a minute in a street fight, but I guess the other part got too heavy for him.

Meanwhile, Arlen Specter tried to get his top prosecutor, Dick Sprague, to bring me to trial on first-degree murder on DeGeorge. Sprague told him he didn't even have a case of manslaughter and to go try his own losers. Specter was trying to build himself up in the political world on the Teamsters' back.

There were 3,000 people there and a lot of shooting. How can you say anybody shot what? Nobody found any guns. Those charges against me lingered in the system from 1967 to 1972. Finally, they took me to court to pick a jury and begin the trial. I had my character witnesses there. They were all different labor guys, a guy from the steelworkers, my buddy John McCullough from the roofer's union who got whacked just before my trial in 1980, and some others. Before we picked a jury, the judge put me on the stand and asked me how many times the Commonwealth asked for a postponement of the trial, and I told him "sixty-eight." Then the judge asked me how many times I asked for a continuance and I said "none," and he called it a disgrace and said a motion was in order.

My new lawyer, Jim Moran, got the judge to throw it out on the first speedy trial motion in Pennsylvania. While that motion was going on, the Commonwealth tried to give me a *nolle prosse* and I told them to stick it because with a *nolle prosse,* sure it drops the charges, but they can always reindict you. My advice is to take a dismissal from a judge if you can get it, not a *nolle prosse* from the D.A. That's what I got on the thing.

When I lost that election in 1968 on account of being in jail for four months I went to work to fill an unexpired term as a business agent. It's good work. You service the people. You make sure the company lives up to the contract. You have certain barns to cover. You process grievances. You defend people that the company is trying to fire. If a union is run right you don't have too many discharge cases. Stealing or accidents where you were negligent, then you're done. The company has some rights, too.

I remember one Polish guy I defended who had a gambling problem. The company caught him stealing Holland hams. At the hearing I told him to keep his mouth shut and let me do the talking. The company manager took the stand and testified that he saw the Polish guy take ten cases of hams off the dock and load them into his personal truck. The Polish guy looked at me and said out loud, "Frank, he's a fucking liar. There were only seven." I promptly made a motion to withdraw the grievance and took the management representative aside and we worked out a letter of resignation stating that the Polish guy was resigning from the company for personal reasons.

When you think about it, even before Jimmy did, I had the first taste of how it was going to be under Fitz. I was the first one who got to feel how Jimmy got to feel when Fitz betrayed him later on. It was a minor thing compared to what he did to Jimmy, but I'm still not happy with it. I lost my own election and I lost my local on account of being in jail. And I was sitting in jail for four months on account of Fitz. After I got out of jail I was out there with no union position. I got no respect at all from the man and he was the one who put me in the thing in the first place. I was trying to take care of a job for him, risking my life in a fire fight, getting indicted, and all he did for me was to hang up on me.

chapter twenty-two

Pacing in His Cage

From the brochure "Questions and Answers about Federal Correctional Institutions":

"Question 41: How can I take care of my business while in confinement?"

"Answer: You must appoint someone else to run your business while you are confined."

Jimmy Hoffa lived by his own rules, and he would soon develop his own answer for Question 41.

The Federal Correctional Institution at Lewisburg, Pennsylvania, that Jimmy Hoffa entered on March 7, 1967, was amusingly depicted in the movie *Goodfellas* as a place where Italian mobsters were able to live comfortable lives with their own cooking facilities, an endless supply of good food, good wine, and fine cigars. Their battle cry was "Let's eat." Surely, in a place like that, Jimmy Hoffa would have little trouble learning the ropes and figuring out the most efficient way to pull the strings that extended from the rolling farmland of central Pennsylvania to his puppet regime and the new general vice president, Frank Fitzsimmons, as well as strings that extended beyond Fitzsimmons to Hoffa's former hand-picked staff at "the marble palace," Teamsters headquarters in Washington, D.C.

The prison rules allowed for a total of three hours of visitation a month from a list of nonlawyers. The visitation list was restricted to family members. Inmates were permitted

no phone privileges in those days. Letters were permitted to
be written to only seven people from a list of relatives and
lawyers. All letters in and out were screened. No union officer
was permitted to visit or write to Jimmy Hoffa. There was
no limitation on visitation from lawyers working on active
cases. Hoffa's son was a lawyer for the union and so was not
restricted to the family member list; he could see his father as
often as once a week.

Although the appeals on the jury-tampering case had been
exhausted, the appeals on the Chicago case were still pending
when Jimmy Hoffa first walked into Lewisburg for delousing,
photographing, fingerprinting, and outfitting in blue denim.
In addition, Hoffa would be eligible for a parole hearing in
two and a half years — in November 1969. All of this legal
activity meant that Hoffa could receive visitations from a
number of lawyers. Frank Ragano was among those lawyers
who visited Hoffa, consulted on the issues, and carried
messages back to both the union and mob figures. Attorney
Morris Shenker represented Hoffa on the machinations
of his parole strategy and on another matter: the delicate
maneuvers involved in securing a presidential pardon, from
what would later be revealed as the corrupt administration of
President Richard M. Nixon. Bill Bufalino regularly visited
Hoffa in his role of lawyer and adviser.

The tight restrictions on visitation hamstrung those
inmates without the financial resources, battery of lawyers,
or power of a Jimmy Hoffa. Many young men did not have
relatives who could afford to make the trip to Pennsylvania.
They could not use up their three hours of allotted visitation.
Jimmy Hoffa would arrange for "job interviews" for such
men with Frank Sheeran. The young inmate would meet with
Frank Sheeran in the dining hall that served as the visitation
room. They would sit at a table next to Jimmy Hoffa, who
would be consulting with one of his many lawyers.

I'd pull on my shirt and the kid would know that was a signal
to go to the buck house so Jimmy and I could get a little

business done. The guard would look the other way. They made out all right at Christmas, those guards. I think every day was Christmas for some of them in the old days. I saw it tighten up quite a bit over the years when I went to school in the eighties and nineties. I think it was on account of the publicity and the new type of inmate, especially the drug dealers like the Jamaicans and those Cubans that Castro had kicked out.

There was one kid named Gary that Jimmy asked me to help get a job in construction. If they had a job waiting for them they had a good chance at making parole. Gary should have stayed in. When he got out somebody put a whack on him. He was a friend of Tommy Barker, the one that claimed later on when I had my trial in 1980 that I told him to whack a guy named Fred Gawronski for spilling a bottle of wine on me at a bar in Delaware. Joey McGreal was in there with Jimmy for a while toward the end. Joey had settled down a lot and was good company. Tony Pro was already in waiting for Jimmy. They were still very close when Jimmy came into Lewisburg. Charlie Allen, the rat, was in there for bank robbery. His real name was Charlie Palermo, but he changed it to Charlie Allen. He was "Blinky" Palermo's nephew. Blinky used to control boxing in America.

Charlie Allen is the one the FBI wired and used to set me up in the late seventies when they were trying to get everybody on their little list for something so they could squeeze us for information on Jimmy's disappearance. They made a deal with Allen to get me even though they knew he was a baby-rapist and a sodomizer of his own stepdaughter from the time she was five, and they hid that information from my attorney and me. Charlie Allen's in jail in Louisiana for that one. Can you imagine how much they wanted me when you think of who they used to get me?

At my 1980 trial, my 1981 trial, and my 1982 trial Charlie Allen claimed he was Jimmy's bodyguard in jail and that he got cut on the cheek defending Jimmy from a rape. That would have made Jimmy laugh if he was listening to the trial in heaven. Allen got cut when he got caught trying to steal some candy bars from a black guy's candy stash. As far as who took care of who, it was the other way around. Jimmy looked out for Charlie Allen. He's one of those that Jimmy felt sorry for and asked me to help get a job so he could make parole. I even got him a job. I let him hang around with me. I let him drive me places. Then later on I put him on the payroll at Local 326 as an organizer. I used him as a barking dog, but I'm the one he turned on when they caught him again for making methamphetamine. They let him slide on that, but he couldn't get out from under the baby rape because it wasn't federal.

For $3 you could join the inmates for lunch. Wednesday lunch was spaghetti and meatballs. Jimmy loved spaghetti and meatballs. I would give Jimmy my meatballs for a treat. Jimmy loved ice cream, too. Sometimes it would be just a social visit between us. We wouldn't even have business. One time he got on me about all the watermelon Bill Isabel and I used to eat at the suite in the Edgewater in Chicago. Jimmy didn't know we had spiked the watermelon with two quarts of rum and plugged it back up. He learned about that trick in Lewisburg from some of the people from Brooklyn with Tony Pro who were doing it.

There was a lot happening on the outside on his appeals and all for Jimmy to talk to me about. I made some drops to Attorney General John Mitchell after Jimmy got out, too, but while he was in Lewisburg there was money going down to Mitchell for Jimmy to get parole or a pardon. The people would take care of the money part from the Vegas skim or from Jimmy's own money. Russell was very big in Vegas, places like Caesar's and the Desert Inn. When Jimmy went in everybody was trying to help him get out — Russ, Fitz, Carlos, Santo, all of them. Jimmy complained that maybe Fitz was dragging his heels, but in the beginning he didn't suspect Fitz of betrayal, just maybe not being aggressive enough, sitting on his rear end, enjoying the job too much.

Right after Jimmy went in somebody sent a message to Allen Dorfman. He was pulling out of his driveway and some people jumped off and fired shotguns into the body of his Cadillac. That's not the way you kiss somebody; that's a straight message job.

Dorfman had balls. He was in charge of the pension fund. Nobody was going to scare him into anything. More likely, Jimmy and I thought it was mostly a message for Fitz from some people.

Everybody knew Fitz had no balls. If they fired the shotguns at Fitz's car he might overreact and run into the arms of the feds. This way, Fitz got the message through what they did to Dorfman. A lot of times when a guy is kissed, it's a message for somebody else.

After that Fitz didn't keep an eye on the pension fund and he let people get away with a lot. The loans didn't have the proper security behind them. They just didn't even bother to make the payments on a lot of them under Fitz. And why should Dorfman care anymore if Fitz wasn't going to back him up.

Later on, when I was in jail in the early eighties, I got some bad news about Allen Dorfman. Jackie Presser was head of the Teamsters and he set Dorfman up. Presser was a dry snitch for the FBI, a snitch they keep undercover. He doesn't wear a wire or testify, but he let's the feds have everything he hears and he puts out everything the feds tell him to. He put the word out that Dorfman was a rat, and that to save himself from jail Dorfman was going to cooperate with the feds. They used silencers on Dorfman in an outdoor hotel parking lot in broad daylight in Chicago. What I don't get is how Chicago fell for the idea that Dorfman was a rat. When I was in Chicago twenty years before that, everybody in Chicago knew Presser was a rat. I guess it was a case of when in doubt have no doubt. But it was a bad hit. I'm not saying Chicago did the hit, but it could not have been done in Chicago without Chicago's approval. Allen Dorfman lived his life a certain way and he was no rat. He was very loyal to Jimmy.

Allen Dorfman's attorney was quoted as saying about the ex-Marine combat veteran: "The idea that he would capitulate or throw in the towel is anathema, impossible." The U.S.

attorney in charge of the pending cases against Dorfman confirmed that "Dorfman was not cooperating with us at all."

In school Jimmy talked a lot about Partin. Frank Ragano was supposed to be getting an affidavit from Partin that the government set Jimmy up. There was a D.A. in New Orleans who arrested Partin, and they were supposed to get that D.A. off Partin's back in exchange for the affidavit. The same D.A. arrested Walter Sheridan for bribery, and that was supposed to help Jimmy by making Sheridan look bad in the papers. All that help came from Russell's and Jimmy's good friend, Carlos Marcello, the boss in New Orleans who had the D.A.

That was the same D.A. that was arresting everybody for the JFK assassination. Sometimes a friendly D.A. acts like a bird dog to flush rats out of the weeds. When the rat surfaces to cooperate with the D.A., then the people know what to do. I don't know about that D.A. I was never a party to any discussions about him. But he did arrest Partin and Sheridan during this time.

About a year after Jimmy went in, Bobby Kennedy announced that he was going to run for president. As far as I could tell that didn't affect Jimmy at all because Jimmy was already supporting Nixon from jail, getting deliveries of cash down to Mitchell and the Nixon campaign. Jimmy was just glad that Bobby was no longer the attorney general.

Everybody approved of Lyndon Johnson's attorney general, Ramsey Clark. He was the opposite of Bobby Kennedy. He didn't bother anybody. He was the one they used to call Pamsey Clark. He was against wiretaps.

A couple of months later Bobby Kennedy got it from the terrorist. I know Jimmy lost no sleep over that, but Jimmy hardly mentioned it. I think all of Jimmy's focus was on getting out. He kept up with events through all the papers that he always read, but he didn't waste his breath on what was happening on the outside unless it had something to do with getting him out. I do believe Jimmy hated jail way more than he ever hated Bobby.

After a while of spending every night after lockdown in a small cell with nothing to do but think about it, Jimmy knew in his gut he was getting double-crossed by Fitz. Then Jimmy started hating Fitz. But he couldn't let on to Fitz, because he still needed his help to get out.

The biggest problem Jimmy ended up having in jail was with Tony Pro. Pro was in for extortion. I heard it was something about a trucking company owner who was having problems with his men slowing down on the job. The guy paid Pro, and the drivers went back to full speed. That kind of thing was known to happen once in a while. Only something went wrong and Pro went to jail for it.

Jimmy and Pro were sitting in the dining room one day and Pro wanted some kind of help about his pension from Jimmy, and Jimmy couldn't give it to him. It had something to do with the different charges they each had. Under the pension law you have some extra problems if you go in for extortion, but not if you go in for the things Jimmy went in for. Pro couldn't see why Jimmy was going to get his and he couldn't get his. Pro couldn't understand why Jimmy couldn't get that pension thing worked out for him. Somehow one thing led to another and Jimmy supposedly said something about "you people," like he was better than Pro. Pro said something about ripping Jimmy's "guts out." I heard the guards had to break it up. From that day to the day they both died, Jimmy hated Pro and Pro hated Jimmy more.

I never liked Pro. His brothers Sam and Nunz were good people. Whenever Pro couldn't hold office on account of some conviction or other, he'd appoint one of his brothers. Still and all, Pro was always a strong and loyal supporter of Jimmy Hoffa. Before Jimmy's jury tampering trial, Pro helped Jimmy raise a lot of green stamps for expenses. Jimmy had Pro's vote on the executive board any time he wanted it. Pro always gave speeches praising Jimmy.

Pro was with the Genovese family, and from time to time Russell was acting boss over that family, and Pro was way down lower than Russell in the thing, not even close in rank. So I guess Jimmy figured that since he had Russell with him and the two of them were so close, he didn't have to concern himself about Pro. Russell really and truly liked Jimmy a lot. It wasn't just show. It was sincere. Russell respected a man who was hard but fair, like himself. Both Jimmy and Russell's bond was their word. Once they told you something, you could count on it. Whether it was good for you or bad for you, there is no doubt you could count on it.

I wasn't there for the hollering match with Pro, but I was there when Bill Bufalino walked out on Jimmy. Bill would come regularly from Detroit to Lewisburg just so Jimmy could give him a hard time. They were talking about Partin one day at lunch and Bufalino got fed up with it. I heard him say, "No, I'm not fired. I resign." He just walked out. He never came back to jail again to see Jimmy as far as I know. Bill was still a lawyer for the union anyway under Fitz, but from now on he wasn't with Jimmy; he was with Fitz. Bill knew he could do all right without Jimmy. Bill had a jukebox local that he was president of and a lot of other businesses. Bill was very well off. Russell was the godfather to Bill's daughter.

After a while it was getting to be like Jimmy was one of those tigers you see at the Philadelphia Zoo that spends his time just pacing in his cage, all day long, back and forth, looking at the people.

Jimmy Hoffa's first application for parole was turned down in November 1969. Having defeated Hubert Humphrey in 1968, Richard M. Nixon was at that time completing his first year as president and John Mitchell was completing his first year as attorney general. At the time of his 1969 parole application, Hoffa's appeal of his Chicago conviction was still pending. As a result of the five-year Chicago sentence still hanging over Hoffa's head, the parole board denied Hoffa's application. It is unlikely that Hoffa expected to make parole the first time he applied, anyway, no matter how much influence he thought he had with the new administration.

Hoffa's next parole eligibility date was March 1971. If Hoffa were to make parole at that 1971 hearing he would be out from behind bars in time for the July 1971 Teamsters Convention in Miami Beach, where he would be a shoo-in to be reelected International president. He would no longer need to pull strings from a long distance away. Moreover, he would be in power under favorable circumstances, the likes of which he had never before had. Hoffa easily would win a five-year term in 1971, and Nixon easily would be reelected to a four-year term in 1972. Jimmy Hoffa would control the most powerful labor union in the nation while having an ally in the White House, an ally whose attorney general, instead of hounding him, accepted his cash. An ally with whom he could do business and get a lot accomplished for his union and his comrades.

Very early in 1971 Frank Fitzsimmons said that he would run for president if Jimmy Hoffa did not make parole in March. This was a direct challenge to Jimmy Hoffa, because Hoffa had every right to run for president from the jailhouse. The crimes for which he had been convicted did not fit the list of the Landrum-Griffith Act of offenses that disqualified a convict from holding office for five years. As long as Hoffa held a union office of some kind at the time of the election he could run for president. While in jail Hoffa still held several union offices, including president of the International itself. After his announcement Fitzsimmons sought a conditional endorsement from the executive board at its January 1971 meeting in Palm Springs, California. Fitzsimmons wanted a vote of approval for his candidacy for president if Hoffa did not get his parole. The executive board refused to endorse Fitzsimmons even conditionally.

At Hoffa's March 1971 parole board hearing he was represented by his lawyer-son James P. Hoffa and by attorney Morris Shenker. Hoffa had a deposition from Partin delivered to his attorneys. It was hot off the press, as Partin had just given it. This is the "twenty-nine-page confession" Hoffa spoke about in his autobiography. Hoffa's legal team, however, overruled Hoffa and decided not to use it. One can only assume that his lawyers understood that all parole boards everywhere look with disfavor on any inmate who protests his innocence. As far as a parole board is concerned, the matter of guilt has already been established by a jury, and an inmate who continues to protest his innocence is one who has not been rehabilitated by his prison experience and who is not exhibiting remorse for his misdeeds. Such a parole applicant is viewed as incorrigible. Perhaps Hoffa's own son had a better chance of making Hoffa accept sound legal advice than other lawyers had been able to.

In any event, Hoffa lost before the parole board and was told he could not reapply until June 1972. Hoffa would miss the July 1971 Teamsters Convention. If he ran, he would have to run from prison.

During the hearing the parole board appeared to focus negatively on the fact that Hoffa was still president of the Teamsters. Under their rules, a request for a rehearing based on new evidence could be made within ninety days. That left Hoffa with a very slight glimmer of hope that he might still have sufficient time to get paroled before the July convention. But how would Hoffa come up with new evidence? In the end would he have to run from jail? Or would he have to settle for the 1976 International Convention?

On April 7 Hoffa went on an unescorted four-day furlough to spend Easter with his wife, Jo, who was recovering at the University of California Medical Center in San Francisco from a sudden heart attack. Hoffa stayed at the San Francisco Hilton, and in defiance of the rules of his four-day furlough held important meetings with Frank Fitzsimmons and other Teamsters officials and advisers, including his Local 299 stalwart and Strawberry Boy pal, Bobby Holmes. All that Hoffa did in the months that followed these San Francisco meetings had to have reflected what went on there.

chapter twenty-three

Nothing Comes Cheap

In May I got a call from John Francis that he had a present all wrapped up to bring to the party. John had become Russell's driver. He was very good people. John and I became very close. John was my driver on a number of matters I took care of for Russell. John was very reliable. He had good timing. On certain matters you might get dropped off on a corner and go into a bar, and John would drive once around the block. You'd go to the bathroom and on the way out you'd kiss a certain party in the bar, and you'd come back out and there would be John.

John's nickname was The Redhead. He was from Ireland. He had done hits over there with the IRA. John lived in a suburb of New York. The Redhead knew a lot of the Westies. They were a gang of Irish cowboys from the Hell's Kitchen section on the west side of New York. Drugs got that outfit. And unnecessary violence. Those two go hand in hand. John had something to do with drugs once in a while just to pick up some money, but he kept it from Russell or he never would have been Russell's driver.

I don't know who recommended John to Russell in the first place. It had to be somebody out of New York. Russell had a lot of business in New York. For twenty-five years Russell kept a three-bedroom suite at the Consulate Hotel, and I would say he went to New York three times a week. He'd cook for us in his suite. I can hear him giving it to me now: "You shanty,

Irishman, what do you know about cooking?" A lot of times he went to New York on jewelry business with the cat burglars. Russell used to carry around one of those jeweler's lenses that he would use on his good eye. But Russell had all kinds of other businesses going on in New York. He had garment businesses like making parts for dresses and dresses themselves, trucking business, union deals, restaurants, you name it. His main hangout was the Vesuvio Restaurant on Forty-eighth Street in the theater district. Russ owned a silent piece of that and a piece of Johnny's Restaurant across the street.

When I got the call from John Francis in May that he had a present for the party, I drove up to the Branding Iron Restaurant at 7600 Roosevelt Boulevard. John handed me a black suitcase. It must have weighed a hundred pounds. I'm not sure if this half-million I was taking down was Jimmy's money he got from Allen Dorfman on the pension fund. It could have been points Dorfman was collecting for Jimmy while Jimmy was in school and putting aside for him on pension fund loans. Maybe the money came from Russ and Carlos and them out of the Vegas skim. That was not my business.

I put the bag in the backseat of my big Lincoln. I already had put the seventy-five-gallon gas tank in the trunk, so that if the Feds followed me they'd have to stop for gas and I could just hit a switch and go to the extra tank and keep on cruising.

I cruised on down to the Washington Hilton. It's about 150 miles to Washington from Philly, a straight shot through Delaware and Maryland on I-95. I always had a CB radio going to warn me about Smokies that had radar set up. But with a package this size I didn't bother with the speeding.

I got down there and parked and carried my own bag into the lobby. I didn't need a bellhop for this. I sat in an easy chair they had in the lobby. After a little while John Mitchell walked in through the front door. He looked around and saw me sitting and sat down in the next chair over. He talked about the weather and asked me how the drive was. It was all chitchat so the thing wouldn't look so obvious. He asked me if I was in the union and I told him I was president of Local

326 in Wilmington. (See, by that time I had won the 1970 election and got my local back. Having time to campaign and not being in jail I won by a three-to-one margin.) He asked me where in Wilmington and I told him our office was down by the train station. He wished me a safe drive back to the union hall. Then he said, "Nothing comes cheap."

He stood up holding the suitcase. I said to him, "Don't you want to go somewhere and count it?" He said, "If I had to count it, they wouldn't have sent you." He knew his business, that man.

I heard Mitchell was putting pressure on Partin, too. The Department of Justice was jamming Partin up on stuff. But I think this money was for the parole or the pardon, not Partin. Technically, the half a big one was for Nixon's reelection.

What Jimmy didn't know at that time, and what came out later, was that Sally Bugs brought a half a big one down from Tony Pro on behalf of Fitz. Russ didn't even know about that. It was to get Jimmy out, too, only on a parole that had a restriction on it that would keep Jimmy from running for union office until his entire prison sentence expired in March 1980.

If he had to wait to run until 1980 Jimmy would have been away from running the union for thirteen years. In thirteen years Jimmy's old supporters would have been replaced and by then he'd be sixty-seven anyway. Back then, the rank and file didn't vote for International president or any of the other officers. The voting was done by the delegates to the convention in an open ballot. The delegates listened to their rank and file back home in their locals, but they listened mostly to Jimmy or whoever had put them in their positions. By 1980 Fitz could have eliminated a lot of Jimmy's delegates and a lot of them would have retired anyway and Fitz would have put his own supporters in, like his son Richard Fitzsimmons, who was still with 299 in Detroit. Today the rank and file votes the officers in directly by secret ballot.

So Mitchell and Nixon were getting both ends on the thing.

On May 28, 1971, Audie Murphy was killed in a small plane crash while viewing the location of a business deal he was involved in with the Hoffa forces. Whatever help Jimmy Hoffa expected from Audie Murphy in dealing with Ed Partin went down with Murphy's plane.

Six days after Murphy's crash and a couple of weeks after Mitchell told Frank Sheeran that "nothing comes cheap," Frank Fitzsimmons, accompanied by young James P. Hoffa, held a press conference at the Playboy Plaza Hotel in Miami Beach. Fitzsimmons announced that he had received a letter from Jimmy Hoffa stating that Jimmy was not a candidate for reelection and that Jimmy was endorsing his old friend from Local 299 in Detroit, the general vice president, Frank Fitzsimmons, for the office of president of the International Brotherhood of Teamsters.

Two weeks later on June 21, 1971, Fitzsimmons addressed the quarterly meeting of the executive board in Miami. Reporters were not permitted in the room, but strangely, Fitzsimmons had allowed newspaper photographers in. Fitzsimmons announced to the board that Jimmy Hoffa had resigned as president and had appointed him acting president until the upcoming convention. At that moment President Richard M. Nixon walked into the room and sat in a seat next to Fitzsimmons. The photographers snapped away.

Two days later, following the new game plan for dealing with the parole board, James P. Hoffa wrote the executive board a letter on June 23, 1971, telling the board that his client had resigned as president of the International Brotherhood of Teamsters, president of Local 299 in Detroit, president of Joint Council 43, president of the Michigan Conference of Teamsters, and chairman of the Central States Conference of Teamsters. Based on this new evidence, James P. Hoffa requested a rehearing before the parole board. In his letter, James P. Hoffa pointed out that his father planned to spend his retirement living on his pension and doing some lecturing and teaching.

A preliminary hearing was held before the parole board on July 7, 1971. Based on the "new evidence" contained in the letter and presented at the preliminary hearing, the parole board granted a full rehearing to be held on August 20, 1971.

When I got to the July 1971 convention in Miami Beach I saw a nice big picture of Jimmy on the wall outside the convention center. I went inside and there was not a single picture of Jimmy anywhere to be found. It was like they do it in Russia. They take a guy and erase him. I grabbed a couple of guys and went back outside and took Jimmy's picture down and brought it in and hung it inside. I hung it in as prominent a place as the picture of Fitz. What I wanted to do was to take Fitz's picture down and put it outside and put Jimmy's picture in the spot where Fitz had put his own picture, but you couldn't do that. The hostilities were in the undercurrent stage. They hadn't broken out in public yet and I wouldn't do anything like that without Jimmy's say-so.

Jimmy's wife, Jo, spoke at that convention in July 1971. She gave everybody Jimmy's best wishes and the place went wild. She got a standing ovation. That was a huge Hoffa crowd. Fitz was lucky he didn't get booed.

The FBI tried to get into that convention as maintenance men, but I spotted them and turned them away. You knew you were right when they never returned with their boss to prove they were really maintenance.

I don't know what I was thinking back then, but I didn't know until now that Jimmy was still president when he went in back in 1967. I must have misunderstood what was going on. I thought Jimmy gave up the job and put Fitz in the job as acting president until he got out. I thought Fitz had both jobs — the vice president and the president. Fitz certainly acted like he was the president all that time whenever I had any dealings with the man. I thought he was the president when he sent me to Spring Garden Street on that shootout. Isn't that something, the things you miss when you have a lot of maneuvering going on.

On August 19, 1971, the day before Jimmy Hoffa's rehearing before the parole board, Frank Fitzsimmons held a press conference and praised President Nixon's economic package as good for the country and good for labor. All the other labor union leaders in the nation who had taken a position, especially AFL-CIO president George Meany, had already come out strongly against Nixon's economic plans.

The next day, August 20, 1971, James P. Hoffa and his client did not get the reception from the parole board that they had been led to believe they would get. Jimmy Hoffa's resignations from his union offices were greeted with a yawn. James P. Hoffa was questioned about the job he held with the International Brotherhood of Teamsters, as if his job had any relevance to Jimmy Hoffa's plans for living if paroled. Next, James P. Hoffa was probed about his mother's job with the International Brotherhood of Teamsters' political action committee DRIVE (Democratic Republican Independent Voter Education). When the recently retired Jimmy Hoffa settled his future monthly pension payments for present value, he received a lump sum of $1.7 million. As that figure was certain to irk Sally Bugs's boss Tony Pro in view of Pro's jailhouse request of Hoffa for help on his pension, the size of Jimmy's lump sum irked the parole board. That topic was explored by the board in hostile language and tone. Finally, Jimmy Hoffa's connections to organized crime were explored in great detail, as if somehow the board were now shocked by it, simply shocked. Despite having voted in July to grant a rehearing on the "new evidence" of Jimmy Hoffa's retirement from all of his union offices and the "new evidence" of his plans to lecture and teach, the parole board voted unanimously to turn down his request for parole. Hoffa was told he could reapply the following year, in June 1972, coincidentally the month and year of the Watergate burglary that brought down Richard Nixon and sent Attorney General John Mitchell and several other White House staff members to jail.

What were the grim possibilities that the "Get Hoffa Out of Jail Squad" were forced to face and to explore? Had Frank

Fitzsimmons orchestrated an elaborate scheme to trick Jimmy Hoffa into resigning from every single one of his many union offices so that Jimmy Hoffa would not be eligible to run for IBT president from jail in July 1971? Had Jimmy Hoffa been led to believe that if he abandoned the idea of running from jail in July 1971 he would gain his freedom from jail in August 1971? Had Hoffa been led to believe that by resigning from his union offices he would be giving the parole board and the Nixon administration a face-saving excuse for paroling him? Did a man who was famous for not compromising fall into this trap out of a desire to return to his heartsick wife and family, to whom he was devoted? Did he fall into this trap because he trusted and believed that with his freedom he could ease back into union positions a little at a time and take back the presidency at the 1976 convention — or sooner if a weak and cowardly Fitzsimmons were literally strong-armed out of office? Had Jimmy Hoffa been outsmarted by the likes of Frank Fitzsimmons for all the world to see? Nixon, Fitzsimmons, and Mitchell all seemed to be playing the same hand, and they seemed to be holding all the aces.

What was Jimmy Hoffa going to get for his money and his support of President Nixon, now that Nixon's parole board had slammed the window shut on his fingers?

At a Labor Day rally in Detroit, President Frank Fitzsimmons publicly urged his new friend President Richard M. Nixon to pardon Jimmy Hoffa.

On December 16, 1971, with no fanfare and bypassing all the normal channels, attorney Morris Shenker filed a petition for a pardon with the White House. Instead of the petition going through the Department of Justice for a response, and for input from the prosecutors and the FBI, and going to the two sentencing judges for their input as the procedures in effect for years required, the petition was marked "approved" by Attorney General John Mitchell.

I went up to Lewisburg to see Jimmy just before Christmas. Morrie Shenker was there with the pardon papers that

Nixon was going to sign. I was at another table with a kid.
A guard looked the other way and they passed the papers
to me as a matter of courtesy, and I read the papers. It
said that Jimmy could get out with his good time and all
in November 1975, but Nixon was letting him out now. It
didn't say one word about Jimmy not being able to run for
office until 1980. I can assure you that I would have picked
that up right away. Jimmy was already planning to run in
1976. I might not have a lot of education, but I had been
reading union contracts and legal documents for a living
for many years. I had read hundreds of documents that
were far more complicated than that pardon. All it said was
that Jimmy was getting out, finally. We were happy people
in that lunchroom, and after a lot of double-crossing by
Partin and Fitzsimmons and Nixon and Mitchell, Jimmy
was finally getting what he paid for. He was getting out for
Christmas. The only thing we were doing was talking about
Jimmy taking a vacation in Florida for a few months to get
squared away before he went back into action. There was no
controversy in Lewisburg that day.

The controversy started when Jimmy got out and went
to Detroit and they handed him the final papers signed by
Nixon and we all got a good lesson when we saw in plain
English that the final double-cross was in. Jimmy couldn't
run until 1980. He would miss the 1976 election. If he had
stayed in and did all his time he'd have been out in 1975
in plenty of time for the 1976 convention. This was before
Watergate, so who knew the thieves we were dealing with. "

An Executive Grant of Clemency reducing Hoffa's sentence
from thirteen years to six and a half years was signed by
Richard Nixon in record time on December 23, 1971. With
his good-time credit the reduction to six and a half years
guaranteed Hoffa's immediate release. That same day Hoffa
walked out of the penitentiary at Lewisburg, Pennsylvania,
and flew to his married daughter Barbara's home in St. Louis
to be with his family for Christmas. From there he returned

to his home in Detroit to register with the federal parole and probation office, as Hoffa still would be "on paper," that is, on parole, until the full six and a half years was up in March 1973. From Detroit Hoffa would be heading to Florida for a three-month respite. While in Detroit, Hoffa and his supporters, including Frank Sheeran, read the following language in the pardon from Richard Nixon:

> . . . the said James R. Hoffa not engage in direct or indirect management of any labor organization prior to March 6, 1980, and if the aforesaid condition is not fulfilled this commutation will be null and void in its entirety . . .

On January 5, 1972, Jimmy Hoffa flew to Florida to his Blair House apartment in Miami Beach. He was greeted at the airport by Frank Ragano as a sign of respect from Santo Trafficante and Carlos Marcello, who could not show their faces for many reasons. Perhaps the most important reason was that a federal parolee is not permitted to be in the company of organized crime figures or convicted felons. On February 12, 1972, on ABC's *Issues and Answers,* Jimmy Hoffa said that he personally would be supporting Richard Nixon in 1972. Until his parole period was over in March 1973, he was going to go along to get along. Jimmy Hoffa had had enough experience by now that he did not trust that Richard Nixon's administration would play fair with his parole if he provoked them by going after Fitzsimmons. Jimmy Hoffa was not going to provoke them.

On July 17, 1972, a month after the Watergate burglary, Frank Fitzsimmons's executive board formally endorsed President Richard M. Nixon for reelection in November by a vote of 19 to 1. The one vote belonged to Harold Gibbons, the vice president who had enraged Hoffa by flying the flag at half-staff in honor of the fallen President John F. Kennedy. Mrs. Patricia Fitzsimmons, Frank's wife, was appointed by Nixon to serve on the Arts Committee of the Kennedy Center for the Performing Arts.

When he was ready, Jimmy Hoffa's plan of attack would be centered on a constitutional challenge to the condition to his pardon. His civil-rights attorneys would argue that the president exceeded his authority by adding a condition to the pardon. Under the Constitution a president has the power to pardon or not pardon, but he has no power, express or implied, to pardon in such a way that his pardon could later be rescinded and the recipient returned to jail. A conditional pardon would give a president more power than the Founding Fathers intended he have.

Furthermore, this particular restriction added a punishment of not being allowed to manage a union. Hoffa had had no such restriction even while in jail. Although the rules of the jail made it difficult to do, it was not forbidden. This new punishment had not been given to Hoffa at the time of his two sentencings, and the president did not have the power to increase a punishment handed down by a sentencing judge.

In addition, this condition violated Hoffa's First Amendment right to freedom of speech and of assembly by putting off-limits a valid and legitimate forum for the exercise of these freedoms.

However, because he hated jail and feared that the Nixon administration would more closely monitor his parole if he filed such a lawsuit, Hoffa played 'possum until his parole expired and he went "off paper" in March 1973. For the time being Fitzsimmons could relax.

A lot of allegations and finger-pointing were to come out of the Nixon White House on the topic of how the restriction ended up in the pardon. John Dean, White House counsel and Watergate witness against his confederates, testified that it had been his idea to stick the restriction language in at the last minute. He testified that he was merely being a good lawyer, because when Mitchell asked him to prepare the papers Mitchell casually mentioned that Hoffa had orally agreed to stay out of union activity until 1980.

The other White House counsel and future Watergate jailbird to be suspected of complicity in the restriction language caper was attorney Charles Colson, special counsel to the president, and the man in charge of the infamous Nixon enemy list. John Dean testified that Colson asked him to initiate an IRS investigation into the finances of Harold Gibbons, the only member of the Teamsters executive board not to vote to endorse Nixon for reelection. A memo from Colson to Dean was produced asking for the audit and calling Gibbons an "all-out enemy." Jimmy Hoffa testified in a deposition, "I blame one man [for the restriction on my pardon] . . . Charles Colson." Colson took the Fifth on the topic during the Watergate hearings, although he did admit discussing the pardon with Fitzsimmons before it was granted. It is hard to imagine that the two men did not discuss something as important as the restriction.

Was the restriction a result of Dean being a good lawyer? Was it Colson and Mitchell ordering the language in such a way that Dean thought it was his own idea to add it? If the topic of a restriction were phrased the right way by his superior, any prudent young lawyer would have added the language on his own. John Mitchell had been a Wall Street lawyer; he knew how to massage an associate.

Shortly after Colson resigned from the White House, and before he went to jail, he returned to private practice. Frank Fitzsimmons took the lucrative IBT legal contract away from Edward Bennett Williams and gave it to Charles Colson, thereby ensuring Colson of a $100,000-a-year retainer, minimum.

Since those heady days, Charles Colson had changed his life and founded a Christian organization that sponsors prison visits and encourages the inmates to follow a spiritual path to redemption. While at Delaware's largest prison to interview Frank Sheeran or some other client I saw a repentant and dignified Charles Colson leaving the prison after visiting with the inmates, Bible in hand.

Jimmy Hoffa, meanwhile, bided his time. Hoffa was going to take no chance that he ever would be sent back to prison. As he wrote in his autobiography, "I spent fifty-eight months in Lewisburg, and I can tell you this on a stack of Bibles:

prisons are archaic, brutal, unregenerative, overcrowded hell holes where the inmates are treated like animals with absolutely not one humane thought given to what they are going to do once they are released. You're like an animal in a cage and you're treated like one."

chapter twenty-four

He Needed a Favor and That Was That

During that first year when he got out, Jimmy had to get permission to go anywhere. He was not allowed to go to union conferences, but he'd get permission to go to California or wherever for some other reason. He'd stay in the same hotel as all the other guys, and he'd run into them in the lobby. I guess you might say Jimmy was lecturing and teaching.

Jimmy was doing a lot of under-the-table campaigning, not that he had to. He was doing a lot of stuff on the telephone. It was more like keeping everybody in line and letting them know he was coming back so they didn't get tempted to go over to Fitz.

I flew down to Florida to see Jimmy for a couple of days at his condominium. I called him from the airport while I was waiting for my rental car. He told me Jo wasn't down there with him and that I should pick up some chili dogs from a Lums along the way so we could have a treat.

After we ate our dogs, we talked about John Mitchell resigning as attorney general to run Nixon's reelection campaign. With that CREEP [Committee to Reelect the President] angle going for them, those boys were going to have a license to print money.

Jimmy told me he was going to get even with Fitz and Tony Pro for that restriction. He said he was definitely coming back. He was already lining up a lawsuit against the restriction, and I told Jimmy I wanted to be a party to the lawsuit. I told him that John McCullough with the roofer's union and some other people in Philly were putting together a testimonial dinner for me. I asked him if he'd be the featured speaker. Jimmy asked me to get them to hold off on the testimonial until he was off paper and then he'd be honored to speak.

At this time Jimmy assumed that he was very strong with the alleged mob. He had Russ, Carlos, Santo, Giancana, Chicago, and Detroit. While he was in Lewisburg he got close with Carmine "The Cigar" Galante, from Queens, the boss of the Bonnano crime family. Galante was very rough. He took no prisoners.

Jimmy thought the only problem he had with their culture was with Tony Pro on account of their beef in school. He figured Pro was supporting Fitz so Fitz would help Pro get his lump-sum settlement with the pension fund and get his mil. Speaking mostly about Pro and Fitz, Jimmy said, "They will pay." Jimmy told me he was going to send a message to Fitz. Jimmy told me he was going to have Pro taken care of. He didn't specify, but I assume that taking care of Pro would be Fitz's message.

"Something has to be done about Pro," he said.

"You get the go ahead and I'll do his house," I said. "I got a good man who can drive me. The Redhead."

"I'll be the driver," Jimmy said. "I want him to know it was me."

When he said he'd be the driver, he took the serious part out of the subject. After he said that, I thought he was puffing, just letting off steam. You don't use a driver that's got a face as well known as Milton Berle's.

The Redhead already had proved himself as a stand-up guy when it came to driving. A little while before I sat down with Jimmy in Florida that spring of 1972 and ate chili dogs, The Redhead drove me on a matter.

Late one night I got a call from Russ to get my little brother and go up to see The Redhead. The little brother was a gun. For something like this I'd have two little brothers. I'd have one in my waistband and a backup piece in my ankle holster. You'd use something like a .32 and a .38 revolver because you wanted more stopping power than you could get with a .22. You certainly didn't want a silencer, which mostly only goes with a .22 to whack a guy you don't want to annoy. You wanted to do some noisy stray shooting all over the place to send the witnesses for cover. But not the kind of noise that a .45 makes, which you could hear in a patrol car blocks away. So you wouldn't use a couple of .45s, even though a .45 has first-class stopping power. Besides, a .45 is not accurate beyond twenty-five feet.

When I hung up the phone and got in my car I didn't know who Russ had in mind, but he needed a favor and that was that. They don't give you much advance notice. They have people that follow a guy. They have people that call in tips. They have people that tap his phone, and they figure out when he's likely to be on the street in a vulnerable situation. They don't want a lot of bodies around between the guy and the street.

A couple of days before the July convention in 1971, where I put Jimmy's picture inside the convention center, Crazy Joey Gallo got a nut from Harlem to kiss the Colombo family boss, Joe Colombo. This matter was done during an Italian-American Civil Rights League rally at Columbus Circle, and poor Joe Colombo lingered in a coma for several years. On top of everything else, Joe Colombo was hit in front of his own family and his own relatives. Handling the matter that way is something that violates protocol. No doubt Gallo had approval to kiss a boss like Colombo, but not that way, in front of his family. I guess that's why they called the man Crazy Joey.

As I understand it, the Colombo thing got sanctioned because Joe Colombo was putting too much attention on the alleged mob by all these rallies and the publicity they brought, and he wouldn't listen to anybody and stop doing them. So he had to go. If Russell had been on the commission I am most certain he would have voted against it. Russell had his own chapter of Colombo's Italian American Civil Rights

League in upstate Pennsylvania. They gave me the man of the year award. I got the plaque up in my room.

Now along comes the man who did a lousy job of kissing Colombo, and now he's running around in New York with all the big shots in show business. He's getting himself in the papers all the time. He'd be out with this movie star or that writer or going to a play with the New York nightlife crowd, and the photographers would be having a field day. Crazy Joey was drawing big-time attention and publicity. That's what they didn't need. He was doing worse things as far as publicity than Joe Colombo ever did. Colombo liked attention and Gallo liked attention even more than Colombo. When you look past all of that, I heard he was shaking down a restaurant in Little Italy so he could afford the lifestyle of the rich and famous that he was running around with, like he was Errol Flynn. Messing around with Little Italy was definitely out.

John Francis, The Redhead, had a stack of pictures of Crazy Joey Gallo from the New York newspapers. I had never met the man, but now I would know what he looked like. John had a diagram of Umberto's Clam House, including the corner door, the Mulberry Street door, and the men's room. The place was owned by a very prominent boss who had his own brother running it. It's moved since those days, but it's still in Little Italy.

Gallo was out on the town for his birthday, and somehow whoever wanted this done had a good idea he was going to end up his night at Umberto's, and they had a good idea where he was going to be sitting — off to the left when you walk in from the Mulberry Street door. Maybe some people had invited him to end up his night there. It was the only joint open at that time of the early morning anyway.

The planning was well done, but it required a good shooter with accuracy. Crazy Joey Gallo would be there with his bodyguard and some women relatives, including his new wife and his sister. Shooting Gallo is one thing. Shooting women is another thing. So you needed very good accuracy, because you wouldn't get closer than about fifteen to twenty feet, and you wouldn't want to hit any women in his party.

There was no way you could get any closer than fifteen feet to the man, or the bodyguard would have his piece in his hand. Gallo had to be suspicious somebody was looking for him. He knew he'd stepped on people's toes and he knew the people he was dealing with. Gallo had to be on his own toes. But he personally wouldn't be carrying a piece. He was a convicted felon and he would never take that chance. New York had a tough gun law, the Sullivan Law. You wouldn't expect any of the women to be holding a piece for him in their purse because these women weren't dates. These were family relatives. There wouldn't be anybody sitting nonchalant at another table looking out for him, or John Francis would have been told that there was another man that was traveling close in the party that night. That means the only one that most likely had a piece on him was the bodyguard. You'd want to take him out first. You had no reason to mortally wound him, so you'd look to shoot him in the back or the seat of his pants and avoid an artery in the neck or his heart. You just wanted to disable him. You most definitely needed a good shooter with some skill here in this matter. And you had to go in alone or you'd have a Wild West shoot-out. And to go in alone, you couldn't use just anybody.

I didn't look threatening or familiar in any way. I looked like just a broken down truck driver with a cap on coming in to use the bathroom, which was not far from the door. I have very fair skin. I don't look like a Mafia shooter.

Another aspect is that you don't do a hit on a man in front of his family. But the thing is, that's the way Gallo did it to Colombo. Right there in front of his family; they turned the man into a vegetable. So that's the way it was going to be for Crazy Joey. He was a fresh kid.

This was before cell phones, so once we left for the thing everything could change by the time we got there. The place could be crowded or he could have left. But he was out celebrating his birthday, drinking, and getting careless. Fighters, when they're drinking, their skills get diminished. And from what I understand, Gallo had a lot of heart. He could scrap. No doubt people were buying him drinks to make sure he stayed put. Then, when the people figured we'd be getting there soon, they would have called it a night and slipped out. Meanwhile, he would have champagne and drinks lined up for him to finish and whatever food he had.

Crazy Joey Gallo had to feel somewhat safe and comfortable in Little Italy. You're not supposed to do any hits in restaurants in Little Italy because a lot of the people are silent partners in the restaurants, under the table. This particular Italian seafood restaurant was outright owned by very important people and it had just opened. And it's bad for the tourist business in Little Italy if people think it's unsafe to go there. Plus tourists might not know how to be good witnesses, and they might not have sense enough to tell the cops that there were eight midgets about three feet tall and they all had masks on.

Anyway, the people had rules, but they were always a little bit ahead of their own rules. Let's say they had the power to waive their rules. They would consider doing a hit in a Little Italy restaurant if they had to. And this was very close to after hours, anyway. By law the bars close at four most nights in New York, and this was either after hours or pretty close to it, so there would not be many tourists from Idaho to worry about. Gallo would not have been an easy man to get to at any other time of day, because everywhere he went at a normal hour there could be newspaper photographers nearby on the prowl angling to get a good picture. Maybe that's why the man went for all that celebrity publicity. It gave him safety. The photographers were better than bodyguards.

John Francis dropped me at Umberto's Clam House on the corner of Mulberry Street and Hester Street in Little Italy. The way something like this worked is John would drop me off. While I went to the bathroom the Redhead would circle around the block, and I'd come out just when he was back. If I wasn't there he'd wait a couple of minutes, but if I didn't come out I'd be on my own. If he ever turned on me, all that John could ever say about the matter is that he dropped me off to go to the bathroom. The Redhead wouldn't see whatever went on inside. He only knew up to a point.

Sometimes you actually would go to the bathroom first as long as you didn't have to pass the person to get there. It gives you a chance to make sure nobody's tailing you. It gives you a chance to look the thing over. It gives you a chance to make sure there's nobody in the bathroom you have to be concerned about. It also gives you a chance to go to the bathroom. You don't want to have to take a leak if you're trying to outrun a couple of cop cars.

But in a thing like this with witnesses right there at the table, you might take a chance on nobody being in the bathroom. You might want to be able to count on the witnesses at the table not seeing anything if it went fast enough without a lot of procrastination. You might just head in the direction of the bathroom and if things looked right you might just go to work. The bartender and the waitresses in a place like this would already know enough not to see anything or they wouldn't be working for these owners. At this hour, the tourists from Idaho would all be in bed.

Anyway, all John could say was that I was going to the bathroom. If you're taking care of a matter outdoors, right on the street, your driver has to be parked right there waiting for you, and he can see what it is. Sometimes you need him to be standing out there right on the sidewalk to dispose of the piece or to scare the witnesses, but indoors, like inside doing a house, you want to work alone. That way, at the worst, you can always claim self-defense. My whole time with the people, I never trusted anybody enough that I would take care of a matter with another person in the room. A driver only knows as much as he knows, and that's good for everybody, including the driver himself. A guy's facing the electric chair and he's liable to break down and weaken. If you do it yourself you can only rat on yourself.

There were some alleged mob figures hanging out on the corner whose job it was to greet Crazy Joey and his party when they arrived. It would make Joey less suspicious if somebody walked in the door. When they saw our headlights they dispersed. Their part was done. None of these Little Italy people or Crazy Joey and his people had ever seen me before.

When we came to New York, Russell and I would be uptown at Vesuvio's or at Monte's in Brooklyn with the Genovese people.

I walked in the Mulberry Street door. I went straight ahead toward the clam bar, and I kept my back to the Mulberry Street side of the room where Gallo was. I turned and ended up facing the table with the people. I was a bit startled to see a little girl with the people, but sometimes you saw that in the fighting overseas. A split second after I turned to face the table, Crazy Joey Gallo's driver got shot from behind. The women and the little girl dove under the table. Crazy Joey swung around out of his chair and headed down toward the corner door to the shooter's right. Could be he was trying to draw fire away from the table, or could be he was just trying to save himself, but most likely he was trying to do both. It was easy to cut him off by going straight down the bar to the door and getting right behind him. He made it through Umberto's corner door to the outside. Crazy Joey got shot about three times outside of the restaurant not far from the corner door. Could be he had his piece in his car and he was going for the car. He had no chance of making it. Crazy Joey Gallo went to Australia on his birthday on a bloody city sidewalk.

The stories that are out there say that there were three shooters, but I'm not saying that. Maybe the bodyguard added two shooters to make himself look better. Maybe there were a lot of stray shots being fired from the two guns that made it seem like there was more than one shooter. I'm not putting anybody else in the thing but me.

The important thing is that John Francis was right there and he never panicked. He had his experience with the Irish mob in London. John Francis had no job or anything. He lived by his wits. And he had them.

John headed back to Yonkers the very long way, after first making sure there was no tail and after changing cars. Quite naturally, the next thing he did was to toss the pieces in the river at a spot he knew about. There's a spot like that in the Schuylkill River in Philly; if they ever send divers in they'll be able to arm a small country.

Later on, I heard some Italian guy took credit for the whack they put on Gallo. That's okay by me. Maybe the guy wanted to be a celebrity. Probably the guy turned rat or something. The rats always load up their résumés so the government treats them with more respect. The government loves a rat that gives them a chance to solve the big ones, even if the rat was just a low-life drug dealer who wouldn't know a big one from his left nut.

Now before The Redhead died of cancer it was told to me by a good source that he implicated me in fourteen hits that he claimed I did with him while he was the driver, including Crazy Joey Gallo. It was in the eighties when he was dying and I was in jail at the time. I don't know for sure; maybe John was stand-up. But if John did talk when he was delirious I don't mind that. John was dying of cancer and he was in a lot of pain and full of medication, and he didn't want to die in jail. The Redhead was in no mental state to testify to the truth against anybody. John was good people. I don't blame a man who wants to make his peace.

Russell trusted John and me both with important errands like the fresh kid. The other bosses would never want a hit like that linked to their families. That's how gang wars start. The New York families were ultra-Italian. The Commision knew that Russell had a very liberal attitude about non-Italians. Two old-time Irish guys with a lot of combat experience was a benefit Russell was able to provide for important matters like Gallo. The Commission always gave Russell anything really big. Besides, Russell was close to Colombo and supported the Italian American Civil Rights League.

It was during that time that Jimmy was doing his politics on the sidelines. He became very big in prison reform. He was sincere about it, but it also gave him a lot of opportunities to do his campaigning. One time Jimmy used Charlie Allen for something during a prison-reform fundraiser. It was a drop.

Charlie Allen got out of Lewisburg after Jimmy did and Jimmy asked me to take care of him. I already knew Allen

slightly from downtown. I first met him when I was out
of office after the DeGeorge thing. I was driving a truck
for Crown Zellerbach. Allen had done an armed robbery
and he needed to get out of Philadelphia. I drove him up
to Scranton in my truck and dropped him off with Dave
Osticco. Dave had been with Russ for many years. Dave
kept Allen in a safe house until the heat got so bad for
Allen back in Philly that he decided to turn himself in. If
I'm not mistaken that armed robbery is the one he went
to Lewisburg on. After Jimmy asked me to help him out
I used Allen to drive me places. My status was now at the
point where I had a driver and people did things for me and
showed me respect in certain ways.

The one thing Charlie Allen really did do that he testified
about at my trials was to make a delivery to John Mitchell
from Jimmy Hoffa for CREEP. Jimmy was still keeping all
the lines of communication open to Nixon. Jimmy was at a
prison-reform fundraiser in Washington. His parole officer
allowed Jimmy to travel to Washington for something like
that. Jimmy would invite people he wanted to do business
with to these affairs. Jimmy would also invite people he had
been to school with who could talk about prison life. Jimmy
made sure I had Charlie Allen there with Allen's partner,
Frank Del Piano, at this particular affair in Washington.
Jimmy had Alan Cohen, a political mover from Philadelphia,
there, and Jimmy and Alan gave Charlie Allen $40,000 in
cash to give to Mitchell for the Nixon campaign. Later on it
came out that Mitchell only handed over $17,000 of that cash
contribution to the CREEP. Mitchell palmed $23,000. Like I
said, he knew his business, that man.

Three or four years later the feds got Charlie Allen to talk
to them. In one of his very early conversations with them he
told the FBI the truth about this incident. This conversation
with the FBI was about a year before he agreed to wear a wire
to trap me. In the beginning he probably didn't realize they
wanted him to go way overboard against me on the Hoffa
disappearance. At least in the beginning he was sticking up
for me on the Hoffa case, not that somebody way down the

chain like him would have known anything about my business anyway. I had been taking pretty good care of Charlie Allen from the time he got out until the day I caught him wearing a wire in 1979.

Excerpt from an official FBI report, known as a 302, produced by the government in Frank Sheeran's trials pursuant to Federal Court Rules. (Allen's mistake as to the approximate year he made his delivery of the money to Mitchell is deleted from the excerpt and was cleared up in a subsequent 302 dated November 4, 1977):

HOFFEX

On September 22, 1977, PH 5125-OC [Charlie Allen] advised SA [Special Agent] HENRY O. HANDY, JR. and SA THOMAS L. VAN DERSLICE as follows:

When asked the last time he saw AL COHEN, source responded, "when he gave me a suitcase full of money to give to JOHN MITCHELL." Source remembers attending a testimonial dinner in Washington, D.C. at a "very big beautiful hotel" right in Washington, D.C. The purpose of this dinner was to raise funds for prison reform which was of great interest to JIMMY HOFFA. HOFFA was in attendance at this dinner. . . . During this dinner FRANK DEL PIANO, also known as TONTO, and source were approached by HOFFA and AL COHEN. HOFFA told source to "take this money to John Mitchell." At this point Cohen handed a suitcase to source who described it as a black satchel approximately two feet long and one foot wide. Source did not look inside because "you don't do that to Jimmy." He remembers, however, that the bag was very heavy. Upon receiving the satchel, source and DEL PIANO left the hotel and had entered a waiting limousine without knowing where they were going. The car took them to a "big beautiful house" outside of Washington and source was met at the door by John Mitchell. Source addressed MITCHELL and stated "JIMMY sent me." MITCHELL took the satchel, said "thank you" and closed the door. Source re-entered the limousine and returned to the hotel.

Of all the different jobs and things I did in my time, looking back my favorite part was being president of Local 326. When I was incarcerated the local made me Honorary President for Life. They didn't have to like me, but they did respect me and they respected the job I did for them. I got them their own charter through Jimmy. Before that they were run by Philadelphia. In 1979 I got them a new building that is their headquarters to this day. I took care of them day to day on their grievances and the enforcement of their contracts. We had over 3,000 members when I went to jail. Today it's more like 1,000.

Our old office before 1979 was at 109 East Front Street, a rundown neighborhood by the railroad station. That whole area is improved now. Toward the end of 1972 I got a visit at that old building from a very prominent lawyer I knew who was very big in the Democratic Party. He wanted to talk to me about the upcoming 1972 race for the United States Senate.

Earlier in the year the incumbent United States Senator Caleb Boggs had stopped by and asked me to allow him to speak to the membership. I told Boggs that he was too much against labor. He denied that he was against labor. He was a Republican and he said that since the Teamsters were supporting Nixon for reelection, he ought to be given a shot to speak to the rank and file. Boggs had been the governor and a congressman before he became senator. I don't think he ever lost an election. Everybody liked him. He was a very personable man with a good reputation, but as far as I could tell he was for the corporations in Delaware. I took it to the executive board and we decided not to invite him.

When his opponent Joe Biden asked if he could speak to the membership I took it to the executive board and got their feelings about it and nobody opposed it, so I said sure. Biden was on the County Council and he was a Democrat and the County Council had some very good people on it for labor. Joe Biden was a young kid compared to Boggs. He came and gave his spiel and he turned out to be a very good talker. He gave a really good pro-labor speech to the rank and file at that membership meeting. He took questions from the floor and handled himself like somebody many years older. He said his door would always be open to the Teamsters.

So when this prominent lawyer I knew stopped by my office a little before Election Day I was already in Biden's corner. The lawyer had another guy with him who worked inside the *Morning News* and the *Evening Journal*. They were two papers that were put out by the same company. They were basically the same paper and they were the only daily newspapers in Wilmington.

Wilmington is in the very northern part of the state and was more liberal than the southern part. Delaware, being a very small state, had maybe 600,000 people back then. Over half of them lived in the northern county and the rest in the two southern counties. The Mason-Dixon line runs right through Delaware. For years they had segregated schools in the two southern counties. They had some out-and-out segregation in the north too but mostly the north had customs that were more like a northern city like Philadelphia. At that time — and maybe even today — nearly every newspaper buyer in the state read the Wilmington newspaper.

The lawyer explained to me that Senator Boggs had put together some ads that were going to run in an advertising insert in the paper every day for the last week before the election. Boggs was claiming that Joe Biden had distorted Boggs's voting record, and the ads were going to show what Biden had said about Boggs alongside of Boggs's actual voting record or whatever. The lawyer didn't want those newspapers to be delivered. The lawyer was very good people. He was very smart. He was experienced and he knew that both sides of an election played their games. The corporations played plenty of games over the years, telling their workers who to vote for, pulling strings behind the scenes.

The guy who was there who worked on the paper said that he wanted to put up an informational picket line, but he didn't have any good people that worked with him in the newspaper he could trust to walk the line. I think they had a union already, but this line was going to be for a different union. I told him I would hire some people and put them on the picket line for him. They were people nobody would mess with.

The idea behind an informational picket line is that you're trying to organize the company, or you're claiming that the company is unfair and won't sit down and negotiate with the union, or that the company is putting pressure on the workers not to sign union cards. You might be trying to force an election to replace the union they already have, like Paul Hall and the Seafarers did against Jimmy Hoffa. Any time you see the words "Unfair to Labor" on a picket line that's an informational picket line. You can't put on your signs that you're on strike because you're not a recognized union yet, and that would violate the rules of the National Labor Relations Board.

I told my friend the lawyer and the guy he had with him that they could count on me to get it handled. I always had a lot of respect for that lawyer and I thought Biden was better for labor anyway. I told him that once we put up the picket line I would see to it that no truck driver crossed that picket line. The Teamsters would honor the informational picket line of the other union, whatever name they used.

The line went up and the newspapers were printed, but they stayed in the warehouse and they never were delivered. The newspaper company called me up and wanted my men to go back to work. I told them we're honoring the picket line. He asked me if I had anything to do with the blowing up of a railroad car that had material that was going to be used in the printing of the newspaper — whether it was paper or ink or some kind of other supplies, I don't know. But no people got hurt in the bombing. I told him we're honoring the picket line, and if he wanted to hire some guards to keep an eye on his railroad cars he should look in the Yellow Pages.

The day after the election the information picket line came down and the newspaper went back to normal and Delaware had a new United States Senator. It's hard to believe that was over thirty years ago.

There have been things written about this incident and I am always mentioned in them. They say that this maneuver is what got Senator Joe Biden elected. Especially the Republicans say that if those newspaper inserts from the Boggs side got delivered inside the newspapers it would have made Joe Biden look very bad. The Boggs ads coming as they almost did that last week there would have been no time for Biden to repair the damage. I have no way of knowing if Joe Biden knew if that picket line thing was done on purpose on his behalf. If he did know he never let on to me.

I do know that when he became the U.S. Senator, the man stuck by his word he gave to the membership. You could reach out for him and he would listen.

chapter twenty-five

That Wasn't Jimmy's Way

Jimmy Hoffa's time in a cocoon ended in March 1973, when his parole ended. He was no longer on paper. He was now free to come out as a butterfly and travel wherever he wished and say whatever was on his mind.

In April 1973 at a Washington banquet, Jimmy Hoffa ascended the podium and announced that he was going to launch a legal challenge to President Nixon's restriction on his pardon. In his announcement Jimmy Hoffa surprised no one when he asserted that he intended to challenge Frank Fitzsimmons for president of the Teamsters at the 1976 convention.

Jimmy Hoffa's timing was right in at least one other respect. Fitzsimmons would no longer have the friendship and backing of a strong president in Richard Nixon. The very month of Hoffa's announcement was an especially grim time for Nixon, as the Watergate scandal steamed ahead. As a result, Nixon had more concerns than Jimmy Hoffa. Nixon's inner circle was in the midst of a mad scramble to control the Watergate burglary. At the end of the month that Hoffa announced his planned legal challenge to the pardon restriction, Nixon's chief of staff at the White House, H. R. (Bob) Haldeman resigned. Haldeman would later go to jail. A month earlier, Charles Colson, Nixon's special counsel, had left the White House for private practice, to reap the Teamsters' legal business before going to jail. Soon the Arab oil embargo would grip the country and give Nixon still more to worry about.

Following Hoffa's announcement of the legal challenge and his plans to run in 1976, Frank Sheeran gave his friend and mentor a colorful endorsement, "I'll be a Hoffa man 'til the day they pat my face with a shovel and steal my cufflinks."

There was no way Jimmy could lose come 1976. It wasn't just a matter of the delegates being for Jimmy; the rank and file was even more for Jimmy. If that wasn't good enough, not too many people in the union had favorable things to say about Fitz. He was weak and that's why Jimmy put him in. What Jimmy didn't consider was that his weakness would be a very appealing character trait to certain people in the alleged mob.

Jimmy's supporters gave a testimonial dinner for Jimmy for his sixtieth birthday in February 1973. They held it at the Latin Casino in Cherry Hill, New Jersey, the same place mine would be held a year or so later. I was right there, front and center, and there was a strong turnout even though Fitzsimmons didn't want anybody to go. Harold Gibbons was the only member of the executive board who showed up. Like they did at mine, they had a professional photographer there. Jimmy got me to pose in a number of pictures with him, including one of us shaking hands that I prize to this day.

I visited Jimmy at Lake Orion right after he had that problem in Miami at a private meeting with Tony Pro. At that meeting in Miami Jimmy wanted to get Pro's support in 1976. Instead what he got was a threat from Pro that he'd kidnap Jimmy's granddaughter and rip Jimmy's guts out with his bare hands. In Miami after the meeting Jimmy told me he was going to ask Russell to let me do what I had to do against Tony Pro. This time he didn't say anything about being my driver on the thing. Jimmy was serious now. Jimmy and Pro hated each other and they were both capable of doing to each other what they said they were going to do. It was a matter of who got off first.

I came to Lake Orion to follow up on the Miami thing. Jimmy mentioned again that something had to be done about Pro, but he didn't tell me to talk to Russell or do anything. Then Jimmy said that Fitz wasn't a made man and he didn't need approval from anybody to take care of Fitz. Jimmy said he was already lining up a cowboy to do what he had to do against Fitz if it came to that.

I knew Jimmy had some recent contact with Charlie Allen and I said, "You're not thinking of using Allen, are you?"

Jimmy said, "Hell no. He's a bullshitter. All talk."

I said, "I know that. I'm glad you know that."

(Neither one of us mentioned Lloyd Hicks at that time, but I certainly thought about it. Lloyd Hicks was an officer with a Miami local. Hicks was a part of Rolland McMaster's faction, and McMaster was one of those who left Jimmy for Fitz. McMaster was the kind of person that Jimmy hated for desertion. When Jimmy and Pro met in Miami, Lloyd Hicks bugged the meeting room for McMaster. Hicks went out to the bar, got a few drinks in him, and went around bragging that he was going to have a tape of the meeting between Jimmy and Pro. Which would then be of interest to Fitz. Which would then make Jimmy flip out more than a little bit.

Later that night they found Hicks with I don't know how many bullets in him, but more than one gun's worth, that's for sure. It was like there were two shooters doing the man's house. If Hicks had a tape he no longer had a tape. At that particular time The Redhead and I happened to be in Miami on Jimmy's side of the matter.)

At Lake Orion Jimmy told me he was working on his lawsuit to get rid of the restriction and he was going to file it after he got some more ammunition. I said I'd be a plaintiff on that part of the lawsuit that would be brought by active Teamsters who wanted Jimmy back in the union. Jimmy told me he was going to have a money drop for me in a couple of months to Mitchell as soon as he got some things straightened out. He told me to remind him when my testimonial dinner was scheduled, because he was going to be there no matter what. I told Jimmy I had been holding up on the dinner, waiting for when it would do him the most good. Jimmy told me he appreciated my loyal support. He knew I was running for reelection of Local 326 and he offered to help, but I told him I wasn't going to have any problem with my local.

Later that year in October I got a call from Jimmy to go over and see The Redhead. I went to the Branding Iron and he had another suitcase for me. It wasn't as heavy as the last one, but it had some heft. It had $270,000 in it. I drove down to the Market Inn. I didn't even have a drink. As soon as I walked in a guy came up to me who I didn't know and he said he was going to take me where I had to go. We got in his car and drove up to an impressive house. I got out and rang the bell and Mitchell answered the door. I handed him the bag and he handed me an envelope with an affidavit in it. This time, no chitchat. I drove back up to Philly and met Russell at a restaurant and he read the affidavit that Mitchell had given me in the envelope and took care of it after that.

I, JOHN W. MITCHELL, being duly sworn, depose and say:

1. That neither I, as Attorney General of the United States, nor, to my knowledge, any other official of the Department of Justice during my tenure as Attorney General initiated or suggested the inclusion of restrictions in the Presidential commutation of James R. Hoffa.

2. That President Richard M. Nixon did not initiate with or suggest to me nor, to my knowledge, did he initiate with or suggest to any other official of the Department of Justice during my tenure as Attorney General that restrictions on Mr. Hoffa's activities in the labor movement be a part of any Presidential commutation for Mr. Hoffa.

John W. Mitchell (S)
Sworn to before me this 15th day of October, 1973

Rose L. Schiff
Notary Public, State of New York

A little more than a year later, while this affidavit was still wending its way through the court system on behalf of its purchaser, the man who swore an oath to its truth, John W. Mitchell, would be convicted of perjury and obstruction of justice as a result of his outright lying under oath in the Watergate cover-up.

With the affidavit in hand, an affidavit as yet untainted by its author's perjury conviction, Jimmy Hoffa put his campaign in overdrive.

On February 16, 1974, Hoffa accused Fitzsimmons of "traveling all over the country to every damn golf tournament there is, when being president of the Teamsters is an 18-hour-a-day job."

In a television interview Hoffa pointed out that "Fitzsimmons is crazy. He goes to a shrink twice a week and he's running a union for more than two million Teamsters?"

Hoffa began regularly referring to Fitzsimmons as "crazy" and a "liar."

In retaliation, Fitzsimmons fired Hoffa's wife, Josephine, from her union position and she lost her $48,000-a-year income. At the same time Fitzsimmons cut off James P. Hoffa's $30,000-a-year legal retainer. Chuckie O'Brien, who had grown up in the Hoffa household as a foster son and called Hoffa "Dad," kept his Teamsters job. O'Brien became increasingly close to Fitz and increasingly estranged from Hoffa. Jimmy Hoffa, an earnest family man, was outspokenly disappointed in O'Brien's divorce and strongly disapproved of O'Brien's gambling habit and spendthrift ways. Jimmy Hoffa refused to support O'Brien for president of Detroit's Local 299 and the split widened.

On March 13, 1974, Hoffa filed his much-anticipated lawsuit. This time, instead of his usual cast of yes-men lawyers, he used a renowned civil-rights attorney, Leonard Boudin. In his suit Hoffa claimed that he had no knowledge of the restrictions at the time he walked out of prison on December 21, 1971, and had never agreed to them. Furthermore, even if he had agreed to them, the president lacked the constitutional authority to restrict his or any other person's pardon in such a way.

There is an old maxim that young lawyers learn: "If you can't beat them on the law, beat them on the facts." Here, the argument that Boudin was making on his client's behalf was an argument that he and many other constitutional scholars considered a winner. That left the government to argue the facts and Jimmy Hoffa, through his actions, unwittingly provided the government with a factual argument.

Hoffa and his special friends had provided Boudin the facts to allege in the lawsuit to supplement the legal argument. Accordingly, the lawsuit claimed that the restriction did not originate from a proper source, such as the attorney general, but had "originated and derived from no regular clemency procedure but was caused to be added to said commutation by Charles Colson, Special Counsel to the President, pursuant to an agreement and conspiracy."

In a television interview after his legal papers were filed, Hoffa expounded on that part of his lawsuit: "I'm positively sure that he had a hand in it and I'm positively sure that he was the architect of the language. . . . He did it to ingratiate himself with Fitzsimmons. And in doing so got the job of representing the Teamsters. And Fitz did it, through Colson, to be able to keep the presidency of the International Union."

To which Fitzsimmons responded: "I didn't know nothing about them restrictions."

To which Colson added: "That's just plain malarkey. . . . I advised Mr. Fitzsimmons I think the day before Hoffa was to be released that he was going to be released under the conditions that seemed to be in the best interest of the labor movement and the country at the time. I never told him what, what those restrictions were."

And if Colson is to be believed, Fitzsimmons's curiosity was not at all aroused and he never asked, "Restrictions, what, what restrictions?" But as to all of this stuff that lawyers call "he said, she said," the government would have an opportunity to argue that it was beside the point. On July 19, 1974, Judge John H. Pratt of the United States District Court in Washington, D.C., responded to the factual allegations made by Hoffa and found against him. Judge Pratt held that even if the Colson-Fitzsimmons conspiracy were proven, the president's signature on the restriction held the day "for the same reason [that] one cannot attack the validity of an Act of Congress on the grounds that the Congressmen who voted in favor of it did so for improper motives."

This loss left Hoffa with no choice but to appeal to the next judicial level, where the argument there would focus on the law, the constitutional issues raised by Boudin. Hoffa and Boudin were very optimistic that their legal arguments would prevail on the appellate level. However, the appeal would take another year or more. A decision would not come until late 1975.

On August 9, 1974, less than a month after Hoffa lost that first legal round in Judge Pratt's courtroom, Nixon threw in the towel. He resigned from office and was replaced by Vice President Gerald R. Ford, who had been handpicked by Nixon a few months earlier to replace Spiro T. Agnew. Agnew had resigned when it was discovered that, even as vice president, he had continued to be on the payroll of crooked public works contractors in Maryland, where he had been governor. The day after Nixon resigned the new, handpicked president, Gerald R. Ford, who had been one of the seven members of the Warren Commission, pardoned Nixon for any crimes he might be charged with. Ford put no restrictions on Nixon's pardon.

Now all Jimmy Hoffa had to do was trust in the appeal.

There is no doubt Jimmy expected to win that court case, and everyone expected him to win it in time to take back the union practically on the same day as America's bicentennial celebration. Jimmy could have done nothing for a couple of years, let his lawyers handle the appeal, and coasted into office. But that wasn't Jimmy's way. Jimmy's way was to fight even if he didn't have anybody to fight with.

chapter twenty-six

All Hell Will Break Loose

In his book *The Teamsters,* Steven Brill makes the point that by 1974 the Central States Pension Fund of the Teamsters Union had more than $1 billion dollars loaned out for commercial real-estate ventures, including casinos. This was only 20 percent less than was loaned out by the financial powerhouse, Chase Manhattan Bank. "In short," said Brill, "the mob had control of one of the nation's major financial institutions and one of the very largest private sources of real-estate investment capital in the world."

Control of the president of the Teamsters ensured control of the pension fund and ensured favorable treatment in union contracts. For many years after Hoffa disappeared and after Fitzsimmons stepped down the mob continued to control the office of the president of the IBT by controlling delegates who voted at the election. As late as 1986, Commission member and Genovese family boss, Anthony "Fat Tony" Salerno, was convicted of rigging the election of Teamsters president Roy Williams. The FBI had bugged the Palma Boys Social Club in New York and Fat Tony was convicted with his own words. Frank Sheeran and Fat Tony would be inmates together at the same federal prison hospital in Springfield, Missouri, in the late eighties, when Fat Tony was dying of cancer.

Also in prison with Sheeran and Fat Tony was a tattooed, muscle-bound, outlaw biker named Sailor. Like Fat Tony, Sailor was dying of cancer, and because he had only a few months left to live he was given a hardship release. According to Sheeran, Fat Tony arranged for $25,000 to be delivered to him on his release. In return for the money Sailor drove to Long Island and murdered a civilian witness who had testified against Fat Tony. While Russell Bufalino had gotten religion at Springfield prison hospital, preparing himself for the next life, Salerno had no such epiphany.

In 1975, at the time of Jimmy Hoffa's disappearance, Fat Tony was the boss of the very crime family to which Tony Pro belonged, the Genovese.

Frank Sheeran Appreciation Night was October 18, 1974. About six months before my banquet there were some murmurs floating around that Jimmy might not be so good for pension fund loans in the future. This talk was mostly coming out of Tony Pro's area, because he was campaigning against Jimmy. I talked to Russell about what I was hearing here and there, and Russell said there's only so much money the Teamsters can lend out, anyway, and pretty soon that well would run dry no matter who was in charge of it. Jimmy was always good to deal with. Russell said there were problems from Tony Pro and some others in Kansas City, but Jimmy had a lot of support from his old friends. Russell was for Jimmy and he told me that after his trial he'd take me to see Fat Tony Salerno, Tony Pro's boss. Tony Pro had control over two or three locals in north Jersey, but Fat Tony had way more than that as far as influencing delegates.

Meanwhile, Russell had to win his own trial in upstate New York. A couple of Russell's people had a cigarette vending machine business there. They were getting a lot of competition from this other company in Binghamton, New York. Russell's people tried to talk to the two owners of the company in Binghamton about putting some of their profits on the table. The owners of the other company did not go for the idea of making Russell's people silent partners. Then one night, the two owners of the other company allegedly got worked over. The next thing you know Russell and about a dozen others in his family were arrested for extortion. Some of the ones they arrested got dismissed for lack of evidence, but they took Russell and about half a dozen other ones to trial. I went up to the trial and I sat down in the first row. It was a three-week trial and I sat there every day to support Russell. The jury could see that Russell had friends in the courtroom. On April 24, 1974, Russell and the other ones were all found not guilty. This was the same spring that Jimmy filed his lawsuit. Spring 1974 was a charm for this Irishman's friends.

After his victory Russell took me to New York and we met with Fat Tony Salerno at the Vesuvio. Russell and I told him that Tony Pro and Jimmy had a personal beef over Tony Pro's pension, but that we would appreciate any help Tony could give to Jimmy later on at the 1976 convention. Fat Tony always had a cigar in his mouth. He said he would not stand in Jimmy's way. He would not try to tell Pro what to do, but he was not with Pro on this issue. Jimmy had done a lot of good in the past.

Around May or June of 1974 I got a surprise visit at my Local 326 office down by the train station. Who should waltz in but John Mitchell. I didn't ask the man how he found me or how he even knew who I was. He said he only had a minute and he just wanted to say hello and to tell me that I should "Tell Jimmy I was asking for him. Tell him to just enjoy his pension and play with his grandchildren and to forget about running." I said, "Thanks for stopping by. Next time I see him I'll tell him what you said."

Meanwhile, things were heating up in Detroit at Local 299. Jimmy's old pal from the early years, Dave Johnson, was still president. The plan was for Dave not to retire until Jimmy was ready to take over the International. But Fitz was putting pressure on Dave to retire early. That way Fitz could appoint his own son Richard as president of the local. Jimmy needed his own man in there in 299 until he got the restrictions off. When the restrictions came off, Dave Johnson was supposed to appoint Jimmy as a business agent to Local 299. That way Jimmy would be a delegate to the 1976 convention and that would make him qualified under the constitution to run against Fitz for president of the International.

Dave Johnson started getting hang-up calls at home with people laughing into the phone. Somebody fired a shotgun at the window of his office down at the union hall. About a week before Jimmy lost his first round in court on the restriction lawsuit, somebody blew up Dave's forty-five-foot cabin cruiser. It was all a message from Fitz and his people.

Fitz's son Richard announced that he was going to run for president of Local 299 against Dave. Richard claimed that Jimmy himself was responsible for the explosion that blew up Dave's boat. This kind of thing would only make a man like Dave Johnson stronger. Dave was good people. He stayed in there as president and they made a deal and made Richard the vice president. Later on somebody blew up Richard's car, but Jimmy would never have blown up Fitz's son's car. Jimmy wouldn't want to put his own son on the front line and expose the kid to retaliation.

Jimmy put the word out that he was going to run no matter what the judges ended up saying. If he lost in his appeal he was just going to defy the restrictions. If they wanted to try to put him back in jail, the ball would be in their court. No matter what, Jimmy was running in 1976. Some people put together an organization called HOFFA, for How Old Friends Feel Active.

Jimmy was no rat. But Jimmy could puff. Jimmy started saying things like he was going to call in all the bad loans that Fitz, "the fat old man," had made. A lot of those loans had gone to build casinos for the alleged mob; only under Fitz they were careless with their payments. With Jimmy they always made their payments on the loans. As crazy as it sounds, Jimmy kept saying in public that he was going to expose the alleged mob connections that Fitz had. Jimmy said he was going to expose everything once he got back in office and got his hands on the records. It sounded like Jimmy was going to forfeit some of these loans and take over some of the casinos the way Castro did.

I kept telling Russell that this was just Jimmy's way; that Jimmy was only puffing. Russell told me to tell Jimmy to relax and stop drawing attention to his friends. Russell mentioned one time that there had already been all that talk about Jimmy ratting to the McClellan Committee and getting Dave Beck indicted so he could get Beck out of the way and take over. Dave Beck was president of the International just before my time. I didn't know whether to believe that one about Jimmy or not, but I doubted it. Still, Jimmy was going to have a problem if he kept that loose talk up about exposing his friends.

On the campaign trail, Jimmy Hoffa often stung like a swarm of bees. Hoffa was quoted in the news as accusing Fitzsimmons of "selling out to mobsters and letting known racketeers into the Teamsters." He made bold accusations against Fitzsimmons and organized crime that mirrored the language from Hoffa's autobiography, scheduled for release six months before the 1976 election: "I charge him with permitting underworld establishment of a union insurance scheme. . . . There will be more and more developments as time goes on and I get my hands on additional information."

To keep his nose clean and to avoid the appearance of having his own conflicts of interest, Jimmy Hoffa negotiated himself out of coal mining interests he had in northeastern Pennsylvania. If he continued to be in a management position as to the Teamsters who hauled the coal, Hoffa would not appear as lily-white as he needed to appear if he were to continue to sling mud against Fitzsimmons and the "underworld."

They closed the Latin Casino for Frank Sheeran Appreciation Night. The Latin was where I used to go with Skinny Razor and the downtown crowd in the old days on Sunday nights. Frank Sinatra had been a regular performer. They had all the big stars over the years — Al Martino, Dean Martin,

Liberace. The same stars that played in Vegas played at the Latin. That was the only nightclub around.

John McCullough of the roofer's union had put the banquet together. There were 3,000 people there eating prime rib or lobster and an open bar. It was a Friday night and a lot of the Catholics still ate fish on Friday so they had the choice of lobster, but the prime rib was excellent. The guests included the men from the different Teamsters locals and my old war buddies and some people from management, all kinds of people. The president of Local 676, John Greely, gave me a plaque as Teamsters Man of the Year. John McCullough announced all the high-ups that were in the room and he mentioned all the FBI agents that were outside in the trees with their binoculars. Even if you had a ticket that night you didn't get in unless you knew somebody. We would refund your money and confiscate your ticket if you didn't know anybody.

Jimmy Hoffa was the featured speaker, and he presented me a solid gold watch with diamonds all around it. Jimmy gave a terrific speech telling everybody there what good work I had done on behalf of the working men and women in Pennsylvania and Delaware. Jimmy looked around on the dais and said, "I had no idea you were this strong." Mayor Frank Rizzo was up there on the dais. Cecil B. Moore, the head of the Philadelphia NAACP, was up there. The former D.A., Emmett Fitzpatrick, was on the dais. The dais was loaded with dignitaries from politics and labor.

My wife, Irene, and all four of my daughters were there at the front table. My youngest, Connie, was only eleven at the time. Dolores was nineteen. Peggy was twenty-six. Mary Ann was twenty-eight. They all looked very proud of me that night. Jimmy made Irene come up on stage and he gave her a dozen roses. She was embarrassed to go up and he kept coaxing her until she gave in.

There was a front table off to the right of the table from Irene and my daughters. This was Russell's table. His wife, Carrie, was the only woman at that table. Dave Osticco and Guf Guarnieri, the high-ups from Russell's family, were there. Angelo Bruno and a couple of his people were there at Russell's table. All of downtown was there at another table.

Russell had bet me that I was going to louse up my speech. I ended my speech by saying, "Thank you all from the bottom of my heart. I know I don't deserve all of this tonight, but I have arthritis and I don't deserve that either. See, Russ, I didn't mess up my speech." Russell waved to me and everybody laughed.

For entertainment John McCullough had lined up the Italian singer Jerry Vale. He sang all the old Italian songs he was famous for singing, like "Sorrento" and "Volare." Then he sang some Irish songs that McCullough had put him up to. He did a special number on Russell's and my favorite song at that time, "Spanish Eyes." If you didn't know who was singing you'd think it was Al Martino.

As part of the show they had the Golddigger Dancers with legs up to their shoulders. They were good-looking girls. Everybody kept kidding me to go up on the stage and mix it up with the dancers. The Latin was packed and they didn't have a dancefloor or I would have danced with the most beautiful girls in the house, my daughters.

We all posed for our own photographer that night, and while we were getting our pictures taken Jimmy said to me, "I truly had no idea you were this strong, my friend. I really appreciate all the support you have given me over these years. I'm glad you're on my side. Frank, when I get back in, you're going right along with me. I need you around me. If you'll take the job I'm going to make you an International organizer with an unlimited expense account."

"I know you mean it, Jimmy," I said. "It would be my honor to serve as an International organizer someday." That would have been my dream come true.

John McCullough had limos to take my family home and I took Jimmy back to the Warwick Hotel. There was no way I was letting Jimmy go back to his hotel alone in a limo. We didn't talk about anything important. All our important talking had been done the night before.

The night before, we had our own private party at Broadway Eddie's. Broadway Eddie's was a small bar with a few tables at the corner of Tenth and Christiansen. The bar is still there, but under a different name. That night the bar was closed to the public and you needed a special invitation to get in. My good friends from downtown and from upstate were all there to show their appreciation for Frank Sheeran. Naturally, Jimmy would be at that private affair, too. If anybody had the place under surveillance the whole thing looked like it was built around me. But it was actually put together for a meeting with Russell and Angelo to talk to Jimmy. Russell had asked me if Jimmy would attend a meeting with special friends of mine. Jimmy said, "Is it important to you?" I said, "Yes." And that's how the thing at Broadway Eddie's was set up.

Jimmy had gotten into Philly from Detroit that afternoon. I guess he flew in, but he didn't have the private plane at his disposal anymore. Fitz had that. I picked him up at the Warwick Hotel and filled Jimmy in on the meeting Russell and I had with Fat Tony Salerno. Jimmy was happy about that part. We got in my big Lincoln and drove out to Jersey to see John Greely at Local 676. Greely was a Hoffa man, and Jimmy wanted to touch base with him about something. While Jimmy was meeting with Greely I waited outside. Then we went to Broadway Eddie's

There were about sixty people at Broadway Eddie's that night. The only ones who were at a table eating were Angelo, Russell, Jimmy, and me. The rest were at the bar. Trays of food kept coming out of the kitchen for the people at the bar. Jimmy was having spaghetti and meatballs, and I was having raviolis. The four of us were sitting in a row. When you wanted to talk you had to lean out a little bit. Angelo was on the end next to Russell, and Jimmy was between Russell and me.

Angelo didn't say anything and I didn't say anything the whole time. They knew I was for Hoffa. I had Hoffa stickers all over my Lincoln. There was no prolonged conversation about what they were there for. I would imagine Jimmy knew why he was asked to be there, but I don't know.

"What do you want to run for?" Russell asked.

"It's my union," Jimmy said.

"You only have four years to wait. You could run in eighty. That would make sense."

"I could run now. I've got the people with me."

Jimmy wasn't being fresh, but he was being firm. Russell didn't say anything about the way Jimmy was campaigning and the things Jimmy was going around saying about the alleged mob. But Jimmy had to know that such talk in public would be of concern to Russell. Jimmy knew about Joe Colombo and the publicity he brought and Crazy Joey Gallo. Jimmy knew how all of Russell's problems began with the publicity from Apalachin. At least Jimmy should have been wondering what was causing Russell to go from being behind Jimmy and meeting with Fat Tony to help Jimmy in 1976, and now talking this way about things.

"What are you running for?" Russell said. "You don't need the money."

"It's not about the money," Jimmy said. "I'm not letting Fitz have the union."

Russell didn't say anything for a minute. He just ate in silence. People didn't say no to Russell and he usually never had to ask twice.

Jimmy said, "I'm going to take care of the people who've been fucking me."

Russell turned to Jimmy and was now facing Jimmy and me both. "There are people higher up than me that feel that you are demonstrating a failure to show appreciation," and then he said so softly that I had to read his lips, "for Dallas."

Jimmy did not respond to that.

Russell turned away and made some small talk with Angelo and that meant the meeting was over. We finished eating. I sat there thinking that this was it. The people had talked among themselves and Russell was now speaking for them, and they were against Jimmy running and Russell was, too. Tony Pro had won the battle for their hearts and minds. I had the feeling that it wasn't that Jimmy was running that was costing his support among his friends; it was the way he was running.

I didn't know how serious it was for Jimmy until Jimmy and I were getting ready to leave. Russell took me aside and said, "Some people have a serious problem with your friend. Talk to your friend. Tell him what it is."

"I'll do my best. You know yourself, Russ; he's tough to talk to."

"He's got no choice."

"Jimmy's pretty high up himself," I said.

"You're dreaming, my friend. If they could take out the president, they could take out the president of the Teamsters."

Jimmy liked the Warwick Hotel. It was around Seventeenth and Walnut, a short ride from Broadway Eddie's in my Lincoln with the Hoffa stickers. I went up to Jimmy's room with him to have that talk with him, but Jimmy started talking first.

"Everybody wants Hoffa to back down. They're all afraid of what I know. I got a package here I want you to take down to the Market Inn." Jimmy handed me a small satchel, not too heavy. It had no name on it. Whoever it was for would know enough to come for it.

"That reminds me, Jimmy," I said. "I've been meaning to tell you this before; Mitchell stopped down the hall last spring and told me to tell you not to run. He said to enjoy your pension and your grandchildren."

"That doesn't surprise me. That fucking Mitchell already told me, 'Don't even think about using what you think you know.'"

"I didn't know what Russell was going to say to you tonight, Jimmy," I said. "But I know they mean it, Jimmy. On the way out tonight Russell told me to tell you what it is."

"If anything unnatural happens to Hoffa, I can tell you all hell will break loose. I've got more records and lists ready to be mailed out to the media than you can imagine. I've had too many motherfuckers in my life I thought I could trust. I need more people like you. And I have them now. I know who my friends are."

"Jimmy, you're doing a lot of puffing that has people concerned."

"That's just the tip of the iceberg, the tip of the iceberg. Let me tell you — Dallas, did you hear that word tonight? Remember that package you took to Baltimore? I didn't know it then, but it turns out it was high-powered rifles for the Kennedy hit in Dallas. The stupid bastards lost their own rifles in the trunk of a Thunderbird that crashed when their driver got drunk. That pilot for Carlos was involved in delivering the replacements that you brought down. Those fuckers used both of us on that deal. We were patsies. What do you think of that? They had fake cops and real cops involved in it. Jack Ruby's cops were supposed to take care of Oswald, but Ruby bungled it. That's why he had to go in and finish the job on Oswald. If he didn't take care of Oswald, what do you think they would have done to him — put Ruby on a meat hook. Don't kid yourself. Santo and Carlos and Giancana and some of their element, they were all in on Kennedy. Every single one of the same cast of characters that were in on the Bay of Pigs. They even had a plot to kill Castro with Momo and Roselli. I've got enough to hang everybody. And every last bit of it comes out if anything unnatural happens to me. They will all pay. All those who fucked me will pay."

I sat there with the satchel in my lap. Jimmy would sometimes get on a kick and there was no stopping him. You just listened. But I never saw him like this before. I never saw anybody like this before. This time it was unreal. There was nothing for me to say even if I was inclined to do any talking. If the room was bugged I didn't want my voice on anything. Picking up high-powered rifles — man, oh, man.

"You don't know the half of it. Fitz's stupidity is only exceeded by his arrogance. They thought Hoffa was going to drop off the face of the earth. None of them have got an ounce of balls to face me. My Irish friend, there are things I can't tell you because it would cost you your life to know them. There are secret things I have known, seen, and supported that would rock this nation."

Jimmy then went on to tell me alleged things about our good friends, not pertaining to this. Things not for publication. I can't say I knew them all, anyway, but I knew most of them and I suspected some of the others. None of it was my business or his business. It was time for me to get out of there. In case the room was bugged I said, "I heard none of that was true, Jimmy."

"Don't worry about that. I've got records in the hands of the right people and the motherfuckers know I've kept records on all of it. And I've got it all in safe places."

"Jimmy, do me a favor and keep some bodies around between you and the street."

"Bodyguards make you careless."

"I'm not saying bodyguards. Just travel with people. You came to this thing in Philly alone."

"I'm not going that route or they'll go after my family."

"Still in all, you don't want to be out on the street by yourself."

"Nobody scares Hoffa. I'm going after Fitz and I'm going to win this election."

"You know what this means, Jimmy," I said softly. "McGee himself told me to tell you what it is."

"They wouldn't dare," Jimmy Hoffa said out loud.

On the way to the door, Jimmy said to me, "You watch your ass."

chapter twenty-seven

July 30, 1975

I reported back to Russell that Jimmy was still running in 1976. I reported what Jimmy said about having records and lists that were going to make their public appearance in case something unnatural happened to him. I didn't go into all the details, all the wild things Jimmy had said. These were things I didn't need to know. Russell made a comment about Jimmy's thinking being "distorted."

"I don't understand this," Russell said. "I don't understand why he just doesn't go away."

I made the drop for Jimmy at the Market Inn and called him to tell him. I really can't tell you that what was in the package was money. I didn't look. After that I was afraid to have too many conversations with Jimmy, because I would only have to repeat them to Russell. I got the feeling from all this that Jimmy was being ruled by his ego and by his feeling of revenge. I guess he figured that if he waited until 1980 to run, Fitz would retire and Jimmy would never get a chance to humiliate Fitz at a convention, to rub his nose in it. I guess that Jimmy was not too happy with the way things looked with our friends. After the meeting at Broadway Eddie's and the approach that Russell took about wanting Jimmy not to run, Jimmy had to figure that Tony Pro was making progress in that part of the campaign.

After the thing I could never understand them wanting to hurt Jo and the kids by making Jimmy disappear. While they would do whatever they had to do, people like Russell and Angelo would not want to hurt the immediate family. Make them suffer not knowing, not having a decent funeral and having to wait so many years under the law to be able to declare Jimmy dead before they could get his money. Unless Tony Pro had the final say and got the okay from Fat Tony. That we'll never know for sure. Pro already threatened to kill Jimmy's granddaughter. Who talks like that about a man's grandchildren?

In April 1975 rumors were circulating at a Teamsters convention that Jimmy Hoffa was cooperating with the FBI. The *Detroit Free Press,* in a December 20, 1992, article, attributed these rumors to Chuckie O'Brien, the alleged driver of the car that Jimmy Hoffa was in at the time of his disappearance. An FBI 302 from the FBI file on Jimmy Hoffa's disappearance, the HOFFEX file, confirms the existence of this rumor and a plausible reason as to why it may have had a basis in truth: "It has been rumored among sources that Hoffa, while attempting to gain control of the Teamsters, may have provided information to the Government in exchange for a favorable decision concerning the lifting of his Union restrictions."

- On May 15, 1975, Jimmy Hoffa testified at a grand jury investigation into "no show" jobs at his former Detroit Local 299. Hoffa took the Fifth. Afterward, when questioned by a reporter, Hoffa said he was "damn proud of it." That same day Jimmy Hoffa attended a meeting at his son's law office with his son and Detroit mobster Anthony "Tony Jack" Giacalone. Giacalone tried to broker a meeting between Hoffa and Tony Pro, and Hoffa refused to attend. Giacalone then asked for Hoffa's help in obtaining records that were going to be used by the government against Giacalone for an alleged insurance scam indictment. Hoffa turned down Giacalone's request.

- At the end of May, Frank Fitzsimmons threatened to put Local 299, Hoffa's former local and power base, into trusteeship and have it run by a monitor, who would report to the Teamsters headquarters in Washington.

- On June 19, 1975, Jimmy Hoffa's ally and good friend Sam Giancana was assassinated in his Chicago home five days before his scheduled testimony before the Church Committee on the mob's role in a CIA plot to assassinate Fidel Castro.

- On June 25, 1975, a Local 299 supporter of Frank Fitzsimmons named Ralph Proctor was attacked from behind as he walked out of a restaurant after lunch. Proctor never saw what hit him. Proctor was beaten and knocked unconscious in broad daylight. Proctor's higher-up in the Fitzsimmons camp, Rolland McMaster, said, "We had that kind of crap happen. I put investigators on it, but they didn't find out anything."

- On the afternoon of July 10, 1975, Frank Fitzsimmons's son Richard Fitzsimmons relaxed in Nemo's bar in Detroit. Richard was vice president of Local 299, and in that capacity he had been given a 1975 white Lincoln Continental for his union duties. After finishing his last drink at Nemo's, Richard left the bar and was walking toward this parked Lincoln when the car exploded. Richard narrowly escaped being injured, but his white Lincoln was blown to bits.

- On the afternoon of July 30, 1975, Jimmy Hoffa disappeared.

The whole thing was built around the wedding. Bill Bufalino's daughter was getting married on Friday, August 1, 1975. That was two days after Jimmy disappeared. People would be coming in from all the families around the country. There would be over 500 people there. Russell and I and our wives and Russell's sister-in-law would be driving in a straight line that went through Pennsylvania, most of the way through Ohio, and then a right turn north to Detroit, Michigan.

Because of the wedding Jimmy would be inclined to believe that Tony Pro and Russell Bufalino would be in the Detroit area so they could meet with him in the afternoon he disappeared. The thing with Tony Pro wanting his million-dollar pension was a decoy. Pro didn't care about his pension so much. They just used the pension beef to get Jimmy to come out.

Jimmy had a meeting that was arranged by Tony Giaccalone for 2:30 at the Machus Red Fox Restaurant on Telegraph Avenue outside of Detroit on July 30, 1975. Tony Pro was supposed to get there at 2:30 with Tony Jack. The whole idea was for Tony Jack to make peace between Tony Pro and Jimmy. Jimmy left for that meeting, and Jimmy was seen in the parking lot of the restaurant, but Jimmy never came home from that meeting.

By the time of the wedding everybody was talking about Jimmy's disappearance. I got to talking with Jimmy's old-time buddies from Local 299, Dave Johnson, the president who got his boat blown up, and Bobby Holmes, the old Strawberry Boy who used to be a miner in England. They both asked me, practically at the same time, if I thought Tony Pro had it done.

The next morning, Russell suggested I call Jo to encourage her and console her. Maybe Russ could see I didn't want to do this, so he said, "It would look funny if you didn't call her." So I called Jo and she had been crying. I told her, "Jimmy will come back home. Look at that time when Mr. Bonanno disappeared. Joe Bananas. He came back home in a few weeks. After the people came to terms." I told her more besides. What kind of man makes a call like that?

chapter twenty-eight

To Paint a House

The pilot stayed put in the plane. I stepped in. The pilot turned his head away even though I knew him. He'd been around the block enough times with our friends to know not to look at my face. I looked out the window at the grass airstrip at Port Clinton, Ohio, and saw my black Lincoln with Russell sitting in the passenger seat. Russell had already started to nod off to sleep.

Port Clinton is at the southern tip of Lake Erie. It's a fishing village just east of Toledo, a little over 100 miles from the city of Detroit by car. To drive around the lake to the Georgiana Motel in Detroit could take almost three hours back then if you stretched it and took a little bit of a roundabout route. To fly over the lake and land near Detroit would take maybe an hour.

If you want to know what I felt sitting in that plane, I'm sorry to admit, but back then I felt nothing. It wasn't like I was heading into battle. The decision was made to paint the house and that was that. Sure, I don't feel good about it if I think about it now. I'm in my eighties. Back then, you start feeling too much and no matter how much nerve you have the nervous tension builds up in you and you get confused. Maybe even act stupid. The war taught me how to control my feelings when it was called for.

The sad part of it is that the whole matter could have been stopped by Jimmy any time he wanted, but he kept sailing into the storm. He could have sunk a lot of people in the same boat with him if he kept going in that direction. We all told him what it is. He thought he was untouchable. Some people are like that. Like my father thought he was untouchable when he tossed me the boxing gloves.

But everybody bleeds.

Was I still concerned for my own health and Irene's health the way it crossed my mind last night at Brutico's when Russell told me what it was going to be today? Not even a little bit. They had only two choices. Kill me or put me in the thing. By putting me in the thing they got a chance to make sure they could trust me. By being there to take part I could never do anything back to them. I would be proving, in the best way you could prove it, that it had never been my intent to go out and kiss Tony Pro or Fitz for Jimmy. Russell understood these things. He saved my life over and over again. I had seven contracts out on me over the years and Russell was able to square every one of the beefs.

Even though he was a boss, Russell himself had to do what he had to do. They took care of bosses, too. I didn't sleep at all that night at the Howard Johnson's, pondering these things, but I always came up with the same answer. If they had decided not to use me in the thing Jimmy would have been just as dead and no doubt in my mind I'd have been dead along with him. They even told me that later on.

After what seemed like a quick up and down I got out of the plane the way I got in, alone, with the pilot looking the other way.

My wife, Irene, Russell's wife, Carrie, and Russell's wife's older sister were in Port Clinton at a restaurant having coffee and smoking cigarettes while they thought Russell and I had gone to do some of Russell's business. We already had done some business on the way out and we would stop to do more business on the way home. Among other things, they knew Russell always had his eyepiece with him to look at diamond jewelry. When we got back together in three hours they would never think I could have driven to Detroit and back in three hours, when it would take three hours one way by car just to get to our motel in Detroit.

It wasn't something that entered my mind, but there was no doubt about my boarding this plane again safe and sound when I was done with my errand. There's no way they would put the women in the middle of an investigation if something unnatural happened to me in Detroit. I'd be hooking back up with my black Lincoln in Ohio and Russell and I would pick up the women. You might analyze it that the women being in Port Clinton was insurance and gave me a psychological comfort zone, but that kind of thinking never entered my mind.

Besides, I had a piece in my back under my belt. Even today at my age in a nursing home, there's still nothing wrong with my second finger.

I landed at the Pontiac airfield, a small one just north of where everything was going to take place. It's gone now; if I'm not mistaken it's a housing development. You didn't need a flight plan to land in those days and they kept no records.

There were two or three cars in the lot. One of them was a Ford with the keys sitting on the floor mat just like Russell said. It was plain and gray and a little dusty. You would never expect to find a flashy car that would attract attention in a situation like this. It was a loaner. Cars would be taken off lots and the owners would never know about it. Hotels were good. Long-term parking at airports was good. An inside man could make himself a nice note here and there providing loaners for cash customers.

I had the address and the directions from Russell. I knew Detroit pretty good from working for Jimmy, but these directions were real simple. I was to get on Telegraph Road, which is Route 24, a main artery into Detroit. It was a sunny day, hot enough for the air conditioner. On my right I drove past the Machus Red Fox Restaurant, which is on Telegraph Road. I took a left off Telegraph Road onto Seven Mile Road. I drove a half-mile on Seven Mile, crossed a roadway bridge over a small creek. I made a right and down that road there was another roadway bridge, then a footbridge nearby, and then I made a left and there was the house with brown shingles, a high backyard fence, and a detached garage in the back. The houses in the neighborhood weren't far away but they weren't on top of each other either. I checked the address. I'd been driving just a few miles.

Like I said, on the way to the house, going south on Telegraph Road, I passed by the Machus Red Fox Restaurant where Jimmy would be waiting in vain for me to show up for our 2:00 appointment. The restaurant was set back quite a way in the parking lot. When I passed it I wasn't concerned that Jimmy would spot me. Because of my size and the good posture I still had in those days before I got bent over by the arthritis, I sat with my head up close to the roof of a car, and people had to take a close look to see my face. Nobody ever identified me in this matter.

I was supposed to be sitting there in the restaurant when the two Tonys showed up for their 2:30 appointment with Jimmy. Only Tony Jack was getting a massage at his health club in Detroit. Tony Pro meantime wasn't even in Michigan. He was in New Jersey at his union hall playing Greek rummy, with the FBI no doubt sitting across the street from the union hall keeping an eye on him.

The house was just a few miles from where Jimmy's remains would go. Everything was going to be very close to everything else, all of it a straight shoot. You most definitely couldn't go driving around any kind of distance and making lots of turns with Jimmy's body in a car. The writers that claim I shipped the package in a fifty-five-gallon drum to a dump site in New Jersey or to the end zone in Giants Stadium never had a body on their hands. Who in their right mind would transport such a high-profile package a block longer than was necessary, much less across the country?

And this theory that somebody hit Jimmy inside Tony Jack's son's car is another idea that is just plain crazy. You kiss somebody in a car and you never get the smell out of the interior. It becomes a corpse car. All the body chemicals and body waste gets released into a small space. The death smell stays in the car. A car is not like a house in that respect. A house doesn't retain the death odor.

The house with the brown shingles was another loaner. Could be some old lady lived there by herself and never knew her house was being borrowed for an hour. People like chiropractors would know when people would be out of town so that burglars could unload their houses. Might even be that somebody in the Detroit outfit had a chiropractor who treated an old lady who lived there alone. They would know she wouldn't be home, and they would know her eyes were so shot she would never notice anybody had been there when she did get home, much less smell anything. The house is still there.

When I pulled up to the house, I could see a brown Buick at the end of the single-lane driveway. I pulled in and parked my Ford in the driveway behind the Buick.

I went to the front and walked up the steps. The front door was unlocked and I walked in. Sally Bugs was already in the small vestibule inside the front door, looking up at me through his Coke-bottle glasses. He had thick, curly black hair. I closed the door behind me. We shook hands.

All the books say the New Jersey brothers Steve and Tom Andretta were involved. I heard one of them is deceased now and one of them is still alive. Two young good-looking Italian guys were in the kitchen at the back of the house. They both waved to me then turned their heads away. One of the kids down the hall was the Andretta brother who's gone now. No need to use the other kid's name. They both had good alibis anyway.

The way I remember it, on the left in the hall there was a staircase to the upstairs. On the right there was a living room and a dining room that had rugs on the floor, not wall to wall. There were no rugs in the vestibule or the long hallway leading from the vestibule to the kitchen. Probably they had picked up the rugs if there were any. There was just a piece of linoleum in the vestibule. I don't know how it got there.

I knew of these people as Pro's people, but I had never met them before that day. These were not my social friends. There was no reason to talk. Later during the different Hoffa grand juries we got to see each other a little bit. I walked down the hall to the kitchen. I looked out the back door just to get a feel for the backyard. The high fence and the garage gave the backyard some privacy.

I walked back down the hall to Sally Bugs in the living room. He was peeking through the curtains. "This Chuckie is late," he said in that north Jersey accent.

Jimmy Hoffa's foster son, Chuckie O'Brien, and I were going to be part of the bait to lure Jimmy into a car with Sally Bugs, Tony Pro's right-hand man. Sally Bugs was a squat little guy. Even with a piece in his hand, Sally Bugs was no match for me. Without being told I knew that there was no reason for Sally Bugs to get in Chuckie's car other than to keep an eye on me. To make sure I didn't spook Jimmy not to get in the car. Jimmy was supposed to feel safe with me in Chuckie's car so he'd go to this house with brown shingles and walk right in the front door with me as his backup.

"Here's a car. Is that Chuckie?" Chuckie O'Brien had long sideburns and a paisley shirt with a wide collar and lots of gold chains on his neck. He looked like he belonged in *Saturday Night Fever*. Chuckie was an innocent bystander. If Chuckie knew anything to hurt anybody, he'd have been gone to Australia the next day. No way would they have him in that position. Chuckie was known for bragging and boasting. He used to make himself bigger than he was, but he had to look between his legs to find his balls. He could not be trusted with anything worth knowing. If he suspected anything he'd be too nervous when we picked up Jimmy and Jimmy would sense it. All he knew was that he was taking us to pick up Jimmy — a man who helped raise him, a man he called "Dad" — and then driving us all back here to an important meeting with important people. He would just be at ease with Jimmy, acting normal. I always felt sorry for Chuckie O'Brien in this whole thing and I still do. If anybody deserves to be forgiven it's Chuckie.

My presence there would be the thing that would start out putting Chuckie at ease so he'd act normal with Jimmy. Chuckie was driving Tony Jack's son's maroon Mercury, not the kind of car that spells trouble. That familiar car would put

Jimmy and Chuckie both at ease. Jimmy was expecting Tony Jack and so his son's car would be normal. Chuckie picking me up at the house where we were going to come back for the meeting would also put Chuckie at ease.

Everybody being at ease was an important feature, because Jimmy was as smart as they come at smelling danger from all his years in bloody union wars and knowing the people he was dealing with. He was supposed to meet Tony Jack and Tony Pro in a public restaurant with a public parking lot. Not many people change a public meeting place to a private house on Jimmy Hoffa — even with me in the car. Even with his "son" Chuckie driving.

I said, "That's him."

Chuckie parked in the street at the front door. The two good-looking guys stayed at the back of the house, down the hall in the kitchen. Sally Bugs got in the backseat of the four-door maroon Mercury right behind Chuckie, introduced himself, and shook Chuckie's hand. I sat in the front passenger seat. Jimmy would be sitting behind me. Sally Bugs would be able to see us both.

What was going to happen to Chuckie after all this was over? Not a thing. He'd keep his mouth shut about what little he did know out of fear and embarrassment. Chuckie was never known for sticking his neck out. He was the only one in the Hoffa family to keep his job under Fitz.

"What the fuck is this?" Sally Bugs asked. He pointed to the floor in the rear. "It's wet back here."

"I had a frozen fish," Chuckie said. "I had to drop off a fish for Bobby Holmes."

"A fish, how do you like that?" Sally Bugs said. "The fuckin' seat is wet back here." Sally Bugs took out a handkerchief and wiped his hands.

We got there in less than fifteen minutes.

The parking lot was clearing out. Most of the lunch crowd had finished and were gone already. We saw Jimmy's green Pontiac off to the side on our left as we pulled in. There were trees along Telegraph Road in those days that gave the lot a little privacy.

"He must still be inside," Chuckie said. "I'll get him."

"Don't bother. There's a spot over there," Sally Bugs said, "on the other side of the lot."

Chuckie drove to where Sally Bugs had pointed. From there we could see Jimmy and get to him before he got to his car. It was believed he had started keeping a piece in his glove compartment.

"Let him finish whatever he's doing," Sally Bugs said. "Keep the motor runnin'. When he heads over there to his car, we'll pick him up."

We sat and waited a minute. Then Jimmy came from the area of the hardware store behind the restaurant walking toward his car. He was wearing a pullover short-sleeve sport shirt and dark slacks. He was looking around impatient while he walked, looking for me or for the two Tonys. He most definitely didn't have his piece on him. Not in that outfit.

Chuckie slowly pulled up to Jimmy. Jimmy stopped. He was showing rage in his eyes, that look of his that could make any man respect him.

Chuckie said, "I'm sorry I'm late."

Jimmy started yelling, "What the fuck are you even doing here? Who the fuck invited you?" He was jabbing his finger at Chuckie.

Then Jimmy looked at Sally Bugs in the rear seat behind Chuckie. "Who the fuck is he?"

"I'm with Tony Pro," Sally Bugs said.

"What the fuck is going on here? Your fucking boss was supposed to be here at 2:30." Jimmy started pointing at Sally Bugs.

A few people going to their cars in the parking lot started looking over at us.

"People are staring at us, Jimmy." Sally Bugs said, and then he pointed over at me. "Look who's here."

Jimmy lowered his head and looked in the other side of the car. I lowered my head so he could see me and waved at him.

Sally Bugs said, "His friend wanted to be at the thing. They're at the house waitin'."

Jimmy put his hands down and stood there squinting. Seeing me there, Jimmy instantly would believe Russell Bufalino was already in Detroit sitting around a kitchen table at a house waiting. My friend Russell wanting to be there would explain the sudden last-minute change in plans in Jimmy's mind. Russell Bufalino was not the man to conduct a sit-down in a public place he didn't know like the Red Fox. Russell Bufalino was old school. He was a very private person. He'd only meet you in public in places he knew and trusted.

Russell Bufalino was the final bait to lure Jimmy into the car. If there was going to be any violence, anything unnatural, Russell would not be there.

Jimmy would believe it was safe to get in the car. He would be too embarrassed at his outburst even to think about not getting in the Mercury with us. He would be too embarrassed to insist on driving his own Pontiac with the piece in it. The psychology of the matter was played to perfection. They knew how to get under the man's skin. Jimmy Hoffa had been forced to wait for me for a full half-hour, from 2:00 to 2:30, only because he was stuck waiting for the 2:30 meeting. And then he waited his standard fifteen minutes for the two Tonys besides. Waiting forty-five minutes made Jimmy nuts like it was supposed to and then to compensate for all the bull he put out, he got cooperative like he was supposed to.

Not to mention he was now impatient as only Jimmy could be. Jimmy went around and got in the backseat behind me. I heard that Jimmy's hair that the FBI analyzed for DNA turned up in the trunk. Jimmy was never in the trunk, dead or alive.

There was no sign of a piece anywhere on Jimmy as he got in. With me finally sitting there as backup like I was supposed to and with us now going to a meeting with Russell Bufalino it would have been the height of disrespect for Jimmy to go and get his piece out of his own car if he had one in it. Plus Jimmy was a convicted felon now and he didn't need a gun on him if he didn't need one.

"I thought you were supposed to call me last night," Jimmy said to me. "I waited in front of the restaurant at 2:00 for you.

You were going to be sitting in my car with me when they showed. I was going to make them get in for the sit-down."

"I just got in," I said. "We had a delay in plans." I wasn't lying to Jimmy. "McGee had to rearrange things so that we could do this meeting right. Not sitting in a car."

"Who the fuck is Pro?" Jimmy yelled at Sally Bugs, regaining his steam. "Sending a fucking errand boy?"

"We'll be there in two minutes," Chuckie said, trying to be a peacemaker. Even as a kid there was never any fight in Chuckie. He couldn't fight to keep his hands warm.

"I called Jo," Jimmy said to me. "You could have left a message."

"You know how McGee is about the telephone when it involves his plans," I said.

"Somebody could have told me 2:30," Jimmy said. "At the very least. With all due respect to McGee."

"We're almost there already," Chuckie said. "I had to run an errand. It's not my fault."

We passed the footbridge and pulled up in front of the house and everything looked normal for a meeting. The same two cars were there, the brown Buick and the gray Ford, to signify to Jimmy that people were already inside waiting. I was disappointed when I saw the two cars still there because if either one of the cars was gone, that would have meant that the matter would have been called off.

The house and the neighborhood were not threatening in the least. It was a place you'd want your kids to grow up in. The garage in the rear was detached, which was a nice touch. Nobody was asking Jimmy to go in that house in secret through an attached garage. Jimmy and I were walking right in the front door in broad daylight with two cars parked right there in the driveway.

Time was of the essence. The thing had to be done on a schedule. There were alibis to consider. There's only so much time Tony Jack could spend getting a haircut and a massage. Plus I had to reconnect with Russell and the women in Ohio.

Chuckie pulled up the driveway and stopped near the brick steps to the front door.

Jimmy Hoffa got out of the rear door of the maroon Mercury. I got out of the front door at the same time. Sally Bugs would not be important enough to be going to a meeting like this. So Sally Bugs stepped out of his rear door and went around the Mercury and got in the front passenger seat. Jimmy and I headed for the steps while the Mercury backed on out to go the way we came. Chuckie drove away with Sally Bugs sitting in the shotgun seat. And that's the only point Sally Bugs could ever talk about. He knew only up to that point. Anything else he thought he knew was hearsay.

Russell told me that Chuckie dropped Sally Bugs off at Pete Vitale's office. Pete Vitale was an uncouth old-timer from Detroit's Purple Gang who owned a meatpacking plant where a body could be cut up and an industrial incinerator where a body could be burned up.

Jimmy Hoffa always walked out front, way ahead of people he was walking with. He took short steps but he was fast. I caught up to him and got right behind him the way you get right behind a prisoner you're taking back behind the line, and when he opened the front door I was right behind him up the front stoop and into the small vestibule, shutting the door behind us.

Nobody was in the house but the Andretta brother and the one that was with him, and they were down the long hall in the kitchen. You couldn't see them from the vestibule. They were there as cleaners to pick up the linoleum they had put down in the vestibule and to do any clean-up that might be necessary and to remove any jewelry and take Jimmy's body in a bag to be cremated.

When Jimmy saw that the house was empty, that nobody came out of any of the rooms to greet him, he knew right away what it was. If Jimmy had taken his piece with him he would have gone for it. Jimmy was a fighter. He turned fast, still thinking we were together on the thing, that I was his backup. Jimmy bumped into me hard. If he saw the piece in my hand he had to think I had it out to protect him. He took a quick step to go around me and get to the door. He reached for the knob and Jimmy Hoffa got shot twice at a decent range — not too close or the paint splatters back at you — in the back of the head behind his right ear. Back of his head, he could spin like half a turn. It all depends.

My friend didn't suffer. I took a quick look down the hall and listened to make sure nobody was going to come out and try to take care of me. Then I dropped the piece on the linoleum, went out the front door with my head down, got in my loaner, and drove back to the Pontiac airport where Russell's pilot was waiting for me.

The planners had timed the operation in Detroit to take an hour from start to finish.

Russell told me that after the two guys got done cleaning the house they put Jimmy in a body bag. Protected by the fence and the garage they took him out the back door and put him in the trunk of the Buick. Then they took Jimmy to be cremated. Russell told me the two cleaners picked up Sally Bugs at Pete Vitale's meat-packing plant and drove to some other airport, I don't know which, where the three of them flew back to Jersey to report to Tony Pro.

Once again, the pilot never looked at me. It was a quick up-and-down flight.

Russell was sleeping in my big black Lincoln at the small airfield in Port Clinton. We picked up the ladies and pulled into Detroit a little before 7:00. We picked up a Detroit police tail just inside the city limit. On account of the wedding they were on the lookout for people like us in out-of-state plates in big Lincolns and Cadillacs.

The only thing that was said between Russell and me that night about the particular matter was back there at the airstrip in Port Clinton, Ohio, after I slid behind the wheel and started up my Lincoln.

Russell woke up and winked his good eye at me and said softly with his raspy voice, "Anyway, I hope you had a pleasant flight, my Irish friend."

"I hope you had a good sleep," I said.

chapter twenty-nine

Everybody Bleeds

On August 4, 1975, five days after the disappearance of Jimmy Hoffa, the FBI made note of a meeting at the Vesuvio Restaurant at 163 West Forty-eighth Street in New York City. Present at the meeting were Anthony "Fat Tony" Salerno, Russell Bufalino, Frank Sheeran, Anthony "Tony Pro" Provenzano, and Salvatore "Sally Bugs" Briguglio.

New York had turned it down. They didn't sanction it, but they didn't oppose it either. "If you did it you were on your own"–type of thing. It couldn't have been done without Detroit's sanction, because it was their territory. Same for Chicago because they were close by and there was a lot of tie-in between Chicago and Detroit. The purpose of this meeting at the Vesuvio five days after Jimmy disappeared was to report to Fat Tony Salerno to tell him how the whole thing was done. Fat Tony was very satisfied. If New York had been involved in it, Fat Tony would already know how it was done and we wouldn't have been there reporting to him. Also, you wanted to let him know if there were any loose ends. You don't do a whole lot of talking. Just enough so that if something else needs to be done it can be ordered by Fat Tony, who was the top guy. Homicide detectives were all over the place. They try to be nonchalant but they can't help themselves; they peek. Charlie Allen drove me up and he waited at a table in another area and drank coffee. Sally Bugs sat at a different table in that area.

That first meeting at the Vesuvio went fine and then Tony Pro asked for another meeting to take place right after the first meeting. This one was about me. At this second meeting, Tony Pro made the claim that I knew all along that Jimmy wanted him whacked. Tony Pro claimed that he heard that Jimmy had asked me to kiss him and Fitz.

Tony Pro looked at me and said, "If it was up to me, you'd have gone, too."

"That works both ways," I said. "Everybody bleeds."

Tony Pro also complained that I was telling people at the wedding that he was capable of killing Hoffa. Tony Pro and I then got up from the table. I waited where Charlie Allen was, and Tony Pro sat down with Sally Bugs while Russell talked to Fat Tony about the whole thing. Russell came out from the partitioned area and got me and left Tony Pro sitting behind. On the way back to where Fat Tony was Russell said to me, "Deny it." I got back there and Fat Tony Salerno started off telling me he didn't believe I would be thinking about kissing a made man for Jimmy Hoffa and that was it. Russell Bufalino once again had taken care of his Irishman. Then they got Tony Pro and told him there was nothing to it.

Then Tony Pro started complaining to them about some time that I made him look bad. There was a joint council convention banquet in Atlantic City a few months before Jimmy disappeared. It was Pro's joint council. Fitz was supposed to be a speaker at the testimonial banquet, but Fitz canceled his visit. He wouldn't come to Atlantic City because he was afraid of me. Pro was hot talking about it to Russell and Fat Tony. He never took his eyes off me the whole time. Pro said, "You made me look bad. I didn't have the president. The president speaks at every joint council banquet everywhere in the country, except at mine. Fitz told me he heard you were going to give him a kiss for your friend Hoffa if he showed his face in Atlantic City." I told Pro, "If I was going to kiss Fitz for anybody he'd be long gone. I'm not your pimp. I can't straighten out your affairs. It's not on me if Fitz is a pussy and has no confidence that you can't protect him in Atlantic City with all your muscle." Russell told us to shake hands at once. That was not an easy thing to do. But if I ever said no to Russell I wouldn't be here now. We shook, but I hated Pro for the whole thing, all of it.

Then, like I was getting fire from all sides, Russell and I left the Vesuvio and began walking down Forty-fifth Street to Johnny's place and we bump into Pete Vitale. He was coming the other way from Johnny's, heading for his meeting with Fat Tony at the Vesuvio. Pete Vitale knew I didn't care for him a little bit, and he always thought I was making fun of him when I talked because I stammer like him. Pete Vitale gave me a hard look. He stopped and took his time so he wouldn't stammer and he said, "If it was up to me, the next time I see you and your friend is the next snowstorm in Detroit."

I knew what he meant. In the old days when there was a lot of coal in use, we threw ashes under the wheels to give the tires traction in a snowstorm. I had to laugh, hearing this tough talk again. I made sure I talked fast and stammered. I told Pete Vitale, "L-L-Like I just told your midget friend. That works both ways. Everybody bleeds."

Russell told us to knock it off.

We walked away and I said to Russell, thinking of Pete Vitale's industrial incinerator in Detroit, "Like you said, 'Dust to dust.'"

Then Russell whispered to me that he knew what I was thinking, but that Pete Vitale's incinerator was too obvious. He said that it was the first place they'd look and it was. He said they cremated Jimmy at a funeral parlor in Detroit that the Detroit people were close to. During the investigation I read that the FBI checked out the Anthony Bagnasco funeral parlor in Grosse Pointe Shores, because the Detroit people used it. I don't know if when Russell told me it was a funeral parlor he said that because he wanted to throw me off about Pete Vitale. He didn't want to have to square another beef like he did with Tony Pro. He didn't want me shooting my mouth off about Pete Vitale's incinerator to Jimmy's friends. Or it could have been that they took Jimmy to the funeral parlor. I don't know if they had an inside man at the funeral parlor who took charge of Jimmy and got him to a crematorium — maybe put him in the same box with somebody else they were cremating. But I do know that this detail was none of my business and anybody who says they know more than this — except for the cleaner who is still alive — is making a sick joke.

The day before that Vesuvio meeting with Tony Pro I had had a worse meeting. I had stopped by my ex-wife Mary's place in Philly to drop off some cash for her. When I walked into her kitchen my next-oldest daughter, Peggy, was there visiting her. Peggy was twenty-six. That was twenty-eight years ago.

Peggy and I had always been very close. When she was a little girl she used to like to go to dinner with me at the club. Then later on she used to like to go out to dinner with Russell and Carrie and me. Once a newspaper photographer took a picture of Russell going into a restaurant with Peggy in Bristol, Pennsylvania, but they had to cut Peggy out of the picture because she was a minor.

Peggy could read me like a book. Mary and Peggy were watching all the Hoffa disappearance news on the TV. Peggy looked up at me when I walked in and saw something she didn't like. Maybe I looked hard instead of worried. Maybe she thought I should have stayed in Detroit to work on finding Jimmy. Peggy asked me to leave the house and she said to me, "I don't even want to know a person like you." That was twenty-eight years ago and she doesn't want to have anything to do with me. I haven't seen Peggy or talked to her since that day, August 3, 1975. She has a good job and lives outside of Philly. My daughter Peggy disappeared from my life that day.

chapter thirty

"Those Responsible Have Not Gotten Off Scot-Free"

The FBI put 200 agents on the Hoffa disappearance and spent untold millions of dollars. Ultimately, seventy volumes of files were compiled containing more than 16,000 pages that came to be known as the HOFFEX file.

Early on, the FBI focused on a small group of people. Page three of a memo in the HOFFEX file identifies the following seven men: Anthony "Tony Pro" Provenzano, age fifty-eight; Stephen Andretta, age forty-two; Thomas Andretta, age thirty-eight; Salvatore "Sal" Briguglio, age forty-five; Gabriel "Gabe" Briguglio, age thirty-six; Francis Joseph "Frank" Sheeran, age forty-three; and Russell Bufalino.

Add Tony Giacalone and Chuckie O'Brien to the list, and the FBI had a total of nine suspects.

As if they had dead certain inside information, the FBI proved relentless in their belief that this handful of known suspects on page three of the HOFFEX memo had abducted and killed Jimmy Hoffa. Wayne Davis, a former head of the FBI in Detroit, was quoted as saying, "We think we know who's responsible and what happened." Kenneth Walton, another former head of the FBI in Detroit, said, "I'm comfortable I know who did it."

A federal grand jury was convened in Detroit six weeks after Jimmy Hoffa's disappearance. All nine of these men appeared, and they were all represented by Bill Bufalino. They all took the Fifth. Frank Sheeran took the Fifth on every question he was asked, including whether the prosecutor's yellow pen was yellow. After taking the Fifth, Stephen Andretta was given limited immunity and forced to testify. He refused to answer questions and did sixty-three days in jail for contempt of court before finally agreeing to answer the prosecutor's questions. Stephen Andretta set a Detroit record by leaving the grand jury room more than one thousand times to consult with his lawyer, Bill Bufalino. Chuckie O'Brien was called and took the Fifth, and he, too, was represented by Bill Bufalino. When asked how he could represent these uncooperative men who were suspected of killing his former client, Bill Bufalino said that Jimmy Hoffa "would have wanted it that way."

Today the FBI is quite satisfied that by now they have punished the guilty parties. The former assistant director of criminal investigations for the FBI, Oliver Rendell, said, "Even if it's never solved, I can assure you that those responsible have not gotten off scot-free." The current head of the Detroit FBI office, Special Agent John Bell, said with respect to the Hoffa suspects, "Remember, the government didn't convict Al Capone for bootlegging. They convicted him of tax evasion."

- In 1976, a year after Jimmy Hoffa disappeared, Tony Provenzano and Sal Briguglio were indicted for the 1961 murder of Local 560's Secretary-Treasurer, Anthony "Three Fingers" Castellito, a man who had grown up with Tony Provenzano on New York's Lower East Side. The murder had been ordered by Provenzano and had been committed by Sal Briguglio, a young hood named Salvatore Sinno, and an ex-boxer named K. O. Konigsberg. The day after the murder Tony Provenzano was in a wedding chapel in Florida marrying his second wife.

- The importance of the Hoffa case to the FBI was not lost on the prison inmates of America.

Anyone who knew anything about anyone on the short list of nine suspects whose names appeared in the newspaper with regularity knew that the government would make terrific deals of leniency in exchange for information. As a direct result of the Hoffa investigation, Salvatore Sinno came forward to admit his role in the fifteen-year-old murder and to turn on his accomplices. Sinno said that Sal Briguglio had been rewarded with Castellito's union job and that Konigsberg had been given $15,000. Tony Provenzano was convicted of Castellito's murder in 1978 and sent to Attica. The *New York Times* quoted an FBI source as saying, "These are all direct spinoffs from our Hoffa investigation." The *Times* then quoted O. Franklin Lowie, head of the FBI's Detroit office: "I don't care how long it goes. We'll stay on it. If enough people get their toes stepped on, someone will say something. It's still just a question of getting the break we need." Although his toes had been stepped on for life Tony Provenzano said nothing and died in Attica ten years after his conviction at the age of 72.

• In 1976 Tony Giacalone was convicted of income tax fraud and served a ten-year sentence. Two months after that conviction the government released to the media embarrassing tapes from a bug in place from 1961–64 that revealed that while Jimmy Hoffa was helping Tony Giacalone bribe a judge with $10,000, Tony Jack was plotting with his brother Vito "Billy Jack" Giacalone and Chuckie O'Brien's mother, Sally Paris, to get Josephine Hoffa drunk while her husband was out of town and steal Hoffa's strong box full of cash from his Florida condo. The plot was foiled when Hoffa returned home unexpectedly and found the plotters in his house with his wife passed out. They all claimed they were looking after her. In 1996 Tony Giacalone was indicted for labor racketeering, but his poor health led to many trial postponements. Giacalone died in 2001 at the age of 82 with the trial on these racketeering charges still pending. The Reuters headline for Giacalone's obituary read: "Reputed U.S. Mobster Takes Hoffa Secret to Grave."

- In 1977 Russell Bufalino was convicted of extortion. A con man named Jack Napoli had obtained $25,000 worth of jewelry on credit from a New York jeweler affiliated with Russell Bufalino. To get the jewelry Napoli posed as a friend of Bufalino's, although Bufalino had never heard of him. Bufalino held a meeting with Napoli at the Vesuvio. At the meeting, the seventy-three-year-old Bufalino threatened to strangle Napoli with his bare hands if Napoli failed to make good on the $25,000 he had stolen. As a direct result of the Hoffa investigation, Napoli had been wearing a wire.

- Bufalino went to jail for four years. When he got out in 1981, he met with two men and the three of them conspired to murder Napoli. Before the murder was to occur, one of those men, Jimmy "The Weasel" Frattiano, made a deal with the FBI and turned on Bufalino. Frattiano testified that at a meeting about Napoli in California, Bufalino said, "We want to clip him." Russell Bufalino, by then seventy-nine years old, was handed a fifteen-year sentence. While in prison he had a severe stroke and was transferred to Springfield prison hospital where he turned to religion; he died at the age of ninety in a nursing home under the FBI's watchful eye.

- The most the FBI could get on Chuckie O'Brien was receiving a car from a trucking company with whom his local had a contract, and falsifying a bank loan application. He served a ten-month sentence in 1978.

- Thomas Andretta and Stephen Andretta each served twenty-year sentences for a 1979 labor-racketeering conviction. For many years they had been squeezing cash out of one of the nation's largest trucking companies in exchange for labor peace. Tony Provenzano was convicted with them but he was already serving enough time for ten men his age. One interesting side note is that the defense subpoenaed Steven Brill, author of *The Teamsters,* in an effort to learn what a turncoat witness against them had told Brill, but Brill had never interviewed that particular witness.

- Gabriel Briguglio served seven years for labor racketeering and extortion.

- Based on two cases brought by the Department of Labor and the FBI, in 1982 Frank Sheeran received sentences totaling thirty-two years.

At one point during these efforts to step on toes James P. Hoffa was quoted as saying, "Only now does there seem to be some fruit from the investigation and there is some consolation from certain prosecutions. It does show the FBI is trying. But I hope the FBI renews its efforts to solve the case with regard to the disappearance of my father and not think justice has been done by putting certain suspects in jail on other cases."

What is it that made the FBI so dead certain about this list of nine "certain suspects" that they were putting "in jail on other cases"? With all their resources and their ability to investigate anywhere in the land, why were all the FBI agents and the Department of Justice's resources so narrowly focused for so long on such a small group of "certain suspects"? Why was the entire government effort, which included Department of Labor investigators and accountants, hovering over this small group? As a former prosecutor I can only ask the obvious question: Who was talking to the FBI?

❝ They watch the federal buildings. If they see you go into a federal building and you don't report it to somebody, you've got a problem. Sometimes I think they have people inside the federal buildings, like secretaries, but I never was told exactly how it worked. All I was told by Russell was that if I ever went into a federal building, even to answer a subpoena, I had better tell somebody in the family as soon as possible. You're not going there for tea.

In some way they heard Sally Bugs was going into a federal building and having contact with the FBI and he was not telling anybody. Now, he knew better. They confronted him and he admitted going in to see the FBI, but he denied telling them anything. Confronting him like this would cause the FBI to pull back a little bit. If he was wearing a wire they would pull it. If they were tailing him they would pull the tail.

I had heard that Sally Bugs might have been a little nervous about the Castellito murder indictment on top of the Hoffa investigation. Sally had a liver problem, and maybe it made him look a little yellow in the face. I heard he was afraid he had cancer, which would make certain people concerned about his mental toughness. Maybe Tony Pro was in a bad mood because he was on trial for taking a kickback on a loan. ❞

Provenzano was on trial for taking a $300,000 kickback on a $2.3 million loan to the Woodstock Hotel in New York's theater district. The loan proceeds came from his local's cash reserve. *New York Post* reporter Murray Kempton wrote, "Local 560 is a cash register." When Provenzano's indictment was handed down, Victor Riesel, the courageous labor reporter whom Johnny Dioguardi had blinded with acid twenty years earlier, reported in his syndicated column that it had been Provenzano's plan to run for president of the International in 1981 when Fitzsimmons retired, and to do that he needed the popular Jimmy Hoffa out of the way. Seizing and keeping power was the same reason he had needed the popular Anthony "Three Fingers" Castellito out of the way in 1961. And on both occasions he had used Sal Briguglio.

They didn't tell me much. They just told John Francis and me where to be. For the noise factor we both had .38s tucked in our belts against our backs. By this time I trusted The Redhead to work anywhere any time with me. On March 21, 1978, Sally Bugs was walking from the Andrea Doria Social Club, which was a block from Umberto's Clam House in Little Italy. He was alone. How they knew he was going to walk out alone from that place at that time I never heard, but they had their ways. Sally Bugs wore thick glasses and that's how he got the name "Sally Bugs," because he looked bug-eyed in the glasses. I didn't know him too well, but there was no mistaking those big glasses on a guy about 5'7". I walked up to him and said, "Hi, Sal." He said, "Hi, Irish." Sally Bugs looked at John because he didn't know The Redhead. While he was looking at John for an introduction, Sally Bugs got shot twice in the head. He went down dead, and John Francis pumped about three more into him for the effect of the loudness and the impression of a shoot-out to scare away anybody that had an idea to look out his window after the two shots.

In something as well planned as this, where they have to take into consideration that there could be agents in the vicinity, they've got people sitting in a car to drive you away and get rid of the guns. Time is of the essence, and you're out of there before the man hits the ground practically. They've got lots of backup on the scene. Backup is very important. You need people in crash cars to pull out from the curb and crash into any FBI cars.

In the newspaper they said that two hooded men knocked Sally Bugs to the ground first and then shot him. How two hooded men got close enough to Sally Bugs to shoot him the paper did not say. Sally Bugs was not blind. He could see good out of those glasses. Why the two hooded men would waste their time knocking him down to the ground first the paper did not say. Were the shooters hoping that on his way to the ground Sally Bugs would pull out his own piece and shoot them? Very likely the witness thought Sally Bugs was knocked down first because when you do it right he goes down very fast without any suffering. Most certainly the eyewitness knew enough to put hoods on the gunmen, so no one would have any doubt about him. Besides, eyewitness identification has been proven by statute as very erratic.

Bugs was another case of when in doubt, have no doubt.

And maybe now Tony Pro figured I did him a favor and we were all square on that beef he had with me. That I don't know. 🙶🙶

From my experience on both sides of this issue, I know that when a suspect asks for a deal, the prosecution asks him for an offer of proof, an outline of what the suspect has to offer. The things the suspect will be able to tell the authorities must be on the table before the authorities are in a position to know whether the information is worth offering a deal to obtain. From the beginning of the Hoffa investigation, Salvatore Briguglio appeared to be a man with something he wanted to get off his chest.

In 1976, during the waiting between lineups for the Detroit grand jury, a Michigan state police detective named Koenig kept an eye on the Andretta brothers and the Briguglio brothers. His attention was drawn to Sal Briguglio. Koenig said, "You could see that his brain was in turmoil and he was having difficulty coping with it. We all agreed he'd be the one to focus on."

In 1977 Sal Briguglio's need to talk manifested itself in discussions with Steven Brill, author of *The Teamsters*. Brill wrote in a footnote: "Salvatore Briguglio and I talked in 1977 with the ground rules that I would not reveal our discussions. On March 21, 1978, he was murdered. Our talks, which were conducted privately, were rambling and touched on the murder only occasionally. Even then, he only passively confirmed with a nod of his head certain relatively minor aspects of the crime that I put before him. He offered no elaboration and never revealed enough to implicate anyone except possibly himself."

In 1978, only a few days before Sal Briguglio was murdered his need to talk led to a recorded interview with Dan Moldea, author of *The Hoffa Wars*. Moldea described Briguglio as appearing "worn and tired, showing the strain of the enormous federal pressure he was under." Moldea quotes Briguglio as saying, "I've got no regrets, except for getting involved in this mess with the government. If they want you, you're theirs. I have no aspirations any more; I've gone as far as I can in this union. There's nothing left."

Did Sal Briguglio tell the FBI as much of the plot as he was in a position to know? Did the FBI then leave Sal Briguglio on the street to obtain an admission on a wire from the suspected killer?

Why did law enforcement sources immediately direct newspaper reporters' attention away from Provenzano as a suspect and betrayal as a motive? For example, Carl J. Pelleck of the *New York Post* reported the next day: "Investigators say the mob probably ordered the killing to get control of Provenzano's Local 560 — one of the largest in the nation — and its lucrative pension and welfare funds, which they would then parlay in investments in legalized gambling in Atlantic City." Why did law enforcement offer up another suspect who was in jail? Pelleck wrote: "They also were not discounting the possibility that the hand of Mafia boss Carmine Galante might be behind the Briguglio slaying plot."

Why won't the FBI release its file to the public whom it serves, the public that pays its bills? Is the FBI embarrassed?

In 2002, following intense pressure from the media and from Hoffa's children, who had unsuccessfully taken a lawsuit for access to the FBI Hoffa file all the way to the U.S. Supreme Court, the FBI released a 349-page summary of the Hoffa case. On September 27, 2002, the *Detroit Free Press* wrote,

"The *Free Press* obtained the new Hoffa information as a result of a decade-long legal battle. It is the first public disclosure of the FBI's own summary of the case. However, the report was heavily censored. Names were removed. Portions of interviews with potential witnesses were blacked out. Pages were missing from the report."

In March 2002 the FBI, while keeping its sixteen-thousand-page file close to its vest, released fourteen hundred pages of it to the *Free Press*. In the final sentence in its article concerning these pages the newspaper made the observation that, "the documents suggest that the FBI's most significant leads ran out in 1978."

That was the year Sal Briguglio was silenced.

chapter thirty-one

Under a Vow of Secrecy

> **❝** I can't put my drinking on the Hoffa disappearance. I didn't need an excuse to drink back then, but I was drinking heavily, I know that. **❞**

The *Philadelphia Bulletin* profiled Frank Sheeran on February 18, 1979, seven months before his Philadelphia RICO indictment. The headline read: "A Tough In Deep Trouble." There was a photo of Sheeran with the caption "History of Violence." The article said Sheeran was "a man noted for using his hands so well he did not need to carry a gun . . . a man so large police once found it impossible to handcuff his hands behind his back." The only other photo in the article was that of Jimmy Hoffa captioned, "Close Ties to Sheeran." The article emphasized "the FBI considers Sheeran a suspect in Hoffa's disappearance in 1975." The reporters quoted an unidentified Philadelphia lawyer who observed that Sheeran never cared about the vintage of his wine: "It just had to come from a grape. I never saw such a big man so able to crawl into a bottle of wine. He drinks incessantly."

On October 27, 1979, a month after his indictment and several months before his RICO trial, the *New York Times* also ran a profile and included a photo of Sheeran sitting at a bar with a whiskey in front of him. The article quoted

Sheeran, "Anything I got I owe him. If it wasn't for Hoffa, I wouldn't be where I am today."

An FBI 302 report quotes Charlie Allen on those years immediately following Jimmy Hoffa's disappearance: "Sheeran is a very heavy drinker and is drunk almost every day of the week."

The report also contains Charlie Allen's opinion of the kind of person who could have been in a position to kill Jimmy Hoffa: "It had to be somebody that knew him to set him up, you know, it had to be somebody he knew really good to get him in the car. Jimmy was a powerful man and you just didn't walk up to him and take him like that, you know, it had to be somebody that really knew him to get him in the car and do whatever they did."

In 1977 they took me in front of another grand jury. This one was in Syracuse. The FBI gave me advice that it was time for me to be a rat. The federal judge gave me limited immunity, so I had to answer questions at the grand jury. They had the Andretta brothers there, too, and they asked me if I knew them. I said I keep meeting them at grand juries. The prosecutor asked me if Russ ever had me shoot anybody. Later on that week they asked Russ if Frank Sheeran had anything to do with whacking anybody, and Russell said, "Not to my knowledge. To my knowledge the Irishman is a big pussycat."

They asked me questions about the pad Jimmy had at Lake Orion with "Russ & Frank" written on it. They asked me questions about the Pad, a private club in Endicott, New York, for Russ's family. I told them I went to the Pad to play the Italian fingers game "Amore" to see who gets to be boss and underboss to decide who gets to drink the wine. They asked me about matters I had done with a guy named Lou Cordi. They had particulars. After the grand jury, Russ told me that to die in peace Lou Cordi had done a deathbed confession.

Like with John Francis, nobody blamed Lou Cordi for talking while he was dying and under medication, making his peace.

They had me in Syracuse for nine hours. They heard a lot of the lessons on testifying that I had learned from Jimmy: "If you could refresh my recollection on that matter I might be able to recall what you want me to recall, but at this particular time I do not recall the particulars of that particular matter."

About a year later I was standing in the Cherry Hill Inn in Jersey getting ready to leave after having a few drinks, when my driver, Charlie Allen, leaned over and asked me, "Did you kill Jimmy Hoffa?" I said, "You rat, motherfucker," and the FBI came out of the walls to surround Allen to protect him. The restaurant was crawling with agents who had been listening in on Allen's wire. They thought I was going to whack him on the spot.

Whenever anybody says, "Did you . . . ?" it's time to pick up your check and leave. The only way Charlie Allen asks that particular question at that particular time is that the feds decided it was time he got around to asking it.

I had a .38, so while they were surrounding Allen I ran to my Lincoln and drove up the off-ramp of Route 72, bucking traffic. I got to the Branding Iron and gave my piece to a woman friend I knew. She put it in her purse. They walked in and she walked right past them and out the door.

They asked me to go out to their car with them. I did and one of the agents said they had me for two life sentences and 120 years. I said, "How much time do I get off for good behavior?"

The agent said that if I wore a wire against Russ and Angelo I would be guaranteed to be back out on the street in ten years. I told him, "This must be another case of mistaken identity."

The agent said they had me nailed solid for two murders, four attempted murders, and a long list of other felonies, and if I didn't cooperate and let them protect me I'd end up dead from the mob or I'd die in jail. I said, "What will be will be."

The way they got me in the first place is that they caught Charlie Allen operating a methamphetamine lab in New

Jersey. Naturally, Allen didn't want Angelo or Russell to know he was moving meth. Naturally, Allen didn't want to go to jail forever on the meth lab, and naturally, Allen knew the feds would do anything to get me because of the Hoffa case. The feds ended up giving Allen two years in jail. But then the State of Louisiana got him for life for baby-rape of his stepdaughter.

I had a RICO indictment against me that named about twenty unindicted coconspirators, including Russell and Angelo. Angelo was already whacked by the time the case went to trial, but there were a lot of other important people who did not want to see the government convict me of crimes I allegedly did with them, or they could be next. On the first day of my federal RICO trial in February 1980, the FBI went to my attorney, F. Emmett Fitzpatrick, to warn him that they had gotten word from one of their sources that my unindicted coconspirators were concerned that when I got convicted I was going to flip and so they had a contract out on me. I told Emmett to ask them who had the contract so when I saw the guy coming I could get off first.

One of the murders they put on me was the Fred Gawronski shooting that Tommy Barker had already beaten on self-defense. Charlie Allen claimed I ordered the hit because Gawronski spilled wine on me. Emmett beat Charlie Allen to death on cross-examination.

During a break in the trial I saw an agent named Quinn John Tamm talking to my teenage daughter, Connie. I asked the prosecutor, "Hey, Courtney, how many murders do you have on me?" He said, "Two. Why?" I said, "If Tamm ever talks to one of my daughters again you're going to have three." Later on, somebody jumped from behind a bush and threw a blanket over Tamm. Blanketing a guy is a message to let him know how vulnerable he is. It startles a guy and by the time he gets the blanket off him the guy who threw it is long gone. Tamm came to court and called me a "motherfucker." I just smiled.

After Emmett called his last witness for the defense, I said, "You've got another witness."

"Who?" Emmett said.

"Francis," I said.

"Francis who?" Emmett said.

"Francis me," I said.

I always believe in testifying and making eye contact with the jury, especially if the government is painting a picture of you that you would have a guy whacked for spilling wine on you. Can you imagine what they have to be thinking when you look into their eyes?

"Jury Acquits Sheeran on All Charges," they said in the headline in the *Philadelphia Bulletin*.

My big problem was a couple of smaller offenses. They had my voice on the wire that Charlie Allen was wearing when he was on the payroll of Local 326.

I had a problem with a crane company. The manager had fired two of my shop stewards and he wouldn't negotiate with me. The grievance hearing was coming up and I didn't want this company manager showing up at the hearing. They claim I told Charlie Allen to give the guy a tune-up. Allen had me on tape saying: "Break both of his legs. I want him laid up. I want him to go to the hospital." After that secret taping the FBI put a fake cast on the guy's leg, and they had him show up at the hearing on crutches. The feds got me for that one in a state trial in Delaware.

The FBI also got me in that state for picking up dynamite from Medico Industries, a Pennsylvania manufacturer of ammunition that had big contracts with the government. Russell was a silent partner in Medico. The dynamite was for blowing up the office of the company that the guy with the fake broken leg worked for. I got a total of fourteen years.

The other big problem I had was that the FBI took down the license plate number from my black Lincoln that I had in Detroit when Jimmy disappeared. The feds found out that I bought the car from Eugene Boffa, who ran the company that leased truck drivers to freight companies and paid them substandard wages. I paid under the market value for the car, and I didn't have all my receipts for the monthly payments I made in cash. They claimed I got the black Lincoln as a bribe to let Boffa pay substandard wages and fire some people. They claimed I got a white Lincoln a year later and that I got $200 a week from Boffa. They had a tape from Charlie Allen that had me saying that I split the $200 with Russell and "to hell with my union." By then with Jimmy gone, everything was different.

After that conviction I told the *Philadelphia Inquirer* on November 15, 1981, that "the only man who was perfect got nailed to the cross."

Agent Quinn John Tamm got the last laugh and he told the reporter I had "more lives than a cat until now."

I was sixty-two years old and I got eighteen on top of the fourteen for thirty-two. I had bad arthritis and it looked like I would die in jail.

I did my federal time first. I spent the Reagan years as the president's guest. They sent me to the United States penitentiary at Sandstone, Minnesota. It's up near the Canadian border, and they get wicked wind up there. In the winter the wind-chill factor can go to seventy below zero.

Every so often the FBI would show up and call me out in the middle of the night. That's the time snitches get called out when they think everybody else is asleep. The FBI waits for you in a separate building far away from the inmate population. To get from your block to where the FBI waits you have to walk outside a quarter of a mile. They have a yellow rope for you to hold on to to keep the wind from blowing you down. The wind chill goes right through a normal person. If you have arthritis and you're walking real slow it's an experience.

My old army buddy Diggsy Meiers swears that he got his arthritis because when he fell asleep in a foxhole in Monte Casino I stole his blanket. Those foxholes were filled with rainwater that was frozen over and you had to kick through the top layer of ice to get into the hole to avoid the shrapnel. I think that's how we both got the arthritis to start with. In jail I kept getting more and more hunched over as the arthritis ate at my lower back and pressed on my spinal cord. I went into jail 6'4" and I came out 6'0". You didn't have to talk to the FBI when they came, but you did have to go to them. They told me that they would move me closer to my daughters if I cooperated so it wouldn't be so hard for them to visit me. I wear a ring on my right hand that has the birthstone for each one of my four daughters. They would tell me I had the keys to the prison in my pocket if I cooperated, and I would turn around and head back down that yellow line to my block. The next day I would call my lawyer to go on record that I had had a visit from the feds so nobody would have no doubt.

I met some good people in school at Sandstone. There was an old guy from Boston who was in for doing the Brinks job around 1950. In its day it was the biggest heist ever pulled. They put millions on the table. It took about seven years to solve, but they got them. They had a list of suspects right away, like they did with us. For seven years they just kept hauling them down for questioning, banging away until finally one of them broke and brought them all down.

Sally Bugs's brother, Gabe, was in Sandstone. He went about 5'2". Gabe had nothing to do with what happened to Jimmy. He wasn't even there, but the FBI kept him on the list because with Sally Bugs talking the feds would have figured he'd leave his brother's name out. So they kept his brother's name in.

When things got really bad with my arthritis, the warden at Sandstone sent me to Springfield in Missouri. That's a prison hospital. Fat Tony Salerno was there dying of cancer. He couldn't control his urine. Russell was there in a wheelchair on account of his stroke. With Russell there, I was back with my teacher, and I had the best teacher around. The old man played bocce from his wheelchair. He was older than I am now and he could still hit for his age. Every once in a while he'd give me a little shot when I beat him at gin. McGee loved his ice cream and I would make sure he got some every day, because you only got commissary privileges once a week. I would pay whoever had commissary that day to get me some ice cream for Russ. When I was in Springfield my daughter Connie had her first baby and Russell came out to the bocce court and gave me the good news. Russ had heard it from his wife, Carrie.

A couple of times when we were alone together we talked about Jimmy. I learned more about the thing, too, a few details. Neither one of us wanted to see things go as far as they did. We both felt that Jimmy did not deserve that. Jimmy was a nice man with a nice family.

One Sunday I was heading to the bocce court and I saw Russell being wheeled to the chapel by one of the attendants. I said, "Where are you going, McGee?"

"To church," Russell said.

"To church?" I laughed.

"Don't laugh, my friend. When you get to be my age you'll realize there's something more than this."

Those words stayed with me all these years.

By 1991 I needed surgery or I would become paralyzed, so they let me out on early parole on a medical hardship. I was seventy-one. I was still on paper and the FBI kept trying to get my parole violated. They wired a guy who used to deal in sports tickets. His wife left him and she had all the money. She was going to divorce him, but he wanted her whacked before the divorce was final so he would end up with everything. He offered me $25,000 down, $25,000 after she was whacked, and then he would really take care of me after the settlement of her estate. I said, "I suggest you get a good marriage counselor."

They finally got me on parole violations for drinking Sambuca with the alleged Philly boss, John Stanfa. You float three coffee beans in the Sambuca; one for yesterday, today, and tomorrow. I didn't have much of a tomorrow left, but the FBI was still after it. At the hearing they played the wired guy's tapes, saying I should have turned him in for wanting his wife whacked. I was seventy-five and they ordered me back to jail for ten months. The day I got violated I held a press conference to let the world at large and certain people downtown and upstate know that I was no rat. I was not going to fold and be a rat just because they were sending me to jail at my age and in my condition. I wanted all the people I did anything with over the years to know that I was not weakening in my old age, like John Francis and Lou Cordi did before they died. And I wanted the FBI off my back in jail; no more late-night visits. I told the reporters I was going to write a book to prove that Richard M. Nixon did it to Jimmy.

While I was in jail I got a letter from Jimmy's daughter, Barbara, asking me to tell what happened to Jimmy "under a vow of secrecy."

I got out on October 10, 1995, and my wife Irene died of lung cancer on December 17. I got worse and worse with my hunched-over walking and my dropped right foot in the brace, and before you knew it I couldn't get very far with my two canes. I had to use a walker everywhere I went. My three daughters that have anything to do with me were concerned that if I died I couldn't be buried in a Catholic cemetery. I pictured Russell going to chapel at Springfield and telling me that there was "something more than this." My daughters arranged a private audience for me with Monsignor Heldusor at St. Dorothy's Church in Springfield, Pennsylvania. I met with him and we talked about my life and he forgave me for my sins. I bought a green casket and the girls bought me a crypt in a Catholic cemetery. The older girls are happy that their mother, Mary, will be buried in the crypt with me when she goes from her Alzheimer's.

I have a small room in a nursing home. I keep my door open. I can't stand to have a door closed.

Afterword

I heard Frank's lawyer, Emmett Fitzpatrick, say to Frank at one of Frank's birthday parties, "You're a hell of a man with a telephone in your hand, Frank. What would you care if they sent you to prison. As long as they gave you a telephone in your cell, you'd be happy. You wouldn't know you were in jail."

During the years I spent on this project Frank Sheeran called me repeatedly throughout the day, practically every day, to talk about practically everything. He referred to nearly anyone he spoke about as being "good people." He ended nearly every conversation by telling me, "Everything is copacetic." I could always tell when he was having second thoughts about having admitted something — the number, the volume, and the nervous energy of his social calls increased. Occasionally, he would try to take back what he said. But his nerves would eventually settle down and he would be comfortable, even pleased, with having made the admission, with having told someone.

Frank got especially nervous as the day approached for our planned trip to Detroit to find the house where Jimmy Hoffa was hit.

In February 2002 I drove Frank to Detroit. At the time he was living by himself in an apartment in a Philadelphia suburb. He told me that he had just started having a lot of nightmares, mixing incidents in the war with incidents and

people from his life in the mob. He began to "see" these
people when he was awake, and he called them "chemical
people," because he believed they were from a chemical
imbalance that would be fixed when he got his medicine
checked. "There are two chemical people in the backseat. I
know they're not real, but what are they doing in the car?"

The drive west through Pennsylvania and Ohio into
Michigan was a nightmare for me when he was awake. If he
wasn't talking about the "people" he was critical of my driving. At one point I said to him, "Frank, the only good thing
about having you here in the car with me is that you're not
calling me on the telephone." Fortunately, he laughed.

We took two days for the drive. At the motel the first night
he made me keep the door open between our rooms. Ever
since jail he didn't want to be alone behind a closed door. The
next day in the car he slept a lot and became much improved.
I began to think that all he needed was some good restful
sleep, which he rarely got alone in his apartment.

When I saw the Detroit skyline I nudged him awake. He
took one look at the skyline and barked at me: "You got a
piece?"

"A what?" I said.

"A piece," he demanded.

"What do you mean a piece?"

"A P-I-E-C-E piece." He made his hand into a gun and
made as if to fire the gun into my floorboard.

"What would I be doing with a piece?"

"Lawyers have pieces. You're allowed to have a permit."

"I don't have one," I yelled back. "I'd be the last person you
know to have one. What do you want a piece for?"

"Jimmy had friends here. They know I was on the other
side of this thing."

"Frank, what are you trying to do? Scare me? Nobody
knows you're here."

He grunted, and I began to calculate the approximate ages
of Jimmy's former Detroit allies. As I settled down, I had the
image of Jimmy's "friends," if any were still alive, in wheel-
chairs stalking us.

When we got to our motel I was relieved to see and meet Frank's former fellow inmate and the man who was going to write the book in 1995 blaming the Hoffa hit on Nixon, John Zeitts. He had driven there from his home in Nebraska to visit Frank out of respect, and he would now spend the night in Frank's room. He would change the bandage on Frank's bedsore. At dinner that night at a steak house, Frank looked over at me and winked. "You got a piece?" he said and the two of them laughed. Frank told me that John had been a prisoner of war in Vietnam. That night I was entranced by the story of John's escape from the Viet Cong. He bore long scars all across his torso. The Viet Cong liked to slice a prisoner's skin because a certain type of fly would lay its eggs in the open wound. John would find maggots oozing out of his body years later.

That night alone in my motel room I wondered if I had waited too long to make this Detroit trip. I knew better than to rely on Sheeran's help in finding the house. The next morning I asked John to help us, but he did not know there was a house. It was not part of anything in the fantasy version he had worked on with Frank in 1995. I had my notes with me and found the general directions that Frank had given during an editorial meeting we'd had with Eric Shawn at Fox News. Amazingly, they were almost as solid in 2002 as they had been in 1975. The only thing missing from my notes was a final left turn onto the street opposite a footbridge that was mentioned. It turned out that the footbridge was in a golf course on the right. It took a few passes before I saw the bridge at all, finally noticing it from a parallel road on the other side of the course, a road that was on higher ground and overlooked the links. I drove back around to the original road and saw the problem at once. I said a few Hail Marys.

Over the years a chain-link fence had been built, and the fence made the bridge less noticeable than in the directions Sheeran had given me some time back. While we were stopped near that footbridge at a T intersection I got out of the car, looked down the street to my left, and spotted the rear of a house at the end of the block on the right that had the kind of backyard Sheeran had described. Of course, I thought, being on a golf course the footbridge could have had no significance to the directions except that it was at the bridge that a left turn had to be made. I made the turn and drove to the front of that house. The steely, tense look on Sheeran's face told me at once that this was it. He studied it and confirmed that it was with a nod of his head and a grunt of "Yeah." It was a very quiet street, a perfect house in a perfect street. The only thing that bothered me about the house was that it was brick and Sheeran had described a house with brown shingles. It wasn't until after we returned home and I developed the photos I had taken that I realized that the top half of the house was all brown shingles on the rear and on the side of the house that you see as you approach it from the footbridge.

On the return trip east from Detroit it was evident that Sheeran had settled down. There were no "chemical people" and no complaints about my driving. We found the airport at Port Clinton, took some photos, and drove home in one day. Shortly after this trip I helped his daughters get him into an assisted living facility. I accompanied Frank and his daughter Dolores to a doctor who prescribed medication to control the "chemical people," and I never heard about them again. I never again saw him in as distraught and nervous a condition as he was in heading in to Detroit without a "P-I-E-C-E piece."

The next trip we took together was to find the company grounds in Baltimore where he had picked up a load of war matériel for the Bay of Pigs invasion and where he had delivered rifles just prior to the John F. Kennedy assassination. Before we went down to Baltimore he told me the name of the place was the Campbell Brickyard. He had a general idea where it was, but we couldn't find it. Finally, I drove into the Bonsal Cement Plant to ask if anyone knew about the brickyard. As we entered there was something familiar about the plant to Sheeran. Inside the office I learned from a female employee that when her father had worked there Bonsal had been the Campbell Cement Company, but she didn't know of any Campbell Brickyard. We drove around the grounds. Some new buildings had been erected. Sheeran pointed to an older structure and said, "That's where the soldiers came out of to load the truck." I took a picture and we returned to Philadelphia.

Some things did not go as smoothly as the trip to Baltimore.

It has been my experience that when an adult who has developed a conscience in his childhood wants to get something off his chest the route to confession is usually a circuitous one with many fits and starts, with roadblocks and red herrings and hints and glimpses of the truth. Often the person drops a hint and wants the questioner to figure it out. A good example of such an interrogation is the notorious case of Susan Smith, who drowned her two sons in her car in a lake and blamed a "black carjacker." For nine days Sheriff Howard Wells displayed the patience and skill of a superb interrogator who knows how to avoid pitfalls, maintain a rapport, and follow the hints until it is time to confront the truth.

There were certain things that Frank Sheeran expressed to me that I knew would interfere with the clearing of his conscience. He didn't want the three daughters that still were in his life to think any worse of him than they already might. His deceased wife, Irene, had assured his youngest daughter that Frank didn't have time to kill Hoffa, because Irene was convinced he was "with her." Frank didn't want Barbara Crancer to think he was some kind of ogre because he had called her mother two days after her father's disappearance to express his concern. Frank didn't want to offend Russell Bufalino's widow, Carrie, or anyone else who might be alive. He didn't want people that he had been involved with over the years to think he had gone soft in the end like John Francis and Lou Cordi. He said, "I lived my life a certain way. I don't want people thinking I went the other way." Another time he said, "Even though he's dead, if I would say that about Russ, as close as we were, there are other people out there who know I know things about them." In the interview, I kept the focus on the Hoffa case.

About two years into the interview process, after Sheeran had admitted to me that he was the shooter in the Hoffa case but about a year before going to Detroit to find the house, my agent scheduled a meeting at Emmett Fitzpatrick's office with Eric Shawn, a senior correspondent with Fox News who was knowledgeable on mob matters, and his producer, Kendall Hagan. It was our intention to get Frank comfortable with one correspondent that he could trust. At the meeting, consistent with the protection of his rights, Sheeran was going to utter for the first time to anyone besides me the words: "I shot Jimmy Hoffa."

Two nights before the meeting I arrived at Sheeran's apartment to spend the night in his guest room. Without comment Sheeran handed me a typewritten letter purportedly signed by Jimmy Hoffa in 1974 following Frank Sheeran Appreciation Night. More than half of the letter contained things Sheeran had told me all along, starting with the 1991 aborted interviews. The rest contained things that more easily could be read to bolster the fantasy version of events that he had promoted with his friend John Zeitts. I assured Frank that at some point I would check the authenticity of this letter.

The meeting went well. When Shawn asked if he thought he could find the house, Sheeran gave us the directions and mentioned "the footbridge." This was the first time he had ever revealed the directions to me. His deepened voice and hard demeanor was chilling when, for the first time ever, he stated publicly to someone other than me that he had shot Jimmy Hoffa two times in the back of the head. To everyone in the room it had the ring of truth. Fox News did some preliminary independent research and confirmed the historical value of Frank Sheeran's account of the last ride of Jimmy Hoffa.

Soon thereafter, I contacted the renowned forensic lab of Dr. Henry Lee. They assured me they could determine the authenticity of Hoffa's signature and could lift latent Hoffa prints from the letter. However, I would have to contact the FBI and obtain Hoffa's prints and handwriting exemplars for them. At that time we had no publisher and the book had yet to be written. I did not want to alert the FBI and have the story leak out before there was a book in the stores. I decided to put the matter on a back burner. Later on when we got a publisher I explained all this and the publisher told me that, coincidentally, they had published Henry Lee's book. I gave them my e-mail correspondence with Lee's lab and hoped that because of the publisher's relationship the lab would make the necessary requests of the FBI themselves. The publisher contacted the lab and sent them the letter. There was no need for exemplars or prints; when the letter was put under a special light it turned out to be a laughable forgery. The paper it was typed on was manufactured in 1994, not 1974. The signature was inked over a faint photocopy of an authentic Hoffa signature. Even though the letter was not at all central to the book and could be removed easily, and even though the editor assigned to the book had no doubt that Sheeran had killed Hoffa, the publisher decided to cancel the book. I was upset at Frank until my now former editor suggested that I got off easy, considering what Sheeran had done to some other friends in his life. He said, "If you can't trust a man who murdered one of his best friends, who can you trust?" He asked me to be sure never to give Sheeran his phone number.

When the dust settled and I confronted him Sheeran conceded that the letter had given him insurance, a way out if he ever needed it. It was to him a loose thread he could unravel any time the heat got to be too much for him. If a grand jury were convened he could expose the letter and that would cancel out everything else in the book.

My agent, Frank Weimann, told Sheeran over the phone that if he wanted to get another publisher he would have to come clean and stand behind the book. Weimann sent Sheeran a hard copy of his e-mail to the former publisher, which said, among other things: "I am willing to stake my reputation on this book for many reasons, not the least of these is that *The Irishman* is of historical significance. Frank Sheeran killed Jimmy Hoffa."

In the aftermath of losing the book deal Frank's generous
and delightful girlfriend and constant companion, Elsie, sadly
passed away following surgery. Her room had been across the
hall from Frank's at the assisted living facility where they
met. On occasion I had taken the couple to dinner, and it
was always a lot of fun. Frank teased her about her love of
food. He claimed he had fork marks on his hand from the
time he made the mistake of reaching over to taste her dish.
Although his daughters and I never told Frank of Elsie's
passing, he learned it somehow. Around that time his health
took a dramatic turn for the worse, and he was repeatedly
hospitalized. He was in severe pain and became bedridden.

At the hospital he sensed that he was dying, and he
expressed to me that he didn't want to live the way he was
living. In our conversation about doing a video to stand
behind the book, as Weimann had suggested, he said: "All
I want now asking [sic], Charles, is keep the pain at a mini-
mum, keep me dry, and let the Man upstairs do what He
wants to do. I can't be livin' like this."

After speaking by phone with Emmett Fitzpatrick, Frank
Sheeran decided to go on videotape and stand behind the
material in the book, including what happened to Jimmy
Hoffa on July 30, 1975.

Although I agreed to make it as easy on him as possible,
he now publicly would be endorsing the truthfulness of that
material. I said to him, "All you're going to have to do is back
up what the book says. That's all. Will you be prepared to do
that, do you think?" He answered, "I might as well." As I left
him that night he said in reference to his having received the
visiting priest's sacraments, "I'm at peace." I said, "God bless
you. You'll be at peace standing behind the book."

The next day he said that the FBI will "have me [sic] a
hard time to question because they can't make me travel
anywhere." Because of his health and medical needs he did
not expect that any prosecutor would bother to indict him.

When I turned the video on he became hesitant and with-
drawn. I told him: "You're hesitating, right? I don't want to do
it if you're hesitating." He said, "No, I'm not hesitating." I said,

"If you're heart's not in it, forget about it." He replied: "It's something that you've got to work yourself into. I'm going to do it." He asked for his mirror to check his appearance.

We discussed that he had given his confession and received communion the day before. He said, "And I had it last week, too."

I said that he was now facing his "moment of truth." I gave him the galley copy to hold up to the camera. And then, without any of our normal protective language, I got down to it and said: "I'm going to get it now, okay. Now, you read this book. The things that are in there about Jimmy and what happened to him are things that you told me, isn't that right?" Frank Sheeran said: "That's right." I said: "And you stand behind them?" He said: "I stand behind what's written."

I immediately asked him a question about what Jimmy Hoffa was like and that caused him to say that Jimmy, ". . . did not — what can I say — did not — You have to go into questions, then one question leads to another. — Let the book speak for itself." I knew that he wouldn't want to delve into details, especially about Jimmy Hoffa, but it was hard not to talk in some detail.

Unfortunately, the camera battery died, and it was awhile before I discovered it and plugged the camera in. Furthermore, to make him comfortable or at his request I stopped the tape from time to time and turned on an audio tape recorder. Still, ample material was recorded. In reviewing the recordings, both audio and video, there are a number of segments that are revealing of the man himself, some of his deeds, and the interview process.

At one point he asked me to be sure to specify in the book that whenever he was intimate with a woman other than his wife it was at a time that he was single. He said that to say otherwise "don't serve no literary purpose. . . . That's not going to win no Pulitzer Prize. . . . Make sure to note I was single."

Looking at the cover of the book he said, "I think the title sucks." I said, "But they're the first words that Jimmy ever spoke to you, right?"

"Yeah," he admitted and dropped that topic.

While he was looking at a photo of Sal Briguglio I mentioned that we would be following our plan to urge the FBI to release their file so that whatever Sally Bugs had told them would corroborate the book. I said the photo was taken "[b]efore you took care of him. You know what I mean?"

"Yeah," he said.

"Did that picture of Sally Bugs stir up anything in you?" I asked.

"No, not really," he said. "Water under the dam."

I told him that if he got well enough Eric Shawn wanted to take us for lunch at Monte's Restaurant in Brooklyn where he had picked up "the package."

"Yeah," he said, "the package, yeah — for the — for Dallas." Later we returned to the topic of lunch at Monte's, and I said that when we go, "We'll see where you picked up those rifles."

He said: ". . . [Y]ou're right, and have a little angel spaghetti with oil and garlic." I told him that I'd like to see him dipping his Italian bread into his red wine. "You got a picture of that," he said.

I mentioned the place where he made drops "for the politicians." I asked: "What was the name of that place?"

He promptly replied, "The Market Inn" and said, "See, my memory's there, Charles."

The most significant moment for me came when he revealed something brand new. It began when we were looking at a photo of the house in Detroit, and he said: "They're supposed to be the original people. They were there originally . . . But they never testif—" He followed that with mumbling and said, "They wasn't involved." Whenever he was being extra careful with his words and making some of them inaudible I knew it was a topic I would likely return to. When I mentioned in the form of a question that the house was a loaner like the car, he ignored the question twice and then said, "Well, I don't have to worry about being indicted." Based on my experience with him it seemed to me that his response might be an indication that he was mulling over whether to tell me something new.

A little later I pointed out the photo of the house in Detroit "where Jimmy died — got hit." He volunteered a comment that sounded like there was a "guy" involved in the house that I had not known about. It was a mumbled and swallowed comment that seemed to stop in mid-sentence. Later I had the tape analyzed by an audio expert; it sounded to him like ". . . that's the house that the guy did his letters to." The audio problem was compounded by the fact that Sheeran's fifty-year-old full dentures no longer fit because of his dramatic weight loss. Immediately after making the comment Sheeran said, "I'm only going by what you got in the book, so —" He had made dismissive comments like this before when there was something additional that he wasn't sure he wanted to tell me. Unless he knew that the "guy" was dead he would not want to reveal his identity.

At the time it sounded to me that the "guy" had "lent" them the house, but today I don't hear an "n" on the CD that the audio expert made for me.

At any rate, after some short chitchat about his friend John calling to see how he was and a brief cell phone call from my stepson, I followed up.

"All right. But that house was on loan, huh?" I said.

"Yeah. The people that owned it . . ." he paused.

"They didn't know anything about it," I said, which is something he had told me years earlier and that was already in the book.

"Yeah," he said. "The people that owned it, yeah. There was a real estater —" This brand-new revelation of the existence of some kind of real-estate broker or agent was followed by a lengthy pause during which I said nothing. Then he said, "They lived there at the time." "Uh huh," I said.

"And they were never. They were never — never questioned."

"But they didn't know anything about it, did they?" I said.

"No, of course not," he said with an exaggerated emphasis that made me think that the "real estater" did know something. But this was not the time for me to press and cross-examine. We had an agreement, and he had lived up to it.

"Okay," I said.

"I, I, I only said — what you got printed that's the story."
And with that comment I knew there was more to it, and that
it was going to be difficult for me to let it drop entirely.

"I understand," I said. "I'm not questioning you anymore.
I'm just curious. When you said the real estate—"

"Uh-huh," he said attentively.

"The real-estate broker. I — You hadn't told me that. So," I
laughed. "That's okay. No problem. . . ."

"Yeah," he took his glasses off.

"All right," I said as Sheeran turned, gave the camera a hard
look, and began smoothing his hair. I knew that was my cue
to turn it off, and I did. What comes next is from an audio
recording.

In a short while my curiosity had the better of me. Even
though my heart wasn't entirely in it, I couldn't resist. I had
to make one last respectful try at the "real estater."

"Now," I said. "You got my interest about this realtor that
you mentioned."

"About the what?" he said.

"The realtor that you mentioned on the house in Detroit.
You'd never mentioned that to me before."

"What's that?"

I sensed he was having a problem with my use of the word
"realtor." I should have stuck closer to his terminology. I knew
better. I said, "The real — the real-estate guy on the house in
Detroit. You said there was a real-estate guy involved. You
don't want to talk about that, huh?"

He mumbled and swallowed a few words that I strained to
hear, but could not. And then he made up his mind and said
clearly, "No. Well, you got enough, Charles."

"I got enough," I said.

"Be satisfied, Charles."

"I'm satisfied."

"You got enough. Don't be probing."

Indeed, I had more than enough. But there's nothing like
the whole truth. If I had somehow known that in a few days
Frank Sheeran would take such a dramatic turn for the worse
I might have pursued it. But he'd told his son-in-law, I'm

checking out, Mike. It's lost now, unless the FBI file has a reference to it, and the FBI releases its file.

It seems likely to me that the house was a rental unit in 1975, because of the advanced age of the owner, a single woman who bought the house in 1925. Perhaps a realtor acted as her rental agent and had a key. Perhaps a realtor was simply the elderly woman's friend and had a key. Perhaps the house had a For Sale sign. In any event, the existence of a realtor could explain more than just the key. It could explain why the planners felt comfortable letting people park in the driveway. If it were a rental unit or if it were listed for sale it would be normal for strangers to park in the driveway and walk into the house.

Frank Sheeran died six weeks after that interview. During that time my wife and I drove the three hours from our home to visit him at least once a week, and I visited him alone a couple more times a week. His head was bent and he barely looked up, but he smiled broadly when he heard our voices. He would allow me to feed him a little bit of Italian water ice and would sip water from a straw my wife held for him, but basically he had shut down. He refused to eat. I last saw him on December 6, 2003. My stepson, Tripp, and I had visited, and I told him that I was going to Idaho and I would see him after the New Year. His last mumbled words to me were, "I'm not going anywhere."

I got the call from his daughter Dolores the night he died, December 14, 2003. It was the day U.S. soldiers captured Saddam Hussein. When I heard about Saddam's capture my first thought was, "I wonder what Frank thinks of this." He was always on top of the news. When the Columbine story broke and the police were waiting outside the school as the killers continued to shoot inside, Frank said to me, "What are those cops waiting for? They would tell six of us to take a tank and we'd go take the tank." That was the soldier talking. When influential Delaware lawyer Tom Capano got sentenced to death for murdering his girlfriend and dumping her body at sea when she tried to break off their romance, Sheeran said: "You don't kill somebody over something like that. They don't

want you any more, you just leave." That was the expert on
the subject. When our embassies in Africa were blown up
in the late nineties and a man named Osama bin Laden was
suspected of being behind it, I said, "They should take that
guy out. I'm sure he did it." Now the mob legend spoke, "If he
didn't do it, he thought about doing it." And that was plenty
good enough.

Obituaries in both the *Philadelphia Inquirer* and the
Philadelphia Daily News made mention of the fact that Frank
Sheeran had long been a suspect in the Hoffa disappearance.

I flew back for the funeral and at the viewing a man I had
seen bending over the casket to kiss Frank's forehead came
up to me. He said he knew I was writing Frank's book. His
daughter had been Frank's housekeeper, and she used to see
us working together, sitting in the sun on Frank's patio. He
said that he had been Frank's cellmate in Sandstone. "Can
you imagine the little bit of room I had in a small cell with
that big guy?"

"He had it rough at Sandstone," I said, meaning the effect
the cold had on his arthritis.

"He brought it on himself. He took no crap from anybody.
He never could keep his mouth shut. One time he told me
some guy who worked in the laundry wouldn't give him a
hat. He told me to get the guy to come over to the wall, and
he'd let go of his canes and balance himself against the wall
and punch the guy and knock him out. I told him, 'Here, let
me punch him for you.' I ended up getting five months in
the hole for that punch. I never should have been in jail in
the first place. Even Frank said that. They wanted Angelo's
underboss, his New Jersey underboss, and they had to have
a conspiracy so they threw me in to it. It's not that I didn't
do anything. I tied the guy up and I worked him over, but he
deserved it. Still you don't get fifteen years for that."

"They loaded up on Frank, too," I said, "because they were
trying to squeeze him on the Hoffa case."

"Yeah. There was a book that came out called *The Teamsters*.
I'd be in the upper bunk reading it, and Frank would be down
below. I'd say something like 'What are you doing carting the

body to New Jersey, couldn't you get rid of it in Detroit?' It would get him going, 'What are you saying up there?' "

And so in prison Frank Sheeran was a hardened, deadlier version of the rebellious schoolboy who planted the Limburger cheese in the radiator and who broke the jaw of the principal with one knockout punch. As he said often and repeated on the last videotape, "I gave it eighty-three years of hell and I kicked a few asses; that's what I did."

In that last videotape I reminded him of the time when, in my presence, he had responded to a media representative who asked him if he felt his life had been exciting that his life had not been exciting, but had been "exacting." He had expressed remorse for parts of his life and told the man that after he did something he wondered if he "did the right thing or not." Although it's not on the video, he actually ended his conversation with the man by saying, "If I did all the things they allege I did and I had to do them over again I would not do them."

After reminding him about that conversation I said, "Well, you're at peace now, Frank, and that's the important thing."

In his bed he was looking at a photograph of himself taken with Jimmy Hoffa on Frank Sheeran Appreciation Night.

"Time goes back a lifetime, doesn't it?" he said.

"Yes it does," I said.

"Who could — who could — who could forsee — Who could forsee then in this picture that you and I would be talking here today?"

to the 2005 first paperback edition

"The real estater . . ." Those three little words had given me chills when I videotaped the big Irishman for the last time. The taping was a formality, an affirmation, analogous to putting a signature on the confession that already existed on audiotape. I did not anticipate that still more confession would spill out during the session. But then as the character Sarah said in *The Right to Remain Silent*, my novel based on interrogations I had conducted that solved major crimes: "[C]onfession is one of the necessities of life, like food and shelter. It helps eliminate psychological waste from the brain."

When I tried to get more details about "the real estater" out of Sheeran he cut me off. No probing allowed. Sheeran's caginess was due to his deeply held beliefs. He confessed in order to relieve his guilt and save his soul, but he never wanted anyone to call him a rat. Sheeran said the word "rat" with such contempt in the ordinary course of conversation that my partner, Bart Dalton, and I adapted it for use in our law practice.

While Sheeran hated rats and would not be one himself, he bore no malice toward John "The Redhead" Francis who, dying of cancer and not wanting to die in jail, implicated himself and Sheeran in the killing of Salvatore "Sally Bugs" Briguglio and Joseph "Crazy Joey" Gallo. Because Francis had already implicated himself, Sheeran would only confirm Francis's involvement. But it would take a lot of skill and hard work to get Sheeran to implicate even a dead man in anything the man was not already at least suspected of doing. Sheeran often spoke of someone's family, including his own daughters, needing his protection from bad publicity. Sheeran told me: "You got enough, Charles. . . . Be satisfied, Charles. . . . You got enough. Don't be probing."

The next day we prayed together, and then he stopped eating. A man who "painted houses" and determined the life expectancy of more than two dozen other men — not counting those he killed in combat — determined his own. And so the "real estater" would remain nothing more than an intriguing slip of the tongue.

Until one day in fall 2004, when I spoke by phone to retired New York City Police Department detective Joe Coffey, the man who solved the Son of Sam and Vatican Connection crimes, along with countless other high-profile cases, and who co-wrote *The Coffey Files*. A mutual friend, the mystery writer and retired NYPD detective Ed Dee, put us together. While knowledgeable about the mob, Coffey had never heard of John Francis. He said he would check him out with a mob confidant he still had in the former Bufalino family. I couldn't tell Coffey much about John Francis that wasn't already in *The Irishman* so I sent him a copy.

I called Joe in February 2005. He hadn't read the book.

"But," Joe said. "I did look into that real estate guy. Like you told me, he was very close to Russell Bufalino."

"What real estate guy?"

"What's-his-name, the driver. He wasn't merely a driver. He was big in his own right. He had a commercial real estate license. He was independently wealthy from it. He was very close to Bufalino and to Sheeran. He might have driven for Bufalino, but he wasn't really a driver per se."

"John Francis? The Redhead?"

"John Francis. That's it. Very big in real estate. Independently wealthy."

Chills. The chills I got as a young prosecutor when the truth would lead to more truth, snowflake by snowflake until it became an avalanche.

In 1972, on orders from Bufalino, Francis drove when Sheeran killed Gallo. In 1978, again on orders from Bufalino, Francis fired, too, when Sheeran shot Briguglio. Does there exist any possibility that this member of that very tight trio of Bufalino, Sheeran, and Francis was left out of some role in the 1975 Hoffa hit? I suppose there's a possibility. But one thing we now do know is that John Francis was a "real estater," and not a fly-by-nighter, but an independently wealthy commercial "real estater," the kind of man who must have had connections far and wide.

After the first edition of *The Irishman* was published in 2004, a Detroit newspaper reporter tracked down the son of the owner of the house in which Sheeran shot Hoffa. The house had belonged to a now-deceased woman who bought it in 1925 and sold it in 1978, three years after Hoffa's disappearance. Her son told the reporter that his mother moved out several months prior to the murder and let a single man, whom neighbors described as "mysterious," rent a room in the house. Are there dots that connect "real estater" John Francis to an unsuspecting "real estater" in Michigan to that "mysterious" boarder?

It would be helpful to read the FBI file to see what, if anything, it says about John Francis's possible role in Hoffa's disappearance. In 2005 I filed a Freedom of Information Act request for the file on Francis and the others, including Sheeran, the Andretta brothers, Briguglio, and Chuckie O'Brien. If possible, I also wanted to corroborate Briguglio's role as a confidential FBI informant. But I anticipate as little success with my FOIA request as the Hoffa family and the Detroit newspapers had with theirs. While individual agents are top notch, as an institution the FBI sometimes behaves more like an armed public relations agency than a public service agency. The FBI would be too embarrassed to divulge that Briguglio was an informant and that they failed to protect him. As Kenneth Walton, who headed the Detroit FBI from 1985 to 1988 said about Hoffa, "I'm comfortable I know who did it, but it's never going to be prosecuted because . . . we would have to divulge informants, confidential sources."

If I do end up getting any of the file, which could take years, the censor's black ink will probably cover the FBI's failure to protect its informant, and the file will not be worth the cost.

However, if the FBI were to give relevant portions of its file to the Oakland County district attorney, David Gorcyca, there could be no black ink. He is the brother law enforcement officer to whom they turned over the Hoffa case on March 29, 2002, when they threw in the towel. It would be an insult if the FBI blackened his pages.

Unfortunately, despite at least three requests by Gorcyca beginning in June 2004 for relevant portions of the file that deal with Sheeran, Briguglio, and the Andretta brothers, none of the requested portions of the FBI's seventy-volume, sixteen-thousand-page file have been released to the DA. Gorcyca wrote me, "It is obvious on the local level something is seriously up with their reluctance to cooperate." He spoke of "old stereotypes about the FBI," and said he was "incensed." But all he can do is ask. Since Oakland County has no standing grand jury, Gorcyca also asked the feds to convene a grand jury to call as witnesses the last living participants identified by Sheeran: Tommy Andretta and Chuckie O'Brien. That request was denied.

Just before the first edition of *The Irishman* came out, Fox News followed leads they read in an advance copy of the book. They got permission from the current owners of the house where Sheeran confessed he shot Hoffa to allow forensic lab specialists to spray Luminol, a chemical agent that detects evidence of blood, iron oxide, on the house's floorboards. The boards tested positive, revealing eight tiny indications of blood in a trail that exactly matched Sheeran's confession. The blood trailed from the vestibule down the hallway that leads to the kitchen.

Two shots to the back of the head produce relatively little blood. Even though I knew that the forensic lab Fox News hired felt there was an insufficient quantity of blood for DNA testing; that nearly twenty-nine years had elapsed and that a prominent forensic pathologist, Dr. Michael Baden, felt that the biological components of Hoffa's blood needed for DNA testing would have degraded due to environmental factors; that there were "cleaners" to make sure no blood was left behind; that linoleum had been placed on the vestibule floor to catch any "paint" that did spatter; and that the body was carried out in a body bag, I got caught up in the hope and the hype. I wanted a DNA test to prove the blood was Hoffa's. Maybe the linoleum dripped as the cleaners carried it out.

The Bloomfield Township Police Department read portions of *The Irishman*, then ripped up sections of the floor and sent them to the FBI lab to see if the blood's source could be positively identified. On February 15, 2005, Chief Jeffrey Werner announced that the FBI lab found human male blood on the flooring, but that the DNA in the blood did not match Hoffa's. At the press conference Gorcyca made it clear that while this did not corroborate Sheeran's confession, it did not refute it either.

Dr. Baden, former Chief Medical Examiner of New York City, commented, "Sheeran's confession that he killed Hoffa in the manner described in the book is supported by the forensic evidence, is entirely credible, and solves the Hoffa mystery. Nothing about this latest finding speaks against the confession and the overwhelming weight of the evidence."

After nearly twenty-nine years, finding another's blood could mean anything from a boy with a nosebleed to the house being used by the mob for other murders, as was the case with the Gambino family's house of death described in Gene Mustain and Jerry Capeci's fine book about that family, *Murder Machine*.

Eight months earlier, in mid-June 2004, I had received an unsolicited letter from Professor Arthur Sloane, author of *Hoffa*, a biography I'd relied on for information about Hoffa and the Teamsters. Although this 1991 work offers a different theory on the Hoffa disappearance, Sloane wrote after reading Sheeran's confession: "I'm fully convinced — now — that Sheeran was in fact the man who did the deed.

And I'm impressed too by the book's readability and by its factual accuracy in all areas on which I am qualified to pass judgment." When I called to thank him he said to me: "You have solved the Hoffa mystery."

When Sheeran and I found the house in 2002, I did not bother to try to enter. As an experienced homicide investigator and prosecutor I never dreamed there would be forensic evidence nearly three decades after the murder. As a recognized expert in interrogation I was certain I had found the house — a house burned forever into Frank Sheeran's memory — and I didn't want anyone challenging the confession in this book on the grounds that we had seen the interior and had been influenced by it. Friends have said that I have an uncanny knack for interrogation, and I was willing to test that. Let the snowflakes fall where they may.

In a visit arranged by Fox News, I entered the house for the first time after *The Irishman* had shipped to the stores. The current homeowner, Ric Wilson, his wife, and one of their sons were present. (During our visit Wilson and his son recognized me as the man who was outside their house in 2002 taking the photo that appears in this book.)

I opened the front door and entered a small vestibule. As soon as I entered I got those old chills I got as a homicide investigator when I viewed a scene, and it added to my understanding of the crime.

Sheeran described a "small" vestibule, and I wrote the word "small"; this vestibule was very small, indeed, and had a box canyon feel to it. It became instantly obvious that the only person who could have killed Jimmy Hoffa was the man who brought him in, and Hoffa would have entered this strange house only with his friend, the loyal "Hoffa man," Frank Sheeran. There was no escape from this vestibule for Jimmy Hoffa.

Directly in front of the vestibule on the left I saw the staircase that leads to the second floor. The staircase was so close it gave the appearance of crowding the vestibule, and it blocked the view of the kitchen and most of the hallway.

It hid the cleaners. It effectively cut off the back door as an escape option. With no time to think, the only way out was the way Jimmy Hoffa tried to get out, the way he'd come in.

To the right of the staircase was a long hallway leading to the kitchen. On the right side of the hallway were two rooms: the living room and then the dining room. At the end of the hallway there was that kitchen out of whose back door the body of Jimmy Hoffa was carried in a body bag to be placed in the trunk of a car and taken away to be cremated at what Sheeran called an "incinerary."

The interior was now revealed to be precisely as Sheeran had described to me and as I had written. Except for one important detail. There was no back door out of that kitchen. My heart sank.

"Sheeran told me Hoffa's body was carried out a back door," I said to Fox News correspondent Eric Shawn.

"Look — there's a side door on the left at the top of the stairs to the cellar," he said. "And the last indication of blood stopped in the hall just before the stairs down to the cellar. He must have meant this door."

"No. He said a back door. At the end of the hallway and through the kitchen leading to the backyard. A back door. This door goes to the driveway alongside the house. It's a side door."

I went to the living room and asked Ric Wilson if there had ever been a back door to the backyard through the kitchen. He said, "I took that back door out in 1989 when I renovated the house. I got that back door still sitting in my garage." Chills again; snowflake by snowflake.

In some jurisdictions a credible confession alone suffices to convict. In others there needs to be one added piece of corroborative fact. Here we already had the fact that in 1999, Sheeran confessed to me that he lured Hoffa into the rear passenger seat of the maroon Mercury — even though Hoffa always insisted on the front "shotgun" seat. The driver of the car, Hoffa's foster son, Chuckie O'Brien, denied Hoffa was in that car and passed a lie detector test.

On September 7, 2001, the FBI announced that a hair recovered from the headrest of the rear passenger's-side seat and saved all these years recently had been DNA-tested and was indeed Hoffa's hair. Sheeran's confession and that piece of important forensic corroboration would have been more than enough to convict Sheeran. I put four men on death row with less evidence than I amassed against Sheeran out of his own mouth.

Interestingly, O'Brien's alibi had already been shot full of holes by the FBI. To my eye, this also corroborated Sheeran's confession. Sheeran told me that O'Brien was an innocent dupe and truly believed he was taking Hoffa to a mob meeting. And that is likely why O'Brien did not have a planned and well-thought-out alibi.

Sheeran's lawyer, former Philadelphia district attorney F. Emmett Fitzpatrick, warned Sheeran in front of me that he would be indicted. They discussed how Sheeran's health would likely delay the proceedings against him.

Among the kind letters I received after publication of the first edition of *The Irishman* was one from Stan Hunterton, a Las Vegas attorney. As a young assistant U.S. attorney in Detroit in 1975 he drafted the search warrant for the maroon Mercury and successfully argued against the mob lawyer's motion to have the hair and anything else seized from the car returned to the car's owner. (Nice work, Stan, in preserving that hair until DNA science could catch up with it.) In his letter Stan congratulated me on getting "the first confession concerning the assassination" of Jimmy Hoffa.

In February 2002, five months after the FBI announced finding Hoffa's DNA in the strand of hair, Sheeran and I searched for and found the house of death. This find was additional corroboration of Sheeran's confession. The house's location and exterior features were just as Sheeran described.

And now with the book in stores, the home's interior turned out to be just as Sheeran had described as well. Further, we now know that the homeowner at the time of the shooting was living elsewhere. A lone boarder is much easier

to plot and plan around than a family full of people coming
and going. The snowflakes mounted.

More chills were in store, and they wouldn't all be mine. The
avalanche was about to start.

Sheeran confessed that in 1972, on orders from Bufalino,
he walked into Umberto's Clam House in New York's Little
Italy alone, and with two guns shot the place up, killing
"the fresh kid," Crazy Joey Gallo. I intensely interrogated
Sheeran on this "matter." The prevailing story, derived from
informant Joe Luparelli, was that three Italians associated
with the Colombo crime family to which the rebellious Gallo
crew belonged — Carmine "Sonny Pinto" DiBiase and two
brothers known only as Cisco and Benny — were down the
street at a Chinese restaurant. Luparelli saw Gallo arrive at
Umberto's. Luparelli then walked to the Chinese restaurant
and encountered the three Italian men. He told them that
Gallo was in Umberto's. Sonny Pinto impulsively announced
that he was going to kill Gallo, as there was an "open"
contract out on Gallo. He told Benny and Cisco to get guns,
and when they returned with the guns the three Italian men
stormed into the Mulberry Street side door at Umberto's,
guns blazing as if it were High Noon at the OK Corral. The
three alleged Italian gangsters wounded Gallo's bodyguard,
Pete Diapoulos, in the buttocks and killed Gallo as he fled.

After I exhausted all my cross-examination skills on
Sheeran, I was satisfied that although Sheeran's confession
went against all the books, a movie, and every reference on
the Internet, he was telling me the truth about killing Crazy
Joey, and like everything else he confessed to me it was going
in the book. It seemed to me that Luparelli was providing
disinformation to the FBI and to the public. Perhaps he had
some personal motive or personal gain to sell this story to
the authorities — maybe he owed a lot of money he couldn't
pay and needed to get off the street. Likely on orders,
Luparelli was shifting the blame away from the mob bosses
who ordered and sanctioned the hit in case Gallo's crew was
thinking about a vendetta against the Genovese family, too,

rather than just against their own family, the Colombos, with whom the Gallo crew was already feuding.

Sheeran told me long ago that no mobster associated with one boss paints a house in another boss's territory without the express approval of that other boss. For example, Hoffa could not have been killed in Detroit's territory without the approval of both the Detroit boss and the Chicago boss, as Chicago's territory overlapped Detroit's. Down south, Carlos Marcello ran such a tight territorial ship that he would not permit a mobster from another family to visit New Orleans without his express approval, much less allow him to paint a house there.

Umberto's Clam House was owned by a high-ranking Genovese family capo, Mattie "The Horse" Ianello, who was at the restaurant at the time of the shooting. Ianello had been a codefendant of Sheeran's on the list of top twenty-six mob figures in the civil RICO lawsuit brought by Rudy Giuliani a few years later. Clearly, the Genovese family, at least, if not Ianello personally, would have to have sanctioned the hit in Ianello's restaurant. Unless it were some crazy impulsive and unsanctioned act, the eyes of the Gallo crew, now led by his brother, Albert "Kid Blast" Gallo, would narrow on Ianello and the Genovese family. It was well-known that the Bufalino family did a lot of work with the Genovese family, a family that included Tony Pro. And so Luparelli told the authorities and wrote in a book that it was "a spur-of-the-moment-thing."

In any event, not one of the three Italians was arrested for Gallo's killing on Luparelli's information, because his statement was never corroborated in a single detail. In fact, "Benny" and "Cisco" were never identified further.

Following publication of *The Irishman*, the shooting of Crazy Joey Gallo by a lone gunman, and not by three gunmen, was corroborated in an article posted on www. ganglandnews.com by author Jerry Capeci, who checked the original news accounts of the Gallo hit. As a young reporter for the *New York Post*, Capeci said he "spent a few hours at Umberto's Clam House on Mulberry Street in lower

Manhattan during the early morning hours of April 7, 1972." Capeci wrote that Al Seedman, legendary chief of detectives for the NYPD, had walked out of Umberto's and announced to the reporters that all the carnage was the work of a lone gunman.

Capeci wrote in his second edition of *The Complete Idiot's Guide to the Mafia*, published in 2005, "[I]f I were forced to make a choice [about who killed Gallo], I'd say Frank Sheeran did the work." As to Hoffa he wrote: "Sheeran's account has the ring of truth."

And then fortune brought me something special. Eric Shawn of Fox News called. Based on a tip from an old news hand at Fox he had learned about an eyewitness to the Gallo shooting. She was a respected journalist at the *New York Times* who wished to remain anonymous. He called her, and she admitted she had been there and witnessed the shooting. He said, "I understand three Italian types came in and started shooting." She said, "No, it was a lone gunman." He directed her attention to Capeci's Web site and to a postage-stamp-size photo of Sheeran taken in the early seventies, around the time of the Gallo hit, the same photo that appears in this book. She said, "Oh my God, I've seen this man before. I have to get this book." Shawn immediately walked from Fox News on Forty-seventh Street to the New York Times building on Forty-third and delivered a copy.

I told this story to Ted Feury, a friend of mine and retired CBS executive. Ted said, "I know her. She was the best grad student I ever had at Columbia. She's a terrific gal, very bright, a great journalist, and as honest as they come. I'll call her."

The three of us had dinner at Elaine's in New York. Although many people close to this eyewitness in her profession know of her involvement in "the matter," she told us that she still wanted anonymity. The eyewitness drew a diagram of the scene for us, including where her table was in relation to the Gallo party, and said, "There were a lot of shots that night, and I heard those shots for a long time afterward." She confirmed that it was, indeed, the work of a lone gunman, "and he wasn't Italian, that's for sure." She described him as

an Irish-looking man fitting Frank Sheeran's general descrip-
tion and facial features, his distinctive height and build, and
his approximate age at the time. She flipped through a collec-
tion of photos I had, including photos of other gangsters, and
when she saw an enlarged version of the black-and-white
photo of Sheeran taken around the time of the Gallo shooting, she said: "Like I told Eric Shawn on the phone, it's been
a long time, but I know this much. I've seen that man before."
In answer to my question she said, "No, not from a photo in
the newspaper. I've seen him in the flesh before." I showed
her black-and-white photos of a younger Sheeran, and she
said, "No, too young." An older Sheeran, "No, too old." Then
she looked again at the photo of Sheeran taken around the
time of the Gallo hit, and she said with palpable fear, "This
picture gives me chills."

The meeting at Elaine's was more social than business. Ted
and the eyewitness were regulars.

Elaine Kaufman sat at our table and told us that Gallo
used to frequent her restaurant with the actor Jerry Orbach,
who played Gallo in the movie *The Gang Who Couldn't
Shoot Straight*, and Orbach's wife at the time, Marta. Marta
had contracted to write Gallo's biography. Elaine said that
Gallo always gave her what she called "the eyelock." And
she demonstrated it. She said he stared directly into her eyes
whenever he talked to her about the travails of owning a
restaurant, and it was hard to get away from him or his gaze.

Like all restaurants, the lighting at Elaine's is subdued.
I wanted to formally interview the eyewitness alone and
on tape, show her the still photos in better lighting and
show her a video of Sheeran in color — "in the flesh." I
wanted to run by her the things I'd read that conflicted
with Sheeran's confession. Due to our mutually busy
schedules nine months elapsed before I met with her at
her New York–area home. I brought my photo collec-
tion and a video I'd made of Sheeran on September 13,
2000, when he was seventy-nine. Although he was twenty-
seven years older than he'd been at Umberto's, it was in color
and it was Sheeran "in the flesh."

"I was eighteen at the time," the eyewitness said, "a freshman in college in Chicago. It was probably spring break. I was with my best friend. We were visiting one of her brothers and his wife. They lived near Gracie Mansion. We'd gone to the theater. I think we saw *Equus,* and then we probably drove around and did some sightseeing. None of us were drinking. We were underage, and my friend's brother and his wife didn't drink when they were out with us. We ended up at Umberto's about twenty minutes before the shooting.

"No way were there only seven people there besides the Gallo party, if that's what some book says. It was pretty crowded for that time of night, with people at maybe four or five tables and a couple of people sitting at the bar. Maybe people left after we got there and before it happened, that I don't know. We came in the front door — the one on the corner of Hester and Mulberry. There were no tables to the left on the Hester Street side. They were all in front of you as you walked in — between the bar on the left and the Mulberry Street wall on the right. We were sitting toward the back. I was facing Hester Street. My best friend sat to my right. Her brother and his wife sat opposite us. They faced the back wall and the side door off Mulberry. I remember the Gallo party to our left because of the little girl, and because I thought that the girl's mother was very pretty. Besides the little girl there were two or three women and two or three men. I don't remember seeing the faces of the men.

"Our seafood had just arrived when I noticed a tall man walk in through the Mulberry Street door. I could see the door easily. The door was just off my left shoulder. He walked on a diagonal to the bar, walking right in front of me — the whole way in my direct line of vision. As he walked past me I remember being struck by him. I remember thinking he was distinctive — quite tall and a handsome man. He stopped at the bar not far, at all, from our table. I was looking down at my plate of food when I heard the first shot. I looked up, and that same man was standing there facing the Gallo table with his back to the bar. I can't say I remember a gun in his hand, but he was definitely the one doing the shooting.

There's no doubt about that. He was calmly standing there while everybody else was ducking.

"The Gallo party didn't know what hit them.

"It was Sheeran. That man is the same man in this photo. Even the video looks more like the way he looked that night — even though he's much older in the video. Oh, it was him. I'm positive. In those news photos [circa 1980] you showed me he looks bloated and fat, but not in the video. In this photo he looks like a clown [a photo published in *Newsweek* in 1979.]"

I told her that Sheeran had done a lot of drinking and became bloated after he was forced to kill Hoffa in 1975, and she said, "That's the year I came to New York to go to grad school in journalism at Columbia."

She then went on with her account. "My friend's brother yelled for us to get down. Other people were screaming to get down, too. Besides the gunshots the thing I remember most when I was down on the tile floor was the crashing of glass. We stayed on the floor until the shooting stopped. When the shooting stopped my friend's brother yelled, 'Let's get out of here,' and we got up and ran out the Mulberry Street door. There were a lot of others shouting "Let's get out of here," too, and they ran away when we did.

"We ran up Mulberry. There was nobody on Mulberry firing at any getaway car, if that's what the bodyguard claimed. Our car was parked near the police station. On the drive home we speculated about whether we had just been in a robbery or a mob hit. Nobody wanted to stereotype Little Italy, but we thought it was mob related. I don't remember if we heard it on news radio on the way home, but we saw it in the papers the next day. It was pretty horrible. I think if my girlfriend and I had been there alone we might have gone back the next day, but her brother and his wife were very protective and didn't want us involved in any way."

This Gallo witness with a journalist's memory and eye for detail told me that she had not read any of the stories that had cropped up over the years. She didn't like thinking about it or talking about it. She had never heard about the "three Italians" until Eric Shawn had mentioned them. She said, "That's ridiculous. There's no way three Italians burst through that side door on Mulberry Street and started shooting. I'd have seen them come in. If there were three men we'd have been too scared to get up and run away. If we did get up we wouldn't have run out that side door."

I closed the session by asking her again how sure she was that Sheeran was the man she had seen that night. She said, "I'm positive. He's definitely the man I saw that night."

This positive eyewitness identification sealed it; if I were the prosecutor in this case, I would have just heard the cell door slam. Although the identification was made many years after the fact, she was a budding journalist who had an opportunity to see the killer and to form a mental image of him before he became a threat with a gun in his hand. Eyewitnesses confronted with a gun often remember only the gun.

As a result of her identification, I decided to buy as many books as I could find on Gallo. It's been a while; many are used, out of print. Their versions of that night at Umberto's often border on the silly. However, a 1976 book written by Pete "The Greek" Diapoulos, Gallo's bodyguard, was more revealing.

In *The Sixth Family,* Diapoulos writes that Gallo's birthday celebration began that night at the Copacabana, the famous New York nightclub. Don Rickles was the entertainer that night, and he paid his respects to Gallo. At the Copa, Gallo had an encounter with "an old timer, Russ Bufalino, a regular greaseball." In Bufalino's lapel Gallo spotted an Italian-American Civil Rights League button. True to Bufalino's love of jewelry, this button had a diamond in it. Joe Colombo, Bufalino's friend and fellow boss, the man Gallo ordered hit, had been in a coma for ten months. Gallo said to Bufalino, "Hey, what're you doing with that? You really believe in that bullshit league?"

Diapoulos wrote:

> You saw how Bufalino's chin went, his back going very straight, turning away from us. Frank [Bufalino's companion] with a very worried

look, took Joey by the arm. "Joey, that's nothing
to talk about here. Let's just have a few drinks."

"Yeah, we'll have a few drinks."

"Joey, he's a boss."

"So he's a boss. So am I a boss. That make him
any better than me? We're all equal. We're all
supposed to be brothers." "Brothers" came out
like it was anything but.

"Joey," I said, "Let's go to the table. Let's not
have a beef."

Diapoulos identified Bufalino's companion, the one "with
a very worried look" who took Gallo by the arm, as a man
named Frank. Diapoulos described how the "beef" got
started: "Champagne was still being sent over. A wiseguy
named Frank sent some. He was with an old-timer, Russ
Bufalino, a regular greaseball, the boss of Erie, Pennsylvania."

And Frank Sheeran, Russell Bufalino's regular companion
on their drives to New York, always described Gallo as "a
fresh kid." Frank had reason to know. Because this incident
at the Copa reflected on Bufalino, it was the kind of detail
Sheeran would have omitted in his confession to me.

Joseph D. Pistone, the real-life Donnie Brasco, told me
that when he was working undercover for the FBI he used to
hang out at the Vesuvio. There he met Bufalino and Sheeran.
They came in every Thursday. The Vesuvio was a long walk
or a short ride from the Copa. Gallo's birthday party at the
Copa began at 11 P.M. on a Thursday night. By 5:20 on Friday
morning Joey Gallo was dead.

Russell and Frank in New York City at the Copa the
night Crazy Joey Gallo got "fresh" with the wrong people
and had his house painted. Like Jimmy Hoffa's, and all the
other houses Frank Sheeran confessed to painting, the Gallo
mystery is solved.

One of Frank Sheeran's daughters, Dolores, told me after
the release of *The Irishman*: "Jimmy Hoffa was one of only
two people my father cared anything about. Russell Bufalino

was the other one. Killing Jimmy Hoffa tortured my father the rest of his life. There was so much guilt and suffering my father lived with after the disappearance. He drank and drank. At times he couldn't walk. I was always afraid to face that he did it. He would never admit it until you came along. The FBI spent almost thirty years torturing my father and scrutinizing his every move in order to get him to confess.

"Having him for a father was a nightmare. We couldn't go to him with a problem because of our fear of the horrible things he would do to fix it for us. He thought he was protecting us with the way he handled things, but it was just the opposite. We didn't get protected by him because we were too afraid to go to him for protection. A neighborhood man exposed himself to me and I couldn't tell my father. My oldest sister never went with us when my father took us out, because she was afraid he wouldn't bring us back home. We hated the headlines growing up. All of us girls suffer from it to this day. My sisters and I begged him not to write this book, but in the end we gave in. At least I did. He needed to get it off his chest. We had enough headlines about murders and violence, but I told him to tell you the truth. If my father had not told the truth to you no one would ever have known the real story.

"I feel like we've lived under this black cloud forever. I want it to be over. My father is finally at peace now. I would like the same for Jimmy's family. My father killed his friend and regretted it till the day he died. In my heart I always had my suspicions and I did not want them confirmed. Now that I have been forced to acknowledge the life my father lived, I have had to come to terms with it and with all the conflicting emotions the truth has evoked."

And only the truth has made it into this book.

March 2005

Stories That Could
Not Be Told Before

"Zip-a-Dee-Doo-Dah"

On a dreamy midsummer day in Sun Valley, Idaho, my ring-tone rang with the original "Zip-a-Dee-Doo-Dah" from the Disney film *Song of the South*. I had seen its revival, along with *Bambi*, on my first date with my future wife Nancy, chaperoned by her six-year-old son Tripp and four-year-old daughter Mimi, my future stepchildren.

A young woman from the 212 area code said, "Charles Brandt?"

"Yes."

"Please hold for Bob De Niro."

"Zip-a-Dee-Doo-Dah," indeed.

Eight months prior in 2008, *Variety* had trumpeted on its front page that Martin Scorsese and Robert De Niro had made a deal with Paramount for a feature film of *The Irishman*. But then: tick, tock. No Hollywood news in the months that followed, until this call.

As a producer of the film in which he would star as Frank Sheeran, De Niro asked me if I had any material that was not used in the book.

"Plenty," I assured him.

"Can you give me an example?"

"Well, yes. The arrest of certain people and the deaths of certain other people make it safe to go public about certain things Frank told me." I rattled off a few anecdotes.

This led to Paramount flying me to Manhattan for a meeting with Scorsese, De Niro, and the screenwriter Steve Zaillian, an Oscar recipient for *Schindler's List*.

I sat facing them with my back to the floor-to-ceiling window in a room on the thirty-seventh floor of Le Parker Meridien Hotel on 57th Street. We were just down the street from Carnegie Hall and across the wide street from Scorsese's Sikelia Productions. We were uptown from De Niro's Tribeca Productions and from my high school on East 15th Street. My 1959 graduation from Stuyvesant High School, where James Cagney and Thelonious Monk had gone, had been held at Carnegie Hall. Although Scorsese, De Niro, and I went to different high schools, I was about to be right at home. We all grew up Italian in New York at the same time, the dawn of rock and roll, the era known today as Doo Wop. "Ooh . . . ooh . . . ooh, Florence . . ."

Scorsese sat on my left on a couch perpendicular to mine with Zaillian to his left making notes on a draft of his script, which I had not seen. De Niro sat on a wing chair across a heavy wooden coffee table from me. He was in arm's reach of Zaillian and occasionally tapped Zaillian's shoulder asking, "Did you get that?" It was 5:30 p.m. There was fresh fruit and cookies. The room had the coffee smell and the casual feel of a corner luncheonette. And we were the guys who hung out there.

"The interrogator," I said, "gets a dose of his own medicine."

Paramount had scheduled us for an hour, but the questions these three artists asked me were so thorough and I had so much material that we sat without break for four hours until 9:30 p.m. No dinner.

At one point during their questioning I explained that an obscure movie I'd seen in 1961 at the Steel Pier in Atlantic City had caused me in 1991 to ask Frank a seemingly innocent question that led to a chilling answer of historic importance.

"What obscure movie?" Scorsese asked.

"Believe me, you wouldn't know it. No one saw this movie but me and that was nearly fifty years ago."

"What was the movie?" he insisted.

"*Blast of Silence.*"

He laughed. "Recently the French asked me to write something about it. I'll send you a DVD."

Some of the material I gave them was new, events that had happened during the years after the 2005 epilogue had appeared. But most was old, dating from 1991; material I'd kept as close to my chest as a bulletproof vest. This is essentially what I told them of the old and the new:

Integrity Test

Just in time for the epilogue to the first paperback edition's 2005 release, retired NYPD organized crime homicide detective Joe Coffey told me that John "The Redhead" Francis had been a wealthy commercial realtor, and I used that information in the epilogue. A month after that publication, Coffey wrote a letter to the editor of *Playboy*. His letter endorsed an article I'd written based on Frank's confession to shooting the "fresh kid" "Crazy Joey" Gallo at Umberto's Clam House in Little Italy.

The Gallo murder had been Coffey's case and he believed it had been solved by Frank's confession. But one incident still left the taste of ashes in his mouth all these years later. Coffey wrote *Playboy* that among those helping Gallo celebrate his birthday at Umberto's was the *Law & Order* actor Jerry Orbach, who had refused to cooperate with Coffey's homicide investigation.

To thank Joe Coffey for his letter to *Playboy* endorsing Frank Sheeran's confession to killing Gallo, I called his home in New York from my home in Sun Valley.

"The creep showed up with a lawyer," Coffey said, referring to Jerry Orbach. "He wouldn't let me ask him a single question."

"Orbach," I said, "I learned at a book signing, went to high school in Bufalino territory. Anybody who ever lived in northeast PA knows enough to keep his mouth shut."

Coffey grunted. "Well, the Gallo case is solved," he said. "But it could have been solved back then if Orbach cooperated."

Coffey revealed one of the reasons he knew Sheeran was telling the truth about killing Gallo. It wasn't just the eyewitness identification by a *New York Times* editor. Coffey explained that he had a law enforcement purpose when he allowed the story of a trio of Italian gunmen to circulate. Coffey used the bogus story as an integrity test. It would filter out phony tips. He'd hang up on an informant looking to sell "information" about three Italian gunmen because Coffey knew the shooter was a large lone gunman and he wasn't Italian.

"It was Sheeran," said Coffey.

I asked: "Did you ever read my book?"

He hesitated.

"I sent you one after you told me that The Redhead was a commercial realtor?"

"Oh, you mean Johnny Francis."

"That really helped me a lot. I quoted you in the paperback edition. Did you ever read it?"

"No, I didn't." He laughed. "But I did send the book to my source in the Bufalino family. Only he already read it. All the Bufalino guys up there read it. This old-time Bufalino guy told me he was shocked. He couldn't believe Sheeran confessed all that stuff to you. It's all true. They're all shocked up there."

"Sheeran was very remorseful," I said. "You've seen that over the years."

"Definitely."

Were Frank alive when I hung up with Detective Coffey, I would have called him to share the news. Gallo case closed. Bufalino family vouches for you. "It's all true."

I took from my file a candid snapshot of Frank and me sitting at the head of the table at a fellow Teamster's retirement party. Someone snapped the two of us at the moment Frank had confessed to killing Crazy Joey.

"Why did Russ have so much faith in you?" was my initiating question.

"If I tell you that," he said, smiling like a leprechaun, "I have to tell you something else."

"C'mon, Frank. Don't leave me hanging here. Now's as good a time as any to get it all out."

He lowered his voice. His lips barely moved. "Ever heard of Joey Gallo?"

"Sure," I said, "Crazy Joey."

"A fresh kid," he said.

"I don't get it. Why did Russ have so much faith in you?"

"I handled that matter myself. The Redhead was my driver on the thing. He dropped me off and drove around the block once. If I wasn't outside when he got back, he'd drive off. I'd be on my own. That's the way you do it."

In the candid snapshot, I'm pressing in toward him, tape recorder in hand, to hear his soft voice amid the beer-bottle racket of the party. In the photo Frank had that faraway flashback look he got sometimes after confessing to something new.

When I decided to include in the book Frank's confession that he killed the "fresh kid," I never dreamed that the Gallo hit's inclusion in the book would be anything but a headache. I knew I'd have to contend with the worldwide-accepted version that a trio of Italian gunmen stormed Umberto's, shot Gallo's Greek bodyguard in the butt, and killed Gallo as he ran out onto Hester Street. It was troublesome enough for the credibility of the Irishman that, like Forrest Gump, Frank had been involved in so many things at such a high level.

My decision to keep the Gallo confession in the book turned out to be an opportunity for both Frank and me to pass Detective Coffey's integrity test.

But I didn't know that heading toward publication of the first edition. For all I knew there was a *New York Times* editor out there who would come out from underneath an Umberto's table and say she'd seen three Italian gunmen blazing away at Gallo. What if she identified a photo of some Italian? The book wouldn't be the only thing that would go right down the drain in yet another Hoffa fiasco.

Very much at stake was my hard-earned reputation. In my law practice, my ability to attract referrals from other lawyers, judges, and the public depended entirely on my reputation. People knew of me as a former president of the Delaware Trial Lawyers Association; a former chief deputy attorney general; a novelist; a writer of opinion pieces; and a speaker and writer on the arts of interrogation and cross-examination. My reputation was such that although I was a non-political public figure I was asked by the party chairman to run for governor as a Democrat and then twenty years later by the other party chairman as a Republican. Getting exposed as a sucker, a naïve believer in what a known liar told me, could damage all I'd built.

I could have left Gallo where he lay on Hester Street. But I spent thirteen years as a member of our Supreme Court committee that investigates lawyer ethics violations. I helped investigate and clear then-senator Joe Biden on a failure to disclose a law school plagiarism incident when he applied to the Delaware Bar. When I was editing to publish, my background in legal ethics told me loud and clear that if it turned out Frank was lying to me about Gallo, the public had a right to know that and to disbelieve everything else Frank told me.

However, I confidently believed Frank. As the candid photo shows, I was inches from him when he confessed this to me. I saw his eyes. I heard the way he spoke. After all, I didn't just have him on the witness stand for an afternoon. Over many years I challenged Frank that it was etched in stone, in books and in movies, that three Italian gunmen did the "piece of work." But Frank stuck to his guns, both of them. And I knew my subject.

I never dreamed that the Gallo hit's making the final cut would be rewarded by validation of Frank four times.

First, of course, was the miraculous eyewitness, a respected *New York Times* editor who positively identified Frank as the lone gunman. This distinguished journalist graciously allowed herself to be interviewed on camera by PBS, albeit without showing her face and anonymously. She said the photo of Sheeran they showed her was "definitely" the man who killed Gallo.

Second, the chief investigating officer Detective Coffey pronounced the case closed after reading my *Playboy* article.

Third, Gallo's Greek bodyguard's book supplied the account of an altercation earlier that night at the Copa among Russell, Frank, and Crazy Joey, who was behaving like a "fresh kid."

Fourth, the Bufalino family rendered its verdict: "It's all true."

With Frank's credibility established on the Gallo matter in opposition to popular history that sharply contradicted Frank, I anticipated writing a short update to the book, adding Coffey's closing of the Gallo case and the blanket endorsement from the Bufalino family insiders, the most credible of men on all these subjects. But I would hear much more from and about the Bufalino family, and the short update would lengthen into these pages.

The Irishman had to be a shock to those Bufalino men, loyalists of La Cosa Nostra and its *Omerta* code of silence punishable by death. "When in doubt, have no doubt." All along I knew that Frank was telling the Bufalino guys and the Philly guys we'd meet with at social clubs, and his friend the Chicago godfather Joey "The Clown" Lombardo — who called him frequently in my presence — that he and I were working on a whitewashing book, what Frank called "my side of this thing." They were led to believe we were writing a defense to all the books that put Frank in the Hoffa murder. Russell Bufalino had allowed Frank to tell one and all that Russell gave Frank permission to write a book with me. As Frank put it, "As long as it don't hurt nobody." But Frank and I knew what we were really doing. At times in the company of these made men and their bosses I felt like an undercover.

Looking at that "fresh kid" photo of Frank and me, I was relieved that these Bufalino guys hadn't falsely accused me of double-crossing Frank on our whitewashing book; breaking down Frank to get his confession; taking advantage of his age; preying on his conscience. After all, depending on the interrogation tactic I was using at any given time, he would call me "Mr. Prosecutor" or "Holy Roller." He said I was the "toughest prosecutor" he'd ever dealt with.

Detective Coffey's news was exhilarating on every level. There were heavy snowflakes starting to fall in northeastern Pennsylvania. A blizzard would come.

Third Ring

On May 31, 2006, exactly two years after the release of my book's original hardcover edition, Big Billy D'Elia, the underboss who'd become the godfather of the Bufalino family on Russell's death twelve years earlier, got indicted by the feds for laundering drug money. Big Billy was Russell's nephew, and had been his daily companion. In 1972 Russell had made up three diamond-encrusted three-dollar gold-coin rings for himself, for Frank, and for a third person whose identity I'd left out of the book. These rings signified an inner circle of three.

The third ring was for Big Billy D'Elia.

Billy had been taught well by his uncle Russ and knew how to handle this annoying federal indictment. Billy promptly ordered hits on both investment banker witnesses scheduled to testify against him. Fortunately for the targets, the hit man to whom Billy had given the order was wearing an FBI wire. Billy got caught the same way his uncle Russ got caught, giving an order to a man on a wire to do what both Brutus in Shakespeare's *Julius Caesar* and the Mafia call "a piece of work."

Now Billy was facing two counts of the far more serious conspiracy to murder federal witnesses. At fifty, and with the government's case on tape, Billy would die in jail.

In 1991, fifteen years before these indictments, Frank had introduced me to Big Billy D'Elia at a Mafia sit-down at the Mona Lisa Restaurant on 6th Street in South Philly. Frank was fresh out of jail. And Billy was heir apparent to Russell. Billy was a tall, easygoing man, very pleasant. I had no reason to dislike him, but it was clear over the ensuing years that he didn't like me at all.

For instance, after a birthday party luncheon for Frank at an Italian restaurant near the Philly airport, Frank called me at home: "You know what Billy said to me after you left the party? He said to me, do I trust that guy. I said do I trust that guy, if it wasn't for that guy I'd still be in jail for nine more years. Do I trust that guy?"

"Hold on, Frank," I demanded. "Hold on. Back up here, please. What did the godfather of the Bufalino family say about me? That's all I care about."

Frank had taught me how his friends think: "When in doubt, have no doubt." And here was Big Billy doubting me. Everyone at that table with Frank, Billy, and me and prominent Philly and Bufalino guys knew that I was writing Frank's book.

"Aw, he's just trying to get a rise out of me," Frank said. "You got nothing to worry about. I never liked that motherfucker, and he never liked me."

"Is that part supposed to be reassuring?"

"No, no, no," Frank said. "I never liked that motherfucker, and he never liked me."

During my years with Frank, I was in Billy's company from time to time, but he rarely spoke to me, as if I might be wired. When the hardcover first edition of my book was days away from being released, my wife, Nancy, received an FYI email from a former paralegal of mine, Diane, who had dated a friend of Billy's. Diane forwarded to Nancy a copy of an email Billy's friend had just sent her. It closed with the following warning: "P.S. Billy is not happy with Charlie."

I tried to reassure Nancy: "Billy's had no access to the book yet. It's not on the shelves. I'm sure Billy's imagining that it incriminates him."

"I felt better," Nancy said, "when Frank was alive."

Nancy knew that I followed Frank the ballroom dancer's lead, dancing around certain delicate issues. More than once Frank said, "You can't write that about Russell because he was involved with other men in the thing. They're going to wonder if I say that about Russell, as close as we were, what would I say about them. And they're not pussycats, either." On other occasions he'd say that I couldn't use some relatively minor material about Russell as long as his wife, Carrie, was still alive. Carrie has since passed.

Frank insisted that Billy's name not appear in the book and I complied. Even now I won't reveal Billy's Mafia nickname. In the book I didn't even reveal that Billy was the source of the information that John "The Redhead" Francis, while dying of cancer, admitted to authorities to painting many houses with Frank. I didn't mention that Billy was the third man, along with Frank and Russell, to wear the gold-piece ring.

Nancy had seen how protective Frank was of me. After sessions at his apartment near Philly, Frank would invariably say: "Call me when you get home. I want to be sure you got home okay."

"Once Billy reads the book," I said to Nancy, "Billy will be, as you heard Frank put it many times: 'copacetic.'"

Nancy knew it wasn't merely certain delicate matters about certain men that I omitted. I omitted myself, too. I didn't want to be seen as taking credit for any interrogation techniques I used.

I grew up in a predominantly Italian family. Even though we were Perry Como Italians, true-crime headlines fascinated me. I'll never forget a young salesman named Arnold Schuster who spotted Willie Sutton, a wanted bank robber, on a Brooklyn street and ran to get a cop and claimed the reward. Mafia boss Albert "The Mad Hatter" Anastasia, famous for being killed in a hotel barber's chair in 1957, was the godfather of what would come to be called the Gambino family. Willie Sutton had no relationship with the Mafia. But Anastasia was "not happy with" Arnold for taking credit on TV. He had Arnold shot to death in front of his house as a lesson for the youngsters of New York, including me.

Three years before this book's release I learned a lesson from one of Frank's co-conspirators, Chuckie O'Brien.

Chuckie didn't let any grass grow under his feet following the September 7, 2001, FBI announcement that DNA testing confirmed that it was Hoffa's hair that had been found in the maroon Mercury in 1975. This was the car that Chuckie long ago admitted to exclusive use and control of on the afternoon Hoffa disappeared.

From his home in Florida, O'Brien called Frank as soon as he heard the DNA news. He asked to meet Frank at a bar in the Philly airport. O'Brien couldn't have cared less about the FBI and its DNA test. His only fear was that certain people might decide they were "not happy with" Chuckie.

At the airport bar Chuckie reassured Frank that he was not going to be intimidated by this finding. He was stand-up. Hoffa's hair could have gotten there in any number of ways.

"The hair," Frank explained to me after the airport meeting, "could have been transferred person-to-person. After all, the Mercury belonged to the Giacalone kid. These were close friends of Jimmy's. They were always hugging each other, and all. You could get a hundred witnesses to them hugging each other right out in public. Chuckie's got nothing to worry about."

O'Brien flew home no doubt satisfied that he would not fall victim to "When in doubt, have no doubt." Two days later came 9/11 and interest in the Hoffa hair ended.

One important reason I omitted some of my interactions with Frank is that in my role as father confessor I sometimes had to show Frank less respect than his friends would approve of. A lack of respect is their culture's biggest sin; it's punishable by instant death. Not even pushiness is pardonable. I wasn't pushy often. When I was, it was mostly trying to get Frank to open up about his war experiences.

Frank was never angrier with me than when I pressed him on his 411 combat days.

"I wouldn't even talk about it to my jury in my RICO trial to save my ass from jail. Emmett wanted me to. I'm going to talk about it to you so you can sell books?"

My job was to keep reminding him of the benefits of getting it all out. And it helped that I'm Catholic. Ultimately, Frank allowed me to be pushy because every time he revealed something new, he felt better; he felt a physical release.

Bottom line, I kept the details of my role out of the book because I didn't want anyone, especially not Billy, to get too big a dose of being "not happy with Charlie."

Our family motto was: When in doubt, leave it out.

1991

In addition to leaving out my role and my tactics as interrogator from March 1, 1999, to December 14, 2003, nearly five years, I also left out the details of my earlier time with Frank in 1991.

To that year I devoted these four sentences:

I conducted the first interview in 1991 at Sheeran's apartment, shortly after my partner and I were able to secure Sheeran's premature release from jail on medical grounds. Immediately after that 1991 session Sheeran had second thoughts about the interrogative nature of the interview process and terminated it. He had admitted far more than he was happy with. I told him to get back in touch with me if he changed his mind and was willing to submit to my questioning.

All of that is true, but it's prudently brief.

Right from the start with Frank Sheeran in 1991, the going was rough. My partner, Bart Dalton, and I visited him in jail to have him sign medical releases we'd need in order to file for early parole on medical grounds. Twice before Bart had driven alone the fifty miles each way to the prison. On both occasions Frank refused to sign anything. Frank demanded of Bart that instead of filing for medical parole, we file civil rights lawsuits against the FBI, the federal and state prosecutors, the federal and state trial judges, the prison warden, and a rattled-off list of other officials guilty of "cruel and unusual punishment" in violation of the Eighth Amendment to the Constitution. By our visit we were double-teaming our rebellious client.

One advantage I felt I had was the firm way I'd handled Sheeran ten years earlier, in 1981. Right after Frank had beaten his RICO trial in Philadelphia, he engaged me to represent him in Wilmington on his labor racketeering charges in federal court. I stood with him at his arraignment. We entered pleas of not guilty. There were half a dozen Mafia co-defendants, led by Genovese capo Tony Provenzano's man Eugene Boffa and including Bobby Rispo of the Philly family. Each had an opulent big-city lawyer, men with diamond cuff links and monograms on their starched white shirts.

In the hallway after the arraignment, Frank took me aside and said: "I like the way you handle yourself, and all. I got no problem with the fee. D-d-don't take this wrong, but that up-front part of the money for motions and stuff like that. You don't need to do any of that paperwork. These other lawyers in there, they'll put all that together and you just sign your name, that's all."

"Frank," I said. "You're going to have to get yourself another lawyer. I quoted you a fee in my office and you accepted it. Once an issue arises about my fee, I'm done. I won't represent you or negotiate with you. I'm sure you can find another lawyer to do it the way you'd like it done. But what you propose is never how I work on behalf of my clients. When I prepare motions for a client, I know whose side I'm on. I have no idea whose side any of these people are on."

Before he could answer I turned and left.

As if to prove my point, a month later the U.S. attorney revealed that the Philly guy, Bobby Rispo, had turned government informant months earlier. Rispo was a man on a wire the whole time this group of lawyers met with all their clients to discuss strategy, with the government listening in. It sounded unconstitutional to me — an invasion of the attorney–client relationship — but it was upheld in a reported decision, *United States v. Boffa, et al.*

Ultimately Frank was convicted and got eighteen of his thirty-two years on these charges. I was sure Frank remembered all of that when he decided to hire me to get him out on medical parole.

The door to the jail conference room opened and a strong odor of disinfectant wafted in, no doubt caused by an inmate mopping the hallway. I was surprised to see Frank get rolled into the jail conference room in a wheelchair pushed by the former president of the Delaware chapter of the Pagan Motorcycle Club.

Years earlier, when I practiced homicide defense work before restricting my practice to medical cases, I went across the Delaware River and represented this Pagan successfully in a double murder of witnesses in New Jersey. A Pagan and his Pagan mama had been left in the salty Pine Barrens of South Jersey, each shot in the head by another Pagan, but not by my client. My client, a sad case of a champion high school heavyweight wrestler lost to the 1960s drug epidemic, was now in jail on drug charges. He was glad to see me, and he engulfed me in his bulging rock-hard arms. I thought this was a good thing for Frank to see, an endorsement from a satisfied client.

As if I were still teaching junior high English in Queens, I patiently explained to Frank that the medical parole hearing was a quiet internal procedure held in this very conference room. There would be no lawyer for the state, no press, and no fanfare. None of his FBI agents, prosecutors, or judges would be informed that we'd filed for his release.

As I talked, the largest face on the largest head I've ever seen looked gray and hard, his cold and dry blue eyes glaring at me. We hadn't seen each other in a decade. His tough skin was as gray as the granite of the Delaware courthouse in which he was convicted and he seemed to be getting grayer as I talked. I'm sure he was breathing, but there was no way to tell.

"Frank," I said. "You're in a wheelchair. Bart and I are medical malpractice lawyers. That's all we do now, and we know how to present medical evidence. You need spinal surgery for your severe stenosis. You've got the best neurosurgeon in Philly, Fred Simeone, ready to do the surgery at Penn. Then you'll need extensive aftercare, physical therapy and nursing services. The warden of this jail doesn't want to have to provide you the special aftercare you'll need. He'd be pleased to have you wheeled out of here on medical parole. The three-member civilian parole board will be on our side. In fact, there won't be any other side but our side. If, on the other hand, we file any of these lawsuits you want us to file, all of your favorite law enforcement authorities will band together behind the scenes to ensure that you serve every last second of your sentences."

As if he hadn't heard me and with a voice as icy cold as his glare, in a monotone through clenched teeth he embarked on a monologue clearly written for him by a jailhouse lawyer. Every sentence began with: " I want you to sue . . ." Like a cop who gets a broadcast of two men fighting on a corner and takes his time getting there so the men can wear themselves out, I let him drone on about all those he wanted us to sue.

When he seemed done, I said: "Frank, are you finished?"

"Yeah," he grunted. "I'm finished."

"I wish you could hear yourself talk. Then you'd know you weren't making any sense at all."

I had his attention.

"We're putting in for medical parole," I continued slowly and deliberately. "And that's all we're doing. If we fail and if you can find a lawyer stupid enough to file these frivolous lawsuits, go right ahead. Bart will be back in a week to pick up these papers and if you want us to represent you, they'd better be signed. Guard, we're out of here."

The next week 6'3", athletically built Bart Dalton drove to the jail alone. On his return he was gravely concerned for my safety: "All he would talk about was you," Bart said. "I'm really worried for you. No one's ever talked to him that way before. And gotten away with it. He kept saying that over and over. I tried telling him you were doing it for his own good, but he wouldn't listen. It was like I was squaring a Mafia beef. Not practicing law. I'm really worried. He never stopped talking about you. Remember, he had Fred Gawronski killed for coming late to a meeting and spilling wine on him."

"Not to mention," I said, "that he's a prime FBI suspect in Hoffa. Well, did he sign the papers?"

"He did."

"Nice job. Then this one counts, doesn't it? Let's spring him."

Of course, we did.

In gratitude Frank took our paralegals and us to lunch with some tough Teamsters who looked as if they'd just stepped off an informational picket line, eight guys named Rocco. Since he'd left the cold and gloomy jail, Frank had improved and was able to get around using a cane. We were in the back room of his former hangout, Vincente's restaurant in the Little Italy section of Wilmington, referred to by mobsters on FBI tapes as "the wine shop." It was a place where a gangster once sent over a bottle of Dom for my daughter Jenny Rose at her sixteenth-birthday family dinner party.

At one point Frank told us that his daughter had a cat that liked to jump on his lap while he was watching football. So he bought a squirt gun. He imitated how he would shoot the cat with a spray of water, and his imitation gave me chills. I felt the chills again in Detroit in 2002 when he imitated shooting my rental Cadillac floorboard with a "P-I-E-C-E piece."

As though we weren't there, Frank and his pals did a lot of reminiscing, marveling that they were still alive and impugning the masculinity of particular judges and FBI agents. As to one agent they really disdained, John Tamm who never had a hair out of place, the one Frank had "blanketed" during his RICO trial, it was observed by a thick-lipped man in a black suit, black shirt, bright red tie, and red pocket handkerchief: "I know what Tamm's problem is. I'll tell you what Tamm's problem is. His whole life he's fightin' gayism."

One of Frank's other pals, a closed-mouth knock-around guy named Franny who had delivered Frank's fee to me, looked deep in thought. I was to learn that Frank and Franny had been buddies since kindergarten. Suddenly Franny lifted his wineglass and said with a tear in his voice: "Frank, may the feds leave you alone." "Hear, hear," came the unanimous reply. "Hear, hear," Bart and I echoed.

After the luncheon Frank took me out of earshot of his guests.

"I'm tired of being accused over Jimmy. Every article they got. Th-th-they got six books out there and they all put me in the thing. See."

Frank added that while in jail he'd read my detective novel, *The Right to Remain Silent*, published by St. Martin's Press in 1988 and optioned by Tri-Star Pictures, but never exercised. Its hero, Detective Lou Razzi, is a master interrogator. It's based on major cases I helped crack through interrogation, such as *State v. Fullman*. It's a pro-law-and-order book where a central character calls confession "one of the necessities of life, like food and shelter. It helps eliminate psychological waste from the brain." After publication it was announced in the Delaware news that the realistic novel had prompted a letter to me from President Ronald Reagan commending *The Right to Remain Silent* for its "forthright stand on improving the protection of law-abiding citizens." Frank had seen this article about the Irish American president liking my book.

"I liked your book, too," Frank the Irishman said. "I want to write a book and I want you to write it for me. I want to tell my side of this thing."

My training and instincts told me at once that, at least subconsciously, Frank had a latent desire to confess.

Our past encounters told me that, as well. After the firm hand I'd used on him just before Bobby Rispo was revealed to be on the FBI's side of that thing; after the even firmer hand I'd used on him in the jail conference room regarding his medical parole; and now after his exposure to Lou Razzi, the master interrogator hero of my law-and-order novel, there was no question in my mind that he knew better than to pick me to tell his "side of this thing." He'd shared space in jail with some of the real-life criminals in that book, men I had put in jail.

A latent desire to confess to a person in authority was a concept I had been taught very early in my former law enforcement career by a seasoned Wilmington PD homicide detective, the late Charlie Burke.

"How do you get so many confessions?" I asked Burkie.

"They want to tell you, Choll," Burkie answered.

I thought he was kidding.

This was after he'd gotten a murder confession out of the burglar Randolph Dickerson. Randolph had used a screwdriver he'd jimmied a window with to stab to death the old woman who lived alone and supplemented her Social Security by selling Bibles. The Bible saleslady had entered her apartment and surprised her upstairs neighbor Dickerson in the act of rifling her dresser.

"Randolph needed to get this murder off his chest, Choll. The man needed to get this murder off his chest." Burkie liked to repeat himself. "It's the damn heroin. Believe me, he's not a bad guy. But you most definitely gotta let 'em know who's boss. They gotta know you're boss, Choll."

Burkie didn't rely much on textbook technique, although some of the books out there are terrific. Burkie had faith. I became a believer in a desire to confess to an authority figure. It became a phenomenon I would rely on and would see countless times before this luncheon celebration at "the wine shop" and Frank's post-luncheon request that I write his book and tell his "side of this thing," this Jimmy Hoffa "thing."

Working on both sides of criminal law I came to appreciate, as many have for millennia, that conscience, as ministered to by religions, 12-step programs, and psychiatrists, and as dramatized by artists like Shakespeare, is an element of human nature. Alcohol and drugs can anesthetize it, but it lies beneath the skin, waiting to be skillfully brought to the surface.

However, even when a murderer displays a desire to confess, it's the heart and soul that want to confess. Meanwhile, every cell in the body doesn't want to. That's because it's the body that will end up in jail or strapped to a gurney. There are often at the same time these opposing pulls at work inside a mind full of guilty knowledge.

Thanks to my being inspired in my final year at Brooklyn Law School by the exploits of reporter Mike Wallace on the then-brand-new *60 Minutes* TV show, interrogation and cross-examination became my passion. By degrees in my legal career I went from cross-examining drug-addled burglars to cross-examining expert witness neurosurgeons. But whether I'd get Frank to open up, whether I'd plumb the depths of his "side of this thing," was going to depend on how deeply remorseful this Roman Catholic was.

Mona Lisa

We set up a meeting at Frank's garden apartment in Springfield near Philadelphia. It was October 1991, well before his surgery. I figured at the worst I'd end up with material for my next Lou Razzi novel.

Frank opened the door, leaning on a cane for support. He was wearing his "uniform" of navy-blue cotton sweatpants, a matching sweatshirt, and a flat gray tweed cap announcing the truck driver he still was in his heart. In keeping with the truck-driver theme, a country music station played in the background. Standing behind Frank was a short pudgy red-faced man about Frank's age in a solid brown suit, with a starched yellow dress shirt and a red-and-gold club tie. My heart sank.

Rule number one, you want your subject alone.

Frank let me into his well-cared-for two-bedroom apartment, which smelled faintly medicinal, and said: "This is my lawyer, Charlie Brandt. This is my other lawyer, Jimmy Lynch, 'The Catholic.'"

Jimmy Lynch, The Catholic, reached out his hand and said: "Hiya Cholly, howya doin.'"

I felt a return of hope hearing his nickname. Catholics make a sacrament out of confession.

I went to the bathroom and heard the phone ring. When I came out I saw a very respectful Frank Sheeran on the phone, nodding and saying yes, yes, and yes to someone who turned out to be Big Billy D'Elia, the underboss to Russell Bufalino.

On hanging up Frank said to Jimmy, "That matter, we gotta go do it now."

"Now?" Jimmy protested.

"You do it when they want you to do it, not when you want to do it. They don't give you no notice, either."

"What are we going to do with Cholly?"

"Guys," I said quickly. "I brought work from the office. I'll do it right here at the dining room table until you get back."

"No," Frank said. "We'll bring him along. It'll be good."

Frank took off his hat and sweatshirt and put on a starched bright white-on-white dress shirt with his monogram FJS on the cuffs. Over this he wore a black vest. He retained his sweatpants.

The Catholic drove. Frank had shotgun, and I had the backseat. I would later learn that a trusting Jimmy Hoffa had also sat in the backseat on his last ride. Frank's massive head of white hair blocked my view. Not a single word was spoken, and I had no idea where we were going. I knew that if Frank was being set up for a hit, both The Catholic and I would go with him. Finally we reached South Street, and soon I recognized my favorite store in Philly, the Tower Record store on the corner of 6th Street. We made a right turn at Tower and ended up across the street from the Mona Lisa restaurant. A rap on the car window startled me. An Italian American man directed us to a spot where we wouldn't get a parking ticket.

At speaking engagements, people ask me if I ever was fearful during my time with Frank. "Once," I say, "when we walked into the Mona Lisa restaurant and the lock on the door snapped behind us." That loud crack got my heart's attention. Later Frank would confide that he'd experienced that scary snap of a restaurant door locking behind him when he reported to Angelo Bruno at the Villa di Roma to answer for the plot to torch a laundry for Whispers.

The Catholic and I were invited to sit at the bar. Just past the bar was a large round table. Seated alone was John Stanfa, the newly crowned godfather of the Philly crime family, a royal descendant of "Chicken Man" Testa who was dethroned by a nail bomb planted beneath the front steps of his house; and of Angelo Bruno who was toppled by a shotgun blast to the head while sitting in a car parked in front of his house. Mrs. Bruno had rushed out and yelled, "Call Simeone," the surgeon who was to operate on Frank, but it was much too late. John Stanfa had been Angelo Bruno's driver that night and was shot in the shoulder by a pistol to neutralize him the way Frank shot Gallo's bodyguard in the butt.

Frank later told me that he was almost killed when "Ange" had his house painted. That night Frank was having dinner at Cous' Little Italy Restaurant. Angelo came over to Frank's table and asked Frank to drive him home if John Stanfa didn't show up soon. But Stanfa arrived and Frank stayed put.

"Why do you say you'd have been killed?" I asked.

"They knew they couldn't just shoot me in the shoulder. They'd have to shoot me another way."

From that embarrassment, John Stanfa worked his way up and later succeeded "Little Nicky" Scarfo as family boss. Little Nicky was then doing a number of life sentences for multiple murders he had ordered. John Stanfa, born and raised in Sicily, owned the Mona Lisa. Seventeen years earlier in 1974 all of the above-named Philly bosses were among the three thousand guests at the Latin Casino paying their respects to Frank Sheeran at his Appreciation Night.

Stanfa signaled Frank where to sit as others slid off their bar stools and joined the table.

I knew enough not to ask, but I easily could glean that we were at a trial and that John Stanfa was the judge. Stanfa had a very restrained and humorless demeanor.

Frank, the plaintiff, alleged that two men in the Philly family collected loan shark payments for him while he was in "school," and now "wouldn't come up with the green stamps." For their part, the two men claimed that as they collected the "vig" they gave Frank's money, fifteen hundred dollars a week, to the prior Philly godfather, Little Nicky Scarfo. From prison Little Nicky testified that the two had given him none of Frank's money. Big Billy D'Elia, who was then pretty much running the family as the underboss for godfather Russell Bufalino, represented Frank.

The bar was free and there was food laid out for us at a separate table. I was struck that it was bread and Italian cold cuts for sandwiches, and not the soulful feast of hot aromatic red gravy dishes my immigrant grandparents Rosa and Luigi DiMarco would have spread out at their Staten Island family farm. But then again, this was a courtroom.

The round trip to the Mona Lisa, the trial, and the camaraderie that went with it would last for five hours. I thought I saw Stanfa crack a smile at the end. Outside after the trial I shook

Billy D'Elia's hand for the first time. Big Billy looked like a businessman in a Brooks Brothers suit, more American than Italian, very relaxed. I've wondered since if I was on surveillance film.

We got into The Catholic's car. Frank announced with pride and reeking of Chianti: "I won the thing. Look at the respect I get. They only do this for Italians. That's the respect I get. That they hold me in. You got some green stamps coming out of this thing, Jimmy. Those two gotta pay me fifteen hundred dollars a week each till I tell them they can stop."

From the backseat I marveled at the unique form of justice, and wondered, Shouldn't I be in for a third?

After a pause, Frank continued, "Franny's got problems, though, Jimmy. Some things came out about Franny, some things Franny's been doing."

"What do you mean, Frank? Franny's good people. I don't want to see anything happen to Franny."

From the backseat I didn't want to see anything happen to Franny, either. This was the same Franny who had brought me my fee when Frank was in jail, and who at lunch following Frank's release had made a toast with a tear in his voice for his buddy from kindergarten.

On the cool autumn drive in the dark on the way back to Frank's apartment Jimmy kept pleading the case for Franny. Frank kept fending Jimmy off by repeating that he had "no control over the matter."

Eight years later when Frank and I resumed our meetings on March 1, 1999, I learned that nothing did happen to Franny. Frank hinted that he'd protected Franny. He explained: "Franny has a nice wife and a nice daughter." I took that occasion to remind Frank that I have a nice wife and two nice daughters. And a nice son.

We weren't back at Frank's apartment for five minutes when, true to his name, The Catholic announced he was too upset about Franny to stay and that he was going home to bed. I saw it as a good sign that Frank had this man with a conscience among his friends. With The Catholic putting his camel-hair topcoat back on and heading for the door I now had Frank Sheeran, FBI suspect in the Jimmy Hoffa murder, all to myself.

We were good to go. We already had made a deal to share the "profits" of a very unprofitable book that would tell his "side of this thing," a book that would whitewash him. Frank had assured me that Russell had given him approval to do the book "as long as it don't hurt nobody."

From the start I believed that the book project was, in reality, Frank's excuse to talk. And I was open to his opening up all the way. I tossed the whitewashing book out the door behind Jimmy Lynch as he left. I intended to be the facilitator, the catalyst for as much of the truth as Frank wanted to get off his chest. Of course, there is a danger to that, but I was willing to assume the risk.

That long night alone with Frank took some ups and downs, but finally Frank uttered his first words that amounted to an admission of guilty knowledge about Jimmy Hoffa:

"People don't think the FBI knows what the fuck they're doing; the FBI knows what the fuck they're doing."

That compound sentence was the gate swinging wide open for details to flow. Frank had framed the issue for us. Now he was compelled to explain why "the FBI knows what the fuck they're doing."

Without my knowing it, Sheeran was referring to and endorsing the FBI's Hoffex memo. It was something I'd never heard of. It was something I would read about later in the Steven Brill and Dan Moldea books on Hoffa's disappearance. It was something I wouldn't actually see until after this book's publication.

Bob Garrity, the FBI Hoffa case agent during the heart of the investigation, had written the memo a few weeks after Hoffa's disappearance.

I was privileged to meet Bob Garrity in 2005, fourteen years after Frank's Mona Lisa trial, when Bob bought my paperback at a book signing. He asked me to make it out to "Bob Garrity."

"How do I know that name?" I looked up.

"I was the Hoffa case agent. I read the hardback twice."

In the Hoffex memo, which formed the basis for the other books written on the Hoffa murder, Garrity had put together an accurate list of suspects, including Sheeran and Bufalino.

"Please sit with me," I asked.

Bob was wearing a Pittsburgh Steelers shirt as a security rep for the NFL team. The photo my wife took of us sitting together hangs on my wall.

"We always liked Sheeran for it," Bob said. "The Hoffa family thought the sun rose and set on Frank Sheeran." Frank also knew that the Hoffa family idolized him, and that knowledge made his guilty conscience all the harder to bear in silence.

But he had no choice until I came along at the right time and with the right skills.

To a man, all the suspects listed in the Garrity Hoffex memo pushed what I call the *Miranda* mute button on the remote. They each refused to allow the FBI to ask any questions. Bob Garrity and the FBI, using informants, knew whodunit, but had no way to penetrate the stone wall of silence to learn who done what. And so the Bureau mercilessly pursued those on the list for whatever else, however unrelated, they could get on them.

The relentless work Bob and others had put into the case would pay off for me in Frank's apartment that night. Fear of getting caught helps trigger guilt. The FBI's relentless pressure had been an aching weight on Frank's inferno of a conscience, and I got the benefit of the FBI's work.

That momentous night in 1991 a tired Frank had lowered himself onto a gray corduroy La-Z-Boy recliner. And there he settled while I sat close to him, nothing between us. Since I hadn't seen Bob Garrity's memo and hadn't read any of the books about the Hoffa case, I had no theory to guide me, no scenario to envision.

I was helped by the Chianti that Frank drank at the Mona Lisa. *In Vino Veritas*, in wine there is truth. The Chianti likely made him more talkative, and the joy of his legal victory made him more effusive. Jimmy Lynch The Catholic's pleas on behalf of Franny also helped. It set a moral tone. Our session lasted a full five hours after the five hours we'd spent with his Mafia trial. When I left for home I had a big chunk of what happened to Jimmy Hoffa. I had at least a notion of what each man on Bob Garrity's Hoffex list had done.

Eight years later in 1999 Frank would tell me that only one on the Hoffex list of nine suspects was innocent. That was Gabe, the brother of Sal "Sally Bugs" Briguglio. Frank was to tell me that he was in "school" with Gabe and that Gabe assured him that his brother Sally had not "turned rat." Frank observed about his gunning down of Sal Briguglio: "It was a bad hit."

That night in 1991 in his living room, in an intimate atmosphere with no tape recorder in my hand and taking no notes, I helped Frank open up to describe the Hoffa murder as taking place in a "loaner" house in Detroit; to admit that a gun was used; to admit that he was present at that house in Detroit during the killing; that he was there on orders from Russell; that he had flown there on a private plane; and that the body was cremated by the Andretta brothers serving as "cleaners." Frank admitted that he was there as a member of the murder conspiracy. This made him as guilty of murder as if he had pulled the trigger. But he was vague and evasive about whether he had actually pulled the trigger, and I let him slide on that for now.

I knew he felt, from his wary intensity, a genuine remorse. I'd get him on tape next time.

As well, I let slide for now those tough-to-get answers whose questions had to be framed as opinion in order to let the cat out of the bag: "No, no, not what you did. I'm just asking what you think might have happened. In your opinion. It's only an opinion. Everybody's entitled to an opinion."

I thought I would nail down the loose ends at our next session, never dreaming it would take place almost a decade later.

That autumn night Frank never denied that he knew who pulled the trigger; at one point he claimed it might have been two Sicilian war orphans brought in from Windsor, Canada. But he was forced by my follow-up questions to retract that opinion. As well, under my questioning he retracted the claim that he was there "to keep an eye on the thing for Russell."

That the murder weapon was a gun came slowly. He first suggested it might have been a wire clothes hanger and gave me a jolt when he put his good foot into the small of my back to demonstrate on me how a bent hanger would be used to cut off a man's air supply.

When he finally confided that it was a gun, I could sense strongly that he wanted to tell me he had pulled the trigger of that gun, and I was confident that he'd tell me eventually. But I had to be careful and take it slow. He was, after all, a dangerous man, and we hardly knew each other.

Frank's demeanor, especially his sad eyes, showed that he was contrite, driven by guilt, and the more Jimmy Hoffa was mentioned the more profound the guilt. These were eyes in sharp contrast with the cold eyes I'd seen in jail. Eight years later when we resumed our sessions I was to learn that Frank's father studied for the priesthood and his mother went to mass every morning. It didn't surprise me.

Frank's third daughter Dolores, who along with her sisters opposed even the whitewash book, but became a friend for life after this book was published, told me that at their mother's funeral, her older sister Peggy told Dolores that in reality she'd never thought her estranged father killed Jimmy Hoffa. It was guilt that was torturing him those four days after the murder when Peggy said to him in her mother's kitchen: "I don't even want to know a person like you." It was intense guilt that made him think Peggy had caught him. Till the day he died he thought she had seen right through his eyes to his soul.

Blast of Silence

Deliberate silence has its role in certain aspects of interrogation. I successfully used a long silent ride back to the police station in the dark in a car full of homicide detectives I'd discreetly told not to utter a single word, to keep perfectly silent in the presence of the young man in handcuffs sitting next to me, to let him stew while he used his knees to wipe his tears. I used this silent treatment to scare an easy confession out of this non-shooter accomplice we had just seized from his girlfriend's apartment in the serious wounding of a patrol cop in the head by a .22 rifle in a Jack-in-the-Box robbery. When our drive was over and we were standing in the back court-yard outside the police station, I broke our silent treatment and said: "Wait." I looked him up and down, showing a little sympathy, and said to the homicide detective cuffed to him: "Ah fuck it. Let him tell his side of it." And out it poured: "I didn't even have a gun. It was Pinky shot him."

However, the overwhelming majority of the time I preferred to keep a dialogue going. Keep him talking about anything. Don't give him time to reflect on what he's saying. Keep the mouth moving, and hopefully, the truth will find its own way out.

Meantime, as if at a poker game, you'll begin to be able to tell when he's bluffing from where his eyes go when he's tell-ing the truth and remembering something and where they go when he's not, when he's making something up; and from the sound of his voice, his body language, and just plain hunches. Like the music teacher who can tell which kid in the choir is slightly off key, you have to be a great listener. As I used to lecture cops: EFW. Every F'ing Word counts. Listen.

This notion of keeping him talking is especially true when your subject is as tired as Frank was from the long day at the Mona Lisa.

As I looked at him that evening in 1991, I decided another question was in order just to keep him alert. Based on the final scene of the obscure movie that I'd seen at the Steel Pier in Atlantic City decades earlier called *Blast of Silence*, and sensing a lull, a literal blast of silence, just to keep him talking as the evening was coming to a close I very "inno-cently" asked Frank why so many people were actively involved: ". . . Tony Provenzano, you, Russell, Tommy Andretta, Steve Andretta, Sal Briguglio, Chuckie O'Brien, Tony Giacalone."

"That way," Frank said, "if you go bad you only know what you did. You can't rat on the other ones before you and the other ones after you."

"That's a great point," I said.

"Precautionary is all," Frank said.

"Also," I said, "I guess, if you handle a high-profile hit like this by yourself you'll stand a good chance of getting eliminated in the end."

"Oh, yeah. You'd have to be out of your mind to do something like this alone."

"It's like a movie I saw once in Atlantic City where the hit man they brought in from Cleveland for a high-profile hit in New York goes to get paid after the hit and gets hit himself."

"Oh, yeah. You'd have to be out of your mind to do something like this alone. They're definitely not going to have a massacre, but a lone cowboy will be disposable."

"Like the lone cowboy Lee Harvey Oswald," I said, laughing.

As if I'd flicked a switch I could see Frank Sheeran look away at once and start to turn to gray granite as he had in jail when I explained our plan for medical parole.

What had I said to trigger this? I leaned in on the edge of my chair.

"I never read any books on the JFK assassination," I continued casually. He was riveted, his eyes no longer sad, now wide. "But it always seemed to me from the second I saw Ruby shoot Oswald on TV that it was Jack Ruby's job . . ." He got grayer and harder as I spoke.

". . . to get rid of Oswald. When that went haywire on the street, Ruby had to finish the job. There's a lot worse than facing a judge for murder."

His massive forearm muscles bulged on the arms of his gray La-Z-Boy.

"If Ruby didn't shoot Oswald" — I switched to loud and aggressive — "he'd be tortured to death, his family, too. Tortured to death."

He was stiff and solid like a gravestone. Then he barely moved his right hand, as if beginning to swat me off. It was the only part of him that moved.

I kept going faster and with more authority to keep him from shutting me up. "When I worked in East Harlem, I used to see cops in uniform with their ties undone, sitting down with made men over espresso. Ruby had cops . . ."

With this, he fully waved me off with his right hand.

With a voice of dry ice he said:

"I'm not going anywhere near Dallas."

Forever I will hear him say those words in that way. The fear in his voice was profound. This revelation coming out of the blue in answer to a meaningless question about the reason for using eight men in the Hoffa murder, as opposed to a single hit man, was surreal. I could not have anticipated it. I wasn't sure I wanted it. At that moment, reading the intense rigidity encapsulating his very being, I decided not to follow up on "Dallas."

"So, in other words," I said slowly, looking into eyes that were confused. He was spooked by his own outburst. "It's like an assembly line. Each one has a job. That way nobody can testify against anybody else. Is that right? Frank? An assembly line. Is that right? Frank?"

"Yeah, that's right."

"Makes sense."

We wrapped it up. Back in Delaware at the end of that startling October day in Philly in 1991 I felt like an explorer returning home by sail from a long voyage to a strange foreign land. I told Nancy and Bart that we needed to come up with a stronger word than *remorse* to describe Frank Sheeran's conscience, a word that combined remorse with torture. I told them Sheeran gave me a big chunk of what had happened to his dear friend and mentor Jimmy Hoffa and that, believe it or not, Sheeran had guilty knowledge about the JFK assassination. I told them what he'd said to me about "Dallas," the innocuous setup that brought these words erupting out of him, and I impersonated the eerie way he'd said these frightening words to me. Nancy and Bart were concerned for me, urging that I not get in too deep. I didn't need my arm twisted.

Anyone would know what was meant by his words, their bizarre context, and his emotional state as he uttered them. Frank Sheeran had something to confess about "Dallas."

A decade or so later, of course, with all the top godfathers of that era dead or in jail, I did want to know what Frank knew about "Dallas" and I found out and reported it in the book: The Mafia was in on the assassination, and Frank played an unwitting role.

In 2012 in a Charlie Rose interview, Robert F. Kennedy Jr. said his father, RFK Sr., believed the Mafia had killed his brother John in Dallas and that he also believed it. RFK Jr. said that RFK Sr. judged the Warren Commission Report to be a "shoddy piece of craftsmanship . . . He publicly supported the Warren Commission Report, but privately he was dismissive of it." RFK Jr. explained: "He was a very meticulous attorney. He had gone over reports himself. He was an expert at examining issues and searching for the truth."

Charlie Rose asked whether RFK Sr. had "some sense of guilt because he thought there might have been a link between his very aggressive efforts against organized crime" and JFK's assassination. RFK Jr. answered: "I think that's true. He talked about that." RFK Jr. went on to point out that Jack Ruby's phone records "were like an inventory" of organized crime figures.

When I subsequently did some research, one name stood out for me. It was Irwin Weiner. Ruby telephoned Weiner on October 26, 1963, twenty-seven days before "Dallas." It could have been an innocent call. Ruby and Weiner were friends. Weiner was a friend of both Frank Sheeran and Jimmy Hoffa. Frank would occasionally refer to a person of great stature on the fringe of the mob as being "big connected." And Weiner was very "big connected." Weiner had been walking with the Teamsters' billion-dollar pension fund manager Allen Dorfman in a Chicago parking lot when Dorfman was gunned down by two hit men. Weiner, an eyewitness, was spared.

Jack Ruby knew so many gangsters personally that in 1959 the FBI unsuccessfully tried to recruit Ruby as a paid confidential informant.

Knowing what Frank had said to me about "Dallas" and the way he had said it from his gray La-Z-Boy two decades earlier made this pronouncement by a representative of the Kennedy family as gratifying as any of the snowflakes that had fallen since my book was published.

"They Wouldn't Dare"

In 1991 when I typed up a synopsis of what Frank had revealed to me, I prudently left out the "Dallas" comment. I had no idea who or what I might be dealing with. I truly never had read a book on the assassination. I was a junior high English teacher when it happened and I was merely relying on memory, common sense, and my life's experiences when I made a casual reference to Oswald as a disposable "lone cowboy."

At our follow-up meeting at Frank's apartment, just the two of us, I handed Frank my synopsis. He sat on his La-Z-Boy. As he read he turned to granite again, sincerely shocked at what he was reading, as if he'd been in an alcoholic blackout during our night together.

Obviously, I had used our whitewashing book partnership to access Frank's truth. But it was done with Frank's voluntary participation every step of the way. Or he wouldn't have come back to me for more questioning in 1999.

When he finished reading, Frank said: "You can't write this stuff. These people in here, they're still alive. Russ is still alive. I'm keeping this."

And at the moment he took it from me, I knew I'd been wise to leave "Dallas" out of it. I especially didn't want Russell to know he'd told me that.

Of course, I still have a copy of the 1991 memo, titled "They Wouldn't Dare." The title came from Jimmy Hoffa's words to Frank in response to Frank warning Jimmy that Russell said to tell Jimmy "what it is." "They wouldn't dare" in that context were the words Frank believed got Hoffa killed. The words became the title of chapter 1 of the book.

"You know where to find me, Frank," I said, "if you change your mind or if these men die."

Eight years later on March 1, 1999, after Frank received "the Absolution thing" from Monsignor Heldusor, I got the call that started the nearly five years of recorded sessions that went into forming the big Irishman's biography, the story of his adventurous and dangerous life, what he called his "exacting life," and his attempt at spiritual redemption and ultimate salvation through confession, his truthful "side of this thing," a side tested and retested over the next five years by my questions and his answers.

During our five years together I successfully used Hoffa's words, "They wouldn't dare," and other imprudent words and deeds of Hoffa in his last year to casually put the blame on Hoffa for his own death, an interrogator's technique. Hoffa knew the rules and the consequences of breaking them and he wouldn't stop. "I'd have killed him myself," I said more than once.

I planted the seed.

I vividly remember the moment this technique paid off and Frank admitted to pulling the trigger. He called my cell phone as I walked out of Cristina's restaurant in Ketchum, Idaho, after lunch in October 2000, almost two years after our new round of interviews had begun.

"That matter we've been talking about . . ." Frank said.

"Sure."

"That matter, you could say that I did it."

"I could say anything, Frank, as long as it's the truth. Did you do it? Are you telling me you did it?"

"Right."

"Are you telling me you shot Hoffa?"

"Right. Yeah."

"Good for you, Frank. You knew I knew it, anyway, but it's best to get it out. God bless you, Frank. Good for you."

House for Rent

Hoffa case agent Bob Garrity and I met in Detroit in the fall of 2005, nearly a year and a half after my book was published, to seek the boarder who lived in the house used to kill Hoffa. We started with the family of Martha Sellers, the deceased single woman who had owned the house. Although a news article referred to a "son" of hers and I repeated that in the 2005 epilogue, she had no son. It was a great-nephew who had spoken to the media. We met with the great-nephew, his sister, and his mother over coffee and cake on fine china served on a silver tray at the spacious home they shared.

The family explained that Aunt Martha's house is just inside the city limits. As a Detroit schoolteacher, Martha had to use it as her official Detroit residence, while she actually lived in a country home outside the city. The family told us that Martha Sellers had as a student in her classroom the incomparable heavyweight champ Joe Louis, the same "Brown Bomber" who helped earn Bobby Kennedy a parachute jump from the Capitol Building.

The family could shed no light on any "real estater," but by then I was confident that John The Redhead Francis was the "real estater" who had secured the house for the hit. I'd learned that five days after Hoffa's disappearance The Redhead was spotted by surveillance as one of those Hoffa conspirators seen reporting one at a time to cigar-smoking Genovese boss and Mafia Commission member Fat Tony Salerno at the Vesuvio.

From the NYPD officer's "observation report":

At approximately 1255 hours the officer observed FRANK SHEERAN enter the premises . . . He was wearing a light blue short sleeved shirt and dark trousers . . . FRANK went on to ask if 'RUSS was in' . . . [THE MANAGER] replied that 'RUSS was in the dining room' . . . FRANK SHEERAN was wearing a yellow metal coin ring, (the coin is surrounded by what appeared to be small diamonds) on his left hand and a yellow metal watch. The face of the watch is square and surrounded by small diamonds . . . A few minutes after JOHNNY FRANCIS had entered the dining room, he returned to the bar and joined FRANK SHEERAN . . . At one point as they conversed, the name JIMMY was overheard being mentioned by FRANK. He was overheard to tell Mr. FRANCIS that the FBI had entered the investigation . . . Several times their conversation turned to a low tone and the officer was unable to intercept . . .

The Redhead's reporting to the bosses in the dining room puts him squarely in the thing.

Martha Sellers's family remembered a boarder, an old man with a cane, who stayed there from time to time, but they didn't know his name and didn't know if he was still there as late as 1975.

These generous people referred us to a lawyer friend of the family who had considered buying the house in the 1970s. I spoke to him by phone. The lawyer recalled that the house had a hardware-store For Rent sign in one of the windows for years, including 1975. So it was, indeed, a rental in 1975, making it easier for strangers to come and go unnoticed by the neighbors. The lawyer knew it was 1975 because that was the year he'd returned to live in Detroit and seriously considered buying the house.

"I remember the old boarder with a cane," the lawyer said. "He was a ghost who always disappeared whenever anyone came to the house. But he was well gone by 1975."

Martha Sellers's great-nephew got our attention when he told us during our cake and coffee that the cellar of the house had an incinerator with very powerful roaring gas jets. It had an opening big enough to put the body of a man in it. As a kid he had burned garbage for his aunt. It was still in use in 1975, but a few years later these home incinerators were banned as a source of air pollution. Bob and I checked out the cellar and found the incinerator's sealed-off chimney, but the incinerator had been removed.

To be thorough, Bob led us to the local post office to see if we could find the mail deliverer from those days who might remember the name of any boarder, but we were sorry to learn that she had passed away.

Bob then took me to lunch at Nemo's bar and showed me the parking spot out front where the Lincoln belonging to Frank Fitzsimmons's son had been blown up two weeks before Hoffa disappeared. Over a beer Bob told me that Hoffa had slapped Chuckie's face at the Thanksgiving dinner before Hoffa disappeared. Hoffa was angry with Chuckie for abandoning his wife for his girlfriend.

Bob told me he was disappointed that I hadn't come forward sooner when Frank was still alive. All I could say was that I understood. But Frank was supposed to be alive when the book came out. Frank chose suicide by self-starvation, not uncommon in nursing homes.

Transit Permit

Next I got a cold call from a Taylor, Michigan, cop named Jeff Hansen who'd read my book. Hansen described a crematorium less than two minutes from the house. It was in the cemetery where Hoffa's mother was buried shortly after her son's disappearance, in an unmarked grave to deter tourists.

But Jeff pointed to another crematorium twenty minutes away as, in his opinion, more likely to be used by the Mafia for the disposal of a body. It was known to be close to a funeral parlor that handled a lot of Mafia funerals, Bagnasco's. Years ago a Bagnasco was gunned down Mafia-style in front of their funeral parlor.

I flew to Detroit and met with Jeff and some knowledgeable people he'd consulted. I learned how breathtakingly easy it was in Michigan in 1975 to legally cremate a body without any paper trail. All that was needed was something called a "transit permit," and in practice it really wasn't needed. These were slips of paper the size of a dollar bill. There were no duplicates, just an original. It would be supplied to a driver by a funeral director, who typically kept a pad of them in his desk drawer. They would get filed nowhere. They would not be given to the crematorium. It was simply a licensed funeral director giving any driver who possessed a "transit permit" permission to drive around with a body. This phrase reminded me of the "letters of transit" in the Michael Curtiz classic film *Casablanca*.

The driver would pull up and hand a groundskeeper ninety-five dollars, often in cash. The body would be in a body bag or cheap pine cremation coffin. The bag or coffin would never be opened. The driver and his helper, or a cemetery groundskeeper if the driver came alone, would lift the body and slide it into the retort, or oven. One of them would flip what looked like an ordinary light switch. In an hour everything, including the body bag or flimsy pine box, would be reduced to cremains, an ash residue in the shape of a body. The groundskeeper would come back in an hour and using a window squeegee he'd push the cremains into a small cream-colored plastic box for pickup by the driver. The ash would have no scientific or other means of identification. Very often the cremains would be abandoned, never to be picked up, and would simply be stacked in a closet for future disposal. In the cemeteries we checked out on this trip to Detroit, I saw stacks of abandoned cremains on shelves. That's how easily it would work if it was done with the cooperation of a Bagnasco peeling off a transit permit from his pad.

Cooperation from the crematorium would make it even easier, self-serve, done in an hour. The groundskeepers would be sent to another part of the vast cemetery to work while the driver and his helper went to work. I flicked a switch at one of these Detroit crematoriums that seemed to be always unattended and heard the roaring oven flame up instantly.

Bob Garrity told me that his FBI team had suspected Bagnasco in the disposal of the body. In fact, as described in a long FBI memo that I obtained from other sources, a very reliable informant close to the Bagnasco family had fingered Bagnasco as the place they brought Jimmy Hoffa's body immediately. Bagnasco had been checked out, but there was really no way to check it out. In the trade, because of its apparent Mafia ties, Bagnasco was known as "two for one Bagnasco." In 2009 Jeff Hansen wrote a book on his findings: *Digging for the Truth*, published by Spectre Publishing.

Frank was never interested in the latest Hoffa dig. He scoffed every time a dig started. Frank said more than once: "If there was a body to be found, they would have found it a long time ago."

Frank agreed that the one cleaner still alive, Tommy Andretta, is the only person who really knows the details. He and his deceased brother Steve disposed of the body. Tommy Andretta of the late Genovese capo Tony Provenzano's local in New Jersey now lives in Las Vegas. But Andretta won't allow anyone to ask him any questions. He keeps the *Miranda* mute button permanently on.

When the hardback edition of *The Irishman* first came out in 2004, Ed Barnes, a Fox News producer and former organized crime investigator for the state of New York, a man who for over twenty years kept two files from his Strike Force days, one labeled Frank Sheeran and the other labeled Russell Bufalino, and who gave me my first copy of the Hoffex memo, flew to Las Vegas. Ed Barnes waited all day in the desert sun in front of Tommy Andretta's orange-roofed white suburban house. When 6'6" Andretta arrived home, Barnes tried to hand him the book and to ask him questions, but Andretta gave Barnes the brush-off, stared straight ahead, and walked through his front door. While Barnes was still standing at the front door, the garage door next to him rolled up. Mrs. Andretta stood there with her hand out. Barnes put the book in her hand and began asking her questions as the garage door rolled back down.

Big Billy's Court-Appointed Lawyer

Shortly after my last trip to Detroit in 2006, Big Billy D'Elia was indicted on the conspiracies to murder the investment banker witnesses against him. Following this indictment there were newspaper reports that Billy was switching from a high-profile criminal lawyer to a court-appointed lawyer. This told me that Billy, who certainly could afford a top-notch lawyer, had begun taking steps to cooperate. High-profile lawyers would not be a party to cooperation with the FBI. It would look bad to their other clients. It could get them killed.

In a few weeks my hunch was confirmed. It was reported that Billy was cooperating and had entered into a plea agreement with the U.S. attorney for a reduced sentence based on his cooperation. I felt a relief that I hadn't felt since Frank got my attention by confiscating my synopsis in 1991 and did who knows what with it. With Billy having too much on his plate to even think about me, I finally felt a freedom to reveal more about my role "in this thing."

Donnie Brasco: Unfinished Business

In the meantime, thanks to *The Irishman*, I got the opportunity to co-author a sequel to the true-crime tour de force *Donnie Brasco: My Undercover Life in the Mafia* (Dutton, 1988) with my longtime idol, the real Donnie Brasco, retired FBI undercover agent Joe Pistone. Joe was a co-author of *Donnie Brasco* with Richard Woodley. In the 1997 Mike Newell film adaptation of *Donnie Brasco*, Johnny Depp played Joe and Al Pacino played Lefty Guns Ruggiero, the principal made man Joe befriended and brought down. They were so close Joe had been best man at Lefty's wedding.

Joe was in danger of a bullet to the head at any time during his six years undercover posing as a jewel thief in the Bonanno crime family. After he surfaced as an agent there had been a half-million-dollar Mafia contract out on Joe, who continues to take precautions. In the trials that followed, Joe was the wrecking ball that ultimately brought down the Bonanno family.

Our book sequel, published in 2007 by Running Press, is called *Donnie Brasco: Unfinished Business* and contains heroic material that Joe wasn't allowed to use in the first book because it came from open cases that he was still testifying in. Hence our subtitle: *Unfinished Business*.

Joe, who grew up tough in Patterson, New Jersey, is the bravest man I ever heard of. We became brothers for life and are regularly in touch. Joe teaches undercover to police and other operatives all over the world, sometimes in countries I never heard of. On the side he produces movies, plays, and TV shows.

Joe told me that while posing as a jewel thief and associate of the Bonannos, he would drop into the Vesuvio on Thursdays. This was the day Frank Sheeran and Russell Bufalino, who did business with jewel thieves, would arrive in town. Joe never overheard any usable information out of their mouths. Joe came on the scene at the Vesuvio at the beginning of Sheeran's intense remorse in 1975. "On Thursday nights," Joe told me, "I'd sit at the bar nursing my drink while Sheeran would get drunker and drunker."

Joe introduced me to his friend the singer and actor Al Martino, who appeared as the singer Johnny Fontane in all three *Godfather* films. I was already a fan of Al's singing from childhood, and Al Martino and I and his wife, Judi, became fast friends. Before his tragic and sudden death from a heart attack in October 2009, Al told me that the character of Johnny Fontane was patterned after his own life, not — as many believe — Frank Sinatra's.

Al said that Albert Anastasia tried to shake him down for seventy-five thousand dollars following the release of Al's giant hit "Here in My Heart" in 1952. Anastasia was The Mad Hatter who had ordered the hit on Arnold Schuster for taking public credit for the capture of Willie Sutton. But Al Martino was a tough guy who had fought in World War II and was wounded in the Battle of Iwo Jima. He had been a bricklayer in the Philly area before turning to singing. Rather than give in to Anastasia, whom he called Anie, Al moved to England. When Anastasia was killed in the hotel barber chair in 1957, Al sought permission from Philly boss Angelo Bruno to return to America. Angelo referred Al to Russell Bufalino, and Al could see at once that Russell was the real power in the American Mafia. As Al put it, "Don't let anybody tell you different, Russell was the boss who got the most respect by far."

Russell gave Al Martino permission to stay in America and instead of demanding anything from Al he helped Al rebuild his career. Al told me that Russell was a silent owner of New York's legendary Copacabana nightclub where we know Crazy Joey Gallo acted like a "fresh kid."

Al flourished under Russell's wing and had big hits including Russ and Frank's favorite "Spanish Eyes," sung at Frank Sheeran Appreciation Night by the popular American tenor from the Bronx, Jerry Vale. Martin Scorsese told me he used the late Jerry Vale's singing in nine of his movies.

Al told me that he expected to get the role of Johnny Fontane in *The Godfather*, but when he did not he was told the director Francis Ford Coppola wanted an experienced actor instead. After Al was rejected he called Russell. A day or so later Robert Evans, the head of Paramount, summoned him. Evans told Al he had the role if he wanted it, but Coppola was going to shoot in such a way that Al's face would often be hidden. Al said he didn't care; he wanted the role. And so his face was often hidden. On the set some of the other actors gave Al a bit of the cold shoulder. But Marlon Brando took Al under his wing, coached him, and flew him to locations in his private jet, acting like a godfather on and off the screen.

I mentioned this when I spoke at the 2011 Sun Valley Writer's Conference. Wanda Ruddy, the wife of Al Ruddy, the producer of *The Godfather*, was in the audience. Wanda introduced herself and told me: "Russell Bufalino had final script approval of *The Godfather*."

It seemed that every time I spoke someone had a Russell Bufalino story, especially in his home base in northeastern Pennsylvania.

Bernie Foglia runs a great homemade Italian restaurant, Villa Foglia in Exeter, Pennsylvania. I had spoken at the nearby library. Afterward, a couple of us went to Bernie's for good food and good stories. Bernie told me that when he was younger and owned a pizzeria he was scheduled for open-heart surgery. Russell heard about it and stopped in. Russell told Bernie he was too young. He urged Bernie to get a second opinion with his own heart doctor and arranged for it. Russell sent Joe Sonken, of the Mafia hangout and seafood restaurant in Florida, to take Bernie for the doctor's visit. Bernie had never met Joe Sonken, but he soon got used to being called Boinie.

At the reception desk the nurse asked the two men if either could speak Italian. She was trying to register an elderly Italian man who had very limited English and she couldn't get through to him that she needed his Social Security number. She wanted someone to explain why she needed it. Bernie offered to help. He learned from the man that he couldn't produce his Social Security number because he had no Social Security card. He'd started off in America as a bootlegger making booze for Al Capone and had learned to avoid all taxes all the time. Capone's downfall.

Suddenly Joe Sonken, who also started off working for Capone, took off his glasses and put his face in front of the old Italian and said, "Remember me, Joe Sonken?"

Bernie told me: "Next thing you know, these two old bootleggers are hugging and carrying on. After that, I was in Atlantic City coming out of a restaurant when I spotted Joe Sonken sitting in a private booth with a beautiful blond. Not wanting to bother him I kept walking toward the door when the blond shouted at me, 'Boinie.' I turned around. Joe Sonken was sitting with Olivia Newton-John. Out front was a Rolls-Royce with the license plate Olivia.

"One time a buddy and I tried to get into the Rainbow Room in New York for dinner and the show, but we were turned away because we had no reservation. We started to walk off, and then I decided to take a shot. I said, 'Russell Bufalino told us to come here.' In a flash the maître d' had the rope off and put us at the best table. To this day I don't know if Russell was somehow connected to the Rainbow Room, but he sure was known."

When I asked questions, Boinie was very careful not to say anything to me about Billy D'Elia. Later, Boinie's lovely sister was in the audience at my talk at the Mandalay Bay Casino in Las Vegas.

At another talk in Bufalino country a man came up to me and said, "When I was young I was a wild kid. Russell came to my father's furniture store and said: 'Everyone likes to shop in your store, but your son is acting wild. If you can't control him, nobody's going to want to shop here anymore.' My father sat on me all through high school. I was never out of his sight until I matured, and now I have my own business."

"What business is that?" I asked.

"I own my own funeral parlor."

We're Going to Win This Thing

Next Joe Pistone introduced me to retired organized crime supervisory special agent Lin DeVecchio, another American hero and friend for life, the grand master of the FBI's Informant Development Program, paid informants being the lifeblood of the organized crime section. Together Lin and I wrote a book about the job Lin and his colleagues did to decapitate the Mafia. I named Lin and his allies the New Untouchables after the original Untouchables, those federal agents who fought Al Capone and earned their name for being honest and incorruptible when Capone tried to buy them off. The 1987 Brian De Palma film *The Untouchables* starred Robert De Niro as Al Capone and Kevin Costner as Eliot Ness, the honest and incorruptible leader of the Untouchables. The honest and incorruptible Lin DeVecchio of the New Untouchables ended up being indicted on four counts of Mafia murders by a glory-seeking Brooklyn DA in a case engineered by the Mafia in revenge for the irreversible damage Lin did to them. Our book is *We're Going to Win This Thing* (Berkley, 2011)

Lin had been supervisor of the legendary Mafia Commission Case and its 1986 landmark trial. Joe Pistone was the Mafia Commission Case star witness, the wrecking ball. Lin's paid confidential informant, the Colombo family's Greg "The Grim Reaper" Scarpa, was the source of the probable cause needed to permit bugging and wiretapping. The colossal case was the Mafia's Waterloo. It permanently liquidated the Mafia's governing body, the Commission. The Commission bosses were convicted by their own words on tape on all 151 counts and given one hundred years each.

Genovese boss Fat Tony Salerno, who presided over the Vesuvio meeting five days after the Hoffa murder, was one of those Commission bosses brought down by the verdict.

Although I couldn't use it because Carrie Bufalino was still alive, Frank told me that while Russell had planned the Hoffa hit to be over in an hour from Hoffa's pickup to his cremation, it had been Fat Tony Salerno who presided over the murder. And although Salerno gave lip service to being neutral between Hoffa and Tony Provenzano, it was in Salerno's best interest to eliminate Hoffa. Salerno's Genovese family dominated the hit, providing four men for the plot: Provenzano, Sal Briguglio, and the two Andretta brothers.

Lin told me that one of the Commission Case RICO counts against Fat Tony Salerno came from a bug planted in Fat Tony's Palma Boys Social Club in East Harlem where a rat bit one of the agents planting a bug in the cellar. The Palma Boys was a short walk from both the Welfare Center in which I worked as an investigator in the 1960s and Joe's Restaurant, the East Harlem bar on whose modified fast-pitch softball team I played. East Harlem was the turf of Genovese traitor Joe Valachi. I got to be on friendly terms with three members of the nearby San Antonio Social Club, the street boss Joe, his younger brother Sonny, and their brother-in-law Moe, who was married to their delightful sister Flo who ran Sonny's candy store. Moe once said to me: "I did more time in jail than you are alive." One time Moe was talking to me about the privileges "the 400" get from detectives that we don't get. "If a cop wants to question you, he sits your ass down and grills you. Mrs. Woodward of the Woodward Stables shoots her husband. She claims she thought he was a burglar. But does she sit for a grilling? Of course not. Because she's part of the 400." I didn't know what the 400 was and said so. Moe explained, "They're the original settlers, the ones that came over on the Plymouth." Little did I suspect that these days at Sonny's would be a dress rehearsal for my time with Frank.

In the 1980s I drove our teenage kids Tripp and Mimi to my old turf. I wanted our youngsters to see another way of life. Moe was gone, but Flo was still running the candy store. She remembered me fondly. While we were catching up an elderly black man who looked like a poor man's Duke Ellington entered carrying his toy poodle. He picked up a *New York Daily News* and dropped twenty cents on the counter and called out: "I owe you a nickel, Flo." "All right, honey," she said.

On a bug in the Palma Boys Social Club, Fat Tony was caught dictating to the Teamsters Union the name of the man Fat Tony

had selected for them as their next president. It was Roy Lee
Williams of Kansas City, who later went to jail. This total Mafia
domination of his union is what Hoffa had feared if he didn't
personally take back the presidency in the 1976 election. And
it's why the Genovese family wouldn't let Hoffa take it back.
They came to own the Teamsters under Frank Fitzsimmons
and they were planning on keeping it for a long time. Victor
Riesel, the courageous reporter blinded by Johnny Dio for
bad-mouthing Hoffa, reported that the Genovese family's
Tony Provenzano was planning on taking over the presidency
in 1981. This plan was ruined by Tony Pro's conviction for
murder in 1978, the local political murder of popular Teamster
Tony Castellito by Sal Briguglio and Kayo Konigsberg, a
murder solved as a result of the Hoffa investigation.

Supervised by Lin DeVecchio, the FBI's roundup of the
Commission bosses on hundred-year sentences obliterated
the Commission for all time. Now that the godfathers were
proven to be answerable to the law, no man of any substance
wanted to wear the FBI target that came with being a boss,
much less a Commission boss. First the insubstantial dregs
like John Gotti rose to the top, and soon there was no top.
With no secret murderous government to enforce its laws,
the Mafia began a descent into anarchy and disintegration.

Before I'd ever met Lin DeVecchio or Joe Pistone, while traveling with Frank and socializing with him, I became an eyewitness to the damage done by the Mafia Commission Case.

Frank and I frequently visited a Philly capo, a made man
I'll call Carmine, at his private social club, members only or
bring a search warrant. The single obvious illegal activity
going on in the club was gambling. It was a "card casino,"
three or four poker games always in progress, with the
house supplying a dealer and getting a cut of every pot, with
Carmine's men watching to ensure the house got every bit of
its money.

The first time Frank and I sat at Carmine's bar in his social
club, Carmine's thick refrigerator box of an underboss, a guy

who appeared to be about forty years old, came over and stood to the left of me to make small talk with Frank who was on a bar chair to my right. The whole time the underboss and Frank conversed over me, the underboss talked to Frank but never looked at him. Instead he stood there six feet away firmly glaring at me as if I were a poker pot he had to keep an eye on, looking me up and down, letting me know he would never forget me. I smiled pleasantly, like the real Mona Lisa. Carmine was among the many who had been told I was writing a whitewashing book for Frank. The underboss would never have done this without being told to do it.

A couple of years down the road, Frank suggested we visit "our friend" because Ralph Natale, the preceding godfather of the Philly family, had been arrested and was cooperating with the FBI, such cooperation by a boss being dramatic evidence of the disintegration caused by the New Untouchables. Frank told me that the rest of the Philly capos had asked Carmine to become the new Philly godfather, the big boss of the whole Philly family that Ange had once run. Carmine asked Frank's advice, but Frank didn't tell me what advice he'd given. I sat in my usual seat, with Frank to my right. Carmine, an athletic-looking dark and handsome man in his fifties, came over and, as he had done many times, rested his big hand on the back of my bar chair.

"How's our friend?" Carmine asked, referring to the imprisoned former Philly godfather John Stanfa. This was the godfather I had met ten years earlier when he was the presiding judge at his Mona Lisa restaurant. He was now serving five life sentences at Leavenworth for murder.

How's our friend, indeed. Giovanni Stanfa ran smack into the New Untouchables and was convicted in November 1995, four years after having become boss in 1991, a short time before I met him. During most of his time as boss he was in a war with Skinny Joey Merlino for control of the Philly family, a war that would not have been tolerated had there been a Commission in New York. Among the casualties was Stanfa's son Joey, who survived a bullet in the cheek when the Merlinos opened fire on John Stanfa's Cadillac. Stanfa's men retaliated, wounding Merlino in the butt and killing "Mikey Chang," whose father Joe "Chickie" Ciancaglini was the Sheeran ally shot in the belly during the rebel shootout in front of the local in 1967. Chickie's other son "Joey Chang" elected to remain loyal to Stanfa. Brother against brother. Frank was very proud that Chickie advised his son Joey from jail that Frank was the only one he should trust and go to for advice. The Merlinos opened fire on Joey Chang in front of his diner, leaving him partially paralyzed. Chickie the father was serving a forty-five-year sentence when Carmine asked Frank about Stanfa, "How's our friend?"

Frank told me that during the Merlino–Stanfa war three Merlinos drove up to his garden apartment as he sat outside. They asked him to remain neutral in the shooting war.

"Did all three of them get out of the car and come up to you?" I asked.

"If more than one got out of the car we'd be talking in jail. There's nothing wrong with my second finger. All three getting out and they'd be gone."

This occurred in 1993 when Frank was seventy-three and using a cane for a dropped foot. Nevertheless, the Merlinos still feared his active involvement in combat on Stanfa's side.

Around the time of that Merlino visit I had a glimpse of Frank's stature as he conducted business at a table in La Veranda restaurant on the Delaware River in Philly. I was seated a distance behind him, and he never knew I was there. This was during the eight-year period I wasn't seeing him. One by one, tough-looking men waited their turn to sit respectfully at his table and get instructions. Had the table been bugged, any one of these meetings was a parole violation, at the very least. The procession was still going on when I left unseen.

In Stanfa's 1995 murder indictment Frank and former representative Henry Cianfrani, who'd served time for racketeering, were named as Stanfa's unindicted co-conspirators. Frank and Cianfrani were picked up on a bug in the Mona Lisa conspiring with Stanfa, but never charged. As Frank was just getting out from doing a year on his parole violation in

1995 for leaving Philly without permission, Stanfa was just going in forever. Frank told me that by leaving Philly without permission from his probation officer he was merely going to Atlantic City to make sure he got an "honest count" of each garbage truck he got a cut from.

On a Mona Lisa tape, John Stanfa was heard to say: "You know what I'll do. I'll get a knife . . . I'll cut out his tongue and we'll send it to the wife. That's all . . . We put it in an envelope. Put a stamp on it . . . Honest to God."

"John's doing good," Frank answered Carmine. "They still got him in Leavenworth. I got a Christmas card from him. Our friend's doing all right."

"Give him my best." Carmine raised his head to look up at the ceiling and said very carefully as if thinking out loud, "You know, I have to admit I wasn't all that close to my children when I was coming up and I was out there maneuvering. But I have to say, I'm really, really close to my grandchildren, really close to them, and I'd never want to do anything that bad that I'd never see them again for the rest of my life."

I was struck that he'd used the word *bad* to describe the things they did. I peeked at Frank. There was a flicker of a smile. Anyone who saw Frank snuggling with his own little grandson Jake or heard Frank talk with pride about his adult grandson Chris Cahill playing league rugby in Russia for the U.S. team would guess that Frank had given "our friend" advice that would lead him to this decision.

As I listened from my bar chair, I thought, Well, you have to act as a judge and you have to order hits to keep discipline. That's your job. And that's what, in these days of RICO, you get convicted for, as Stanfa had. I knew that I was listening to the closing chapter in Philly mob history. The job of boss had been the pinnacle of a life in the Mafia. Men killed or paralyzed one another's sons over it. Now they couldn't give it away.

Thanks to the passage of RICO and other anti-Mafia legislation and the job the New Untouchables did with these laws, there would be no more Appreciation Nights for anyone ever again.

Of course, Carmine didn't take the job. And I have that John Stanfa Christmas card as a souvenir with its Leavenworth postmark.

My sensible wife, Nancy, wouldn't let me put Carmine's anecdote in the paperback's 2005 epilogue so as not to ruffle any feathers, but I've driven by the social club since and it's closed down with a realtor's For Sale sign hanging on it. Somebody must be playing with his grandchildren.

Thanks to Lin DeVecchio I got to know the FBI legend Jim Kossler, the architect of the strategy to investigate whole Mafia families using RICO and the other new laws provided by Congress. Jim told me that early in the Hoffa investigation he stopped suspect Tommy Andretta's car to try to question him. The 6'6" Andretta, feeling the emotions of the moment, broke down and cried like a baby, even while refusing to cooperate.

In interviewing Lin, I learned that John Napoli, who had worn a wire to record Russell Bufalino's threat to kill Napoli with his "bare hands" in a dispute over a diamond, was one of his paid informants. Russell was convicted of extortion, which in turn set off a chain of events that finished Bufalino when, upon his release, he ordered a made man, "Jimmy The Weasel" Fratianno, to kill Napoli in revenge. Bufalino was unaware that Fratianno was a man on a wire and had already begun to cooperate with the FBI.

These unexpected gifts continued to make me grateful. Here, after writing a book with Joe Pistone who had hung out at the Vesuvio as Donnie Brasco keeping an eye on Russ and Frank, I was now writing a book with Lin DeVecchio, the man who'd brought down Russell Bufalino. How the refreshing snowflakes continued to fall from out of nowhere.

Lin also had a bug in Russell's suite at the Consulate Hotel in New York, listening to Russ and Frank. But Russ and Frank were old school and never talked business there. That bug was one of the very few to come up empty.

What shone through on the bug, however, was how close the two men were, as close as blood. Frank told me two anecdotes that illustrate their relationship and that I am now able to talk about. The first involved Big Bobby Marino, the three-hundred-pound hustler Frank was acquitted of murdering in his 1980 RICO trial. Russell had ordered Frank to do the hit without realizing that Marino was doing some loan sharking for Angelo Bruno. After the hit it was revealed that Marino had eighty thousand dollars of Angelo's money in loans on the street. The problem was that no one but Marino knew to whom he'd lent any of the money. That was eighty thousand down the drain, and it appeared to be Frank's fault. Frank was called in by Ange to explain himself. He took the rap and never once mentioned that Russell had ordered the hit.

"I didn't want to embarrass Russell," Frank told me, "for moving ahead with the thing without checking with the people. Russ did try to call it off, but it was too late. I was already on my way."

The other anecdote involved a made man Frank couldn't stand and who couldn't stand him, Raymond "Long John" Martorano. Frank heard that Long John had put a contract out on him. Frank parked in front of Long John's house at about three on a Sunday morning and sat on his horn. When Long John looked out his window, Frank made a hand pistol as if he were shooting Long John. The very next day Russell called a sit-down between Frank and Long John and made Long John withdraw his contract on Frank and made Frank agree to leave Long John alone.

Decades later when I was traveling with Frank, Long John was released following a long sentence. He was about eighty, as was Frank. Out a week and out for a drive, Long John turned a corner in South Philly when a gunman jumped out from between two parked cars firing away. The next day Frank and I went to the Messina Social Club for peppers and sausage. Tut, a very short Italian, 5'4" to Frank's 6'4" in their prime and also about eighty, greeted Frank in a mismatch of an embrace, looked up grinning, and said, "I'm glad to see you out. I thought they'd have you down for questioning on Long John."

"I'm going to use you for my alibi if I get indicted," Frank said.

"I hear he's still alive," Tut said.

"Well, there's my defense right there. If it was me, Long John would be long gone."

When Emmett Fitzpatrick died in 2014, his obituary linked the two enemies: "Mr. Fitzpatrick went on to become a well-known defense attorney representing reputed mobsters, including Raymond 'Long John' Martorano . . . and Teamsters boss Frank Sheeran."

At a book signing near Baltimore, a man familiar with the area told me that the airstrip Frank and I couldn't find had been up the road where there is now a shopping mall with a Gap and an auto dealership. That was the airstrip where Frank had delivered a duffel bag filled with high-powered rifles to a Genovese man shortly before "Dallas." It was great to verify that we had been in the right vicinity after nearly forty years had elapsed since Frank's 1963 delivery.

As Jim Kossler told me: "The families work together sharing their criminal activities. The Gambinos might control an employers association, while the Genovese might control the union of the men who work for the employers."

Frank's revelations to me had established an important but unrecognized Genovese family connection to "Dallas." Frank drove to the Genovese hangout, Monte's Restaurant; met Genovese capo Tony Provenzano, who gave him a duffel bag with high-powered rifles; and was instructed by Provenzano: "Go down to Campbell's Cement in Baltimore where you went that time with the truck. Our friend's pilot will be there. He's waiting for this." Frank delivered the rifles at the airstrip in Baltimore, not to "our friend" Carlos Marcello's pilot, Dave Ferrie, but to another Genovese made man, "another guy I knew from Monte's," now deceased, whose identity Frank refused to reveal to me out of respect for the Genovese man's "nice family." As Frank described it in the book, this Genovese man silently took Frank's trunk key, got the rifles and said good-bye, "and away I went." Frank never got out of his Lincoln.

A dozen years later at the Warwick Hotel, Jimmy Hoffa told Frank that Carlos Marcello's pilot took the rifles to Dallas, without saying how or if they were actually used. Frank assumed Jimmy was correct about Carlos Marcello, Dave Ferrie, and "Dallas" and the rifles.

But Frank was an actual eyewitness to the Genovese role in his pickup of rifles from a Genovese capo, Tony Pro; at a Genovese hangout, Monte's; and his delivery of the rifles to a Genovese made man.

Here we have crucial parts of a conspiracy to kill the president being handled at the highest level of the Genovese family, a family seated on the Commission and led by Fat Tony Salerno. The Genovese family's active participation in something as monumental as "Dallas" could not have occurred without the input and approval of the Mafia Commission that two decades later would no longer exist thanks to the New Untouchables of the Mafia Commission Case.

"I'm Not Going Anywhere Near Dallas"

After RFK Jr. appeared on Charlie Rose, I viewed a documentary: *Did the Mob Kill JFK?* Its featured guest was Notre Dame professor G. Robert Blakey, a man I'd never met, but who'd figured prominently in my books co-authored with Joe Pistone and Lin DeVecchio. Professor Blakey is the Mafia fighter under RFK who continued the fight after RFK was assassinated.

It was Blakey who drafted for Congress and the signatures of Presidents Johnson and Nixon the Mafia-smashing laws I've referred to, laws that empowered agents like Joe Pistone, Lin DeVecchio, and Jim Kossler and their allies in and out of the FBI to prosecute and imprison the powerful and arrogant Mafia Commission bosses like Fat Tony Salerno and the bosses of the somewhat loose geographic territories.

Blakey drafted and Congress enacted three weapons of mass destruction to target the Mafia nationwide: (1) the authorization of wiretapping and bugging whose tapes could be used as evidence; (2) an expansion of the witness protection program to entice cooperating witnesses; and, most important, (3) the RICO statute that created a new kind of conspiracy, making it illegal to belong to the Mafia.

When the godfathers' verdicts in Lin's Mafia Commission Case came in, guilty on all 151 counts, Jim Kossler immediately called Professor Blakey to congratulate him and celebrate with him.

Blakey previously had distinguished himself as chief counsel and staff director to the House Select Committee on Assassinations from 1976 to 1978. This committee had reopened the 1964 Warren Commission Report and in 1978 contradicted the Warren Commission and concluded that Oswald had not acted alone. Without identifying the conspirators in any way, except of course for Oswald, the committee concluded that JFK more likely than not was "assassinated as a result of a conspiracy." However, the House select committee had relied on now discredited claims of acoustic evidence of a fourth shot from a different location from Oswald's three shots, namely, the grassy knoll area closer to where the president was killed.

In the documentary Professor Blakey cited other reasons to support the finding of a conspiracy. He said that eleven months before "Dallas," Angelo Bruno, the Philly boss we know to have been closest to Russell Bufalino, was heard on a then-illegal wiretap saying that "we ought to kill the big one," in context meaning we ought to kill JFK, and "we ought to kill the little one," meaning RFK. Blakey's narration was voice-over for a photo of the man Frank called Ange: the man who ordered Frank to kiss Whispers; the man who held Frank responsible for killing Big Bobby Marino; and the man who referred Al Martino to Russell for permission to return to America.

Blakey concluded the documentary with a position he has personally held since his work as chief counsel to the committee ended nearly forty years ago: "It's my best judgment that he was killed as the result of a conspiracy and the shape and color of the conspiracy is organized crime . . . I think the mob killed Kennedy and got away with it."

In his book *Fatal Hour: The Assassination of President Kennedy by Organized Crime* (Berkley, 1981), co-authored with Richard N. Billings, the committee's editorial director, Blakey, concluded, however, that he could find no evidence that the ruling body, the Mafia Commission, participated in "Dallas."

Two decades later Frank Sheeran provided the missing evidence of Commission participation by putting Genovese fingerprints on a part of the conspiracy.

"I'm not going anywhere near Dallas," Frank said to me in 1991. When he resumed talking to me in 1999, after eight years of silence, I had to use all my skill to get him to go "anywhere near Dallas."

While Frank told me he had suspicions in 1963 because of Jack Ruby's role, Frank wasn't told about a Mafia conspiracy to kill JFK until that night at Broadway Eddie's in 1974. Frank had an impeccable source in Russell Bufalino, who was a serious man speaking in a serious way about the most serious of matters when he warned Jimmy Hoffa in front of Frank:

"There are people higher up than me that feel that you are demonstrating a failure to show appreciation" — and then in a hushed tone — "for 'Dallas.'"

Russell Bufalino was doubly serious later that night when he assured Frank that Jimmy was not immune from having his house painted:

"You're dreaming, my friend. If they could take out the president, they could take out the president of the Teamsters."

Is there any wonder Frank was petrified to go "anywhere near Dallas" that night in 1991 sitting on his La-Z-Boy when I touched a raw nerve by mentioning Oswald and Ruby, especially with Russell still alive?

Till the day he died, on the same hand, Frank wore Russell's gold-piece ring and Jimmy's gold watch. He wore them both as a reminder of his loyalties. The jewelry symbolized the emotional and moral conflicts going on inside him, and those conflicts included "Dallas."

Sheeran is in excellent company with Blakey and RFK, who both had many years of hands-on experience with the Mafia criminal mind at a time when the Mafia had its own secret government with its own laws and judicial system, its own language and ways of thinking, and its own tax-free economy.

Frank's evidence about "Dallas" as described in this book was subject to intense interrogation by me. At his final video-taping just before carrying out his plan to meet his maker by refusing food, Frank spoke again of picking up the bag of rifles "for Dallas" from Tony Provenzano at the Genovese hangout Monte's Restaurant in Brooklyn.

After seeing Professor Blakey on TV I decided to read his still-vibrant thirty-three-year-old book, and that led me to David Kaiser's terrific *The Road to Dallas* (Harvard University Press, 2008) about which Blakey wrote: "Finally a historian, without preconceptions, has looked at the volumi-nous, once secret documents produced . . . in response to the JFK Assassination Records Act of 1992."

As a historian Kaiser read reams of recently released secret documents. Among these were FBI reports from 1989 to 1990. These official reports recount a three-day jailhouse incident in 1989 that implicated Louisiana boss Carlos Marcello as having a role in "Dallas." The three-day incident was significant enough to cause the FBI within a week to reopen for nearly a year the Bureau's long-closed JFK investigation.

The FBI already held an incriminating tape of Marcello from 1981, a tape springing from the insurance fraud inves-tigation that was to put Marcello in jail for his final years. On that tape from a bug in Marcello's office, a "trusted associate" said something to Marcello about the JFK assassination. Marcello cut him off in 1981 the way Frank had cut me off in 1991:

"We don't talk about it in here," Marcello said.

He took his "trusted associate" outside to continue their conversation in private.

Carlos Marcello, it will be recalled, was one of two bosses to whom Mafia lawyer and Hoffa lawyer Frank Ragano delivered a message from Jimmy Hoffa to "kill that son-of-a-bitch John Kennedy."

Anyone writing in support of the Warren Report's conclusions comes up against Frank Ragano, a man in a position to know what he's talking about, and must find a way to discredit him. Vincent Bugliosi, the esteemed Manson family prosecutor and author of *Helter Skelter* (Norton, 1971), wrote a 1,612-page book about "Dallas" endorsing the Warren Commission Report and arguing that there was no evidence of any conspiracy, Mafia or otherwise: *Reclaiming History* (Norton, 2007). It was published a year before Kaiser's book. On page 1,181 Bugliosi points out that the details of lawyer Frank Ragano's story "smack of the truth." But then, by Bugliosi's account, Ragano self-destructs. Ragano, Bugliosi argued, could not keep his story straight about his meeting with Hoffa.

According to Bugliosi, first Ragano said his conversation with Hoffa took place "in the executive dining room of the Marble Palace Hotel in Washington D.C."

Bugliosi goes on to chastise Ragano: "In November of 1992, Ragano told essentially the same story to a national audience in a *Frontline* TV special, but he said the conversation took place not at the Marble Palace Hotel but in Hoffa's office at the Teamsters headquarters in Washington, D.C. Marble Palace Hotel? Jimmy's office? Better make up your mind, Frankie."

If Ragano were alive he would point out that if Bugliosi had dialed 411 — coincidentally, the number of Frank's combat days — the information operator would say: "There is no listing for a Marble Palace Hotel in the Washington, D.C., area." Ragano would add that the Teamsters headquarters building is named the Marble Palace.

Frank Sheeran's eyewitness account of Hoffa and Bufalino's guilty knowledge of "Dallas" at Broadway Eddie's and the Warwick Hotel corroborates Ragano and is corroborated by Ragano.

It's easy to look into the Mafia mind and see the motive upon motive people like Carlos Marcello had for killing JFK.

The disrespect RFK showed the bosses at the McClellan Committee hearings in the years before JFK was elected president drew first blood. When RFK took over the Justice Department in 1961, there had been thirty-five organized crime convictions in the year before. In 1963 there were 288 and rising swiftly. Among those 288 convictions in 1963 was "the highest paid labor boss in America," the Genovese capo Tony Provenzano, who went down for extortion, selling labor peace to trucking companies. It cost Provenzano his pension and led to a mortal rift with Hoffa. Thanks to RFK all the bosses were being targeted by the FBI, the IRS, immigration, the Labor Department, and state and local police. RFK exposed the Mafia in his book *The Enemy Within* (Harper, 1960). New laws were being proposed. Genovese soldier Joe Valachi was paraded before the TV cameras in 1963, a couple of months before "Dallas," for the sole purpose of exposing the Mafia's secrets to the light of day. To the bosses' way of thinking, their survival was at stake. They had no choice but to kill JFK.

Add to these motives the fact that when Carlos Marcello showed up at immigration for his routine check-in as required by law on April 4, 1961, the portly 5'2" senior citizen was placed in handcuffs and kidnapped by RFK. He was deposited by a border patrol plane in Guatemala with no luggage and only pocket money. There he had to fend for himself and sneak back into America. RFK justified his dirty trick in that to avoid deportation to Italy, Carlos Marcello had procured from the Guatemalan government a false Guatemalan birth certificate. RFK took Marcello up on that by dumping him in Guatemala.

To add insult to kidnapping, when Marcello returned from Guatemala, RFK indicted him for fraud against the United States in using the fugazy Guatemalan birth certificate to sabotage his deportation to Italy. On the afternoon of the day JFK was killed by Oswald, a New Orleans jury promptly returned a verdict of not guilty. Before they went into the jury room to deliberate, the judge told them that the president had been assassinated.

Historian Kaiser's 2008 look at the newly released FBI material revealed that by 1989 an elderly Carlos Marcello was serving a lengthy sentence in Texarkana Prison for insurance fraud and bribery of public officials. In February 1989 Marcello had a passing health episode that made him semi-delusional for three days, just as Frank Sheeran had been semi-delusional during our 2002 drive to Detroit to find the house; Frank kept mixing in Mafia experiences with his war experiences due to chemical reactions from the slow metabolism of his medications triggering his subconscious. Frank spoke to these "chemical people" about past events while I drove.

Similarly, as Kaiser described on page 411, again the number of Frank's combat days:

In 1989, an amazing incident in the Texarkana prison where Marcello was serving his sentence led the FBI to reopen the investigation of John Kennedy's assassination. On February 27 Marcello was admitted to the prison medical facility for dizziness, irregular heartbeat, and disorientation. During the next three days he suffered from the delusion that he was back home in New Orleans, and he began speaking to his attendants as though they were trusted associates. He discussed a meeting he had just held with "Provenzano" in New York, he suggested that his men visit a nightclub, and he spoke of an imminent celebration. And on three occasions during a two-day period Marcello remarked: "That Kennedy, that smiling motherfucker, we'll fix him in Dallas . . .we are going to get that Kennedy in Dallas."

See, they really do want to tell you, Choll.

By the time he was interviewed by the FBI, Marcello was lucid and denied everything. But during the three-day incident, he had specifically talked of a "nightclub" and a "celebration" and had identified the places "Dallas" and "New York," and dropped the names "Provenzano" and "Kennedy." And not just any old "Provenzano," but one he'd met with in "New York," the hometown of Monte's in Brooklyn. And who do we know who owned a "nightclub" in Marcello's territory, a territory that included Dallas, Texas? While others such as Sam Giancana, to whom Jack Ruby was tied, had interests in Dallas, the territory was Marcello's. Jack Ruby owned two nightclubs in Dallas. And no one could own a nightclub in Dallas without the oversight of the Dallas boss Joseph Civello, who reported to his godfather, Carlos Marcello.

The two Mafia bosses were so close that in November 1957, the godfather Carlos Marcello sent the Dallas boss Joseph Civello to represent Marcello at the Apalachin conference arranged by Russell Bufalino. It was, of course, a conference of about sixty godfathers from around the country held at a private estate in a small town in upstate New York. The New York State Police raided it; the arrests and headlines that followed constituted the first public exposure of the nation-wide organized Mafia.

Kaiser's single "amazing" paragraph with these revelations from nineteen-year-old FBI reports was published in 2008, four years after Frank Sheeran's words publicly revealed in 2004 that Genovese capo Tony "Provenzano," working out of a Genovese hangout in "New York," Monte's in Brooklyn, and another unnamed Genovese made man were active conspir-ators in "Dallas."

Although Kaiser made no reference to Sheeran or to this book, with Kaiser's account of these newly released FBI reports quoting Marcello, even in a semi-delusional state, about "a meeting he had just held with Provenzano in New York" in the context of what Marcello identified as a "we" conspiracy — "we'll fix him in Dallas . . . we are going to get that Kennedy in Dallas" — the already highly corrobo-rated Frank Sheeran gets validation from these hidden FBI reports. Provenzano meet Provenzano. Frank Sheeran was the first to publicly provide a direct link between the ruling Commission and "Dallas" through the Genovese family's active participation.

As well, Frank's confession validates Marcello's "amazing" words. As Frank did for the suspect list in the Hoffex memo, Frank validates these FBI reports and the Bureau's decision to take the matter seriously.

As Frank Sheeran and so many others taught me in their Mafia graduate school, as a permanent member of the Commission it would be impossible for members of the Genovese family to be involved in something as big as "Dallas" without the rest of the Commission's approval. An example is the Commission's close vote not to kill then–U.S. attorney Rudy Giuliani in the mid-1980s.

And it would be impossible for any member of the Mafia to be involved in a hit in Dallas, Texas, without Marcello's approval. As Joe Valachi testified, no made man could enter Marcello's territory for any reason without prior approval.

Some may protest that Marcello was semi-delusional. Well, of the thousand or so Mafia gangsters Marcello knew, his subconscious picked the name "Provenzano," a very powerful Mafia Teamster from Jersey City, a very powerful member of New York's Genovese family who hung out at Monte's in Brooklyn, to connect to "Dallas"; just as Frank, who knew many hundreds of Mafia gangsters, had connected "Provenzano" to "Dallas." And Marcello threw in a "night-club" for the anticipated "celebration." More important, these revelations weren't just said once in passing. They were repeated as if he were talking to his New Orleans associates. The "we" conspiracy was said three times in a two-day period. What was said was enough for the 1989 FBI to reopen their long-dormant "Dallas" case. Further, the FBI already had the 1981 tape where Marcello terminated in his office any discussion of JFK's assassination.

With the Genovese family's active participation in the plot, as recounted by Frank Sheeran and now by Carlos Marcello, it should be clear that the Commission participated in "Dallas." Marcello put his meeting with "Provenzano" in "New York," the home of the Commission. That Marcello traveled to New York for a meeting means that those with whom he met were higher up than he.

The Genovese family's hands-on involvement makes perfect sense, too. It had a seething personal motive. It had something operatic to prove. It was a Genovese made man from East Harlem, Joseph Valachi, who — betraying the deepest Mafia secrets — had just humiliated the Genovese in televised hearings.

RFK said that "because of Joseph Valachi . . . we know that . . . [the Mafia] is run by a Commission . . . and that the leaders in most major cities are responsible to the Commission . . . and we know who the active members of the Commission are today."

"Because of Joseph Valachi . . ."

In the eyes of the other families, what disgraceful Mafia discipline the Genovese family must possess for a betrayal so unspeakable to emanate from one of their soldiers. The Genovese had to make it right. It's no coincidence that *vendetta* is an Italian word.

Of course, I'm a believer. I heard Frank's dry-iced words: "I'm not going anywhere near Dallas." Instantly and forever, I came to believe that the Mafia conspired to kill JFK. Anyone who heard him say those words in that way would come away a believer, too. As would anyone who took my word for his words.

"Look Up, Charles"

The biggest snowfall of all stormed in suddenly and, as Lena Horne sang it with the Teddy Wilson Orchestra, ". . . from out of nowhere."

I was at our vacation home in the ski resort of Sun Valley, Idaho, watching a Boise State football game when a call came in on my then-listed landline. The young caller identified himself as Frank Pavlico. His name sounded vaguely familiar.

"I was indicted with Billy D'Elia," he said. "For money laundering. I know that you know Billy."

"I do," I said.

"I'm an investment banker. I didn't lose my license. That was part of my deal."

This fast-talking young man sounded like a hustling stockbroker making a cold call.

"Go on," I said.

"I cooperated against Billy. I'm one of those that Billy was going to have killed. But Billy's good with me now."

"That's good."

"Believe me, Billy and I are really close. We've always been family. My father and Russell were best friends. Billy used to babysit me. I grew up calling him Uncle Billy. I still call him Uncle Billy sometimes."

"Okay."

"What I'm getting at is, two newspaper reporters, one from Philly and one from up here in northeast Pennsylvania, want to write my book, but I want you to write it. Billy is good with everything. There's nothing to worry about from Billy. He'll cooperate. He'll help. We've talked about it. He'll help us. You have nothing to worry about."

I said to Frank Pavlico from out of nowhere myself: "I'd say the two reporters are Matt Birkbeck in northeast Pennsylvania and George Anastasia in Philly. They're both excellent writers. I have no interest."

There was a long pause. I thoroughly enjoyed this awkward silence from the "nephew" of Billy.

"How did you know it was them?" he meekly asked.

"They both write about the Mafia and they're both excellent at it. I've moved on. I have other projects."

Getting him considerably off balance by naming the two writers, I decided to take a shot at exposing what young Frank Pavlico was really trying to sell me. Based on Detective Joe Coffey telling me that his source in the Bufalino family said Frank told me the truth, and that all the Bufalino guys had read the book, and knowing that Billy was cooperating with the FBI, I lowered my voice confidentially:

"Besides, I know that Billy already corroborated Frank Sheeran's confession. I don't need to get that from you."

This time there was an even deader silence, an even longer pause. When Pavlico recovered he said in a voice reeking of disappointment, "That would be good for you then, wouldn't it?"

"Yes, it would be good for me," I said.

Now that his scheme to broker Billy's corroboration was busted, Pavlico went on to volunteer, "That was the first question the FBI asked Billy when they went to see him, what happened to Hoffa. He told them to read the book."

"Frank told me the truth," I said. "I didn't have him on the witness stand for an afternoon. I had him to myself for close to five years."

"When your book came out," he said, "Billy gave it to me and wrote in it: 'Sometimes you can believe everything you read.'"

A part of me, the Italian Catholic in me, likes to think that Billy was influenced to cooperate with the FBI to some small degree by the spirituality of Frank Sheeran in his later years as recounted in *The Irishman*; the same way Frank had been influenced spiritually by seeing Russell wheeled into chapel at Springfield prison; the same way my daily involvement with Frank found me lighting candles for him at St. Patrick's Cathedral whenever I visited my mother in Manhattan.

Billy was the godfather of the whole Bufalino family. His decision to cross over represents Lin DeVecchio's Mafia Commission Case in action.

A year or so later on December 13, 2012, Frank Pavlico, while pending trial in South Carolina on a separate fraud case, committed suicide by hanging.

Meanwhile Billy D'Elia exposed two juvenile court judges in Bufalino territory who had a giant conflict of interest. They owned a "piece" of a privately owned juvenile jail that got fees for each prisoner under their roof. They then sentenced their juvenile offenders to jail for minor crimes like shoplifting. It was on *60 Minutes*. The judges likely will die in jail.

Big Billy D'Elia was paroled in 2013, a couple of months after Pavlico's suicide. But he'll never testify against the two living Hoffa conspirators because Billy was not actively involved in the parts they played: Chuckie O'Brien's driving of Hoffa to the house and Tommy Andretta's disposing of the body. As Frank put it in 1991: ". . . if you go bad you only know what you did. You can't rat on the other ones before you and the other ones after you."

If Billy played a role of any kind in Hoffa or in "Dallas," Frank never told me. But Billy's position as underboss made him privy to whatever Russell knew.

Frank was always convinced that Big Billy was a secret informant, what Frank called a dry snitch and what Lin DeVecchio, the professor of informant development, calls a source.

Frank was very close to the boss of the Chicago outfit, Joey "The Clown" Lombardo. In fact, both men were defendants in the civil RICO lawsuit against the Mafia Commission and its co-conspirators, as distinguished from Lin's Mafia Commission criminal RICO case. The civil case's list of co-conspirator defendants, to borrow from RFK Jr., reads "like an inventory" of organized crime figures. Because that's just what it was. As stated, Frank was one of only two non-Italians on the list.

Frank and Joey The Clown often spoke at times when I was present listening to Frank's end of the conversation. It was the nationwide conspiracy right before my eyes. One day I was walking into a publisher's Park Avenue building for a meeting when I got a call from Frank on my cell phone.

"I got a call from our friend in Chicago," Frank said. "He told me it's all around town in Chicago about the man upstate being a dry snitch. Be careful what you say around Billy. He's no good."

"Frank, come on," I said. "I'm only in his company when I'm with you. What could I possibly say around Billy?"

"Never mind, watch what you say around Billy. That's all."

For me there's a personal irony to Billy later crossing over to the FBI and becoming a cooperating witness after conspiring to kill other cooperating witnesses.

Billy always headed the list of those people I figured might think like a Mad Hatter and decide that I had double-crossed Frank, and that I took advantage of Frank's guilty conscience to turn a whitewashing book into a confessional booth. Who can blame me for not mentioning Big Billy until now?

Anyway, this was a book about Frank and everything about Frank at all times was about Frank's desire to repent and his journey of redemption. Confession needs someone to confess to. And I was blessed to be in the right place at the right time and to have this son of a seminarian all to myself.

A short while after my brief but magical conversation with the former murder target Frank Pavlico, I got a frantic call from Frank Sheeran's daughter Dolores. That night the Detroit FBI had visited the Pennsylvania homes of each of the three daughters Frank had remained close to. The FBI agents were looking for an affidavit or a letter or a note, or cassette tape or videotape or film, or anything at all in writing or on tape that Frank might have left with any one of them for safekeeping.

I told Dolores about my conversation with Pavlico. I explained to her that the agents were looking for anything their father left behind that recanted or denied the truthfulness of what Frank had confessed to me, something he'd left in his daughters' care in case he got arrested.

"They need to be secure," I said, "that something like that won't turn up to discredit what their star witness Billy told them."

"Dad never tried to deny anything to us that he told you."

"I know that, but they have to be thorough. That's their middle name."

Dolores, who by now had become a friend for life, laughed and said, "You know, the three of us treated the FBI the way our age differences would dictate. Maryanne was practically grown before Dad had anything to do with Russell. Maryanne all but made the FBI brownies. I had a taste of what Dad went through with the FBI and I was cooperative, but very formal. Connie was born when Dad was completely in with Russell. Connie wouldn't let them in her house and made them talk to her from the porch. She yelled at them that she had nothing of Dad's and for them to call you and leave her alone. She still won't read the book. All she said was: 'Just tell me Dad didn't kill Frank Sindone. I always liked him.' I said, 'No, Connie, Dad didn't kill Frank Sindone.'"

Frank "The Barracuda" Sindone was one of four made men killed by the Mafia Commission in 1980 in retaliation for that year's unsanctioned hit on Angelo Bruno. Because the Bruno hit was seen as an act of greed, Sindone was left in an alley to be found with his mouth stuffed with money. The killing of the four made men who conspired to kill the Philly boss Angelo Bruno may have been the last such law-and-order act of the Commission before the heat from Lin DeVecchio's Mafia Commission investigation began to be felt. In order for there to be a governing body there needs to be communication, and Lin's case put a stop to that.

The day after Dolores called me I got a call from Special Agent Andy Sluss of the Detroit FBI office. He wanted my Sheeran tapes. The request thrilled me. We had a great conversation. I told him what Dolores said about her sisters and his visit and we laughed. He asked me if I needed a subpoena for my tapes. I said I didn't need one, but I'd love one for a souvenir. Promptly in a day or so I got the subpoena, and later when my tapes were copied and returned to me they had the FBI identification and case number on them.

It was at the same instant gratifying and humbling. As my mother, Carolina DiMarco Brandt, always said to me when I gave her a bit of good news about my life, "Look up, Charles." And boy did I.

My law enforcement experience told me during my conversation with Agent Andy Sluss that unlike Detective Joe Coffey in Gallo where all the serious suspects were dead, because Tommy Andretta was still alive and living in Las Vegas and Chuckie O'Brien was still alive and living in Florida, this still was an open case, one that no agent could publicly comment on, the same way Joe Pistone couldn't comment on certain open cases in his first *Donnie Brasco* book, and didn't do so until *Donnie Brasco: Unfinished Business* twenty years later. I was very careful to stay on my side of the street. I never mentioned Big Billy D'Elia or Frank Pavlico or Detective Joe Coffey. However, before we hung up, I couldn't resist.

"I'm not going to ask you what has engendered your recent interest in my tapes," I said. "But I just want you to know that I never liked that motherfucker and he never liked me."

We burst out laughing together, like two men who were, after all, on the same "side of this thing."

Shortly after that perfect moment came the meeting at Le Parker Meridien Hotel with Martin Scorsese, Robert De Niro, and Steve Zaillian, another perfect moment where Scorsese asked me the name of the obscure movie that had led to my mentioning the "lone cowboy" Lee Harvey Oswald. On my flight back to Sun Valley I recognized the connection the movie title had to Jack Ruby's assassination of Oswald. Ruby's .38 fired a Blast of Silence that silenced Oswald.

When I arrived in Sun Valley from my movie meeting in Manhattan there was a FedEx overnight box on my doorstep. It was a DVD of Allen Baron's 1961 film *Blast of Silence* from Martin Scorsese. What a treasure. And what a gripping film noir it is, set in the New York City of my young manhood.

Each of Frank Sheeran's major confessions now has been validated: Gallo by the *New York Times* eyewitness and Detective Joe Coffey; Hoffa by Frank Pavlico and Billy D'Elia and the FBI subpoena of my tapes; and finally "Dallas" as a Mafia Commission conspiracy by Carlos Marcello at Texarkana and Tony Provenzano's participation on behalf of the Genovese family.

As I follow my mother's advice to look up, my mind selects a picture of Frank Sheeran smiling from above. As I've done many times, I thank him. The Irishman is always young and in uniform. It's my favorite picture, posed in Sicily with Alex Siegel who was killed during the invasion of Salerno.

ALEX MCCAUSLAND

Born and raised in New York City, Charles Brandt is a former junior high school English teacher, welfare investigator in East Harlem, homicide prosecutor, and Chief Deputy Attorney General of the State of Delaware. In private practice since 1976, Brandt has been president of the Delaware Trial Lawyers Association and the Delaware Chapter of the American Board of Trial Advocates. He has been named by his peers to both Best Lawyers in America and Best Lawyers in Delaware. He is a frequent speaker on cross-examination and interrogation techniques for reluctant witnesses. Brandt is the author of a novel based on major cases he solved through interrogation, *The Right to Remain Silent*. He is also the co-author of Joe Pistone's *Donnie Brasco: Unfinished Business* and of Lin DeVecchio's *We're Going to Win This Thing: The Shocking Frame-Up of a Mafia Crime Buster*.

For more information on Charles Brandt and his work, please visit his website: www.charlesbrandtauthor.com